COLLOQUIAL JAPANESE

COLLOQUIAL JAPANESE

with Important Construction
and
Grammar Notes

by NOBORU INAMOTO

Charles E. Tuttle Company

Rutland, Vermont Tokyo, Japan

Published by the Charles E. Tuttle Company, Inc.
of Rutland, Vermont & Tokyo, Japan
with editorial offices at
Suido 1-chome, 2–6, Bunkyo-ku, Tokyo

Library of Congress Catalog Card No. 71-133865
International Standard Book No. 0-8048-1581-X

First printing, 1972
First Tuttle paperback edition
Third printing, 1990

PRINTED IN JAPAN

To my wife

Barbara

TABLE OF CONTENTS

PREFACE

The methods and ideas presented in this book were conceived during the dark days of 1942 when several instructors from different relocation camps gathered at the University of Minnesota to organize and conduct an intensive course of study in the Army Specialized Training Program. The only materials available to us were several Kenkyusha dictionaries and a few copies of old Japanese high school textbooks. Our job was to train soldiers to be interrogators, and time was not on our side.

After much trial and error, both during World War II and since, the basic system used here has been refined. Admittedly, it was a difficult task trying to find a middle road between the listing of simple sentence patterns to be committed to memory, and, on the other hand, a detailed expository on Japanese grammar. In this work, both approaches have been adopted. In studying any language, varying amounts of unquestioning memorization of pattern, syntax, etc., are called for. These are clearly indicated herein.

At the same time, because Japanese is a highly logical language, it is possible to explain grammatically most of the basic constructions. Grammar, when used in this manner, can act as a crutch, a tool to further one's understanding. To know the "why?" and the "how?" will enable one to construct sentences more easily and correctly. Be that as it may, REPETITION is strongly urged. The importance of REPETITION cannot be emphasized enough. The basic sentences given at the beginning of the chapter should be repeated so often that they will be committed to memory. The layout used in this book of contrasting translations of Japanese and English, and the method of breaking the sentences down into its component parts, will facilitate memorization.

Vocabulary has been carefully screened, and sentence patterns organized for clear, quick understanding. Useful phrases and expressions for everyday situations have been included. Easy beginning chapters become more complicated as you progress through the book, and each chapter is constructed around two or three basic patterns. Hence, it is necessary to master one lesson thoroughly before proceeding to the next. Covering ground without sufficient understanding would be equivalent to building a house on a weak foundation.

Each chapter is divided into six parts—the main text, a section on new vocabulary from the chapter, additional vocabulary, important construction and grammar notes, exercises, and useful expressions. The additional vocabularies are given to aid in extending the scope of conversation. Important constructions and grammar are made easily understandable by giving adequate examples and comparing them with English. Attempts have been made in this section to avoid theoretical discussions of grammar, and to make the grammar readily usable. Throughout the book, Japanese and English versions have been placed side by side. The reader may use this to his own advantage by covering one portion and translating into English, or vice versa. From Chapter 1 to Chapter 15 more detailed word-for-word translation is given so that one can clearly grasp the pattern of sentence "build-up," the word order, and the exact function of postpositions; in other words, the "structural analysis." Since Japanese word order is so unlike that of English, and yet falls into definite patterns, this unique presentation will be helpful. Also, wherever thought to be of assistance, the formula type introduction is given in bold print for emphasis. The reader should memorize each formula and be able to use it freely. It might be added here that if the reader studies the vocabulary list first and then begins work on the main text for each chapter, progress will be faster. Exercises at the conclusion of each chapter are designed to give practice in usage of the principal construction, words, and grammar discussed in the chapter. Lastly, listed under "Useful Expressions," are popular idioms which should be memorized for everyday use.

At the risk of being criticized as "too stilted" or "too formal," the ordinary polite form is emphasized throughout this book. This form of expression is polite enough to be acceptable in most social situations. A sound knowledge of this will help the reader to make the transition to superpolite or step down to informal expression. Chapter 19 is devoted to the study of the superpolite (or honorific) way of speaking, the usage of which is not uncommon. In order to feel comfortable in more sophisticated surroundings, cognizance of this form, at least a hearing comprehension, is strongly recommended. It is also possible to go down the scale to more familiar (or abrupt) speech. Examples of this have been introduced in this book, not with the purpose of encouraging this style of expression, but merely to illustrate and to expose the reader to it. The writer feels that it is not necessary to belabor oneself to master informal expressions when this can be offensive if used improperly; in other words, why LEARN to be informal? With this limitation in mind, Chapter 20, which stresses familiar expression, is presented. This chapter gives a contrastive study of male and female speech in a familiar situation, but the author is the first to admit that this is insufficient because the speech pattern differs with the principals involved; viz., between male and male, female and female, male and female, etc.

Chapter 15 on "Abraham Lincoln" is presented here with some modifications with the permission of Mr. Naganuma. Acknowledgment is also given to Dr. E. O. Reischauer for his permission to use portions of Chapter 26 of his *Elementary*

Japanese for College Students, with extensive modification. Chapter 19, "Super Polite and Humble Forms," uses Dr. Reischauer's presentation with much addition of this writer's ideas.

This volume, a systematic study of colloquial Japanese, is the crystallization of many years' experience in teaching Japanese to American students. Many independent conclusions have been reached based upon this experience. I feel certain, however, that further study may lead to a more understandable presentation. Therefore, any suggestions or comments by the reader will be deeply appreciated.

I am indeed grateful to the following: Dr. S. Kimizuka, my colleague at the University of Southern California; and to Mrs. Yasuko Mitamura, who, while a tutor of Japanese in the Department of Asian Studies at the University of Southern California, read the manuscript and gave me invaluable suggestions; Miss Sadako Hashimoto, instructor at Tokushima University, who helped with the vocabulary list; Mr. Kitazumi, who worked with me in 1943 and helped develop this approach; Miss H. Kurosu and Miss K. Suzuki of the Tokyo School of Japanese Language, for reading the Japanese sentence examples; George Isted, a graduate student in linguistics, for making the final check; and to my wife, Barbara, who did the typing and patiently edited for me. All have been most helpful, but I alone am responsible for any errors or misinterpretations.

NOBORU INAMOTO

Los Angeles, California

ABBREVIATIONS AND NOTES

Following are some of the abbreviations used in this book:

adj.—adjective
adj. pro.—adjectival pronoun
adv.—adverb
c.v.—conjugating verb
Chi. v.—Chinese verb
conj.—conjunction
I.C. & G.N.—Important Construction and Grammar Notes
idio.—idiomatic expression
inter. adj.—interrogative adjective
inter. pro.—interrogative pronoun
inter. adj. pro.—interrogative adjectival pronoun
interj.—interjection
n.—noun
n.c.v.—non-conjugating verb
nom. case—nominative case
obj. case—objective case
pol. past—polite past
p.p.—postposition
pro.—pronoun
prog. form—progressive form
rel. cl.—relative clause
suf.—suffix
v.—verb
v.i.—verb intransitive
v.t.—verb transitive

Note: 1. The italics in the text are used to indicate new constructions requiring special attention as they appear in each lesson.
2. Hyphens are used in this book merely to indicate the combination of words, suffixes, prefixes, etc., for better analysis and understanding, and to clarify word structure.

3. Capital letters are used at the beginning of the sentence and for proper nouns.

4. English words now commonly accepted as Japanese have been used in this book in their Romanized forms, e.g.,

takushii	(taxi)
basu	(bus)
hoteru	(hotel)
bataa	(butter)
robii	(lobby)

5. English proper nouns have been left unchanged—the reader must, however, take care to pronounce these English names like Japanese words, e.g., *Nyuu Yoo-ku*.

Harvard	*(Haa-baa-do)*
Brown	*(Bu-ra-un)*
San Francisco	*(San Fu-ran-shi-su-ko)*

6. The italicized words in the main text are the new constructions for the chapter, which require special attention.

7. An attempt has been made throughout this book to demonstrate the sentence buildup in the textual section of each chapter. The asterisks are used here to show that the phrase with the asterisk is the composite of the word groups that precede it. This usage begins with Chapter 7.

CHAPTER 1

PRONUNCIATION

Japanese pronunciation is relatively simple to master. Ask a native speaker to pronounce the basic sounds listed on page 21 and repeat after him. Watch the movements of the mouth and enunciate clearly. Then practice the pronunciation of words and sentences. Listen carefully to the pauses, pitch, intonation, etc. After concluding the practice of the basic sounds on the chart, the following points should be noted.

The first line of the chart on page 21 gives the five fundamental vowel sounds, followed by the consonant+short vowel sounds.

a —	approximately	the sound	of		***a***	in "f*a*ther."
i —	"	"	"	"	***i***	in "*i*nk."
u —	"	"	"	"	***u***	in "p*u*t."
e —	"	"	"	"	***e***	in "p*e*t."
o —	"	"	"	"	***o***	in "h*o*rse."

The second line is:

ka —	consonant	***k*** +	vowel	***a.***
ki —	"	***k*** +	"	***i.***
ku —	"	***k*** +	"	***u.***
etc.				

Japanese words are made up of syllables. Syllables are composed of the following elements:

a. vowel (*a, i, u, e, o*)
b. consonant + vowel (*t* + *a, n* + *i, s* + *o*, etc.)
c. ***m*** (or ***n***)
d. combined sounds (*kya, sha, cha*, etc.)

Each syllable is distinctly pronounced with equal duration.

a-ka-i (red)
ku-da-sa-i (give me)
e-m-pi-tsu (pencil)
de-n-sha (street car)
ko-o-gyo-o (manufacturing industry)
hap-pyo-o (announce)

LONG VOWEL SOUNDS: The long vowels are indicated by the repetition of the vowels, as follows:

aa ii uu ee oo

The pronunciation of these is twice the length of the short vowels; it must be kept in mind when pronouncing that these are the prolongation of the initial vowel sound and not another vowel added on—*not* a-a (two a's) or i-i (two i's) etc. For this reason some books adopt the ā, ī, ū, ē, ō method of expressing these sounds. (In the text of this book, hyphens are omitted between the double vowels in the pronunciation guides following new words in the vocabulary lists. Hyphens are also not used preceding the syllable *m* or *n*.)

The length of sound is very important in Japanese because sometimes the meaning will differ if the long vowel is not prolonged enough.

obasan (aunt)	*obaasan* (grandmother)
to (door)	*too* (10)
futoo (unjust)	*fuutoo* (envelope)

DOUBLE CONSONANT: The double consonant is also common. They are *kk, pp, ss, tt,* and *tch.* In this expression, there is a slight pause at the first consonant, which is considered a part of the first syllable; then you continue with the stress on the second consonant.

Bukkyoo (Buddhism) = Buk/kyo-o
gakkoo (school) = gak/ko-o
happyaku (800) = hap/pya-ku

If this rule for double consonants is not followed, not only does the meaning sometimes change, but it may make the word completely unintelligible.

hikaku	= comparison	hikkaku	= to scratch
kite	= coming	kitte	= postage stamp

G SOUND: In the Tokyo area, when the *g* appears in the middle of a word it is produced as a nasal *ng,* as one finds in "king." Since this is a local phenomenon, it is not necessary for the reader to make a conscious effort to produce this. At the beginning of a word, *g* has a harsh sound as in "good."

Examples:

na*gai*	tai*gi*	ama*gu*	rai*ge*tsu	Ei*go*
*ga*kkoo	*gi*ri	*gu*chi	*ge*ta	*go*go

Each syllable is distinctly pronounced with equal emphasis. As one becomes more familiar with the language, the pitch and stress can be acquired. For our purpose here, however, visualize parallel lines. The pronunciation of words is kept flat as if trying to keep your tone within these two lines.

Yokohama = Yo-ko-ha-ma

atarashii = a-ta-ra-shi-i

R SOUND: When *ra, ri, ru, re,* or *ro* comes at the beginning of a word it should be pronounced more like *la, li, lu, le,* or *lo;* a flat *r,* and not the English *r* in which there is a rolling of the tongue. To get this sound, the tip of the tongue lightly drops from the area behind the upper teeth. They are like *r* when they appear in the middle of a word.

*ra*n	*ri*ka	*ru*fu	*re*ki	*ro*ba
Na*ra*	ama*ri*	su*ru*	a*re*	i*ro*

SOUND COMBINATIONS: The chart on page 22 shows compound sounds. These are really two sounds combined as one.

KYA is a combination of *ki+ya.*
SHU „ „ „ „ *shi+yu.*

The *i* is dropped when these combinations are pronounced rapidly.

Other points for consideration in pronunciation will be explained as they appear in subsequent lessons.

INTONATION: As one becomes more familiar with the language, the pitch and stress can be acquired. However, this book will use the system described below to show intonation. When following the intonation line, the rise and drop in pitch are slight.

Kore wa hon desu.

Sore wa hon desu ka.

PITCH ACCENT: There is no stress accent in Japanese, but it has pitch accent, the accented syllable being said at a slightly higher pitch than the other syllables in a word. On occasion, the place where the pitch is required is indicated in this book by a mark (ʹ) over the vowel. Since pitch accent is not easily learned by the student, and because it is possible to understand the meaning even if a different accent is used, the student should make no great effort to remember or to follow the accent marks too closely.

Exercise

Try dividing the following words into their component parts and pronouncing them.

1. mannenhitsu (fountain pen)
2. atarashii (new)
3. kashikomarimashita (certainly)
4. natsu yasumi (summer vacation)
5. arigatoo gozaimashita (thank you)
6. nakereba narimasen (must)
7. seishin seikatsu (spiritual life)
8. juuichinin (11 persons)

9. irasshaimashita (came)
10. gochisoosama deshita (It was a good meal.)

Japanese Romanized Alphabet

(Hepburn System)

Note: The following Japanese alphabet chart is not only used for pronunciation purposes, but it is also used for verb conjugation, so it should be well memorized. (A, I, U, E, O, etc.)

1st BASE	2nd BASE	3rd BASE	4th BASE	5th BASE
A	**I**	**U**	**E**	**O**
KA	KI	KU	KE	KO
SA	SHI	SU	SE	SO
TA	CHI	TSU	TE	TO
NA	NI	NU	NE	NO
HA	HI	FU	HE	HO
MA	MI	MU	ME	MO
YA	I	YU	E	YO
RA	RI	RU	RE	RO
WA	I	U	E	O
M (the only true consonant which stands by itself) N				

VOICED

GA	GI	GU	GE	GO
ZA	JI	ZU	ZE	ZO
DA	JI	ZU	DE	DO
BA	BI	BU	BE	BO
PA	PI	PU	PE	PO

SOUND COMBINATIONS

Note: Words in which the sound combinations appear are given in parentheses.

VOICED

KYA—(*kya*ku)	KYU—(*kyuu*jin)	KYO—(Too*kyoo*)
SHA—(*sha*shin)	SHU—(*shu*jin)	SHO—(*shoo*bai)
CHA—(*cha*wan)	CHU—(*chuu*mon)	CHO—(*choo*choo)
NYA—(kon*nya*ku)	NYU—(*nyuu*in)	NYO—(*nyo*zetsu)
HYA—(*hya*ku)	HYU—(*hyuu*ga)	HYO—(*hyoo*ban)
MYA—(san*mya*ku)	MYU*	MYO—(*myoo*nichi)
RYA—(*rya*kugo)	RYU—(*ryuu*guu)	RYO—(*ryo*koo)

VOICED

GYA—(*gya*kutai)	GYU—(*gyuu*nyuu)	GYO—(*gyoo*retsu)
JA—(*ja*ma)	JU—(*ju*shin)	JO—(*joozu*)
BYA—(sam*bya*ku)	BYU—(*byuu*ron)	BYO—(*byoo*ki)
PYA—(hap*pya*ku)	PYU*	PYO (hap*pyoo*)

* Appropriate Japanese words are not available for these. They are used to represent English used as Japanese (e.g., *myuujikaru*—musical) or Japanese onomatopoeic words (e.g., the wind blows *pyuu-pyuu*).

CHAPTER 2

BASIC SENTENCES

The reader should become so thoroughly familiar with the sentence construction in the main text that he will be able to respond automatically. Commit the following sentences to memory. (Note that in each lesson new constructions requiring special attention are italicized.)

SUBJECT (what) **(A)**	**WA +**	**PREDICATE DESU.** **(B)** **(is)**

=A *is* B.

SUBJECT (what) **(A)**	**WA +**	**PREDICATE DEWA ARIMASEN.** **(B)** **(is not)**

=A is *not* B.

kore wa — as for this (nom. case)
hon desu — (it) is (a) book

1. *KORE WA HON DESU.* — THIS IS A BOOK.

are wa — as for that (nom. case)
nan desu ka — what is (it)?

2. *ARE* WA *NAN* DESU *KA.* — WHAT IS THAT?

akai — red
akai hon — red book
akai hon desu — (it) is (a) red book

3. ARE WA *AKAI* HON DESU. — THAT IS A RED BOOK.

4. SORE WA EMPITSU DESU KA. — IS THAT A PENCIL?

sore wa	as for that (nom. case)
empitsu dewa arimasen	(it) is not (a) pencil
5. *SORE* WA EMPITSU *DEWA ARIMASEN*.	THAT IS NOT A PENCIL.
6. KORE WA KUROI EMPITSU DESU KA.	IS THIS A BLACK PENCIL?
kono kono empitsu wa kuroi desu ka	this as for this pencil (nom. case) is (it) black?
7. *KONO* EMPITSU WA KUROI DESU KA.	IS THIS PENCIL BLACK?
hai kuroi desu	yes (it) is black
8. *HAI,* KUROI DESU.	YES, IT IS BLACK.
9. *SONO* HAKO WA AKAI HAKO DESU KA.	IS THAT BOX A RED BOX?
iie soo dewa arimasen	no (it) is not
10. IIE, *SOO DEWA ARIMASEN.*	NO, IT IS NOT.
11. IIE, AKAI HAKO DEWA ARIMASEN.	NO, IT IS NOT A RED BOX.
kono kono kuroi kono kuroi hon wa	this this black as for this black book (nom. case)
12. KONO KUROI HON WA JIBIKI DESU KA.	IS THIS BLACK BOOK A DICTIONARY?

13. HAI, *SOO DESU.* — YES, IT IS.

14. SORE WA JIBIKI DESU. — THAT IS A DICTIONARY.

Vocabulary List from the Lesson

kore (*ko-re*)* — (pron.) this

wa — (p.p.) a postposition used in nominative case. It has no meaning, but its significance is explained further below, under "Important Construction & Grammar Notes." (This will be referred to in the future as I.C. & G.N.)

nan (nani) — (interrog. pron.) what (?)

desu (*dé-su*) — (v.) to be, (it) is. (Pronounce this word with a silent ***u,*** closer to *des.*)

ka — Japanese equivalent to a question mark. (See I.C. & G.N.)

sore (*so-re*) — (pron.) that

hon — (n.) book

are (*a-re*) — (pron.) that (over there, pointing to something removed from the speaker and the listener).

akai (*a-ka-i*) — (adj.) red (pronounce as ***a-kai***)

kuroi (*ku-ro-i*) — (adj.) black

em-pi-tsu (*em-pi-tsu*) — (n.) pencil

kono (*ko-no*) — (adj.) this (requires a noun)

sono (*so-no*) — (adj.) that (requires a noun)

hako (*ha-ko*) — (n.) box

hai (*há-i*) — yes

soo — "Is that *so?*" (as in English), or, affirmation of what has been stated: "That is *so.*"

* The pronunciation guide is given for those words which might prove difficult on first encounter. A guide for words easy to pronounce has been omitted. Note the pitch mark (′) provided for some words.

iie (*ii-é*) — no

hon dewa arimasen — (It) *is not* (a) book. (See I.C. & G.N.)

jibiki (*ji-bi-ki*) — (n.) dictionary

Additional Vocabulary

This vocabulary is to be used to extend the scope of conversation. Substitute the words for their grammatical equivalents in the text or in the subsitution drill at the end of the chapter.

shiroi (*shi-ró-i*) — (adj.) white
aoi (*a-ó-i*) — (adj.) blue
gakkoo (*gak-koo*) — (n.) school
daigaku — (n.) university
kootoogakkoo (*koo-too-gak-koo*) — (n.) senior high school
chuugakkoo (*chuu-gak-koo*) — (n.) junior high school
shoogakkoo (*shoo-gak-koo*) — (n.) grade school
ano — (adj.) that (over there)
tegami (*te-ga-mi*) — (n.) letter
mado (*má-do*) — (n.) window
ookii (*oo-kii*) — (adj.) large, big
chiisai (*chii-sá-i*) — (adj.) small
tsukue (*tsu-ku-e*) — (n.) desk
isu — (n.) chair
furui (*fu-ru-i*) — (adj.) old
atarashii (*a-ta-ra-shii*) — (adj.) new

Important Construction and Grammar Notes

JAPANESE NOUNS: Except in a few cases, no distinction is made between singular and plural nouns. Hence, *hon* may mean "a book" or "books" as the case may be. Judging by context is important.

KORE, SORE AND ARE: These are demonstrative pronouns. **Kore** is equivalent to the English "this." **Sore** (that) refers to something comparatively near, and **are** (that) refers to something rather far in the sense of "that over there." Note the following examples:

1. **Kore** wa hon desu.	"This," in the hand of or near the speaker, "is a book."
2. **Sore** wa hon desu.	"That," near the person spoken to, "is a book."
3. **Are** wa hon desu.	"That," over there, "is a book."

WA: **Wa** is a postposition. Postpositions are used in Japanese after a noun to indicate the case (nominative, objective, possessive, etc.) of the preceding noun. **Wa** denotes the nominative case. This postposition is used to show what one is talking about, or the subject of the sentence. One may translate **wa** as "as for" or "with regard to."

Kono hon **wa** akai desu.	"This book," or "As for this book," "(it) is red."

KONO, SONO, AND ANO: Meaning "this," "that" and "that" (over there), they are used as ADJECTIVES, and therefore *cannot* stand alone, but must modify nouns. Do not confuse them with **kore, sore** and **are,** which can be used alone.

1. **Kono** hon . . .	This book . . .
2. **Sono** hon . . .	That book . . .
3. **Ano** hon . . .	That book (over there) . . .

SUBJECT OF A SENTENCE: In Japanese the subject is often left out when it is understood by the context of the sentence. See sentences 8, 10, and 13 in the text. In these three examples, the subjects are the same as those in the preceding statements, so they are not repeated. The omission of the subject in Japanese is somewhat like the usage of "it" in English to replace the subject. (See page 39, for more explanation.)

TRUE ADJECTIVES: There are two types of adjectives in Japanese, viz., true adjective and quasi adjective. The latter is a noun used as an adjective and is explained in Chapter 3. True adjectives are easily identifiable because they have the following endings: *ai, oi, ui,* and *ii.* (*Ei* ending words are not adjectives, but nouns.)

ak*ai*	red
kur*oi*	black
fur*ui*	old
ook*ii*	large

A true adjective modifies a noun directly, and is placed before the word it modifies.

DESU: **Desu** is called a verb at times, but it is actually an auxiliary verb of designation. **Desu** is attached only to substantives (noun or noun equivalent) and adjectives. (See further explanation on page 39.) It fulfills the function of making the substantive to which it is attached the predicate of the sentence. **Desu** is used in making the statement "A is B" or "It is. . . ." For example, "That (A) is a school (B)" is expressed as:

Sore (A) wa gakkoo (B) **desu.**

"Kore wa hon **desu**" means "This *is* (a) book."

Desu may also follow a true adjective:

Kore wa **ookii desu**. — This is big.
Are wa **shiroi desu**. — That is white.
Sono gakkoo wa **chiisai desu.**—That school is small.

NEGATIVE OF DESU:

(a) The following formula, as explained above, is used to express statements when the:

$$\text{SUBJECT} = \left(\begin{matrix}\text{is equal to}\\ \text{the same as}\end{matrix}\right) \text{PREDICATE}$$

A *WA* B *DESU*

For example:
I am a student. (I=student)
This is a school. (This=school)
Harvard is a university. (Harvard=university)

(b) The negative of these:

I am not a student. (I$\neq$student)
This is not a school. (This$\neq$school)
Harvard is not a high school. (Harvard$\neq$high school)

When the SUBJECT $\neq$ (is not equal to / not the same as) PREDICATE

(A)	WA	(B)	DEWA	ARIMASEN
(subject)		(predicate)		(is not)

or

(A)	WA	(B)	JA	ARIMASEN

Ja is the contraction of *dewa*. The *dewa* expression is preferable to *ja*. Therefore, the following translations are possible for:

"Harvard is not a high school."

Harvard WA kootoogakkoo DEWA ARIMASEN. (JA ARIMASEN.)

Affirmative	*Negative*
Kore **wa** hon **desu.**	Kore **wa** hon **dewa arimasen.**
Sore **wa** tsukue **desu.**	Sore **wa** tsukue **dewa arimasen.**
Kore **wa** kuroi empitsu **desu.**	Kore **wa** kuroi empitsu **dewa arimasen.**
Harvard **wa** chiisai gakkoo **desu.**	Harvard **wa** chiisai gakkoo **dewa arimasen.**

SENTENCE WORD ORDER AND MODIFIERS:

(a) The usual word order of a Japanese sentence is as follows:

SUBJECT	*WA*	PREDICATE	+	*DESU*
Kore (This	WA	hon book		DESU is)
Columbia (Columbia	WA	daigaku university		DESU is)

(b) Adjectival modifiers come before the words they modify:

SUBJECT	*WA*	MODIFIER	+ NOUN	+ VERB
Kore	WA	furui	hon	DESU
(This		old	book	is)
Columbia	WA	ookii	daigaku	DESU
(Columbia		large	university	is)

Remember that the verb *always* comes at the end of a sentence in Japanese. "I go to school by bus," when translated into Japanese, will have the following word order:

"I (wa)—to school—by bus—*go*."

INTERROGATIVE SENTENCE: A question in Japanese is asked by the addition of **ka** at the end of a declarative sentence. In English the word order changes when an interrogative sentence is formed but in Japanese it remains the same.

1. Kono daigaku wa furui desu. This university is old.
   Kono daigaku wa furui desu **ka.** *Is* this university old?
2. Kore wa shoogakkoo desu. This is a grade school.
   Kore wa shoogakkoo desu **ka.** *Is* this a grade school?

Substitution Drill

I. KORE WA { *(Noun)* GAKKOO / SHOOGAKKOO / CHUUGAKKOO / DAIGAKU / etc. } { DESU / DEWA ARIMASEN

II. { KORE / SORE / ARE } WA { *(Adj.)* AKAI / KUROI / AOI / etc. } EMPITSU DESU

			(*Adj.*)	
	KONO		OOKII	
III.	SONO	GAKKOO WA	CHIISAI	DESU
	ANO		FURUI	
			ATARASHII	
			etc.	

How to Use the Exercise

In order to get the most out of this exercise, the student should first become thoroughly familiar with the basic sentence patterns and substitution drills. Next, go on to the translation exercise, English to Japanese, which, with slight variation, is based on the sentence patterns. Repetition until one can respond almost automatically is the purpose. The next step is the expansion of these basic sentences by "substitution" (instead of **Kore wa hon desu,** now say **Kore wa tsukue, empitsu, isu,** etc. **desu**) and then by "expansion." This last step is accomplished by changing the sentence **Kore wa hon desu** to **Kore wa atarashii hon desu,** etc.

If this book is used in a classroom situation, the instructor should first read a sentence at a time with the group. The instructor should vary the presentation by the above mentioned "substitution" and "expansion" methods. Also a change of pace can be had by switching from a group recitation to an individual one or by a change to making questions from these sentences.

Exercises

This section of the exercise would be most helpful if the student would cover the right column and translate into Japanese. Next cover the left column and translate into English.

1. This is a book.	Kore wa hon desu.
2. This is a dictionary.	Kore wa jibiki desu.
3. That is a desk.	Sore wa tsukue desu.
4. That is a chair.	Sore wa isu desu.

5. That (over there) is a school.	Are wa gakkoo desu.
6. That (over there) is a college.	Are wa daigaku desu.
7. This is not a dictionary.	Kore wa jibiki dewa arimasen.
8. That is not a chair.	Sore wa isu dewa arimasen.
9. That (over there) is not a college.	Are wa daigaku dewa arimasen.
10. This is a big book.	Kore wa ookii hon desu.
11. This is a new dictionary.	Kore wa atarashii jibiki desu.
12. That is an old desk.	Sore wa furui tsukue desu.
13. That (over there) is a large chair.	Are wa ookii isu desu.
14. This is not a large school.	Kore wa ookii gakkoo dewa arimasen.
15. That is not a new dictionary.	Sore wa atarashii jibiki dewa arimasen.
16. That (over there) is not an old chair.	Are wa furui isu dewa arimasen.
17. This school is old.	Kono gakkoo wa furui desu.
18. That pencil is black.	Sono empitsu wa kuroi desu.
19. That dictionary is new.	Sono jibiki wa atarashii desu.
20. That college (over there) is big.	Ano daigaku wa ookii desu.

Translate into Japanese:

Note: (a) In translating English into Japanese, determine, first of all, the subject of the sentence, and follow it with WA.

(b) "IT" is not translatable into Japanese. Instead, determine the true subject, or treat the subject as understood. (See I.C. & G.N. above.)

1. What is this?
2. This is a chair.
3. What is that?
4. That is a small pencil.
5. Is this black pencil new?
6. No, this black pencil is old.
7. What is that (over there)?
8. That is an old desk.
9. Is that a school?
10. Yes, it is. It is a big school.

11. That big school is a grade school.
12. Is that grade school old?
13. Yes, it is an old school.
14. Is that school a high school?
15. No, it is a college.

Answer in Japanese. Give affirmative answers.

1. Kore wa hon desu ka.
2. Kore wa tsukue desu ka.
3. Kore wa akai hon desu ka.
4. Sore wa kuroi hako desu ka.
5. Kono empitsu wa akai desu ka.
6. Sono isu wa furui desu ka.
7. Harvard daigaku wa chiisai gakkoo desu ka.
8. Kono ookii gakkoo wa chuugakkoo desu ka.
9. Kono atarashii hon wa jibiki desu ka.
10. Columbia wa ookii daigaku desu ka.

Useful Expressions

Greetings (Aisatsu)

The following expressions should be memorized and used frequently.

a. OHAYOO (GOZAIMASU)	"Good morning." It should not be used after about 10:00 a.m. *OHAYOO* alone is used when speaking to a friend informally. *GOZAIMASU* is added for politeness.
b. KONNICHI WA	"Good morning" or "Good afternoon." Used in greeting and not in parting. It is used between 10:00 a.m. and evening.
c. KOMBAN WA	"Good evening." It is used when greeting someone.
d. SAYONARA	"Good-bye."
e. OYASUMI NASAI	"Goodnight." An expression used when one departs to retire for the night.

CHAPTER 3

BASIC SENTENCES (*continued*)

NOUN + NO + NOUN	= Formation of Quasi Adjective
NOUN + NO	= Possessive indicating ownership

Eigo	English
Eigo no	of English language
Eigo no hon desu	English language book is

1. KORE WA *EIGO NO HON DESU.* — THIS IS AN ENGLISH LANGUAGE BOOK.

dare	who
dare no	whose
dare no hon	whose book

2. *DARE NO HON* DESU KA. — WHOSE BOOK IS IT?

anata	you
anata no	your
anata no hon	your book

3. KORE WA *ANATA NO HON* DESU KA. — IS THIS YOUR BOOK?

watakushi	I
watakushi no	mine
watakushi no dewa arimasen	mine is not
4. IIE, SONO HON WA *WATAKUSHI NO DEWA ARIMASEN.*	NO, THAT BOOK IS NOT MINE.
sono	that
Eigo no hon	English language book
sensei no	teacher's
sensei no desu	(it) is the teacher's
5. SONO EIGO NO HON WA *SENSEI NO DESU.*	THAT ENGLISH BOOK IS (MY) TEACHER'S.
watakushi no	my
sensei no	teacher's
Eigo no hon	English language book
6. SORE WA WATAKUSHI NO SENSEI NO EIGO NO HON DESU.	THAT IS MY TEACHER'S ENGLISH BOOK.
anata	you
anata no	your
anata no hon wa	as for your book (nom. case)
jibiki desu ka	is (it) a dictionary?
7. ANATA NO HON WA JIBIKI DESU KA.	IS YOUR BOOK A DICTIONARY? (As for your book, is it a dictionary?)
8. IIE, JIBIKI DEWA ARIMASEN. KYOOKASHO DESU.	NO, IT IS NOT A DICTIONARY. IT IS A TEXTBOOK.

donna	what kind of
iro	color
donna iro	what color
9. *DONNA IRO* DESU KA.	WHAT COLOR IS IT?
watakushi	I
watakushi no	my
watakushi no hon wa	as for my book (nom. case)
10. WATAKUSHI NO HON WA KUROI *NO* DESU.	MY BOOK IS BLACK. (As for my book, it is black.)
11. KONO KUROI HON WA KYOOKASHO DESU.	THIS BLACK BOOK IS A READER.
sensei	teacher
sensei wa	as for (the) teacher
anata no sensei wa	as for your teacher
donata desu ka	who is (it)?
12. ANATA NO SENSEI WA *DONATA* DESU KA.	WHO IS YOUR TEACHER? (As for your teacher, who is it?)
watakushi	I
watakushi no	my
watakushi no sensei wa	as for my teacher
13. WATAKUSHI NO SENSEI WA ITOO-SAN DESU.	MY TEACHER IS MR. ITO.
Nihongo no	of Japanese language (quasi adj.)
Nihongo no sensei	Japanese language teacher (or teacher of Japanese language)
14. ITOO-SAN WA WATA-KUSHI NO NIHONGO NO SENSEI DESU.	MR. ITO IS MY JAPANESE LANGUAGE TEACHER.

Vocabulary List from the Lesson

Eigo (*e-i-go*)	(n.) English (language)
Eigo no	(quasi adj.) of English
Eigo no hon	(n.) English book
Nihongo (*Ni-hon-go*)	(n.) Japanese (language)
Nihongo no hon	(n.) Japanese book
dare (*da-re*)	(inter. pro.) who?
dare no	(inter. pro.) whose?
dare no hon	whose book?
watakushi (*wa-ta-ku-shi*)	(pro.) I
watakushi wa	I, or, as for me (in the nominative case)
watakushi no	my (possessive case)
watakushi no hon	my book
anata (*a-ná-ta*)	(pro.) you
donna (*dón-na*)	(inter. adj.) what kind of . . .?
iro (*i-ró*)	(n.) color
donna iro	what color . . .?
kyookasho	(n.) textbook, reader, primer
sensei (*sen-sé-i*)	(n.) teacher (*i* after another vowel *e* is unstressed and is close to *ay* in "s*ay*.")
. . . **-san**	(suf.) honorific suffix comparable to Mr., Mrs. or Miss. Not used when referring to one's own family or self and always used *after* the name.
no	(p.p.) "of"—used to join two substantives. It also denotes possession. (See I.C. & G.N.)
donata (*dó-na-ta*)	(pro.) who? polite form of *dare.*

Additional Vocabulary

boku	(pro.) I (used by men only)
kimi	(pro.) you (used by men only)

zasshi (*zas-shi*)	(n.) magazine
shimbun (*shim-bun*)	(n.) newspaper
seito (*se-i-to*)	(n.) student
namae (*na-ma-e*)	(n.) name
tekisuto	(n.) textbook

Important Construction and Grammar Notes

POSTPOSITION "NO": **No** is a postposition used to join two nouns. When this is done, the first noun is made to modify the second noun, and it becomes an adjective.

Adjectives thus formed are called *Quasi Adjectives*. When analyzed in this manner, the distinction between so-called True Adjectives and Quasi Adjectives becomes apparent. A true adjective, as the name implies, performs its function of adjectival modifier by itself, but a quasi adjective is a noun converted into an adjective by the addition of **no.**

TRUE ADJECTIVE

1. **shiroi** hon — a white book
2. **furui** jibiki — an old dictionary

QUASI ADJECTIVE

1. Eigo **no** hon — an English book
2. Nihongo **no** sensei — a Japanese (language) teacher

Note: In general, when used to form a quasi adjective, **no** is the English equivalent of "of." **Eigo no hon**="book of English" (English book).

POSSESSIVE "NO": The postposition **no** is also used to denote possession. It is equivalent to " 's" in English. For example:

1. sensei **no** hon — a teacher's book
2. watakushi **no** gakkoo — my school
3. Tanaka-san **no** seito — Tanaka's student

Affirmative	*Negative*
Sensei **no** hon **desu.**	Sensei no hon **dewa arimasen.** (It is *not* a teacher's book.)

Watakushi **no** gakkoo **desu.**	Watakushi no gakkoo **dewa arimasen.** (It is *not* my school.)
Tanaka-san **no** seito **desu.**	Tanaka-san no seito **dewa arimasen.** (He is *not* Tanaka's student.)
Sore wa watakushi **no desu.**	Sore wa watakushi no **dewa arimasen.** (That is *not* mine.)

SUFFIX "GO." **Go** means "language" and it is affixed to the names of the countries to indicate the language of that country.

1. Supein-**go** — Spanish language
2. Furansu-**go** — French language
3. Doitsu-**go** — German language

etc.

Similarly, **jin** which has the meaning "people," can be attached to the names of the countries to indicate the people of that country.

1. Itaria-**jin** — Italian
2. Roshiya-**jin** — Russian
3. Chuugoku-**jin** — Chinese

OMISSION OF SUBJECT: While in English a sentence is incomplete without a subject, in Japanese when the subject of a sentence is understood from the context, it is often left out. For example, in the text, sentence 2 shows that the subject *Kore* is understood from the preceding sentence, so this sentence should actually read:

(Kore wa) dare no hon desu ka.

Also in sentences 8 and 9 the subjects are omitted for the same reason.

KUROI NO DESU, KUROI N' DESU, KUROI DESU: **Desu** is normally used with substantives. Hence,

Watakushi wa Eigo no **sensei desu.**
Kore wa furui **tsukue desu.**

When this rule is applied to adjectives and the sentences "The chair is black" and "My school is big" are translated:

Isu wa *kuroi no desu.*
Watakushi no gakkoo wa *ookii no desu.*

No, as used here after true adjectives, gives a nominal meaning. In the former sentence, it stands for *isu*, while in the latter it stands for *gakkoo*. However, in actual usage *no* is often contracted to *n* and it becomes as follows:

Isu wa *kuroi n' desu.*
Watakushi no gakkoo wa *ookii n' desu.*

Finally, even this *n* contraction may be left out entirely so that in colloquial usage ADJECTIVE+DESU is now acceptable.

Isu wa *kuroi desu.*
Watakushi no gakkoo wa *ookii desu.*

Substitution Drill

KORE WA { *(Noun)* ANATA / WATAKUSHI / GAKKOO / SENSEI / BROWN-SAN } NO ZASSHI { DESU / DEWA ARIMASEN }

Exercises

1. This is my magazine. — Kore wa watakushi no zasshi desu.
2. This is your newspaper. — Kore wa anata no shimbun desu.
3. That is Jiro's school. — Sore wa Jiroo no gakkoo desu.
4. This is mine. — Kore wa watakushi no desu.

5. That is yours.	Sore wa anata no desu.
6. That is Jiro's.	Are wa Jiroo no desu.
7. This is not mine.	Kore wa watakushi no dewa arimasen.
8. That is not yours.	Sore wa anata no dewa arimasen.
9. That is not Jiro's.	Are wa Jiroo no dewa arimasen.
10. This is not my book.	Kore wa watakushi no hon dewa arimasen.
11. That is not your pencil.	Sore wa anata no empitsu dewa arimasen.
12. That is not Jiro's Japanese dictionary.	Are wa Jiroo no Nihongo no jibiki dewa arimasen.
13. What kind of book is this?*	Kore wa donna hon desu ka.
14. What kind of newspaper is the *New York Times?**	*New York Times* wa donna shimbun desu ka.
15. What (kind of) color is your pencil?*	Anata no empitsu wa donna iro desu ka.
16. My college is big.	Watakushi no daigaku wa ookii desu.
17. Your magazine is old.	Anata no zasshi wa furui desu.
18. Jiro's teacher is Japanese.	Jiroo no sensei wa Nihonjin desu.
19. Jiro's English teacher is Japanese.	Jiroo no Eigo no sensei wa Nihonjin desu.
20. Jiro's English teacher is Mr. Tanaka.	Jiroo no Eigo no sensei wa Tanaka-san desu.
21. My Japanese teacher is Mr. Tanaka.	Watakushi no Nihongo no sensei wa Tanaka-san desu.
22. That English school is new.	Ano Eigo no gakkoo wa atarashii desu.
23. My English name is Bob.	Watakushi no Eigo no namae wa Bob desu.

* In these sentences (#13, 14, 15), note that the subjects are reversed as follows: *This* is what kind of book? *The New York Times* is what kind of newspaper? *Your pencil* is what (kind of) color?

Translate into Japanese:

1. Is *Life* a Japanese language newspaper?
2. No, it is not a Japanese language newspaper.
3. It is an American magazine.
4. Are these Japanese magazines yours?
5. No, they are not mine. They are my teacher's.
6. This is Miss Ito's newspaper.
7. This new English dictionary is John's.
8. What kind of Japanese dictionary is that?
9. This is an old Japanese dictionary.
10. Mr. Brown is a college German teacher.
11. What is the color of your English teacher's reader?
12. My teacher's reader is red.
13. This Japanese book is old.
14. Mr. Ito is your teacher.
15. My Spanish language teacher's name is Mr. Sanchez.
16. Are you a Japanese language student?
17. No, I am not. I am an English language student.

Answer in Japanese:

(As explained above and on page 54, the subject is often omitted. Therefore, in answering question #1 below, one can simply say, *Watakushi no desu.* However, it is advisable that the reader, in order to become acquainted with the construction, make a complete sentence by saying *Kono ookii hon wa watakushi no desu.* Use a complete sentence with subject and predicate in answering the following. Also use both negative and positive answers wherever possible.)

1. Kono ookii hon wa dare no hon desu ka.
2. Kono ookii hon wa donna iro desu ka.
3. Kono ookii hon wa Eigo no hon desu ka.
4. Kono zasshi wa dare no desu ka.
5. Are wa furui shimbun desu ka.
6. Sono chiisai hon wa jibiki desu ka.
7. Kono Nihongo no hon wa donata no desu ka.
8. Sono jibiki wa kimi no desu ka.

9. Sono jibiki wa kuroi desu ka.
10. Sore wa Eigo no jibiki desu ka.
11. Sensei no hon wa akai desu ka.
12. Sensei no chiisai hon wa donna iro desu ka.
13. Ano shiroi hon wa sensei no desu ka.
14. *Life* wa Nihongo no zasshi desu ka.
15. Anata no sensei wa Itoo-san desu ka.

Fill in the blanks:

1. Watakushi ___ sensei ___ Itoo-san desu.
2. Kore ___ donata ___ shimbun desu ka.
3. Kono ___ wa ookii desu.
4. Sono ___ wa donata ___ desu ka.
5. Kono empitsu ___ akai ___ ka.
6. Ano kyookasho ___ dare ___ desu ka.
7. Itoo-san ___ Nihongo ___ sensei desu.
8. Brown-san ___ kono gakkoo ___ sensei ___ arimasen.
9. Anata ___ kono gakkoo ___ seito desu ka.
10. Watakushi ___ Eigo ___ sensei wa Brown-san ___.

Useful Expressions

Greetings (Aisatsu)

Itoo:	IKAGA DESU KA.	How are you?
Brown:	ARIGATOO GOZAI-MASU. GENKI DESU.	Thank you. (I'm) quite well.
Itoo:	OTOOSAN (OKAASAN) WA IKAGA DESU KA.	How is your father (mother)?
Brown:	OKAGESAMA DE GEN-KI DESU.	Thanks to (your) kind thought, he (she) is fine. (This is a more complete form of answering the question *Ikaga desu ka.*)
Itoo:	DEWA MATA.	I'll see you again.
Brown:	SAYONARA.	Goodbye.

Supplement I

Numerals

JAPANESE NUMERALS	CHINESE NUMERALS
1 hitotsu	ichi
2 futatsu	ni
3 mittsu	san
4 yottsu	shi (yon)
5 itsutsu	go
6 muttsu	roku
7 nanatsu	shichi (nana)
8 yattsu	hachi
9 kokonotsu	ku (kyuu)
10 too	juu

Note (a): Japanese numerals end at 10, and beyond 10 the numerals are read, in general, the same as the Chinese numerals. Japanese numerals are used in counting inanimate objects, or when there is no classifier. (This is explained in Supplement II, p. 69.)

11	juu-ichi	90	kyuu-juu
12	juu-ni	100	hyaku
13	juu-san	200	ni-hyaku
14	juu-shi, juu-yon	300	sam-byaku*
15	juu-go	400	shi-hyaku, yon-hyaku
16	juu-roku	500	go-hyaku
17	juu-shichi	600	roppyaku*
18	juu-hachi	700	shichi-hyaku, nana-hyaku
19	juu-ku, juu-kyuu	800	happyaku*
20	ni-juu	900	ku-hyaku, kyuu-hyaku
30	san-juu	1,000	sen**
40	shi-juu, yon-juu	10,000	ichi-man, man
50	go-juu	100,000	juu-man
60	roku-juu	1,000,000	hyaku-man
70	shichi-juu, nana-juu	100,000,000	ichi-oku
80	hachi-juu		

Eleven is 10+1, or *juu+ichi.*
Twelve is 10+2, or *juu+ni.*
Thirty is 3×10, or *san juu.*
Sixty is 6×10, or *roku juu.*
275 is *two* (100) *seven* (10)+5 or *ni*-hyaku *shichi*-juu go.
591 is *five* (100) *nine* (10)+1 or *go*-hyaku *kyu*-juu ichi.
909 is *nine* (100)+9 or *kyu*-hyaku *ku.*

Note (b): * A phonetic change occurs for these numbers.
** Note the phonetic change for 3,000 (san*zen*).

Keep the following digit terms clearly in mind, and practice reading numerals in Japanese.

1	0	0	0	0	0	0	0
sen man	hyaku man	juu man	man	sen	hyaku	juu	ichi
					6 rop*pyaku*	7 shichi *juu*	5 go
				1 *sen*	9 kyuu *hyaku*	6 roku *juu*	6 roku
			2 ni *man*	5 go *sen*	4 yon *hyaku*	1 *juu*	8 hachi
		7 shichi juu (nanajuu)	4 yom *man*	1 *sen* (issen)	0	2 ni *juu*	4 shi (yon)

Note: In reading figures exceeding 10,000 (which is in the *MAN* category) first determine how many *MAN*'S there are. Then read the remainder. For example, in the number 5,843,000 there are 584 *MAN*'S 3,000, or *gohyaku hachijuu yon MAN*. Therefore, this figure is read:

gohyaku hachijuu yon MAN san ZEN.

As a result of inflation in post-war Japan, when a copy of *The Japan Times* cost *sanjuu-go en* (35 yen) and a pack of cigarettes cost *hachijuu en,* it is necessary to be able to use large figures when counting.

Try saying the following figures in Japanese:

75	235	1,968	9,360	95,406
86	678	2,305	28,469	187,529
116	989	7,586	86,340	468,023

CHAPTER 4

KYOOSHITSU—CLASSROOM (1)

"TE" FORM OF VERB	+	KUDASAI	=	"Please" *(Polite request)*

"TE" FORM OF VERB	+	IMASU	=	"...ing" *(Progressive form)*
	+	IMASEN	=	"Not...ing."

tatte kudasai	please stand up
1. TAKAHASHI-SAN, *TATTE KUDASAI.*	MR. TAKAHASHI, PLEASE STAND UP.
KOSHIKAKETE KUDASAI.	PLEASE SIT DOWN.
hon o yonde kudasai	book (obj. case) please read
2. *HON O YONDE KUDASAI.*	PLEASE READ THE BOOK.
3. *TO O AKETE KUDASAI.*	PLEASE OPEN THE DOOR.
TO O *SHIMETE KUDASAI.*	PLEASE CLOSE THE DOOR.
anata wa nani o shite imasu ka	as for you (nom. case) what (obj. case) (are you) doing
4. ANATA WA NANI O *SHITE IMASU KA.*	WHAT ARE YOU DOING?

watakushi wa	as for me (nom. case)
Nihongo o	Japanese (obj. case)
kaite imasu	(am) writing

5. WATAKUSHI WA NIHON-GO O *KAITE IMASU.* — I AM WRITING JAPANESE.

Kishi-san ga	(it is) Mr. Kishi
to o	the door (obj. case)
shimete imasu	is closing

6. KISHI-SAN *GA* TO O SHI-METE IMASU. — MR. KISHI IS CLOSING THE DOOR.

7. WATAKUSHI WA TO O *SHIMETE IMASEN.* — I AM NOT CLOSING THE DOOR.

minasan	everybody
anata no hon o	your book (obj. case)
mite kudasai	please look

8. *MINASAN,* ANATA NO HON O *MITE KUDASAI.* — EVERYBODY, PLEASE LOOK AT YOUR BOOK.

issho ni	together
yonde kudasai	please read

9. *ISSHO NI YONDE KUDA-SAI.* — PLEASE READ TOGETHER.

moo ichido	once more
itte kudasai	please say (it)

10. *MOO ICHIDO ITTE KUDA-SAI.* — PLEASE SAY (IT) ONCE MORE.

moo sukoshi — a little more
yukkuri — slowly
hanashite kudasai — please speak

11. MOO *SUKOSHI YUKKURI* *HANASHITE KUDASAI.* — PLEASE SPEAK A LITTLE MORE SLOWLY.

Eigo de — in English
hanashite kudasai — please speak

12. EIGO *DE* HANASHITE KU-DASAI. — PLEASE SPEAK IN ENGLISH.

Vocabulary List from the Lesson

tatsu (*tá-tsu*) — (v.i.) to stand, to stand up
tatte (*tát-te*) — ("te" verb form of *tatsu.* See I.C. & G.N.)
tatte kudasai (*ku-da-sa-i*) — please stand up
tatte imasu — (is) standing
koshikakeru (*ko-shi-ka-ke-ru*) — (v.i.) to sit, to sit down
koshikakete kudasai — please sit down (See I.C. & G.N.)
koshikakete imasu — (is) sitting (See I.C. & G.N.)
o — (p.p.) postposition denoting objective case; indicates that the preceding noun is the object of a verb. (See I.C. & G.N.)
yomu — (v.t.) to read
yonde (*yón-de*) — ("te" verb form of *yomu.* See I.C. & G.N.)
yonde kudasai — please read
yonde imasu — (is) reading
akeru — (v.t.) to open
akete (*a-ke-te*) — ("te" verb form of *akeru.* See I.C. & G.N.)
akete kudasai — please open

suru	(v.t.) to do
shite kudasai (*shi-te*)	please do
shite imasu	(is) doing
kaku	(v.t.) to write
kaite (*ká-i-te*)	("te" verb form of *kaku*. Henceforth "te" form of the verb will be called "te" verb.)
kaite imasu	(is) writing
to	(n.) door
shimeru (*shi-me-ru*)	(v.t.) to close
shimete	("te" form of *shimeru*)
imasen	(v.) negative of *imasu*
shimete imasen	(is) not closing
ga	(p.p.) a postposition used in the nominative case. It has no meaning, but it emphasizes the subject. (See I.C. & G.N.)
mina-san (*mi-ná-san*)	(n.) everybody
miru	(v.t.) to see, to look, to look at
mite	("te" form of *miru*)
mite kudasai	please look
issho ni (*is-sho*)	together
moo	more, additional
ichido	once (one time)
moo ichido	once more
iu	(v.t.) to say, to tell
itte kudasai	please say
moo sukoshi	a little more
yukkuri (*yuk-ku-ri*)	(adv.) slowly, leisurely
hanasu (*ha-ná-su*)	(v.t.) to talk, to speak, to relate
hanashite	("te" form of *hanasu*)
hanashite kudasai	please speak
Eigo de	in English

Additional Vocabulary

dore	(inter. pro.) which?
dono	(inter. adj. pro.) which?
asobu	(v.t.) to play, to while away time, to visit
kau	(v.t.) to buy, to purchase
aruku	(v.i.) to walk
ima	(n.) now
nugu	(v.t.) to take off (shoes, hat, coat, etc.)
tomodachi (*to-mo-da-chi*)	(n.) friend

Important Construction and Grammar Notes

"TE" VERB+KUDASAI: The **te** form of a verb plus **kudasai** is the polite request form, and it means:

1. Please write.
2. Please read.

etc.

"TE" VERB+IMASU: The **te** form of a verb plus **imasu** (or **imasen** for the negative) signifies progressive action in Japanese, and it is translated:

1. He is read*ing* (or, he is not reading.)
2. I am play*ing* (or, I am not playing.)

etc.

Tatte, koshikakete, and **yonde** are "te" (and "de") forms of the verbs **tatsu, koshikakeru,** and **yomu,** meaning "to stand up," "to sit down," and "to read" respectively. Some verbs end in "te" and others "de," as explained on the next page.

In studying verbs, it is necessary to know the DICTIONARY FORMS, sometimes called the abrupt present, or the root forms, of the Japanese verbs since all conjugations and voices are derived from this basic form. **Tatsu, koshikakeru,** and **yomu** are the dictionary forms of the verb. This form of the verb is a complete verb. It indicates the present tense and it is less formal (more abrupt) than the **masu** ending. It has the following meanings:

Hon o *yomu* — I read a book. (a statement of fact)
I will read a book. (intention)
I shall read a book. (simple future)

HOW "TE" VERBS ARE FORMED: From the endings of the root form of the verbs, one can obtain a rule for formulating "te" forms of the various verbs.

For instance, the verb **kaku** has a **ku** ending. The "te" form of the verb is formed by changing **ku** to **ite: ka-ite, kaite.** Similarly, *aru***ku** becomes *aru***ite.** For a verb with a **mu** ending, **mu** is changed to **nde.**

Therefore, *yo***mu** becomes *yo***nde.**

With this thought in mind, the following table should be carefully studied and mastered. This table includes all verb endings. The syllables within the brackets indicate the verb ending.

A(u)	"to meet"	tte	(a/tte)	Verbs ending in *U, TSU, RU* change to **TTE.**
TA(tsu)	"to stand"	tte	(ta/tte)	
U(ru)	"to sell"	tte	(u/tte)	
YO(mu)	"to read"	nde	(yo/nde)	Verbs ending in *MU, BU, NU* change to **NDE.**
TO(bu)	"to fly"	nde	(to/nde)	
SHI(nu)	"to die"	nde	(shi/nde)	
SA(su)	"to point"	shite	(sa/shite)	— *SU* changes to **SHITE**
KA(ku)	"to write"	ite	(ka/ite)	— *KU* changes to **ITE**
NU(gu)	"to undress"	ide	(nu/ide)	— *GU* changes to **IDE**

For verbs ending in **-IRU** and **-ERU**, the ichidan verbs, always drop **RU** and add **TE.**

mi**ru**—"to see"—mi**te**
shi**meru**—"to close"—shime**te**

Note: The "te" form of the verb in Japanese is an incomplete verb, having no meaning when used alone. It acquires meaning only when it is used with another verb, as explained in this lesson. Nevertheless, this form is used quite frequently with many different meanings, so it should be thoroughly mastered. Other usages will be explained as they appear.
For verbs *kuru* (to come) and *suru* (to do), which are considered irregular verbs (see page 134) because they do not follow any rule when conjugating, the "te" form should be memorized as:

KURU—*kite*
SURU —*shite*

POSTPOSITION O: This postposition identifies the direct object. Hence, when we say **hon o** it gives the feeling, "here is a book presented for action to be taken on it." In other words, **o** indicates that the preceding noun is in the objective case, so it must be used with a transitive verb, a verb which passes its action onto an object. Or, to put this in another way, a transitive verb requires an object. Note the following word order when an object is introduced.

DIRECT OBJECT + O + TRANSITIVE VERB

1. hon	**o**	yomu.
2. Nihongo	**o**	hanasu.
3. zasshi	**o**	kau.

In this chapter, **kaku** (write), **miru** (see), **akeru** (open), **shimeru** (close), **hanasu** (speak), etc., are transitive verbs. An intransitive verb does not require an object. **Tatsu** (stand), **aruku** (walk), etc., belong in this group.

SUBJECT+DIRECT OBJECT+VERB: This is the usual word order of a Japanese sentence containing a direct object. Place the object close to the verb.

SUBJECT WA + OBJECT O + VERB

1. Watakushi **wa**	hon	**o**	yonde imasu.
2. Anata **wa**	Eigo	**o**	hanashite kudasai.

ASSOCIATING POSTPOSITIONS WITH VERBS: It is often helpful to remember postpositions by associating them with particular verbs. **Yomu** is a transitive verb. Hence, **. . . o yomu.**

GA: This is a nominative postposition similar to **wa,** and it emphasizes the subject, while **wa** is used to denote attention to the predicate. In English, such distinction is made by intonation, for example, "John did it!" or "I'm the boss." In these instances, **ga** is used.

(a) Kore **wa** hon desu.	This is a book.
(b) Kore **ga** hon desu.	This (particular one) is a book.
(a) Kishi-san **wa** to o shimete imasu.	Mr. Kishi is closing the door.
(b) Kishi-san **ga** to o shimete imasu.	(It is) Mr. Kishi (who) is closing the door.

GA is used for a special reason only.

WA is more commonly used to indicate the subject of a sentence. Use **ga** in the nominative case, after interrogative pronouns:

1. Dare **ga** hanashite imasu ka.
2. Dore **ga** hon desu ka.

POSTPOSITIONS IN GENERAL: Postpositions are simple words sometimes referred to as "particles." Their simplicity, however, is a bit deceptive.

It is well for all beginning students to remember that there is no exact English equivalent to them. Instead of giving simple English equivalents, which are often misleading, it is much more helpful to have a clear definition of each postposition. Know why you are using a certain postposition. Students should pay special attention in their mastery by constant use, practice, association, and mimicry. Remember that after EVERY noun, with a few exceptions, there must be a postposition.

Substitution Drill

("Te" verb)

I. ANATA NO HON O { YONDE / MITE / AKETE / KATTE } KUDASAI.

II. ITOO-SAN WA	TATTE KOSHIKAKETE SHITE KATTE ASONDE HANASHITE ARUITE	IMASU (or IMASEN).

Exercises

Note: The subjects "I" and "You" are omitted as understood in the Japanese translations.

1. Please read.	Yonde kudasai.
2. Please read your book.	Anata no hon o yonde kudasai.
3. Please close (it).	Shimete kudasai.
4. Please close the door.	To o shimete kudasai.
5. Please look.	Mite kudasai.
6. Please look at the book.	Hon o mite kudasai.
7. Please write.	Kaite kudasai.
8. Please write English.	Eigo o kaite kudasai.
9. Please write English slowly.	Eigo o yukkuri kaite kudasai.
10. Please buy.	Katte kudasai.
11. Please buy the magazine.	Zasshi o katte kudasai.
12. I will do (it).	Shimasu.
13. I am doing (it).	Shite imasu.
14. I am not doing (it).	Shite imasen.
15. I will play.	Asobimasu.
16. I am playing.	Asonde imasu.
17. I am not playing.	Asonde imasen.
18. I am writing.	Kaite imasu.
19. I am writing Japanese.	Nihongo o kaite imasu.
20. Please speak.	Hanashite kudasai.
21. Please speak slowly.	Yukkuri hanashite kudasai.

22. Please speak slowly in Japanese.	Yukkuri Nihongo de hanashite kudasai.
23. Please speak slowly in Japanese once more.	Moo ichido yukkuri Nihongo de hanashite kudasai.
24. What are you doing?	Nani o shite imasu ka.
25. What are you writing?	Nani o kaite imasu ka.
26. What are you eating?	Nani o tabete imasu ka.
27. What are you looking (at)?	Nani o mite imasu ka.

Translate into Japanese:

1. Please read your book.
2. Please write in English.
3. Please close the door slowly.
4. Please speak slowly once more.
5. I am not speaking English now. I am speaking Japanese.
6. My teacher is reading the Japanese book slowly.
7. Is Mr. Tanaka opening the window now? No, I am opening (it).
8. Who is looking at the magazine?
9. A student is looking at my magazine.
10. Who is walking slowly? Mr. Ito is walking slowly.
11. The English teacher is writing English slowly.
12. Please read together once more.
13. Please read a little more.
14. What are you doing now? Are you reading a newspaper?
15. No, I am not. I am looking at my high school Japanese reader.

Note: The subject "you" is understood for sentences 1–4. Therefore, the Japanese translation, too, can omit the subject.

Answer in Japanese:

1. Anata wa ima hanashite imasu ka.
2. Sensei wa ima tatte imasu ka.
3. Dare ga ima zasshi o yonde imasu ka.
4. Dare ga Nihongo o hanashite imasu ka.
5. Anata wa ima Eigo o kaite imasu ka.

6. Dore ga anata no isu desu ka.
7. Dono hon ga anata no desu ka.
8. Anata wa ima nani o shite imasu ka. Shimbun o yonde imasu ka.
9. Anata no tomodachi wa ima shimbun o mite imasu ka.
10. Anata wa ima watakushi no tegami o yonde imasu ka.
11. Anata wa Eigo de tegami o kaite imasu ka.
12. Anata no tomodachi wa mado o shimete imasu ka.
13. Anata wa dare no hon o mite imasu ka.
14. Anata wa ima yukkuri aruite imasu ka.
15. Anata wa ima tatte imasu ka, koshikakete imasu ka.

What would you say, when . . .

1. You want someone to say something once more.
2. You want someone to speak a little more slowly.
3. You want to find out how his father is.
4. You want to answer that he is fine.
5. You want to find out the name of his Spanish language teacher.
6. You want to know whether his Japanese language primer is a new one.
7. You meet Mr. Ito in the afternoon and want to find out how he is.
8. You want someone to write his name.
9. You want someone to write his name in Japanese.
10. You want someone to write his name in Japanese once more.

Useful Expressions

The Weather (Tenki)

a. II OTENKI DESU NE.	Nice weather, isn't it?
b. TENKI GA WARUI DESU NE.	Awful weather, isn't it?
c. ATSUI DESU NE.	Hot (weather), isn't it?
d. SAMUI DESU NE.	Cold (weather), isn't it?
e. YOKU AME GA FURIMASU NE.	It rains a lot, doesn't it?

Note: *NE* is used at the end of a sentence, asking for a confirmation to a question. It really isn't seeking an answer. It is equivalent to "isn't it so?" "don't you think so too?" or "n'est ce pas?"

CHAPTER 5

ARIMASU—THERE IS

(Pertaining to the existence of inanimate things)

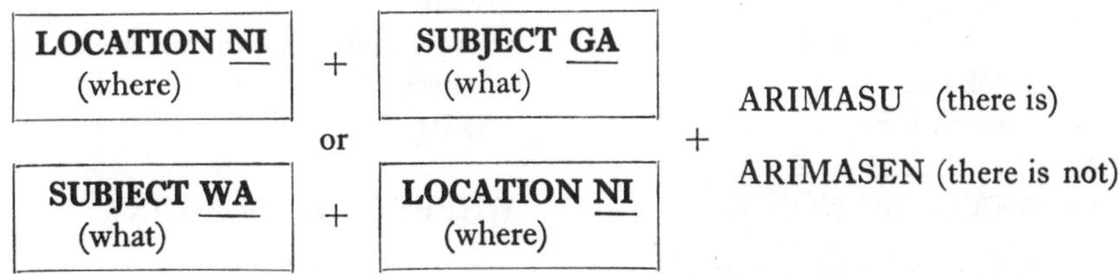

Reminder: The basic sentences in the main text should be repeated until memorized. Use the English sentences on the right side of the page to help you understand the sentence structure.

heya no naka	room's inside
heya no naka ni	in the room
nani ga	what
arimasu ka	is there?

1. *HEYA NO NAKA NI* NANI GA *ARIMASU* KA. — WHAT IS IN THE ROOM?

tsukue ga	a desk (nom. case)
arimasu	there is

2. TSUKUE GA ARIMASU. — THERE IS A DESK.

tsukue no ue	desk's top
tsukue no ue ni	on top of the desk (desk's top)
nani ga	what
arimasu ka	is there?

3. *TSUKUE NO UE NI* NANI GA ARIMASU KA. — WHAT IS (THERE) ON TOP OF THE DESK?

booshi	hat
to	and
kaban	bag

4. BOOSHI *TO* KABAN GA ARIMASU. — THERE ARE A HAT AND A BAG.

anata no	your
anata no hon wa	as for your book (nom. case)
doko ni	where
arimasu ka	is it?

5. ANATA NO HON WA *DOKO NI* ARIMASU KA. — WHERE IS YOUR BOOK?

tsukue no ue ni	on top of the desk
arimasu	there is

6. WATAKUSHI NO HON WA *TSUKUE NO UE NI* ARIMASU. — MY BOOK IS ON TOP OF THE DESK.

7. NOOTO-BUKKU TO HON WA *DOKO NI* ARIMASU KA. — WHERE ARE (YOUR) NOTEBOOK AND BOOK?

8. WATAKUSHI NO HON TO NOOTO-BUKKU WA *TSUKUE NO UE NI* ARIMASU. — MY BOOK AND NOTEBOOK ARE ON THE DESK.

KABAN WA *TSUKUE NO SHITA* NI ARIMASU. — (MY) BAG IS UNDER THE DESK.

anata	you
anata no	your

anata no heya	your room
anata no heya no naka ni	inside your room (your room's inside)
isu ga	chair (nom. case)
arimasu ka.	is there?

9. ANATA NO *HEYA NO NAKA NI* ISU GA ARI-MASU KA. — IS THERE A CHAIR IN YOUR ROOM?

10. IIE, *ARIMASEN.* — NO, THERE ISN'T.

koko	here
koko ni	at this place

11. *KOKO NI* TEREBI GA ARI-MASU KA. — IS THERE A TELEVISION HERE?

12. IIE, KONO *HEYA NO NA-KA NI* TEREBI GA ARI-MASEN. — NO, THERE IS NO TELEVISION IN THIS ROOM.

anata no mae	your front
anata no mae ni	in your front
tomodachi ga	friend (nom. case)
tatte imasu ka	is standing?

13. *ANATA NO MAE NI* TO-MODACHI GA TATTE IMASU KA. — IS A FRIEND STANDING IN FRONT OF YOU?

14. IIE, TATTE IMASEN. KOSHIKAKETE IMASU. — NO, (HE IS) NOT STANDING. HE IS SITTING.

Vocabulary List from the Lesson

Note: These translations are not in the best English. The primary purpose is to convey the *kimochi* or "feeling" of the words or phrases described in the most concise manner. In rendering translations of sentences, however, the reader is expected to use the best English or Japanese of which he is capable.

heya (*he-yá*)	(n.) room
naka (*ná-ka*)	(n.) the inside
ni	(p.p.) postposition indicating location: in, at (See I.C. & G.N.)
heya no naka	the inside of a room, room's inside
heya no naka ni	in the room
aru	(v.) there is (abrupt form of *arimasu*)
arimasu	(v.) there is (used to show existence of inanimate object only)
arimasen	negative of *arimasu*
tsukue (*tsu-ku-e*)	(n.) desk
ue (*u-é*)	(n.) the top part, or, the top; the above part
tsukue no ue ni	on the desk
booshi (*boo-shi*)	(n.) hat, cap
to	(conj.) and (See I.C. & G.N.)
kaban	(n.) bag (lady's handbag, brief case, suitcase, school bag)
doko (*do-ko*)	(inter. pro) where? what place?
doko ni	where? (at what place?)
nooto-bukku	(n.) notebook
shita (*shi-tá*)	(n.) down, the down place, that place which is directly below something
tsukue no shita ni	under the desk
koko	here, this place
koko ni	here, at this place
terebi	(n.) T. V., television
mae (*má-e*)	(n.) the front, the fore, in front place, the before (time), ago (time), past
mae ni	in the front, before (time)

Additional Vocabulary

soko	there, that place
soko ni	there, at that place
aida (*a-i-da*)	(n.) between (in space, or time)
hon no aida ni	between the books
soba	(n.) near, the near place, immediate vicinity
chikaku (*chi-ká-ku*)	(n.) near, includes wider area than *soba*
mannaka (*man-na-ka*)	(n.) dead center, center (also, when loosely used: approximate center)
mannaka ni	in the center
ushiro (*u-shi-ro*)	(n.) rear, back, the behind place
boku no ushiro ni	behind me
uchi (*u-chi*)	(n.) home
hidari (*hi-da-ri*)	(n.) the left side
migi	(n.) the right side
kooen (*koo-en*)	(n.) park
hito (*hi-to*)	(n.) person
sono (ano) kata (*so-no ka-ta*)	that person; this expression is used for the pronouns "he" and "she"
sono (ano) hito	same as above but less polite
teeburu	(n.) table

Important Construction and Grammar Notes

ARIMASU: **Arimasu** is the VERB OF EXISTENCE. It is used to show existence of INANIMATE OBJECTS. It cannot be used with animate things. **Arimasu** can be translated into English as "there is," or "there are."

Desu states the substance. **Arimasu** states existence. **Ni** points and shows EXISTENCE WHERE (see next page).

1. Hon *desu.*	(It) *is* a book.
2. Hon ga *arimasu.*	*There is* a book.
3. Tsukue *no ue ni* hon ga arimasu.	There is a book *on* the desk.

The difference between **desu** and **arimasu** is "it is . . ." and "there is . . ." in English.

NEGATIVE OF DESU AND ARIMASU: The negative of **desu** is **dewa arimasen.** The negative of **arimasu** is **arimasen.** This negates existence of the subject.

1. Hon **dewa arimasen.**	It is not a book.
2. Hon wa **arimasen.**	There is not a book. There is no book.

NI: **Ni** has many uses, but here it will be understood as the postposition indicating location. The formula is LOCATION+NI . . . ARIMASU. It indicates the exact place of location of something or somebody, and is used with **arimasu** (or **imasu**—explained below). It is translated "in," "at," "on," in itself:

1. *Koko* **ni** hon ga arimasu.	Here is a book. (or) **At** this place, there is a book.
2. *Uchi* **ni** arimasu.	(It) is **at** home. (or) **At** home, there is.
3. *Heya* **ni** arimasu.	(It) is **in** the room.

When **ni** is used after these nouns of location, the construction becomes ADVERBIAL with equivalent adverbs in English:

1. *tsukue*—noun "desk"
2. *tsukue no ue*—substantive "top of the desk (desk's top)"
3. *tsukue no ue ni*— adverbial phrase, translated: "on top of the desk"

Similarly:

1. *hon* no *aida* ni—"between the books (or, books' between)"
2. *tsukue* no *shita* ni—"under the desk (or, desks' underneath)"
3. *gakkoo* no *soba* ni—"near the school (or, schools' near)"

WORD ORDER: The word order showing location is as follows:

NOUN + NO + LOCATION (where?) + NI

The word order here is the reverse of English; for example, "in front of the school" in English will be *school's front* in Japanese; "in back of the house" is *house's back.*

1. watakushi	**no**	hidari	**ni**	(my left)
2. uchi	**no**	ushiro	**ni**	(house's back)
3. gakkoo	**no**	mae	**ni**	(school's front)
4. kooen	**no**	naka	**ni**	(park's inside)

SENTENCE WORD ORDER WHEN LOCATION IS INCLUDED: The sentence word order is as follows:

LOCATION (where) NI + SUBJECT (what) GA + VERB

1. Tsukue no ue **ni**	hon **ga**	arimasu
2. Heya no naka **ni**	isu **ga**	arimasu
3. Teeburu no soba **ni**	Itoo-san **ga**	tatte imasu

(In this section, note the usage of the nominative postposition *ga* before the verb.)

—or—

SUBJECT (what) WA + LOCATION (where) NI + VERB

1. Isu **wa**	heya no mannaka **ni**	arimasu.
2. Gakkoo **wa**	kooen no soba **ni**	arimasu.
3. Itoo-san **wa**	sensei no ushiro **ni**	koshikakete imasu.

GA AND WA: As indicated above, the student has noticed that in relation to existence construction, **ga** is the postposition associated with the subject and used with a form of **arimasu** verb when the subject comes just before the verb.

1. Hon no aida **ni** tegami **ga** arimasu.
2. Daigaku no soba **ni** kooen **ga** arimasu.

TO: **To** is a conjunction. Among other uses, it is used to connect two nouns or noun equivalents only, and it means "and." **To,** however, is *never* used to connect sentences.

1. Anata **to** watakushi	you and I
2. Eigo no hon **to** Nihongo no hon	English book and Japanese book

When combining sentences, use **soshite**:

1. Kore wa hon desu. **Soshite** are wa empitsu desu.

Substitution Drill

I. KOOEN { *(Location)* NO NAKA / NO MAE / NO USHIRO / NO MANNAKA / NO CHIKAKU / etc. } *NI* GAKKOO GA ARIMASU.

II. BROWN-SAN WA SENSEI { *(Location)* NO MAE / NO USHIRO / NO MIGI / NO HIDARI / NO SOBA / etc. } *NI* TATTE IMASU.

Exercises

(Beginning with sentence 6, use two patterns given in the text in translating.)

1. in front of me	watakushi no mae ni
2. behind me (in back of me)	watakushi no ushiro ni
3. to his right	ano kata no migi ni
4. to my left	watakushi no hidari ni
5. on top of him	ano kata no ue ni
6. There is a chair in front of me.	Watakushi no mae ni isu ga arimasu.
7. There is a bag under the table.	Teeburu no shita ni kaban ga arimasu.
8. There is a piano in the room.	Heya no naka ni piano ga arimasu.
9. There is a dictionary on top of the desk.	Tsukue no ue ni jibiki ga arimasu.
10. There is a park near my school.	Watakushi no gakkoo no chikaku ni kooen ga arimasu.
11. Where is the park?	Kooen wa doko ni arimasu ka.
12. Where is your television?	Anata no terebi wa doko ni arimasu ka.
13. Where is my room?	Watakushi no heya wa doko ni arimasu ka.
14. Where is Jiro's letter?	Jiroo no tegami wa doko ni arimasu ka.
15. The park is in front of the school.	Gakkoo no mae ni kooen ga arimasu.
16. Your television is in my room.	Watakushi no heya ni anata no terebi ga arimasu.
17. Your room is not in this hotel.	Kono hoteru ni anata no heya ga arimasen.
18. Jiro's letter is between the books.	Hon no aida ni Jiroo no tegami ga arimasu.
19. There isn't a television in this room.	Kono heya no naka ni terebi ga arimasen.
20. There isn't a letter in the bag.	Kaban no naka ni tegami ga arimasen.

21. There isn't a pencil on the desk.	Tsukue no ue ni empitsu ga arimasen.
22. There isn't a school near the park.	Kooen no chikaku ni gakkoo ga arimasen.
23. Jiro is sitting in front of me.	Jiroo wa watakushi no mae ni koshikakete imasu.
24. The friend is standing behind me.	Tomodachi wa watakushi no ushiro ni tatte imasu.
25. He is standing on the chair.	Ano kata wa isu no ue ni tatte imasu.

Translate into Japanese:

1. What is in the small desk?
2. What is under / on top of / in front of / in the back of / in the middle of / on the left side of / on the right side of this table?

Note: It might be helpful to think of the word order of this construction as the opposite of English. "In front of . . ." is: . . . NO MAE NI. (of front in)

3. Your dictionary and notebook are in my briefcase.
4. Where is the teacher's book? It is in the desk.
5. Is Mr. Tanaka sitting in front of you? No, he is standing.
6. There is no TV in the room.
7. Your Japanese letter is in the big box.
8. My school is in front of a large park.
9. My teacher is standing in front of me.
10. The old magazine is under the newspaper.

Answer in Japanese:

1. Kono heya no naka ni nani ga arimasu ka.
2. Anata no tsukue no ue ni nani to nani ga arimasu ka.
3. Anata no uchi wa Tookyoo ni arimasu ka.
4. Anata no shoogakkoo wa New York ni arimasu ka.

5. Kimi no Eigo no hon wa doko ni arimasu ka.
6. Kono gakkoo no mae ni kooen ga arimasu ka.
7. Kono heya no naka ni terebi ga arimasu ka.
8. Anata no empitsu wa tsukue no shita ni arimasu ka. Doko ni arimasu ka.
9. Kono tsukue no naka ni pen ga arimasu ka.
10. Anata no hidari ni dare ga koshikakete imasu ka.
11. Anata no soba ni to ga arimasu ka. To wa anata no ushiro ni arimasu ka.
12. Anata no pen wa poketto (pocket) no naka ni arimasu ka. Doko ni arimasu ka.
13. Kono hon no aida ni Nihongo no tegami ga arimasu ka.
14. Anata no mae ni tomodachi ga tatte imasu ka.
15. Isu to tsukue wa doko ni arimasu ka. Anata no migi ni arimasu ka.

Fill in the blanks with proper postpositions:

1. Soko ___ nani ___ arimasu ka.
2. Watakushi ___ ushiro ___ isu ___ arimasu.
3. Anata ___ uchi wa Nihon ___ arimasu ka.
4. Iie, watakushi no uchi ___ Nihon ___ arimasen.
5. Tsukue ___ ue ___ hon ___ zasshi ___ arimasen.
6. Dare ___ to ___ shimete imasu ka.
7. Tomodachi ___ ima hon ___ yonde imasu.
8. Eigo ___ moo ichido itte kudasai.
9. Anata ___ Nihongo ___ sensei ___ donata desu ka.
10. Anata ___ Nihongo ___ hon ___ yonde kudasai.

Useful Expressions

Introducing People (Shookai)

You (John Brown) are being introduced to Mr. Tanaka by Taroo.

TAROO: TANAKA-SAN, BROWN-SAN O SHOOKAI SHIMASU. Mr. Tanaka, I shall introduce Mr. Brown.

KONO KATA WA BROWN-SAN DESU. This is Mr. Brown.

KONO KATA WA TANAKA-SAN DESU. This is Mr. Tanaka.

YOU: WATAKUSHI WA JOHN BROWN DESU. I am John Brown.

HAJIMEMASHITE. I'm happy to meet you.

(and/or)

DOOZO YOROSHIKU. Pleased to meet you.

TANAKA: WATAKUSHI WA TANAKA DESU. I am Tanaka.

DOOZO YOROSHIKU. Pleased to meet you.

SUPPLEMENT II

Numeral Classifiers

The following is the system of counting or designating the number of people or things with proper "numerators" or "numeral classifiers."

This is equivalent to the English expression of "two *pairs* of shoes" or "ten *heads* of lettuce," etc. In Japanese there are many more classifiers and they are carefully designated. Some objects, however, do not fall into any specific category, or when you have forgotten the classifier, the Japanese numerals (page 44), can often be used for inanimate objects.

hitotsu no kurasu	one class
mittsu no hako	three boxes
futatsu no isu	two chairs

Hyphens are used here to show the combination (or compound) and they are not normally used.

	PEOPLE *-nin*	ANIMALS *-hiki**	BOOKS *-satsu*
1.	hitori	ip-piki*	is-satsu*
2.	futari	ni-hiki	ni-satsu
3.	san-nin	sam-biki*	san-satsu
4.	yo-nin	shi-hiki yon-hiki	shi-satsu yon-satsu
5.	go-nin	go-hiki	go-satsu
6.	roku-nin	rop-piki*	roku-satsu
7.	shichi-nin	shichi-hiki nana-hiki	nana-satsu
8.	hachi-nin	hachi-hiki hap-piki*	hachi-satsu has-satsu*
9.	ku-nin kyuu-nin	kyuu-hiki	kyuu-satsu
10.	juu-nin	jip-piki*	jis-satsu* jus-satsu*
11.	juuichi-nin	juuip-piki*	juuis-satsu
12.	etc.		

* *See note on following page.*

SUPPLEMENT II (continued)

	LONG SLENDER OBJECTS *-hon*	FLAT OBJECTS *-mai*	NUMBER OF TIMES *-do*
1.	ip-pon*	ichi-mai	ichi-do
2.	ni-hon	ni-mai	ni-do
3.	sam-bon*	sam-mai	san-do
4.	yon-hon shi-hon	yom-mai yo-mai	yo-do yon-do
5.	go-hon	go-mai	go-do
6.	rop-pon*	roku-mai	roku-do
7.	shichi-hon nana-hon	shichi-mai nana-mai	shichi-do nana-do
8.	hachi-hon hap-pon*	hachi-mai	hachi-do
9.	kyuu-hon	kyuu-mai	kyuu-do
10.	jip-pon* jup-pon*	juu-mai	juu-do

Note: * represents phonetic changes which sometimes occur for 1, 3, 6, 8, and 10. *Hiki* changes to sam*biki,* rop*piki,* etc. *HIKI* is used in counting animals, fish, insects, etc.

MAI is used in counting flat objects, such as blankets, paper, sheets, bills (paper money), etc.

HON is the classifier used in counting round, slender objects, viz., sticks, pencils, chopsticks, etc.

Other commonly used classifiers are as follows:

DAI is used in counting vehicles, e.g., automobiles *(jidoosha),* bicycles *(jitensha),* motorcycles *(ootobai),* etc. Ichi*dai,* ni*dai,* san*dai* no jidoosha.

HAI is the classifier which is similar to English " ___ful" in "cupful." Note the following phonetic changes:

ippai	(1 cupful)
sambai	(3 cupfuls)
roppai	(6 cupfuls)
jippai	(10 cupfuls)
juppai	(,,)

SOKU is the numeral classifier in counting any footgear, such as shoes *(kutsu),* socks *(kutsushita), geta,* etc. San*zoku* (3 pairs) is the only phonetic change.

Supplement III

Counting and Designating the Number of Various Time Units

The following table shows how to count or designate the number of various time units: "one year . . . ," "one month . . . ," "one week . . . ," "one day. . . ."

	TOSHI (YEAR) *-nen*	**TSUKI** (MONTH) *-getsu*	**SHUU** (WEEK) *-shuukan*	**HI** (DAY) *-nichi, -ka*
1.	ichi-nen	ikka-getsu hito-tsuki	is-shuukan	ichi-nichi
2.	ni-nen	nika-getsu futa-tsuki	ni-shuukan	futsu-ka
3.	san-nen	sanka-getsu mi-tsuki	san-shuukan	mik-ka
4.	yo-nen	yonka-getsu shika-getsu	yon-shuukan	yok-ka
5.	go-nen	goka-getsu	go-shuukan	itsu-ka
6.	roku-nen	rokka-getsu	roku-shuukan	mui-ka
7.	shichi-nen nana-nen	shichika-getsu nanaka-getsu	shichi-shuukan nana-shuukan	nanu-ka nano-ka
8.	hachi-nen	hachika-getsu hakka-getsu	has-shuukan hachi-shuukan	yoo-ka
9.	ku-nen kyuu-nen	kuka-getsu kyuuka-getsu	kyuu-shuukan	kokono-ka
10.	juu-nen	jikka-getsu jukka-getsu	jis-shuukan jus-shuukan	too-ka
11.	juu-ichi-nen	juu-ikka-getsu	juu-is-shuukan	juu-ichi-nichi
12.	etc.			

Note: The term used to designate the number of days is the same as that of the days of the month. (See Supplement V, p. 73.)
Watakushi wa Tookyoo ni **itsuka** imasu—I will be in Tokyo five days.
Watakushi wa Tookyoo ni **itsuka ni** tsukimasu—I will arrive in Tokyo on the 5th.
In the latter example, postposition *NI* is used to indicate specific date or time (see page 124) but none is needed for the former.

SUPPLEMENT IV

Counting and Designating the Number of Various Time Units

	HOURS *-jikan*	MINUTES *-fun*	SECONDS *-byoo*
1.	ichi-jikan	ip-pun*	ichi-byoo
2.	ni-jikan	ni-fun	ni-byoo
3.	san-jikan	sam-pun*	sam-byoo
4.	yo-jikan	yom-pun*	yom-byoo
5.	go-jikan	go-fun	go-byoo
6.	roku-jikan	rop-pun*	roku-byoo
7.	shichi-jikan nana-jikan	shichi-fun nana-fun	shichi-byoo nana-byoo
8.	hachi-jikan	hachi-fun hap-pun*	hachi-byoo
9.	ku-jikan	kyuu-fun	kyuu-byoo
10.	juu-jikan	jip-pun* jup-pun*	juu-byoo
11.	juu-ichi-jikan	juu-ip-pun*	juu-ichi-byoo
12.	etc.		

Note: * represents phonetic change. Hyphens are used in all the charts to clarify word structure.

SUPPLEMENT V

Various Names of Time Units

	MONTH *-gatsu*	DAYS OF THE MONTH *-ka* (up to the 10th) *-nichi*(from the 11th)	DAYS OF THE WEEK *-yoobi*	TIME OF DAY *-ji*
1.	Shoo-gatsu Ichi-gatsu (January)	tsuitachi	Nichi-yoobi (Sunday)	ichi-ji (1 o'clock)
2.	Ni-gatsu (February)	futsu-ka	Getsu-yoobi (Monday)	ni-ji (2 o'clock)
3.	San-gatsu (March)	mik-ka	Ka-yoobi (Tuesday)	san-ji (3 o'clock)
4.	Shi-gatsu (April)	yok-ka	Sui-yoobi (Wednesday)	yo-ji (4 o'clock)
5.	Go-gatsu (May)	itsu-ka	Moku-yoobi (Thursday)	go-ji (5 o'clock)
6.	Roku-gatsu (June)	mui-ka	Kin-yoobi (Friday)	roku-ji (6 o'clock)
7.	Shichi-gatsu (July)	nanu-ka nano-ka	Do-yoobi (Saturday)	nana-ji shichi-ji (7 o'clock)
8.	Hachi-gatsu (August)	yoo-ka		hachi-ji (8 o'clock)
9.	Ku-gatsu (September)	kokono-ka		ku-ji (9 o'clock)
10.	Juu-gatsu (October)	too-ka		juu-ji (10 o'clock)
11.	Juu-ichi-gatsu (November)	juu-ichi-nichi		juu-ichi-ji (11 o'clock)
12.	Juu-ni-gatsu (December)	juu-ni-nichi		juu-ni-ji (12 o'clock)
13.		juu-san-nichi		
14.		juu-yok-ka		
20.		hatsu-ka		
21.		nijuu-ichi-nichi		

CHAPTER 6

KYOOSHITSU—CLASSROOM (2)

(Pertaining to the Counting of Things, both Animate and Inanimate)

NOUN GA + NUMERAL CLASSIFIER + VERB

or

NUMERAL CLASSIFIER NO + NOUN GA + VERB

1. KORE WA KYOOSHITSU DESU.	THIS IS A CLASSROOM.
kono	this
kono kyooshitsu	this classroom
kono kyooshitsu ni (wa)	in this classroom (location)
nani ga	what (nom. case)
arimasu ka	are there?
2. KONO KYOOSHITSU *NIWA* NANI GA ARIMASU KA.	WHAT IS IN THIS CLASSROOM?
3. KOKUBAN TO ISU TO TSUKUE GA ARIMASU.	THERE ARE A BLACKBOARD, A CHAIR AND A DESK.
tsukue ga	as for the desks (nom. case)
ikutsu	how many

tsukue ga ikutsu	how many desks
arimasu ka	are there?

4. *TSUKUE GA IKUTSU* ARIMASU KA. — HOW MANY DESKS ARE THERE?

KAZOETE KUDASAI. — PLEASE COUNT.

5. HITOTSU, FUTATSU, MITTSU—*TSUKUE GA MITTSU* ARIMASU. — ONE, TWO, THREE—THERE ARE THREE DESKS.

kono heya	this room
kono heya no naka	in this room
kono heya no naka ni	in this room (location)
nan-nin no gakusei ga	how many students (nom. case)
imasu ka	are there

6. KONO HEYA NO NAKA NI *NAN-NIN NO GAKUSEI GA IMASU* KA. — HOW MANY STUDENTS ARE THERE IN THIS ROOM?

roku-nin	six (persons)
roku-nin no	six persons (quasi adj.)
roku-nin no gakusei	six students
roku-nin no gakusei ga	six students (nom. case)
imasu	there are

7. ROKU-NIN NO GAKUSEI GA IMASU. — THERE ARE SIX STUDENTS.

Nihongo no sensei ga	as for Japanese teacher (nom. case)
hitori	one (person)
imasu	there is

8. NIHONGO NO *SENSEI GA HITORI* IMASU. — THERE IS ONE JAPANESE TEACHER.

9. KEREDOMO EIGO NO SENSEI WA IMASEN.	HOWEVER, THERE ISN'T AN ENGLISH TEACHER.
watakushi no	mine
watakushi no tsukue	my desk
watakushi no tsukue no ue ni	on top of my desk (location)
nani ga	what (nom. case)
miemasu ka	can be seen?
10. WATAKUSHI NO TSUKUE NO UE NI NANI *GA MIEMASU* KA.	WHAT CAN YOU SEE ON MY DESK? (What is visible on my desk?)
ippon no empitsu	one pencil
to	and
nisatsu no hon ga	two books (nom. case)
miemasu	can be seen
11. IPPON NO EMPITSU TO *NI-SATSU NO HON* GA MIEMASU.	I CAN SEE ONE PENCIL AND TWO VOLUMES OF BOOKS. (One pencil and two volumes of books can be seen.)
or	
EMPITSU GA IPPON (TO) HON GA NI-SATSU MIEMASU.	" "
kore wa	as for this (nom. case)
atsukute	thick and
atsukute kuroi	thick and black
atsukute kuroi hon	thick and black book
desu	(it) is
12. KORE WA *ATSUKUTE* KUROI HON DESU.	THIS IS A THICK AND BLACK BOOK.

issatsu no hon wa atsukute kuroi jibiki desu	as for one book a thick and black dictionary (it) is
13. ISSATSU NO HON WA ATSUKUTE KUROI JIBIKI DESU.	ONE BOOK IS A THICK AND BLACK DICTIONARY.
issatsu no hon wa usukute akai kyookasho desu	as for one book a thin and red textbook (it) is
14. ISSATSU NO HON WA *USUKUTE* AKAI KYOOKA-SHO DESU.	ONE BOOK IS A THIN AND RED TEXTBOOK.
ano hon wa kuroku wa arimasen	as for that book (it) is not black
15. ANO HON WA *KUROKU WA ARIMASEN*.	THAT BOOK IS NOT BLACK.
sono jibiki to kyookasho no iro wa aoku wa arimasen	that dictionary and textbook's color is not blue
16. SONO JIBIKI TO KYOO-KASHO NO IRO WA *AOKU WA ARIMASEN*.	THE COLOR OF THE DIC-TIONARY AND TEXTBOOK IS NOT BLUE.
anata wa kono tsukue no ue ni gosatsu no hon ga miemasu ka	as for you on this desk (location) five volumes of books (nom. case) can you see
17. ANATA WA KONO TSU-	CAN YOU SEE FIVE VOLUMES

KUE NO UE NI GO-SATSU NO HON GA MIEMASU KA.	OF BOOKS ON THIS DESK?
ni-satsu shika miemasen	two volumes only can see
18. NI-SATSU *SHIKA MIE-MASEN.*	(I) CAN SEE ONLY TWO VOLUMES. (Only two volumes are visible)
19. HON GA NI-SATSU *SHIKA ARIMASEN.*	THERE ARE ONLY TWO BOOKS.

Vocabulary from the Lesson

kyooshitsu (*kyoo-shi-tsu*)	(n.) a classroom
ikutsu	(inter. pro.) how many?
kazoeru (*ka-zó-e-ru*)	(v.t.) to count (non-conjugating verb, henceforth referred to as n.c.v.)
kazoete	("te" form of *kazoeru*)
hitotsu (*hi-tó-tsu*)	(n.) one (used only when counting things, or designating the number of things)
futatsu (*fu-ta-tsu*)	(n.) two (used only when counting things, or designating the number of things)
mittsu (*mit-tsu*)	(n.) three (used only when counting things, or designating the number of things)
nan-nin (*nán-nin*)	(inter. pro.) how many persons?
. . . -nin	(suf.) numeral classifier for human beings. Used only in compounds.
iru	(v.) there is (used only with animate things or beings)
imasu (*i-má-su*)	(polite form of *iru*)

roku-nin (*ro-kú-nin*) (n.) six (persons). Used to count people, or to designate the number of persons.

hitori (*hi-tó-ri*) (n.) one (person). Used to count people, or to designate the number of persons.

keredomo (*ké-re-do-mo*) however

mieru (*mi-é-ru*) (v.) (can see), can be seen, (is) visible (n.c.v.)

miemasu (polite form of *mieru*)

ippon (*ip-pón*) (n.) one (long, slender object), phonetic change of *ichi-hon.*

. . . hon numeral classifier for long, slender objects (see Supplement II, p. 70)

ippon no empitsu one pencil

ni-satsu (n.) two volumes (See Supplement II, p. 69)

. . . satsu the numeral classifier for books

ni-satsu no hon two volumes of books

atsui (*a-tsu-i*) (adj.) thick

atsukute ("te" form of *atsui* used connectively, See I.C. & G.N.) thick and . . .

issatsu (*is-sa-tsu*) (n.) one volume, phonetic change of *ichi-satsu*

usui (*u-su-i*) (adj.) thin

usukute ("te" form of *usui*) translated "thin and . . ."

kuroku (*ku-ró-ku*) (adverbial form of *kuroi*)

kuroku (wa) arimasen (negative of *kuroi desu*) not black

Important Construction and Grammar Notes

NIWA: This is the combination of two postpositions, **ni** and **wa. Wa** in this usage does not have the original function of acting as the nominative postposition. It is used to emphasize the location as if to say, "Here, in this room, there is. . . ." The use of **wa** in combination with **ni** is optional.

NI: On page 62, **ni** was explained as the postposition indicating location. We understood it to be translated "in" or "at" in itself. **Ni** can also mean "on" or "to" in the sense of "belonging to . . . ," showing attachment to. This is usually translated as "have." When expressing this it follows the following pattern. **Wa** is optional.

NOUN + NI (WA)	NOUN + GA ARIMASU (or IMASU for animate)	
To a (noun)	there is a (noun)	= . . . has . . .

1. Inu **niwa** ashi **ga** yon-hon **arimasu.**	To a dog, there are four feet. (Dogs **have** four feet.)
2. Kono uchi **niwa** puuru (pool) **ga arimasen.**	To this house, there is no pool. (This house **has** no pool.)
3. Watakushi **niwa** kodomo **ga** futari **arimasu.** (or *imasu*)	To me, there are two children. (**I have** two children.)
4. Watakushi no heya **niwa** terebi **ga arimasen.**	To my room, there is no TV. (My room doesn't **have** a TV.)

Note: The use of "have" in the examples given above does *NOT* show ownership, or possession. This is expressed by *motte imasu.* For example:

1. Watakushi wa Nihongo no jibiki o **motte imasu.**	I **have** a Japanese dictionary.
2. Watakushi wa kaban o **motte imasen.**	I do **not have** a brief case.

KAZOETE KUDASAI: The "te" verb **"kazoete"** is from the verb **kazoeru** (to count). This verb has an *eru* ending as the verb **akeru** in the table, under HOW "TE" VERBS ARE FORMED (p. 51). Since this is an *eru*-ending verb, *ru* is changed to *te.*

NUMERALS: Japanese has two sets of numerals in equally common use. One is purely of Japanese origin, and the other is of Chinese origin. Memorize the table given in SUPPLEMENT I (p. 44).

Notice that the Japanese way of counting only goes up to ten. Beyond ten, use the Chinese numerals.

JAPANESE NUMERALS: The Japanese numerals are the cardinal

numbers used in counting INANIMATE THINGS. *Never* use this form when counting human beings or other animate things.

We use **hitori, futari, san-nin,** etc., in counting people; **ippiki, ni-hiki, sam-biki,** etc., in counting animals; **hitotsu, futatsu, mittsu,** etc., in counting inanimate things in general, or when proper NUMERAL CLASSIFIERS are not known to us; **issatsu, ni-satsu, san-satsu,** etc., in counting books. Memorize the table in SUPPLEMENT II (p. 69).

"THERE ARE TWO CHAIRS": Commonly, this is translated two ways:

SUBJECT GA	+ NUMBER	+ VERB
1. ISU GA	FUTATSU	ARIMASU.
chairs	two	there are

NUMBER + NO	+ SUBJECT GA	+ VERB
2. FUTATSU NO	ISU GA	ARIMASU.
two	chairs	there are

Generally, all modifiers (adverbs, adjectives, or relative clauses) precede the word they modify. However, example 1 above is the ONLY instance in which a modifier (numeral classifier) follows the word it modifies.

In the above example 2, *futatsu*, a noun, is made into an adjective modifier by the use of *no* between *futatsu* and *isu* (both nouns).

IMASU: **Imasu** as opposed to **arimasu** denotes existence of ANIMATE (living) OBJECTS ONLY. Other rules pertaining to **arimasu** apply to **imasu** as well (refer to p. 61).

MIEMASU: **Miemasu,** a polite form for **mieru,** means "can be seen," "can see," or "be visible." Bear in mind that **miemasu** always takes the postposition **ga** and NOT **o** for the object "seen."

1. Gakkoo **ga** miemasu. — A school is visible.
2. Fujisan **ga** mieru. — Mt. Fuji is visible.

ATSUKUTE KUROI HON: When two true adjectives modify the same noun (big black dog, large expensive car, etc.), the first adjective is changed to the **"kute"** form.

This form of adjectives is made by adding *te,* after first converting the true adjectives into adverbial form:

True Adjective	*Adverbial Form*	*"Te" Form*
1. aka*i*	aka*ku*	akaku—te
2. shiro*i*	shiro*ku*	shiroku—te
3. furu*i*	furu*ku*	furuku—te
4. ooki*i*	ooki*ku*	ookiku—te

"Kute" adjectives are translated ". . . and." Hence, *furukute ookii* is "old AND large. . . ."

NEGATIVE OF AN ADJECTIVE: In Chapter 1 we learned to negate a statement concerning nouns:

Hon *desu.*	Hon dewa *arimasen.*

To make a negative of a true adjective:

Akai *desu.*	Aka*ku (wa) arimasen.*
Ookii *desu.*	Ooki*ku (wa) arimasen.*

Rule: Use the adverbial form (see above) of a true adjective plus *wa arimasen* (*wa* is optional).

Affirmative	*Negative*
Kore wa kooen *desu.*	Kore wa kooen ***dewa arimasen.***
Kooen ga ***arimasu.***	Kooen ga ***arimasen.***
Kono kooen wa ookii ***desu.***	Kono kooen wa ookiku (wa) ***arimasen.***
Kono gakkoo wa chiisai ***desu.***	Kono gakkoo wa chiisaku (wa) ***arimasen.***
Sore wa shiroi ***desu.***	Sore wa shiroku (wa) ***arimasen.***

SHIKA PLUS NEGATIVE VERB: **Shika** meaning "only" is always used with the negative verb, and the negative verb becomes positive in meaning. **Shika** is used directly after the word it limits, and replaces the postposition.

1. Issatsu no hon *shika arimasen.*
   one book only there is (There is only one book.)
2. Issatsu no hon *shika miemasen.*
   one book only can see (I can see only one book.)
3. Ano kata wa Nihongo *shika hanashimasen.*
   he Japanese only speaks (He speaks only Japanese.)

Fluency Drill

Empitsu ga arimasu.
Nagai empitsu ga arimasu.
Nagai empitsu ga ippon arimasu.
Koko ni nagakute kuroi empitsu ga ippon arimasu.
Tsukue no ue ni nagakute kuroi empitsu ga ippon arimasu.
Tsukue no ue ni akai empitsu to kuroi pen ga arimasu.
Tsukue no ue ni akai empitsu to nagakute kuroi pen ga arimasu.

There is a pencil.
There is a long pencil.
There is one long pencil.
There is one long black pencil here.
There is one long black pencil on the desk.
There are a red pencil and a black pen on the desk.
There are a red pencil and a long black pen on the desk.

Substitution Drill

I. KONO HON WA { *(Adverb)* OOKIKU / TAKAKU / ATSUKU / etc. } WA ARIMASEN

	(Noun)	*(Numeral Classifier)*	
II.	HON GA	ISSATSU	{ ARIMASU / SHIKA ARIMASEN.
	ISU GA	FUTATSU	
	EMPITSU GA	SAMBON	
	KAMI (paper) GA	GO-MAI	

Exercises

1. There is a book.	Hon ga arimasu.
2. There is a Japanese book.	Nihongo no hon ga arimasu.
3. There is one Japanese book.	Nihongo no hon ga issatsu arimasu.
4. There are 3 chairs.	Isu ga mittsu arimasu.
5. There are 6 sheets of paper.	Kami ga roku-mai arimasu.
6. There are 2 students.	Gakusei ga futari imasu.
7. There are 4 motorcycles.	Ootobai ga yon-dai arimasu.
8. There is one Japanese book on the desk.	Tsukue no ue ni Nihongo no hon ga issatsu arimasu.
9. There are 3 chairs in the room.	Heya no naka ni isu ga mittsu arimasu.
10. There are 6 sheets of paper in the bag.	Kaban no naka ni kami ga roku-mai arimasu.
11. There are 2 students in the car.	Jidoosha no naka ni gakusei ga futari imasu.
12. There are 4 motorcycles in front of the high school.	Kootoogakkoo no mae ni ootobai ga yon-dai arimasu.
13. This book is new.	Kono hon wa atarashii desu.

14. This book is not new.	Kono hon wa atarashiku arimasen.
15. That dictionary is thick.	Sono jibiki wa atsui desu.
16. That dictionary is not thick.	Sono jibiki wa atsuku arimasen.
17. My pen is new.	Watakushi no pen wa atarashii desu.
18. My pen is not new.	Watakushi no pen wa atarashiku arimasen.
19. I can see only one car.	Jidoosha ga ichi-dai shika miemasen.
20. There is only one pair of shoes.	Kutsu ga issoku shika arimasen.
21. There are only 2 dictionaries on the desk.	Tsukue no ue ni jibiki ga ni-satsu shika arimasen.
22. Only 2 students are standing.	Gakusei ga futari shika tatte imasen.
23. He reads only magazines.	Ano kata wa zasshi shika yomimasen.
24. I have only five dollars.	Go doru shika motte imasen.
25. I have only one car.	Jidoosha wa ichi-dai shika motte imasen.

Translate into Japanese:

1. There are three chairs and one desk in this classroom.
2. There are six letters and two pencils in the desk.
3. There are three pencils and six papers in the box.

Note: *Hitotsu, futatsu,* etc. (Japanese numerals), can be used in counting objects that have no specific shapes or forms, and also when the classifier is unknown or forgotten. However, this is never used to count time, money, distance, weight, or living things.

4. What can you see on the desk? I can see one pencil and one pen on the desk.

Note: A sentence with a "can see" construction should be interpreted as "What is visible?" Therefore, this sentence must be rephrased as: "As for you *(wa)*, what *(ga)* on the desk *(ni)* is visible?"

5. What kind of book can you see?
6. I can see only one English book.
7. He can see only four teachers in the classroom.
8. One book is a thick, black dictionary.
9. His pen is old and black.
10. Two magazines are thin and old.

11. This thick book is not blue.
12. This magazine is not old.
13. There is only one desk in this room.
14. There are only five students in my Japanese language class.
15. An English teacher is sitting in front of the room.

Answer in Japanese:

1. Kono kyooshitsu ni nani to nani ga arimasu ka.
2. Koko ni gakusei ga nan-nin imasu ka.
3. Kono kyooshitsu ni seito ga imasu ka. Nan-nin imasu ka.
4. Kono heya no naka ni ookikute kuroi jibiki ga arimasu ka.
5. Kono kyooshitsu no mae ni gakusei ga hitori tatte imasu ka.
6. Anata wa tsukue no ue ni issatsu no hon ga miemasu ka.
7. Anata no futatsu no kaban wa furui desu ka.
8. Kono heya ni Nihongo no seito ga san-nin imasu ka.
9. Koko ni mittsu no mado ga arimasu ka.
10. Kono heya no naka ni Nihongo no seito ga imasu ka.
11. Anata no migi ni sensei ga koshikakete imasu ka.
12. Webster no jibiki wa chiisakute usui desu ka.
13. Anata no pen wa shatsu (shirt) no poketto no naka ni arimasu ka. Doko ni arimasu ka.
14. Anata wa Fujisan ga miemasu ka.
15. Anata no saifu no naka ni Nihon no okane (money) ga arimasu ka. Saifu wa doko ni arimasu ka.

Give the negative of the following and translate:

1. Kono daigaku wa ookii desu.
2. Kore wa gakkoo desu.
3. Anata no kaban wa atarashii desu.
4. Kono hon wa watakushi no desu.
5. Hai, soo desu.
6. Brown-san wa shimbun o katte imasu.
7. Ano kata wa Nihongo o hanashite imasu.
8. Soko ni isu ga futatsu arimasu.

9. Gakusei ga hitori imasu.
10. Kono chuugakkoo wa chiisai desu.
11. Watakushi wa Fujisan ga miemasu.

Useful Expressions

At the Dinner Table (Shokutaku de)

1. Host would say: DOOZO TAKUSAN MESHIAGATTE KUDASAI. In persuading the guest to begin the meal, it means "Please eat a lot."
2. Guest would say: ITADAKIMASU. This is a term used when beginning the meal. It has the meaning of "I am most grateful to receive this food."
3. Host: MOO SUKOSHI IKAGA DESU KA. Host, upon seeing that his guest is about ready for a refill on rice, saké, etc., would ask, "How about a refill (or a little more)?"
4. Guest: MOO KEKKOO DESU. When the host offers you another bowl of rice, saké, etc., and you wish to decline, it means, "I have had sufficient."
5. Guest: TAIHEN OISHIKATTA DESU. "(The meal) was certainly good."
   and/or
   GO-CHISOOSAMA DESHITA. "It certainly was a sumptuous (delicious) meal!" An expression used when you finish eating, or when you are about to depart from a host's place after a meal.
6. Host: O-SOMATSUSAMA DESHITA. When the guest says GO-CHISOOSAMA DESHITA, the host replies, "It wasn't much."

CHAPTER 7

RYOKOO—TRAVEL

"A" WA + "B" YORI + ADJ.	=	larger than smaller ,, more ,, etc.	(*comparative degree*)
"A" WA + ICHIBAN + ADJ.	=	largest smallest most etc.	(*superlative degree*)

RYUUGAKUSEI TO SHASHOO	A FOREIGN STUDENT AND A CONDUCTOR
R: KOKO WA DOKO DESU KA.	WHERE IS THIS?
S: KOKO WA TOOKYOO EKI DESU.	THIS IS TOKYO STATION.
R: TOOKYOO WA TAIHEN OOKII TOKAI DESU NE.	TOKYO IS A VERY LARGE CITY, ISN'T IT?
S: HAI, TOOKYOO WA TAIHEN OOKII TOKAI DESU.	YES, TOKYO IS A VERY LARGE CITY.
Tookyoo to Oosaka dewa dochira ga ookii desu ka	between Tokyo and Osaka which is large(r)
R: TOOKYOO TO OOSAKA	BETWEEN TOKYO AND

	DEWA DOCHIRA GA OOKII DESU KA.	OSAKA, WHICH IS LARGER?
	Tookyoo no hoo ga ookii desu	the side of Tokyo (comparative) is large(r)
S:	TOOKYOO *NO HOO* GA OOKII DESU.	TOKYO IS LARGER.
	ichiban ookii ichiban ookii tokai	largest largest city
	TOOKYOO WA *ICHIBAN OOKII* TOKAI DESU.	TOKYO IS THE LARGEST CITY.
R:	YOI HOTERU NO NAMAE O OSHIETE KUDASAI.	PLEASE TELL ME THE NAMES OF GOOD HOTELS.
	ichiban yoi ichiban yoi hoteru	best best hotel
S:	TEIKOKU HOTERU WA *ICHIBAN YOI* HOTERU DESU.	IMPERIAL HOTEL IS THE BEST HOTEL.
R:	TEIKOKU HOTERU WA DOKO NI ARIMASU KA.	WHERE IS THE IMPERIAL HOTEL?
S:	KOOEN NO MAE NI ARI-MASU.	IT IS IN FRONT OF THE PARK.
	Teikoku hoteru no hoo ga chikai desu	the side of the Imperial Hotel (comparative) is near(er)
	TEIKOKU HOTERU *NO HOO* GA CHIKAI DESU.	THE IMPERIAL HOTEL IS CLOSER.

keredomo	however
kono hoteru no	this hotel's (poss. case)
ryookin wa	rate (nom. case)
*kono hoteru no ryookin wa...	*As for this hotel's (room) rate...
Tookyuu hoteru yori	than the Tokyu Hotel
takai desu	is (more) expensive

KEREDOMO KONO HOTERU NO RYOOKIN WA TOOKYUU HOTERU NO YORI TAKAI DESU.\ — HOWEVER, THIS HOTEL'S (ROOM) RATE IS MORE EXPENSIVE THAN TOKYU HOTEL.

Teikoku hoteru niwa	at (the) Imperial Hotel
yooshiki no heya ga	as for Western-style rooms
arimasu ka	are there?

R: TEIKOKU HOTERU NIWA YOOSHIKI NO HEYA GA ARIMASU KA. — ARE THERE WESTERN-STYLE ROOMS AT THE IMPERIAL HOTEL?

S: HAI, YOOSHIKI NO HEYA *MO* NIHONSHIKI NO HEYA *MO* ARIMASU.\ — YES, THERE ARE BOTH WESTERN-STYLE AND JAPANESE-STYLE ROOMS.

yooshiki to	Western-style and
Nihonshiki no heya dewa	Japanese-style rooms (between)
dochira ga	which
takai desu ka	is (more) expensive

R: YOOSHIKI TO NIHONSHIKI NO HEYA DEWA, — BETWEEN WESTERN-STYLE AND JAPANESE-STYLE

* Note the usage of asterisks here to indicate the composite of phrases which preceded them.

DOCHIRA GA TAKAI DESU KA.	ROOMS, WHICH IS MORE EXPENSIVE?
yooshiki no heya wa	as for the Western-style room (nom. case)
Nihonshiki no heya yori	than the Japanese-style room
takai desu	is (more) expensive
S: YOOSHIKI NO HEYA WA NIHONSHIKI NO HEYA YORI TAKAI DESU.	THE WESTERN-STYLE ROOMS ARE MORE EXPENSIVE THAN THE JAPANESE-STYLE ROOMS.
watakushi wa	as for me
yooshiki no heya ga	Western-style room
suki desu	is likeable
R: WATAKUSHI WA YOOSHIKI NO HEYA GA SUKI DESU. ANATA WA DOCHIRA GA SUKI DESU KA.	I LIKE WESTERN-STYLE ROOMS. WHICH DO YOU LIKE (BETTER)?
Nihonshiki no heya	Japanese-style room
Nihonshiki no heya no hoo ga	the side of the Japanese-style room (comparative)
suki desu	(I) like
S: WATAKUSHI WA NIHONSHIKI NO HEYA *NO HOO* GA SUKI DESU.	I LIKE JAPANESE-STYLE ROOMS BETTER.

Vocabulary List from the Lesson

ryuugakusei (*ryuu-ga-ku-se-i*)	(n.) a student studying abroad
namae (*na-ma-e*)	(n.) name
eki (*é-ki*)	(n.) railroad station
taihen (*ta-i-hen*)	very
tokai	(n.) city, a metropolis
desu ne	isn't it?
dewa	compound postposition. Used in comparison, it means "between" when comparing two, or more, objects.
dochira (*dó-chi-ra*)	(inter. pro.) which (of two); *dore* means "which" (of several)
. . . (A) **mo** . . . (B) **mo**	both (A) and (B) . . . (See I.C. & G.N.)
hoo	(n.) the direction, the side
. . . **no hoo ga**	When combined with an adjective, it gives the comparative degree of the adjective.
. . . **no hoo ga ookii**	bigger, larger (See I.C. & G.N.)
Oosaka no hoo ga ookii desu	Osaka is larger (literally, "the side of Osaka is large")
kooen	(n.) park
ichiban (*i-chi-ban*)	(n.) Number one, the first. When this word is combined with an adjective, the superlative degree of the adjective is obtained.
ichiban ookii	(adj.) largest
ichiban ookii tokai	the largest city
yoi (*yó-i*)	(adj.) good
ryookin	(n.) rate, fare
hoteru	(n.) hotel
oshieru (*o-shi-e-ru*)	(v.t.) to teach (n.c.v.)
oshiete	("te" form of *oshieru*)
oshiete kudasai	Please teach (me). At times it means "Please tell (me)," in the sense of "Please inform me."

keredomo (*ke-re-do-mo*) — (conj.) however

Teikoku hoteru — (n.) the Imperial Hotel

yooshiki (*yoo-shi-ki*) — (n.) western style; *shiki* is a suffix which has a meaning of "style," "model."

Nihonshiki — (n.) Japanese style

takai (*ta-ka-i*) — (adj.) high (in elevation); or high (in price), expensive

yori (*yo-ri*) — "than." When combined with an adjective, it gives the comparative degree of the adjective.

yori takai — more expensive than . . .

suki desu — (v.) (I) like. Use the postposition "ga" after the object that is liked: *obj. ga suki desu.*

Additional Vocabulary

dotchi (*dót-chi*) — (inter. pro.) same as *dochira*

ii — (adj.) same as *yoi*

kirai desu — (v.) (I) dislike, do not like: *obj. ga kirai desu.* Hoteru *ga* kirai desu.

motto (*mót-to*) — more

motto yoi — better

dono (*dó-no*) — (inter. adj. pro.) which? Must be followed by a noun: *dono hon*—which book?; *dono heya*—which room?

yori mo — same as *yori*

kono naka (uchi) de (wa), dore ga . . . — among these, which (of several)?

sono naka (uchi) de (wa), dore ga . . . — among those, which (of several)?

ano hon no naka (uchi) de (wa) . . . — among those books

sekai — (n.) the world

sekai de (wa) — in the world (when comparing things)

kanemochi	(n.) a rich man
Amerika de (wa) (*A-me-ri-ka*)	(n.) in the U.S.A. (when comparing)
shuu	(n.) state
tatemono (*ta-té-mo-no*)	(n.) building (same as *biru*)
toshiyori (*to-shi-yo-ri*)	(n.) old, used only when referring to aged animals, people: *toshiyori no sensei. Furui* is used for old things: *furui zasshi.*

Important Construction and Grammar Notes

COMPARING TWO OBJECTS: Let us say that there are two objects, and we wish to know which of the two is bigger, smaller, older, prettier, etc. How do we ask the question in Japanese? Remember the following patterns:

2 THINGS BEING COMPARED	+	DE(WA) (TO)	+	DOCHIRA GA (DOTCHI)	+	ADJ. NOUN	+	DESU KA

1. Hon to empitsu	**de(wa)**	**dochira ga**	takai	"
2. Tookyoo to Oosaka	"	"	ookii	"
3. Kimi to boku	"	"	chiisai	"
4. Kono biru to ano biru	"	"	furui	"

After the objects being compared, **de(wa)** or **to** is used to give the meaning of "between these things being compared." Note that this usage of **to** is different form the conjunctive **to** (and), where two nouns are connected.

ANSWER: How do we answer the questions above? We may wish to say:

1. The book is more expensive.
2. Tokyo is larger.
3. I am smaller.

—or—

1. The book is more expensive than the pencil.
2. Tokyo is larger than Osaka.
3. I am smaller than you.

WHEN ONLY ONE OBJECT IS MENTIONED in our answer, we say:

1. Hon *no hoo ga* t
2. Tookyoo *no hoo ga* ookii desu.
3. Boku *no hoo ga* chiisai desu.

WHEN BOTH OBJECTS ARE MENTIONED: **Yori** (more than) is used *after* the thing being compared. Note the analysis of the following sentence, especially the word order. In answer to the question:

Tookyoo to Oosaka *dewa (to)* dotchi ga ookii desu ka.
Tookyoo wa Oosaka **yori** ookii desu.

Tookyoo wa—as for Tokyo (the subject)
Oosaka yori—than Osaka (the object being compared)
ookii desu—is large
(lit., As for Tokyo/than Osaka/is large; Tokyo is larger than Osaka.)

1. Hon wa empitsu *yori* takai desu.
   or:
   Hon *no hoo ga* empitsu *yori* takai desu.
   (lit., book's side/than pencil/is expensive)
2. Tookyoo wa Oosaka *yori* ookii desu.
   or:
   Tookyoo *no hoo ga* Oosaka *yori* ookii desu.
3. Boku wa kimi *yori* chiisai desu.
   or:
   Boku no hoo ga kimi *yori* chiisai desu.

WHEN THERE ARE MORE THAN TWO OBJECTS and we wish to know which one is the biggest, smallest, oldest, prettiest, etc., how do we ask the question in Japanese? The Superlative Form is expressed as follows:

1. A to B to C **dewa** (or **to**) **dore ga ichiban** ookii desu ka.
   (Among A, B and C, which one is the largest?)
2. Kono hon no naka **dewa dono hon ga ichiban** furui desu ka.
   (Among these books, which book is the oldest?)
3. Sekai **dewa dare ga ichiban** kanemochi desu ka.
   (Who is the richest man in the world?)

4. Amerika **dewa dono shuu ga ichiban** ookii desu ka.
   (In America, which state is the largest?)

   Note: In the examples 2, 3, and 4 above, *dewa* has the meaning of "of all the books being compared . . .," "of all the rich men in the world . . .," "of all the states in America . . . ." In these instances, *to* CANNOT be substituted for *dewa*.

ANSWERS:

1. A to B to C dewa, A ga **ichiban** ookii desu.
   (Among A, B and C, A is the largest.)
2. Kono naka dewa, kono aoi hon ga **ichiban** furui desu.
   (Among these, this blue book is the oldest.)
3. Sekai dewa John D. Vanderbilt ga **ichiban** kanemochi desu.
   (John D. Vanderbilt is the richest man in the world.)
4. America dewa Alaska ga **ichiban** ookii shuu desu.
   (In the United States, Alaska is the largest state.)

SUMMARY: In comparing, when one, two, or more than two objects are mentioned, the following forms are used:

One Object (. . . NO HOO GA . . .)	**Two Objects** (. . . WA . . . YORI . . .)	**More than Two Objects** (. . . DE(WA) . . . ICHIBAN . . .)
1. Itoo-san *no hoo ga* kanemochi desu.	Itoo-san *wa* Brown-san *yori* kanemochi desu.	Kono machi (town) *dewa* Itoo-san ga *ichiban* kanemochi desu.
2. Kono biru *no hoo ga* takai desu.	Kono biru *wa* ano hoteru *yori* takai desu.	Tookyoo *dewa* kono biru ga *ichiban* takai desu.
3. Kono empitsu *no hoo ga* nagai desu.	Kono empitsu *wa* sono pen *yori* nagai desu.	Sono naka *dewa* empitsu ga *ichiban* nagai desu.

(A) **MO** . . . (B) **MO**+POSITIVE VERB: This construction is used to indicate that "both A and B are . . .," or "A as well as B . . . ."

1. Doyoobi **mo** Nichiyoobi **mo** hatarakimasu. — (I) will work on both Saturday and Sunday.

2. Ano ryuugakusei wa Nihongo **mo** Eigo **mo** hanashimasu. — That foreign student speaks both Japanese and English.

(A) **MO**... (B) **MO**+NEGATIVE VERB: Used with a negative verb, this means "neither A nor B...."

1. Watakushi no heya niwa rajio **mo** terebi **mo** arimasen. — There is neither a radio nor a television in my room.
2. Watakushi no inu wa niku **mo** sakana **mo** tabemasen. — My dog eats neither meat nor fish.

SUKI DESU AND KIRAI DESU: Associate **ga** with **suki desu** and **kirai desu**:

1. Boku wa kono gakkoo **ga suki** desu.
2. Boku wa kono hon **ga kirai** desu.

When you "like" or "dislike" something very much, use **daisuki** and **daikirai.**

1. Aisu kuriimu (ice cream) **ga daisuki** desu.
2. Watakushi wa ano kata **ga daikirai** desu.

Fluency Drill

Ookii desu.

Gakkoo wa ookii desu.

Watakushi no gakkoo wa ookii desu.

Watakushi no gakkoo wa anata no gakkoo yori ookii desu.

Tanaka-san no gakkoo wa motto ookii desu.

Tanaka-san no gakkoo wa ichiban ookii desu.

Tanaka-san no gakkoo wa Nihon de ichiban ookii desu.

(It) is large.

The school is large.
My school is large.
My school is larger than your school.
Tanaka's school is larger.
Tanaka's school is largest.
Tanaka's school is the largest in Japan.

Substitution Drill

I. WATAKUSHI WA ANATA YORI { *(Adj.* or *noun)* OOKII / CHIISAI / KANEMOCHI / etc. } DESU.

II. WATAKUSHI NO HOO GA { *(Adj.* or *noun)* OOKII / CHIISAI / KANEMOCHI / etc. } DESU.

III. WATAKUSHI WA ICHIBAN { *(Adj.* or *noun)* OOKII / CHIISAI / KANEMOCHI / etc. } DESU.

Exercises

1. The U.S. is larger than Japan.	Amerika wa Nihon yori ookii desu.
2. A taxi is faster than a bus.	Takushii wa basu yori hayai desu.
3. My room is more expensive than yours.	Watakushi no heya wa anata no yori takai desu.
4. My pen is newer than John's.	Watakushi no pen wa John no yori atarashii desu.
5. Your school is older than mine.	Anata no gakkoo wa watakushi no yori furui desu.

6. The U.S. is larger.	Amerika no hoo ga ookii desu.
7. A taxi is faster.	Takushii no hoo ga hayai desu.
8. My pen is newer.	Watakushi no pen no hoo ga atarashii desu.
9. My room is more expensive.	Watakushi no heya no hoo ga takai desu.
10. Your school is older.	Anata no gakkoo no hoo ga furui desu.
11. I like the airplane more.	Hikooki no hoo ga suki desu.
12. I like hotels better.	Hoteru no hoo ga suki desu.
13. I like big schools more.	Ookii gakkoo no hoo ga suki desu.
14. I like small dictionaries more.	Chiisai jibiki no hoo ga suki desu.
15. This hotel is the cheapest.	Kono hoteru wa ichiban yasui desu.
16. That house is the newest.	Ano ie wa ichiban atarashii desu.
17. This university is the largest.	Kono daigaku wa ichiban ookii desu.
18. The plane is the fastest.	Hikooki wa ichiban hayai desu.
19. This room is the most expensive in the hotel.	Kono heya wa kono hoteru de ichiban takai desu.
20. This building is the tallest in Tokyo.	Kono biru wa Tookyoo de ichiban takai desu.
21. I am the oldest in the class.	Watakushi wa kurasu de ichiban toshiue desu.
22. Both your room and mine are expensive.	Anata no heya mo watakushi no heya mo takai desu.
23. Both this and that are mine.	Kore mo sore mo watakushi no desu.
24. Both Mr. Tanaka and Mr. Brown are teachers.	Tanaka-san mo Brown-san mo sensei desu.
25. I like both Japanese and Western style rooms.	Nihonshiki no heya mo yooshiki no heya mo suki desu.
26. Neither your room nor mine is expensive.	Anata no heya mo watakushi no heya mo takaku arimasen.
27. Neither this nor that is mine.	Kore mo sore mo watakushi no dewa arimasen.
28. Neither Mr. Tanaka nor Mr. Brown is a teacher.	Tanaka-san mo Brown-san mo sensei dewa arimasen.
29. I like neither this nor that.	Kore mo sore mo kirai desu.

30. Neither your room nor my room has a T.V. — Anata no heya nimo watakushi no heya nimo terebi ga arimasen.

Note: . . . *NI* . . . *ARIMASU* pattern is used here to express "have" as was explained on page 80.

Translate into Japanese:

1. Mt. Fuji is the highest mountain (*yama*) in Japan.
2. What is the name of your school?
3. Between A and B, which is larger?

Note: For A and B, substitute some nouns: chair, desk, pencil, room, etc. For example, between A (the chair) and B (the desk), which is larger?

4. A Buick is more expensive than a Ford.
5. A Cadillac is the most expensive.
6. 50 is larger than 15.
7. Please tell me (teach me) the name of your Spanish teacher.
8. Is that big white house larger than this old building? No, the building is smaller than the house.
9. What kind of books do you like best?
10. Is America larger than Japan? Yes, America is larger.

Note: When translating into Japanese, learn to analyze a sentence by grouping words together with proper postpositions. For example, in translating sentence 1 above, analyze as follows:

Mt. Fuji is the highest mountain in Japan.

a.	Subject (wa)	predicate (desu)	comparison (dewa)
b.	Fujisan (wa)	ichiban takai yama (desu)	Nihon (dewa).
c.	Fujisan wa	Nihon dewa	ichiban takai yama desu.

Answer in Japanese:

1. Nihon dewa dono tokai ga ichiban ookii desu ka.
2. New York dewa dono gakkoo ga ichiban ookii desu ka.
3. California to Illinois to Florida dewa anata wa dono shuu ga ichiban suki desu ka.
4. Anata no gakkoo wa Beikoku de ichiban ookii gakkoo desu ka.
5. Beikoku de ichiban yoi gakkoo desu ka.
6. Anata wa Doyoobi mo Nichiyoobi mo gakkoo e ikimasu ka.

7. Sekai de ichiban takai tatemono wa doko ni arimasu ka.

   Note: *Sekai de ichiban takai* modifies *tatemono* ("in the world-highest-building" is the literal translation, or: "the highest building in the world").

8. New York to Tookyoo dewa dochira ga ookii desu ka.
9. Anata wa Rockefeller-san yori kanemochi desu ka.
10. Nihonshiki no heya to yooshiki no heya dewa, anata wa dochira ga suki desu ka.
11. Texas-shuu to Maryland-shuu dewa dochira ga ookii desu ka.
12. Amerika de ichiban chiisai shuu no namae o oshiete kudasai.
13. Nihon de ichiban takai yama no namae wa nan desu ka.
14. Fujisan wa sekai de ichiban takai yama desu ka.
15. Sekai no tokai no naka de dono tokai ga ichiban suki desu ka.

Make appropriate questions in Japanese to fit the answers:

1. Tookyoo no hoo ga ookii desu.
2. Tookyoo wa ichiban ookii desu.
3. Teikoku Hoteru wa kooen no chikaku ni arimasu.
4. Watakushi wa hon o yonde imasu.
5. Watakushi wa Kyooto ga ichiban suki desu.
6. Kono hon no naka de kore ga ichiban takai desu.
7. Kono tsukue no ue ni zasshi mo shimbun mo arimasen.
8. Sono hoteru wa ookikute takai desu.
9. Anata no kaban wa heya no naka ni arimasu.
10. Kono hoteru niwa yooshiki no heya ga mittsu shika arimasen.

Useful Expressions

Telephone (Denwa)

KOOSHUU DENWA WA DOKO NI ARIMASU KA.	Where is the public telephone?
TANAKA-SAN NO DENWA BANGOO WA NAMBAN DESU KA.	What is Mr. Tanaka's telephone number?

DENWA RYOOKIN WA IKURA DESU KA.	What is the telephone charge?
MOSHI, MOSHI	Hello, I say . . . .
TANAKA-SAN NO OTAKU DESU KA.	Is this Mr. Tanaka's residence?
WATAKUSHI WA BROWN DESU.	This is Brown.
TANAKA-SAN O CHOTTO YONDE KUDASAI.	Please call Mr. Tanaka (to the phone).

SUPPLEMENT VI

In Reference to Various Time Units

Time Units	Past		Present	Future		
	Before Last	Last	Now (This)	Next	After Next	Every
Year	issaku-nen (2 years ago)	kyo-nen, saku-nen (last year)	ko-toshi, kon-nen (this year)	rai-nen (next year)	sarai-nen (year after next)	mai-toshi, mai-nen (every year)
Month	sen-sengetsu, futa-tsuki mae (2 months ago)	sen-getsu (last month)	kon-getsu, kono-tsuki (this month)	rai-getsu (next month)	sarai-getsu (month after next)	mai-getsu, mai-tsuki (every month)
Week	sen-senshuu, ni-shuukan mae (2 weeks ago)	sen-shuu (last week)	kon-shuu (this week)	rai-shuu (next week)	sarai-shuu, ni-shuukan nochi (week after next)	mai-shuu (every week)
Time	kono aida (the other day)		ima (now)	kondo (next time)		mai-do (every time)
Day	issaku-jitsu, ototoi (day before yesterday)	saku-jitsu, kinoo (yesterday)	kon-nichi, kyoo (today)	myoo-nichi, asu, ashita (tomorrow)	myoogo-nichi, asatte (day after tomorrow)	mai-nichi (every day)
Morning	ototoi no asa (morning before last)	kinoo no asa (yesterday morning)	kesa (this morning)	asu no asa (tomorrow morning)	asatte no asa (morning after next)	mai-asa (every morning)
Night	ototoi no ban (night before last)	saku-ban, yuube (last night)	kom-ban, kon-ya (tonight)	myoo-ban, asu no ban (tomorrow night)	asatte no ban (night after tomorrow)	mai-ban (every night)
Hour	ni-jikan mae (2 hours ago)	mae no jikan (last hour)	kono-jikan (this hour)	tsugi no jikan (next hour)	ni-jikan nochi (ato, go) (2 hours from now)	mai-jikan (every hour)

Note: In working with this chart, start with the PRESENT and go to the *Past* or *Future.*

SUPPLEMENT VII

Designating an Indefinite Number of Units with "Suu"

(*Suu* is a Chinese word meaning "a few" or "several." Therefore, *suunen* means "several years"; *suukagetsu* means "several months," etc.)

Time Units	Ago	Hence
Year	suunen mae[1] / zen	suunen ato / go / nochi
Month	suukagetsu mae[2] / zen	suukagetsu ato / go / nochi
Week	suushuukan mae[3] / zen	suushuukan ato[4] / go / nochi
Day	suujitsu mae	suujitsu ato[5] / go / nochi
Morning	suujitsu mae no asa	suujitsu ato[6] / go / nochi no asa
Night	suujitsu mae[7] no ban	suujitsu ato / go / nochi no ban
Hour	suujikan mae[8]	suujikan ato[9] / go / nochi

1. Several years ago
2. Several months ago
3. Several weeks ago
4. Several weeks later
5. Several days later
6. Several mornings later
7. Several evenings ago
8. Several hours ago
9. Several hours later

CHAPTER 8

KEMBUTSU—SIGHTSEEING

2nd BASE of the VERB + TAI	= WANT TO . . . . *(Desiderative)*
2nd BASE of the VERB + NASAI	= POLITE IMPERATIVE
INSTRUMENT + DE	= BY MEANS OF . . . . WITH . . . .
PLACE + E	= IN THAT DIRECTION TOWARD . . . .

KEMBUTSUNIN TO JUNSA	A SIGHTSEER AND A POLICEMAN
Tookyuu hoteru e ikitai desu	to (the) Tokyu Hotel want to go
K: WATAKUSHI WA TOO-KYUU *HOTERU E IKITAI DESU.*	I WANT TO GO TO THE TOKYU HOTEL.
CHIKATETSU TO DENSHA DEWA DOCHIRA GA HAYAI DESU KA.	BETWEEN THE SUBWAY AND THE STREETCAR, WHICH IS FASTER?
J: TOOKYUU HOTERU WA TOOKU ARIMASEN.	THE TOKYU HOTEL IS NOT FAR.

densha de ikinasai	by (means of) streetcar go
DENSHA DE IKINASAI.	GO BY STREETCAR.
K: KONO KADO NI DENSHA GA TOMARIMASU KA.	DOES THE STREETCAR STOP AT THIS CORNER?
J: DENSHA WA KONO KADO NIWA TOMARIMASEN.	THE STREETCAR DOES NOT STOP ON THIS CORNER.
tsugi tsugi no kado tsugi no kado e	next next corner to (the) next corner.
TSUGI NO *KADO E* IKINASAI.	GO TO THE NEXT CORNER.

Kembutsunin to Shashoo — A Sightseer and a Conductor

K: MOSHI, MOSHI. KONO DENSHA WA TOOKYUU *HOTERU E* IKIMASU KA.	HELLO (SAY, IF YOU PLEASE!) DOES THIS STREETCAR GO TO THE TOKYU HOTEL?
S: KONO DENSHA WA *SOKO E* IKIMASEN. TSUGI NO DENSHA GA IKIMASU.	THIS STREETCAR DOES NOT GO THERE. THE NEXT STREETCAR WILL GO.
densha no kippu o kaitai	streetcar ticket (obj. case) want to buy
K: DENSHA NO KIPPU O *KAITAI* DESU.	I WANT TO BUY A STREETCAR TICKET.

Tookyuu hoteru made sanjuu en desu	to Tokyu hotel is thirty yen
S: TOOKYUU HOTERU MADE SANJUU EN DESU.\	IT IS THIRTY YEN TO THE TOKYU HOTEL.
Aoyama-yuki Aoyama-yuki no densha ni norinasai	Aoyama-bound the Aoyama-bound streetcar get on
AOYAMA-YUKI NO DENSHA *NI NORINASAI.*\	GET ON (or TAKE) THE AOYAMA-BOUND STREETCAR.
densha no teiryuujo wa *densha no teiryuujo wa . . . tsugi no kado *tsugi no kado ni . . .	streetcar (quasi adj.) station (nom. case) *as for the streetcar stop . . . next (quasi adj.) corner *at the next corner . . .
DENSHA NO TEIRYUUJO WA TSUGI NO KADO NI ARIMASU.\	THE STREETCAR STOP IS AT THE NEXT CORNER.

On the Aoyama-Bound Streetcar

K: SHASHOO-SAN, KONO DENSHA WA TOOKYUU *HOTERU E* IKIMASU KA.	(MR.) CONDUCTOR, DOES THIS STREETCAR GO TO THE TOKYU HOTEL?
S: HAI, HOTERU E IKIMASU.\	YES, THIS GOES TO THE HOTEL.

* Reminder: these asterisks are used to indicate the composite of phrases which preceded them.

Tookyuu hoteru made	as far as (the) Tokyu Hotel
nampun	how many minutes
kakarimasu ka	will it take

K: TOOKYUU HOTERU MADE NAMPUN KAKARIMASU KA. — HOW MANY MINUTES WILL IT TAKE TO THE TOKYU HOTEL?

watakushi wa	I (nom. case)
hayaku	quickly
hayaku ikitai	want to go quickly

WATAKUSHI WA HAYAKU IKITAI DESU. — I WANT TO GO QUICKLY.

S: HOTERU WA CHIKAI DESU. — THE HOTEL IS NEAR.

JIPPUN SHIKA KAKARIMASEN. — IT TAKES ONLY TEN MINUTES.

KONO DENSHADOORI NO MIGI NI ARIMASU. — IT IS ON THE RIGHT OF THIS STREETCAR LINE.

hoteru wa	the hotel
ookikute	big (and)
atarashii tatemono	new building.

HOTERU WA OOKIKUTE ATARASHII TATEMONO DESU. — THE HOTEL IS A BIG, NEW BUILDING.

Vocabulary List from the Lesson

kembutsunin (*kem-bu-tsu-nin*) (n.) sightseer

junsa (*jun-sa*) (n.) policeman

e (p.p.) directional postposition; "to" (See I.C. & G.N.)

iku (v.i.) to go; same as *yuku*

ikitai (*i-ki-tá-i*) (desiderative form of *iku*) want to go (See I.C. & G.N.)

chikatetsu (*chi-ká-te-tsu*) (n.) subway; or *chikatetsudoo*

densha (*den-sha*) (n.) streetcar, suburban trains

hayai (*há-ya-i*) (adj.) fast

tooi (*too-i*) (adj.) far

de (p.p.) by, with, in, etc., in the sense of "by means of." (See I.C. & G. N.)

densha de by (means of) streetcar

ikinasai (polite imperative form of *iku*) go!

kado (*ká-do*) (n.) street corner

tomaru (v.i.) to stop

Note: This is an INTRANSITIVE VERB. Therefore, it cannot be used in the sense of the English verb, which is transitive: "He stopped the train." There is another verb "to stop"—*tomeru*, transitive, in Japanese.

tomarimasu (polite form of *tomaru*) (it) stops

densha ga tomarimasu The streetcar stops.

tsugi (*tsu-gi*) (n.) next, the next following (*tsugi no hi*—next day; *tsugi no hito*—next person)

tsugi no kado the next corner

shashoo (*shá-shoo*) (n.) conductor

moshi, moshi (idio.) "Hello, oh say, excuse me," (usually spoken in pairs)

kippu (*kip-pu*) (n.) ticket

kau (v.t.) to buy

kainasai (polite imperative of *kau*) buy!

ikimasu (polite form of *iku*) (one) goes

ikimasen (negative of *iku*) (one) does not go

Aoyama-yuki Aoyama-bound, as in "Chicago-bound"

noru (v.i.) to ride

Note: This is another INTRANSITIVE VERB in Japanese. The English verb "to ride" is transitive, and it is possible to say, "Mr. Brown rides a horse." However, when translating such a sentence into Japanese, say, "Brown-san *wa* horse *ni norimasu*." *O* is incorrect. Learn to associate *ni* with *noru*.

norinasai (polite imperative of *noru*) get on, take (in the sense of "take the next car")

teiryuujo (*te-i-ryuu-jo*) (n.) station stop; *basu (densha) no teiryuujo* bus (streetcar) stop. *Eki* is used for train station.

orinasai (polite imperative of *oriru*) get off!

made (*má-de*) (equivalent to English preposition) "up to," or "until"

nan (inter. pro.) what?

-pun (n.) minute (phonetic change from *fun*)

jippun 10 minutes; phonetic change from *juu—fun* (see above p. 72)

nampun how many minutes?

kakarimasu (polite form of *kakaru*) to take, in the sense of "time required"

hayaku (*há-ya-ku*) (adverbial form of *hayai*) quickly, in a hurry

chikai (*chi-ká-i*) (adj.) near

Additional Vocabulary

michi (n.) road

kara from

osoi (*o-so-í*) — (adj.) slow

yomu — (v.t.) to read

deru (*de-ru*) — (v.i.) to leave, depart (n.c.v.) *place O + deru*—leave the place. *Eki O deru.* Associate postposition *o* with *deru* when leaving a place.

mae — (n.) preceding

mae no densha — preceding streetcar

jidoosha (*ji-dóo-sha*) — (n.) automobile

jitensha — (n.) bicycle

hikooki — (n.) airplane

kisha (*ki-shá*) — (n.) train

kisen (*ki-sen*) — (n.) steamship

ootobai — (n.) motorcycle

oriru — (v.i.) to get off (n.c.v.) *vehicle O orimasu*—to get off the vehicle; *basu O oriru.*

basu* — (n.) bus

takushii* — (n.) taxi

Note: *There are many English words used as Japanese words. In pronouncing such words, be sure you pronounce them like a Japanese, e.g.,

typewriter—ta-i-pu-ra-i-taa
escalator—e-su-ka-ree-taa
rice curry—ka-ree-ra-i-su
ice cream—a-i-su-ku-rii-mu
jazz band—jya-zu-ban-do
baseball—bee-su-boo-ru

Important Construction and Grammar Notes

VERB CONJUGATION: Japanese verbs are classified into one of three groups:

1. *Ichidan* (or non-conjugating) verbs
2. *Yodan* (or conjugating) verbs
3. Irregular verbs *(kuru* and *suru)*

NON-CONJUGATING VERBS: The *ichidan* (or non-conjugating) verbs are verbs whose infinitives end in either **eru** or **iru**. As the name implies, the non-conjugating or *ichidan* verb has only one base, its stem. The stem is derived by dropping the **ru** ending of the infinitive, as follows:

miru	"to see"	*mi*-(ru)	*mi*	(the stem)
taberu	"to eat"	*tabe*-(ru)	*tabe*	(the stem)
mieru	"to be able to see"	*mie*-(ru)	*mie*	(the stem)

There are few exceptions. Some *eru* and *iru* verbs belong to the conjugating verb classification, but these are few, and easily memorized (see below). Henceforth, non-conjugating verb may be abbreviated as n.c.v.

EXCEPTIONS: The following verbs are exceptions to the rule that all **eru** and **iru**-ending verbs are non-conjugating.

kiru	—to cut
kaeru	—to return
hashiru	—to run
shiru	—to know
iru	—to need
hairu	—to enter
mairu	—to come (humble form)

Therefore, these are treated as conjugating verbs with the base as follows:

ra
ri
kae ru
re
ro

(See following for detailed explanation of this.)

The "te" form of these verbs assumes the same form as an *ru*-ending verb, i.e.,

uru	becomes	***u-tte****
kiru	"	***ki-tte***

* See page 51 for explanation of the formation of "te" form of the verb.

shiru
etc.

Note: *Kiru* has two meanings: "to wear" and "to cut." *Kiru* as "wear" is non-conjugating. However, the kanji is different. Similarly, *iru* means "is" and "to need." The former is non-conjugating.

CONJUGATING VERBS: All Japanese verbs, except *kuru, suru,* and the *ichidan* verbs mentioned above are *yodan* (conjugating) verbs.

The root forms of the conjugating verbs have either a "consonant + *u*" ending, or a "*u*" ending. For instance:

yo*mu* — to read
ka*u* — to buy

For conjugation purposes, *yomu* belongs to the *ma* column of the Japanese alphabet; while *kau* and other conjugating verbs ending in double vowels belong to the *wa* column (see page 21).

			ma	*yo*ma (1st base)
			mi	*yo*mi (2nd base)
yomu	*yo*	+	mu	*yo*mu (3rd base)
			me	*yo*me (4th base)
			mo	*yo*mo (5th base)
			wa*	*ka*wa (1st base)
			i	*ka*i (2nd base)
kau	*ka*	+	u	*ka*u (3rd base)
			e	*ka*e (4th base)
			o	*ka*o (5th base)

Note: *The double vowel ending verbs, e.g., k*au* (buy), war*au* (laugh), ar*au* (wash) etc. have *WA* as their first base.

SIGNIFICANCE OF CONJUGATION: The importance of conjugation and knowing the proper base is that this forms the base to which different suffixes are attached. For all *ichidan* verbs, verb suffixes are added to the *stem.* For all *yodan* verbs suffixes are added to ONE OF THE BASES. For instance, the "desiderative form" is constructed by adding the "desiderative suffix" **tai** to the STEM of an *ichidan* verb, and to the 2nd BASE of a *yodan* verb, as follows:

1. miru *mi-tai*
2. yomu *yomi-tai*

The polite present is formed by adding *masu*:

1. miru *mi-masu*
2. yomu *yomi-masu* (*masen* is the negative suffix)

The polite imperative is formed by adding *nasai:*

1. miru *mi-nasai*
2. yomu *yomi-nasai*

STEM OF ICHIDAN VERB	+	TAI (Desiderative) MASU (Polite Present) NASAI (Polite Imperative)

miru	mi	+	tai	=	mitai	("I" want to see)
taberu	tabe	+	tai	=	tabetai	("I" want to eat)
miru	mi	+	masu	=	mimasu	("I" see, will see)
miru	mi	+	nasai	=	minasai	(See!)

2nd BASE OF YODAN VERB	+	TAI (Desiderative) MASU (Polite Present) NASAI (Polite Imperative)

yomu	yo*mi*	+	tai	=	yo*mi*tai	("I" want to read)
tomaru	toma*ri*	+	tai	=	toma*ri*tai	("I" want to stop)
yomu	yo*mi*	+	masu	=	yo*mi*masu	("I" read, will read)
yomu	yo*mi*	+	nasai	=	yo*mi*nasai	(Read!)

Note: Other commonly used endings which can be added to each base are found on page 403 as an appendix. These should be memorized by constant practice.

DESIDERATIVE NEGATIVE: The negative of the desiderative, e.g., "do not want to," can be formed in the same way as the negative of an adjective (see page 82):

1. akai desu
   aka*ku* (wa) arimasen. (negative of adjective)
2. mitai desu
   mita*ku* (wa) arimasen. (negative of desiderative)
3. yomitai desu
   yomita*ku* (wa) arimasen. (negative of desiderative)

ZASSHI O YOMITAI DESU AND ZASSHI GA YOMITAI DESU: In the use of desiderative form requiring an object, the postposition **o** is preferred, but **ga** may be used when the object is emphasized.

1. Watakushi wa Kabuki **o** mitai desu.
   I want to see Kabuki.
2. Watakushi wa Kabuki **ga** mitai desu.
   I want to see Kabuki (and not movies).

POLITE IMPERATIVE NASAI AND POLITE REQUEST KUDASAI: The suffix **nasai** expresses a sentiment which has no equivalent in English. It is a command form, but it is not as strong as the English "Stop!" "Go!" "Get out!" It has an element of polite, gentle, admonition, an encouragement, such as when a mother would tell a child, or a teacher would tell a student to:

1. *Tachinasai.*—Stand up!
2. Miruku o *nominasai.*—Drink (your) milk!
3. Hayaku *shinasai.*—Do it quickly!

te + *kudasai* shows a request in which the speaker is requesting a favor of the party being spoken to.

1. Tanaka-san, to o *shimete kudasai.*
2. Kore o *shite kudasai.*
3. Hon o *yonde kudasai.*

POSTPOSITION E: This postposition indicates the direction in which the object is moving or will move, as in "(going) TOWARD . . ." "TO. . . ." Therefore, **e** is used with a verb of movement.

SUBJECT (what) WA + DIRECTION (where) E + VERB

Kono densha	**wa**	Tookyoo eki	**e**	ikimasu.
(This streetcar)		(to Tokyo Station)		(will go).

The difference between *e* and *ni* is that the latter points to specific location, or specific destination, and *e* general direction. However, in actual usage this fine distinction is not made and *e* and *ni* are used interchangeably where movement toward is intended.

POSTPOSITION DE: **De** is used to show the instrument used, "by means of (with) . . .":

1.

SUBJECT WA + INSTRUMENT DE + OBJECT O + VERB (who) (with what) (what)

Gakusei	**wa**	empitsu	**de**	Nihongo	**o**	kakimasu.
(The student)		(with a pencil)		(Japanese)		(writes).
Watakushi	**wa**	me	**de**	hon	**o**	yomimasu.
(I)		(with eyes)		(book)		(read).

2.

SUBJECT WA + INSTRUMENT DE + DIRECTION E + VERB (who) (with what) (where)

Watakushi	**wa**	hikooki	**de**	Nihon	**e**	ikimasu.
(I)		(by airplane)		(to Japan)		(will go).
Tanaka-san	**wa**	Aoyama-yuki no basu	**de**	gakkoo	**e**	ikimasu.
(Mr. Tanaka)		(by means of the Aoyama-bound bus)		(to school)		(goes).

Note: The word order here may be varied as follows:

Subject + Instrument + Direction + Verb
or
Subject + Direction + Instrument + Verb

DE has another function when used with monetary terms. In the following examples **de** means "for," "at the cost of. . . ."

1. Kono pen o go doru **de** kaimashita.
   I bought this pen *for* $5.00.
2. Kono jibiki o gohyaku en **de** urimasu.
   I will sell this dictionary *for* 500 yen.
3. Kore o ikura **de** kaimashita ka.
   How much did you buy this *for?*

It may not be too illogical to think of this *de* as "by means of" and interpret the sentences given above as "bought *by means of* $5.00," "sell *by means of* 500 yen."

HOW MANY VOLUMES (of books), SHEETS (of paper), etc.: When asking how many volumes, sheets, etc., use the following:

		Classifiers	
		nin	(How many persons?)
NAN		*mai*	(How many sheets?)
or	+	*satsu*	(How many volumes?)
IKU		*doru*	(How many dollars?)
		etc.	

Therefore, ***nan-nin, nan-mai, nan-doru,*** etc., or ***iku-nin, iku-mai.***

Fluency Drill

I

Kaimasu.

Depaato de kaimasu.

Depaato de hon o kaimasu.

Depaato de hon o kaimasen.

Depaato de Nihongo no hon o kaimasen.

Depaato de juu doru de Nihongo no hon o kaimasu.

Depaato de juu doru de Nihongo no hon o ni-satsu kaimasu.

I buy.

(I) buy it at a department store.

(I) will buy a book at a department store.

(I) will not buy a book at a department store.

(I) will not buy a Japanese book at a department store.

(I) will buy a Japanese book for 10 dollars at a department store.

(I) will buy 2 Japanese books for 10 dollars at a department store.

11

Ikimasu

Nihon e ikimasu.

Nihon e ikitai desu.

Hikooki de Nihon e ikitai desu.

Brown-san wa hikooki de Nihon e ikitai desu.

Brown-san wa America no hikooki de Nihon e ikinasai.

(He) will go

(He) will go to Japan

(He) wants to go to Japan

(He) wants to go to Japan by airplane

Mr. Brown wants to go to Japan by airplane.

Mr. Brown, go to Japan in (by means of) an American plane.

Substitution Drill

Noun (Instrument)		*(Verb)*
TAKUSHII BASU HIKOOKI etc.	DE	IKIMASU KIMASU KAERIMASU

Noun (Instrument)		*(Verb)*
EMPITSU PEN FUDE (brush) etc.	DE	KAKIMASU

(2nd Base of Verb)		
TABE YOMI KAI SHI KI etc.	+	TAI (DESU) NASAI

Exercises

1. I will go by streetcar.	Densha de ikimasu.
2. I will come in (by) my friend's automobile.	Tomodachi no jidoosha de kimasu.
3. I will go by train.	Watakushi wa kisha de ikimasu.
4. I will go home by subway.	Chikatetsu de kaerimasu.
5. He will go to Japan by plane.	Ano kata wa Nihon e hikooki de ikimasu.
6. Japanese eat with chopsticks.	Nihonjin wa hashi de tabemasu.
7. Americans eat with knives and forks.	Amerikajin wa naifu to fooku de tabemasu.
8. I go to school by streetcar.	Densha de gakkoo e ikimasu.
9. I go to the hotel by subway.	Chikatetsu de hoteru e ikimasu.
10. I will come here by motorcycle.	Ootobai de koko e kimasu.
11. Read your book.	Anata no hon o yominasai.
12. Eat your dessert.	Dezaato o tabenasai.
13. Come here quickly.	Koko e hayaku kinasai.
14. Go home by taxi quickly.	Takushii de hayaku kaerinasai.
15. Get off in front of the hotel.	Hoteru no mae de orinasai.

16. Get on the next streetcar.	Tsugi no densha ni norinasai.
17. Do you want to eat sukiyaki?	Sukiyaki o tabetai desu ka.
18. Yes, I want to eat sukiyaki.	Hai, sukiyaki o tabetai desu.
19. Do you want to see Kabuki?	Kabuki o mitai desu ka.
20. Yes, I do (want to see it).	Hai, mitai desu.
21. Do you want to read this book?	Kono hon o yomitai desu ka.
22. No, I do not (want to read it).	Iie, yomitaku arimasen.
23. Do you want to buy a Kabuki ticket?	Kabuki no kippu o kaitai desu ka.
24. No, I do not (want to buy one).	Iie, kaitaku arimasen.
25. It takes 5 minutes.	Go-fun kakarimasu.
26. It takes 10 minutes to school.	Gakkoo made jippun kakarimasu.
27. It takes 15 minutes by bus to the hotel.	Hoteru made basu de juugo-fun kakarimasu.
28. It takes only 20 minutes.	Nijippun shika kakarimasen.
29. It takes only 20 minutes by taxi.	Takushii de nijippun shika kakarimasen.
30. It takes only 5 minutes by bicycle to the railroad station.	Eki made jitensha de go-fun shika kakarimasen.

31. Get on the bus (taxi, bicycle, train, airplane, steamship, motorcycle).
32. Get off the bus (taxi, bicycle, train, airplane, steamship, motorcycle).

Translate into Japanese:

1. I do not want to go to Japan by plane. I want to go by ship.
2. This hotel room is not large. Is there a larger one than this?
3. Take the next streetcar. Get off at the next corner.
4. This streetcar will not stop in front of the school.
5. How many minutes will it take by subway? It will take 15 minutes.
6. Please go quickly to the classroom.
7. My house is farther (away) than yours. Mr. Brown's house is the farthest.
8. A bicycle is slower than an automobile.
9. I will not go to the station by bus.
10. Is the Tokyu Hotel far from here? No, it takes only 5 minutes by taxi.

Answer in Japanese:

1. Anata wa Nihon e ikitai desu ka.
2. Eki wa koko kara tooi desu ka, chikai desu ka.
3. Densha wa kono gakkoo no mae de tomarimasu ka.
4. Anata no uchi kara gakkoo made densha de nampun kakarimasu ka.
5. Kono machi ni chikatetsu ga arimasu ka.
6. Hikooki to jidoosha dewa dochira ga hayai desu ka.
7. Anata wa mainichi jidoosha de gakkoo e ikimasu ka.
8. Anata wa atarashii jidoosha o kaitai desu ka.
9. Doko kara eki-yuki no basu ni norimasu ka.
10. Nihon-yuki no kisen wa doko kara demasu ka.
11. Watakushi wa hayaku Nihon e ikitai desu. Nani ga ichiban hayai desu ka.
12. Tookyoo kara San Francisco made hikooki de nan jikan kakarimasu ka.
13. Anata no uchi kara gakkoo made tooi desu ka, chikai desu ka.

    Note: . . . ka . . . ka (this construction asks two questions, asking which of the two is correct, viz., "Is it ____ or is it ____?")

    Is it fast, or is it slow?
    Hayai *desu ka,* osoi *desu ka.*
    Is he a teacher or a soldier?
    Ano kata wa sensei *desu ka,* gunjin *desu ka.*

14. Eki-yuki no densha wa kono kado de tomarimasu ka. Koko kara eki made nampun kakarimasu ka.

    Note: " ____ *kara* ____ *made*" expression is often used to say, "from ____ to (up to) ____"

    Koko *kara* New York *made* . . .
    Kugatsu *kara* Juunigatsu *made* . . .

15. Anata wa Indo (India) e ikitai desu ka.
    Anata wa fune de Nihon e ikitai desu ka.
    Anata wa Kabuki o mitai desu ka.
    Anata wa sukiyaki o tabetai desu ka.
    Anata wa New York made arukitai desu ka.

Fill in the blanks with proper postpositions:

1. Kono hoteru ____ puuru ____ arimasen.
2. Anata ____ hikooki ____ Nihon ____ ikimasu ka.
3. Iie, fune ____ ikimasu.

4. Anata ___ nan(i) de gakkoo ___ kimasu ka.
5. Basu ___ gakkoo ___ kimasu.
6. Anata ___ hoteru ___ aisu kuriimu ___ tabetai desu ka.
7. Iie, watakushi ___ aisu kuriimu ___ tabetaku arimasen.
8. Anata ___ aisu kuriimu ___ kirai desu ka.
9. Iie, watakushi wa aisu kuriimu ___ ichiban suki desu.
10. Aisu kuriimu ___ keeki (cake) ___ takai desu.
11. Watakushi ___ tsugi no kado ___ orimasu.
12. Doko ___ basu ___ norimasu ka.
13. Hoteru no mae ___ densha ___ orimasu.
14. Tanaka-san ___ hikooki ___ Nihon ___ ikimasu.
15. Depaato ___ ni doru ___ jibiki ___ kaimasu.

Useful Expressions

Leaving and Returning Home (Aisatsu)

The following expressions are used when you (John Brown) are leaving your home, inn, etc., and the person remaining there (Mrs. Tanaka) responds:

John Brown: ITTE MAIRIMASU. "I am going now." (This is used only when the person is returning to the same place, e.g., husband leaving for work, tourist leaving the inn temporarily, student going to school, etc.) "Sayonara" is not used when you plan to return soon.

Mrs. Tanaka: ITTE IRRASSHAI. "All right, good-bye!" (This expression is used by the person remaining, and wishing a speedy and safe return).

John Brown: TADAIMA (KAERIMASHITA). "Hello! I've just returned," (said upon returning).

Mrs. Tanaka: O-KAERINASAI. "Welcome home!"

Supplement VIII

Telling Time

1. HOUR—JI MINUTE—FUN SECOND—BYO

1 o'clock—ichi-*ji*	7 o'clock—shichi-*ji*
3 o'clock—san-*ji*	9 o'clock—ku-*ji*
5 o'clock—go-*ji*	11 o'clock—juuichi-*ji*

Note: See Supplement IV and V for complete listings of time, minutes, etc.

2. AFTER—SUGI

	HOUR	MINUTES	PAST	
	JI +	FUN +	SUGI	
1:05—	ichiJI	goFUN	(SUGI)*	(1 o'clock, 5 minutes past)
2:10—	ni JI	jipPUN	(SUGI)*	(2 o'clock, 10 minutes past)
6:15—	rokuJI	juugoFUN	(SUGI)*	(6 o'clock, 15 minutes past)

* SUGI may be omitted here. Therefore, for 1:05, *ichiji gofun* is adequate.

3. BEFORE—MAE

	HOUR	MINUTES	BEFORE
	JI +	FUN +	MAE
12:55—	ichiJI	goFUN	MAE (5 minutes before 1:00)
1:50—	niJI	jipPUN	MAE (10 minutes before 2:00)
5:45—	rokuJI	juugoFUN	MAE (15 minutes before 6:00)

4. HALF PAST—HAN

7:30—shichiJI HAN
10:30—juuJI HAN
12:30—juuniJI HAN

5. 9:35—kuJI sanjuu-goFUN
10:40—juuJI yon-jipPUN

Note: 9:35 can also be read as 25 minutes until 10 (or 10 o'clock, 25 minutes before) *juuji nijuu-go-fun mae.*

6. GO-ZEN and GO-GO are the Japanese equivalents to "a.m." and "p.m." These are used BEFORE the time, and not after, as in English.

11:20 a.m.—GO-ZEN juu-ichiJI ni-jipPUN
1:30 p.m.—GO-GO ichiJI HAN

7. GORO and GURAI (KURAI): These two words mean "about" but note the difference in usage as illustrated below.
GORO is used only for indicating the approximate point of time. Therefore, it is used only with words referring to time.

1. *Nan-ji goro* kimasu ka—about what time are you coming?
2. *Roku-ji goro* kimasu—I will come about 6 o'clock.
3. *Hachigatsu goro* Nihon e ikimasu—I will go to Japan about August.

When *goro* is used, since this indicates the approximate point of time, postposition *ni* showing specific time is not used with *goro* (see below).

GURAI, often pronounced as *kurai,* has the meaning of "approximate *length* of time, *quantity* or *amount* of things." This word is used immediately after the number word in the sentence.

1. *San-jikan gurai* benkyoo shimashita.—I studied about 3 hours.
2. *Juugo-nin gurai* kimashita.—About 15 people came.
3. *Go-doru gurai* arimasu.—I have about $5.00.

8. POSTPOSITION NI has another usage of indicating SPECIFIC time. It is used when specific time (either the year, month, day, day of the week, or the hour, as listed in Supplement V) is mentioned. It has the function of: "in" 1964; "on" June 6; "at" 7 o'clock; "on" Friday, etc.

A. Watakushi wa sen kyuuhyaku roku-juuku-*nen ni* Nihon e ikimasu.
B. Nihon-yuki no kisen wa rokugatsu *muika ni* demasu.
C. Nihongo no kurasu wa *hachi-ji ni* hajimarimasu.
(*kurasu*—class, *hajimarimasu*—v.i. begin)
D. Tanaka-san wa *Kayoobi ni* Amerika e kaerimasu.

Note: No postposition is necessary when the time mentioned is vague and NOT specific, i.e., if specific time, day, month, or year is NOT given. For example:

I will go to school tomorrow.
" " " " " next week.
" " " " " next month.
" " " " " next year.
etc.

No postposition is needed after the time element here, since this is a vague reference to time.

Exercises

ANATA WA KYOO NAN-JI NI GAKKOO E IKIMASU KA.
(What time are you going to school today?)

1. I will go at 8:00 o'clock.
2. I will go at 8:15.
3. I will go about 9:30.
4. I will go at 15 minutes to 8:00.
5. I will go at 20 minutes to 10:00.
6. I will go at 10:20.
7. Today, I will go at 1:30 p.m.
8. Today, I will go at exactly 11:00 o'clock.

ANATA WA ITSU GAKKOO E IKIMASU KA.
(When are you going to school?)

1. I will go to school today.
2. I will go to school tomorrow.
3. I will go to school tomorrow about 8 o'clock.
4. I will go to school on Friday.
5. I will go to school on Friday at 8 o'clock.
6. I will go to school tonight.
7. I will go to school tonight at 15 minutes to 7.
8. I go to school every day.

Useful Expressions

Questions Concerning Time

Ima nan*ji* desu ka.	What time is it now?
Nan*nichi* desu ka.	What day (of the month) is it?
Nan*yoobi* desu ka.	What day (of the week) is it?
Nan*gatsu* desu ka.	What month is it?

Nan*ji ni*	. . . at what time . . . ?
Nan*nichi ni* . . .	. . . on what day . . . ?
Nan*yoobi ni* . . .	. . . on what day (of the week) . . . ?
Nan*gatsu ni* . . .	. . . in what month . . . ?
Nan*nen ni*	. . . in what year . . . ?

CHAPTER 9

HOTERU—A HOTEL

3rd BASE OF THE VERB	+	TSUMORI	=	INTEND TO....
VERB or ADJ.	+	KARA (NODE)	=	BECAUSE....

(College Student):

KONNICHI WA. BOKU WA AMERIKAJIN NO DAIGAKUSEI DESU. ANATA WA EIGO *GA WAKARIMASU* KA.	HELLO (or GOOD DAY). I AM AN AMERICAN COLLEGE STUDENT. DO YOU UNDERSTAND ENGLISH?
Eigo ga	as for English
wakarimasen kara	because (I) do not understand
*Eigo ga wakarimasen kara . . .	*because I do not understand English . . .
Nihongo de	in Japanese
hanashite kudasai	please speak
(Clerk): IIE, WATAKUSHI WA EIGO GA *WAKARIMASEN*	NO, SINCE I DO NOT UNDERSTAND ENGLISH, PLEASE

KARA, NIHONGO DE HANA-SHITE KUDASAI.\	SPEAK IN JAPANESE.
(Student): BOKU NO NIHONGO WA HETA DESU.\	MY JAPANESE IS POOR.
II HEYA GA ARIMASU KA.	IS THERE A NICE ROOM?
(Clerk): HAI, ARIMASU.\NAN-NICHI (IKU-NICHI) TOMARI-MASU KA.	YES, THERE IS. HOW MANY DAYS ARE YOU GOING TO STAY?

kono chihoo o	this area (obj. case)
kembutsu shitai	(I) want to sightsee
node	because
*kono chihoo o kembutsu shitai node . . .	*because I want to sightsee this area . . .
futsuka	two days
tomaru tsumori desu	(I) intend to stay

(Student): WATAKUSHI WA KONO CHIHOO O *KEMBUTSU SHITAI NODE,* FUTSUKA *TO-MARU TSUMORI* DESU.\	SINCE I WANT TO DO (SOME) SIGHT-SEEING IN THIS RE-GION, (I) INTEND TO STAY TWO DAYS.

kyoo wa	today (nom. case)
Kinyoobi desu kara	because it is Friday
*kyoo wa Kinyoobi desu kara . . .	*because today is Friday . . .
Getsuyoobi made	until Monday
tomaru tsumori desu ka	do you intend to stay

(Clerk): KYOO WA *KINYOOBI DESU KARA,* GETSUYOOBI MADE *TOMARU TSUMORI* DESU KA.	SINCE TODAY IS FRIDAY, (DO YOU) INTEND TO STAY UN-TIL MONDAY?

Getsuyoobi made	until Monday
tomaru	stay
tsumori dewa arimasen	do not intend

(Student): IIE, GETSUYOOBI MADE TOMARU TSUMORI DEWA ARIMASEN.\ — NO, I DO NOT INTEND TO STAY UNTIL MONDAY.

asatte	day after tomorrow
uchi e	to home
kaeritai node	because (I) want to return
*asatte uchi e kaeritai node . . .	*because I want to return home the day after tomorrow . . .
Nichiyoobi made	until Sunday
tomaru tsumori desu	intend to stay

ASATTE UCHI E *KAERITAI NODE* NICHIYOOBI MADE *TOMARU TSUMORI* DESU.\ — BECAUSE I WANT TO RETURN HOME THE DAY AFTER TOMORROW, I INTEND TO STAY UNTIL SUNDAY.

(Clerk): ANATA NO NAMAE TO TOKORO (JUUSHO) O YADOCHOO NI KAITE KUDASAI.\ — PLEASE WRITE YOUR NAME AND ADDRESS IN THE HOTEL REGISTER.

heyadai wa	as for room rent
ichi-nichi	one day
happyaku en desu	is 800 yen

HEYADAI WA ICHI-NICHI HAPPYAKU EN DESU.\ — THE ROOM RENT IS 800 YEN PER DAY.

(Student): SONO HEYA WA NIHONSHIKI NO HEYA DESU *KA,* YOOSHIKI NO HEYA DESU *KA.* — IS THAT ROOM A JAPANESE-STYLE ROOM OR A WESTERN-STYLE ROOM?

(Clerk): YOOSHIKI NO HEYA DESU.↘	(IT) IS A WESTERN-STYLE ROOM.
hayaku	early
okitai	(I) want to get up
node	because
*hayaku okitai node . . .	*because I want to get up early . . .
hachi-ji	eight o'clock
hachi-ji ni	at eight o'clock
okoshite kudasai	please wake me.
(Student): BOKU WA ASU NO ASA HAYAKU *OKITAI NODE,* HACHI-JI NI OKOSHITE KUDA-SAI. IMA WA NAN-JI DESU KA↗	SINCE I WANT TO GET UP EARLY TOMORROW MORNING, PLEASE WAKE ME AT EIGHT O'CLOCK. WHAT TIME IS (IT) NOW?
(Clerk): CHOODO ROKU-JI NI-JIPPUN MAE DESU.↘ ANATA NO HEYA WA NI-KAI DESU.↘ CHOOSHOKU WA NAN-JI NI TABEMASU KA.	(IT) IS EXACTLY TWENTY MINUTES OF SIX. YOUR ROOM IS (ON THE) SECOND FLOOR. WHAT TIME ARE (YOU) GOING TO EAT (YOUR) BREAKFAST?
hachi-ji han	eight-thirty
hachi-ji han ni	at eight-thirty
tabetai desu	want to eat
(Student): HACHI-JI HAN NI TA-BETAI DESU. SENMENJO TO FUROBA WA DOKO NI ARIMASU KA.	(I) WOULD LIKE TO EAT AT EIGHT-THIRTY. WHERE ARE THE WASHROOM AND THE BATHROOM?
(Clerk): SOKO NI ARIMASU.↘	THEY ARE THERE.

(Student): ARIGATOO. (or ARIGATOO GOZAIMASU). THANK YOU.

(Clerk): DOO ITASHIMASHITE. DON'T MENTION IT.

Vocabulary List from the Lesson

Nihongo ga wakarimasu (I) understand Japanese. (Learn to associate *ga* with *wakaru*. DO NOT say "Nihongo *o wakaru*.")

kara (conjunctive postposition) since, because. (*Kara* cannot be used to begin a sentence. Also remember that, in Japanese, the subordinate clause always precedes the main clause. (See I.C. & G.N.) *Kara* used in this sense follows a verb or an adjective.)

node because. Same as *kara* explained above. (See I.C. & G.N.)

heta (*he-tá*) (n.) unskillful (or poor, in the sense of unskillful at golf, piano, etc.) "Poor in golf or piano" is "gorufu-piano-*ga* heta desu. "I am poor in Japanese" is "Watakushi *wa* Nihongo *ga* heta desu."

nan- what, this is the contraction of *nani*.

nan-nichi (*nan-ni-chi*) how many days (?)

iku-nichi (*i-ku-ni-chi*) how many days (?)

tomaru (*to-ma-ru*) (v.i.) to stay (at some place other than one's home). Also, the abrupt present form (stays, stay) is further used in the definite future sense (will stay, am going to stay). This is true with infinitive forms of other verbs.

tomarimasu (*to-ma-ri-ma-su*)	(polite form of *tomaru*. Also, the definite future form) stays, stay, . . . will stay, . . .am going to stay.
chihoo	(n.) the region, the district
kembutsu	(n.) sightseeing
suru	(irregular verb) to do
kembutsu (o) suru	(Chi. v.) to do (some) sightseeing, to sightsee
kono chihoo o kembutsu shitai	want to sightsee this region (or want to do some sightseeing in and around this region)
tsumori (*tsu-mo-ri*)	(n.) intention
tomaru tsumori (desu)	intend to stay (See I.C. & G.N.)
kyoo	(n.) today
asatte (*a-sát-te*)	(n.) the day after tomorrow
kaeru (*ká-e-ru*)	(v.i.) to return, go back, go home (See I.C. & G.N.)
kaeritai	(desiderative form of *kaeru*) "want to" return, go back, go home
tokoro (*to-ko-ro*)	(n.) place, or residence
juusho	(n.) address, place of residence
yadochoo	(n.) hotel register
heyadai	(n.) room rent (See I.C. & G.N.)
ichi-nichi	one day
asu (*a-sú*)	(n.) tomorrow
asu no asa	(n.) tomorrow morning
okitai	(desiderative form of *okiru*—"to get up") want to get up
okosu	(v.t.) to wake (someone)
desu kara	a full verb (+) *kara* means "because" or "since"
hachi-ji	eight o'clock
ima	(n.) the present, now
nan-ji	what time (?)
choodo (*choo-do*)	(adv.) exactly, just
mae	"of," in the sense of "before"

ni-kai	second floor (See I.C. & G.N.)
chooshoku (asahan, asagohan)	(n.) breakfast
nan-ji ni	at what time (?)
han	attached to time, means "half-past"
tabetai	(desiderative form of *taberu*) want to eat
senmenjo	(n.) washroom
furoba	(n.) room for taking a bath

Additional Vocabulary

yachin	(n.) house rent
chuushoku (hiruhan, hirugohan)	(n.) noon meal, lunch
yuuhan (yuugohan)	(n.) evening meal
benkyoo (*ben-kyoo*)	(n.) study
shigoto (*shi-go-to*)	(n.) work
koojoo	(n.) factory
machi (*ma-chi*)	(n.) town
naze (*ná-ze*)	why (?) used at the beginning of the sentence to ask the reason why.
osoku	(adv.) late, slow
neru	(v.i.) to sleep (n.c.v.)
arau (*a-ra-u*)	(v.t.) to wash
te	(n.) hand, hands
kao	(n.) face
o-tearai	(n.) toilet

Important Construction and Grammar Notes

CHINESE VERBS: In addition to the three classes of Japanese verbs listed in Lesson 7, there is another group of verbs known as Chinese verbs.

These are "noun verbs"—nouns used as verbs by the addition of **suru** ("to do"). The form is:

NOUN + O SURU

The following are some examples of Chinese verbs:

1. *kembutsu (o) suru* . . . to do sightseeing "to sightsee"
2. *benkyoo (o) suru* . . . . to do some studying, "to study"
3. *shigoto (o) suru* . . . . . to do some work, "to work"
4. *sooji (o) suru* . . . . . . to do some cleaning, "to clean"

The use of **o** in Chinese verbs is optional. In this formula, the NOUN portion is a Chinese compound word (*kembutsu, benkyoo, shigoto,* etc.)—thus, the derivation of this term, Chinese verb. See below for other examples of Chinese verbs.

Similarly, English words can be used to form this type of verb:

1. *doraibu suru* . . . . . to drive
2. *booringu suru* . . . . to bowl
3. *dansu suru* . . . . . . to dance
   etc.

CONJUGATION OF CHINESE VERBS: Chinese verbs are conjugated by conjugating **suru. Suru** is an irregular verb, but it is irregular in the sense that the BASES ARE IRREGULAR. Otherwise they are regular, and conjugate like yodan verbs. The four bases are:

se, (sa), shi—1st base
shi —2nd base
suru —3rd base
(*sare*), *sure* —4th base

Hence: 1. the infinitive or abrupt present is *suru.*
2. the polite present is **shimasu** (2nd base + *masu*).
3. the desiderative form is **shitai** (2nd base + *tai*).

The "te" form of *suru* is *shite*, hence:

1. *shite kudasai* . . . please do
2. *shite imasu* . . . (am) doing

TSUMORI: The meaning of this word by itself is "intention." Generally, however, this word is combined with the third base of a verb. (The third base of a verb is the same as the infinitive, or the dictionary form, or the abrupt form.) Thus:

3rd BASE + TSUMORI = (I) intend to . . .

1. Boku wa aruku **tsumori** desu . . . I intend to walk.
2. Boku wa akeru **tsumori** desu . . . I intend to open.
3. Boku wa benkyoo suru **tsumori** desu . . . I intend to study.

THE NEGATIVE: In order to express NEGATIVE INTENTION, simply change **desu** to . . . **dewa arimasen,** or **ja arimasen.**
. . . **tsumori desu** becomes . . . **tsumori dewa arimasen** (. . . do not intend to).

1. Watakushi wa Kyooto ni tomaru tsumori *dewa arimasen.*	I *do not* intend to stay in Kyoto.
2. Ano kata wa fune de kaeru tsumori *dewa arimasen.*	He *does not* intend to return by ship.

Another way of saying this is to make the verb negative*:

3. Watakushi wa Kyooto de *tomaranai** **tsumori** desu.
4. Ano kata wa fune de *kaeranai** **tsumori** desu.

KARA USED AFTER STATEMENTS: In English, one may say:

BECAUSE TOMORROW IS SUNDAY, I shall not go to school.
I shall not go to school BECAUSE TOMORROW IS SUNDAY.

* The making of an abrupt negative of a verb is explained on page 309.

In other words, the subordinate clause (in this case, the REASON) can come either before or after the principal clause. However, in Japanese there is only one way of expressing a subordinate clause:

REASON	KARA NODE	+ PRINCIPAL CLAUSE

Ashita wa Nichiyoobi desu	*kara*	watakushi wa gakkoo e ikimasen.
Hayaku okimasu (okiru)	*kara*	hayaku nemasu.

Kara may be considered a conjunction meaning "hence," "because," "since," or "therefore," and it comes at the end of the subordinate clause, NOT BEFORE, as in English.

NODE: This expresses the obvious cause, reason, excuse of the subordinate clause of the sentence and is often used interchangeably with **kara**. However, **node** does not have the emphasis of **kara** on pointing out the reason.

1. Dempoo o utta **node** Tanaka-san wa sugu kuru deshoo.	Because I sent a wire, Mr. Tanaka will probably come at once.
2. Isogashii **node** iku koto ga dekimasen.	Because I am busy, I cannot go.

"KARA" MEANING "FROM" AND "KARA" MEANING "BECAUSE":

NOUN	+	KARA	=	from . . .

Hikooki wa *Nihon kara* kimasu.	The airplane will come *from* Japan.
Eki no mae kara densha ni norinasai.	Get on the streetcar *from (at)* the front of the station.

VERB ADJ.	+	KARA NODE	=	because . . .

Kono kisha wa Kyooto niwa *tomarimasen kara orinasai.*	Because this train will not stop at Kyoto, get off.

Kono jibiki wa *takai kara* kaimasen.	Because (since) this dictionary is expensive, I shall not buy it.

DOUBLE "KA": A "double **ka**" construction could be either a "conjunctive double *ka*" construction, or a "two question double *ka*" construction—"either . . . or", "whether . . . or":

1. Kore **ka** sore **ka** are.	This, that, OR that.
2. Densha de ikimasu **ka,** jidoosha de ikimasu **ka.**	Are you going on a streetcar, OR in an automobile?
3. Kono hon wa anata no desu **ka,** sensei no desu **ka.**	Is this book yours OR the teacher's?

Examples 2 and 3 illustrate how double questions are asked with ". . . ka . . . ka" construction.

HOW TO HANDLE CHINESE VERBS: You have learned what Chinese verbs are, how they are formed, how they conjugate, and how they are translated. Cañ you use them correctly now? How would you ask such questions as follows in Japanese?

GROUP I

1. What do you do?
2. What are you going to do?
3. What will you do?
4. What are you doing?
5. What are you intending to do?
6. What do you intend to do?
7. What do you want to do?

GROUP II

1. What do you study?
2. What are you going to study?
3. What will you study?
4. What are you studying?
5. What are you intending to study?
6. What do you intend to study?
7. What do you want to study?

The preceeding sentences are translated into Japanese as follows:

GROUP I

1. Anata wa nani o shite imasu ka.
2. Anata wa nani o shimasu ka.
3. Anata wa nani o shimasu ka.
4. Anata wa nani o shite imasu ka.
5. Anata wa nani o suru tsumori desu ka.
6. Anata wa nani o suru tsumori desu ka.
7. Anata wa nani o shitai desu ka.

GROUP II

1. Anata wa nani o benkyoo shite imasu ka.
2. Anata wa nani o benkyoo shimasu ka.
3. Anata wa nani o benkyoo shimasu ka.
4. Anata wa nani o benkyoo shite imasu ka.
5. Anata wa nani o benkyoo suru tsumori desu ka.
6. Anata wa nani o benkyoo suru tsumori desu ka.
7. Anata wa nani o benkyoo shitai desu ka.

Note: Try the same exercise with other Chinese verbs, supplying proper pronouns as a part of your lesson.

TWO POSSIBLE TRANSLATIONS INVOLVING CHINESE VERBS: Following sentences can be translated as follows:

1. I shall study Japanese.
   a. Watakushi wa Nihongo **no** benkyoo **o** shimasu.
   b. Watakushi wa Nihongo **o** benkyoo shimasu.
2. I shall clean the room.
   a. Watakushi wa heya **no** sooji **o** shimasu.
   b. Watakushi wa heya **o** sooji shimasu.

In (a), *Nihongo no benkyoo* and *heya no sooji* are the objects of the verb *shimasu*. The literal translations are "to do Japanese study" and "to do room cleaning." In (b), *Nihongo* and *heya* are objects of *benkyoo shimasu* and *sooji shimasu*. Translations are "to study Japanese" and "to clean (the) room."

In answering the question:

Anata wa saku-ban nani o shimashita ka.

One can answer:

Watakushi wa benkyoo o shimashita.
Watakushi wa benkyoo shimashita.

In this case *o* is optional. However, when the object is supplied one must comply with the pattern explained above.

To the question:

Nani **o** *benkyoo shimashita ka.*

Answer:

Nihongo **o** *benkyoo shimashita.*
— or —
Nihongo **no** *benkyoo* **o** *shimashita.*

KAI: This is a numeral classifier for "times." Hence, **ikkai, ni-kai, san-kai,** etc. mean once, twice, three times, etc. **Kai** is also the numeral classifier for "floors" in a building. Hence:

1. *ikkai* . . . first floor
2. *ni-kai*
3. *sangai*
4. *yon-kai*
5. *go-kai*
6. *rokkai*
7. *shichi-kai (nana-kai)*
8. *hachi-kai (hakkai)*
9. *kyuu-kai*
10. *jikkai*

KAN: **Kan** is a suffix denoting period or duration of time, and therefore it is often attached or placed after various time units:

1. *ichi nen,* or *ichi nenkan*	one year, for the period of one year
2. *ikkagetsu,* or *ikkagetsukan*	one month, for the period of one month
3. *isshuukan*	one week, for the period of one week
4. *futsuka,* or *futsukakan*	two days, for a period of two days
5. *ichi jikan* (*ichi-ji* by itself means one o'clock)	one hour, for the period of one hour
6. *ippun*, or *ippunkan*	one minute, for the period of one minute

7. *ichi-byoo* or *ichi-byookan* — one second, for the period of one second

DAI: **Dai** is a suffix used to denote fare, rental, fee, etc.

1. *heya-dai*. . . . . room rent
2. *takushii-dai* . . . . . . taxi fare
3. *denki-dai* . . . . electric bill

This word, however, cannot be used universally. Hence:

1. *ya-chin* . . . . house rent
2. *funa-chin* . . . . boat fare

At times *dai* and *chin* are interchangeable. Learn by particular association. *Ryookin,* too, has the same meanig of "fare, rate, charge."

1. *heya no ryookin*
2. *takushii no ryookin*

KAERU: According to the definition of verb conjugation established in Chapter 8, page 113, this, being an *eru*-ending verb, should be an *ichidan* verb (n.c.v.). However, this is one of the seven exceptions, and it conjugates as follows:

	RA
	RI
KAE-	RU
	RE
	RO

The "te" form of this verb is: KAE-TTE.

Fluency Drill

I

Suru tsumori desu.
Benkyoo suru tsumori desu.
Nihongo o benkyoo suru tsumori desu.
Daigaku de Nihongo o benkyoo suru tsumori desu.
Nihon no daigaku de Nihongo o benkyoo suru tsumori desu.
Nihon no daigaku de Nihongo o benkyoo suru tsumori dewa arimasen.

(I) intend to do.
(I) intend to study.
(I) intend to study Japanese.
(I) intend to study Japanese at college.
(I) intend to study Japanese at a Japanese college.
(I) do not intend to study Japanese at a Japanese college.

II

Ikimasen.
Ikitaku arimasen.
Samui kara ikimasen.
Samui kara ikitaku arimasen.
Kyoo wa samui kara ikitaku arimasen.
Asu wa samuku naru kara ikitaku arimasen.
Asu wa samuku naru kara yama e ikitaku arimasen.

(I) will not go.
(I) do not want to go.
Because it is cold I will not go.
Because it is cold I do not want to go.
Because it is cold today I do not want to go.
Because it will be cold tomorrow I do not want to go.
Because it will be cold tomorrow I do not want to go to the mountains.

Substitution Drill

	(3rd Base Verb)			
I. WATAKUSHI WA	TOMARU TABERU SURU KAERU etc.	+	TSUMORI	DESU DEWA (JA) ARIMASEN

	(Adj.)		
II. SORE WA	TAKAI OOKII CHIISAI AKAI etc.	KARA NODE	KAIMASEN

	(Verb)		
III. SENSEI GA	IKU KIMASU KAERIMASU IMASEN etc.	KARA NODE	IKIMASU

Exercises

Translate into Japanese:

I. Since I don't understand English, I don't like it.
Since you understand Japanese, read the letter.
Since I speak Japanese, please speak in Japanese.
Since I want to read, I will buy that book.
Since it is twelve o'clock, I want to eat lunch.
Since the day after tomorrow is Tuesday, I will go to school.
Since it is Saturday, I want to do some sightseeing.
Since it is Tuesday, please study.
Since it is exactly six o'clock, I want to eat supper.
Because today is Sunday, I will not go to school.

Because it is 40 minutes before 8:00, it is early.
Because it is 10 minutes after 6:00, it is late.
Because it is big, I will not buy it.
Because it is black, I don't like it.
Because the room is expensive, I will not stay long.

II. I intend to stay.
I don't intend to stay three days.
How many days do you intend to stay?
How many hours do you intend to play?
Are you intending to go straight ahead?
I don't intend to go home.
I don't intend to go home the day after tomorrow.
Do you intend to go sightseeing today?
I don't intend to open that box.
I don't intend to stay until Sunday.
I will play until nine o'clock.

III. I study (work, do sightseeing, etc.).
I don't study.
I want to study.
Please study.
I am studying.
I am not studying.
You study (polite imperative).
I intend to study.

IV. The bus fare is 50 yen.
The room rent is 725 yen.
The train fare from Tokyo to Osaka is 2000 yen.
The streetcar fare is ten cents.
Is the streetcar fare twenty or thirty cents?

V. It is not far.
I want to get up early.
I want to go late.

It is not red.
The school is not near.

VI. Is this yours or mine?
Is your teacher a Japanese or an American?
Is Japanese easy or difficult?
Are you buying or selling?
This is a Ford, or Chevrolet, or Datsun.

Answer in Japanese:

1. Kyoo wa nan-yoobi desu ka.
2. Asu wa nan-yoobi desu ka.
3. Asatte wa nan-yoobi desu ka.
4. Anata wa Beikokujin no gakusei desu ka.
5. Anata no namae to tokoro o oshiete kudasai.
6. Dare ga anata no heya no sooji o shimasu ka.
7. Anata wa Furansugo to Nihongo ga wakarimasu ka.
8. Kono heya wa donna heya desu ka.
9. New York o kembutsu shitai desu ka.
10. Doko o ichiban kembutsu shitai desu ka.
11. Dono hoteru ga ichiban ookii desu ka.
12. Sono hoteru ni tomaritai desu ka. Naze desu ka.
13. Sono hoteru ni nan-nichi tomaritai desu ka.
14. Sono hoteru ni Nihonshiki to yooshiki no heya ga arimasu ka.
15. Sono hoteru no heya-dai wa ikura desu ka.
16. Dochira ga suki desu ka. Naze desu ka.
17. Nichiyoobi no asa hayaku okimasu ka. Naze desu ka.
18. Anata wa Nichiyoobi ni nan-ji ni chooshoku o tabemasu ka.
19. Nichiyoobi no asa nan-ji ni okimasu ka.
20. Choodo juuni-ji ni chuushoku o tabemasu ka.

Formulate questions so that you can obtain the following information:

1. Whether he understands English or not.
2. What is the name of the best hotel and where it is located.

3. I want to get up at 6:30, so can you wake me up.
4. Whether a person is a student or a Japanese language teacher.
5. You want to find out whether a person intends to stay here until the day after tomorrow—and next, how many days.
6. You want to know where he came from and where he is going.
7. You want to find out what he wants to do tomorrow—sightseeing or shopping.
8. You want to know whether there are any Americans staying in this hotel—how many.
9. You want to determine whether your friend has eaten breakfast, if he would like to eat, and where.
10. You want to know the telephone number of the Imperial Hotel, where there is a telephone, and how much the telephone charge is.
11. You want to find out where one buys a Kabuki ticket, how much it is.
12. Find out where the Kabuki theater is, how long it takes by streetcar, the fastest way of getting there.

Change the following sentences into:

a. *tsumori* (intention) construction
b. negative of *tsumori.*
c. *tai* (desiderative) construction
d. negative of *tai.*
e. past tense of *tai.*

1. Watakushi wa ikimasu.
   a. Watakushi wa *iku tsumori* desu.
   b. Watakushi wa iku *tsumori dewa arimasen.*
   c. Watakushi wa *ikitai* desu.
   d. Watakushi wa *ikitaku (wa) arimasen.*
   e. Watakushi wa *ikitaku (wa) arimasen deshita.*
2. Ashita kaerimasu.
3. Kyooto o kembutsu shimasu.
4. Futsuka Kyooto ni tomarimasu.
5. Chuushoku o tabemasu.
6. Asu no asa hayaku okimasu.

7. Te to kao o araimasu.
8. Nihongo o benkyoo shimasu.
9. Komban osoku nemasu.
10. Zasshi o yomimasu.
11. Fujisan o mimasu.
12. Zasshi o kaimasu.
13. Heya ni imasu.
14. Daigaku de Nihongo o oshiemasu.
15. Nihon no hikooki ni norimasu.

Useful Expressions

Degrees of Frequency

The following expressions show the difference of degrees of frequency from "never" to "always." These are commonly used, so master these by constant usage.

1. KESSHITE + (negative verb)=never . . .		*KESSHITE* NIHONGO O HANASHI*MASEN*.
2. HOTONDO + (negative verb)	hardly ever seldom	*HOTONDO* NIHONGO, O HANASHI*MASEN*.
3. TAMA NI	occasionally	*TAMA NI* NIHONGO O HANASHIMASU
4. TOKIDOKI	sometimes	*TOKIDOKI* NIHONGO O HANASHIMASU.
5. TABITABI	often, frequently	*TABITABI* NIHONGO O HANASHIMASU.
6. ITSU-MO	always	*ITSU-MO* NIHONGO O HANASHIMASU.

Note: Postpositions are not used after these expressions.

CHAPTER 10

KAIMONO—SHOPPING

adj. YASUI + NO	=	CHEAP *ONE*
LOCATION + DE + VERB	=	*(place where action occurs)* AT, IN

BROWN-SAN WA KAIMONO O SHITAI KARA GINZA E IKIMASHITA.	MR. BROWN WANTED TO DO SOME SHOPPING SO HE WENT TO THE GINZA.
DAIMARU *TO IU* OOKII DEPAATO NI HAIRIMASHITA.	HE ENTERED A BIG DEPARTMENT STORE CALLED DAIMARU.

iriguchi	entrance
iriguchi de	at the entrance (place of action)
tenin ni	to the clerk
tazunemashita	asked

BROWN-SAN WA IRIGUCHI *DE* TENIN NI TAZUNEMASHITA.	MR. BROWN ASKED THE CLERK AT THE ENTRANCE.
(Tenin): IRASSHAIMASE.	WELCOME!

(Brown-san): TEBUKURO O KAI-TAI DESU. NANGAI NI ARI-MASU KA.	I WANT TO BUY (SOME) GLOVES. ON WHAT FLOOR ARE THEY?
(Tenin): TEBUKURO WA NANA-KAI DESU.	THE GLOVES ARE ON THE SEVENTH FLOOR.
EREBEETAA WA MIGI NO HOO NI ARIMASU.	THE ELEVATOR IS TO THE RIGHT.
(BROWN-SAN WA EREBEETAA NI NORIMASHITA. SOSHITE *NANA-KAI DE* ORIMASHITA.)	(MR. BROWN TOOK THE ELE-VATOR, AND GOT OFF ON THE SEVENTH FLOOR.)
(Brown-san): KONO TEBUKURO WA IKURA DESU KA.	HOW MUCH ARE THESE GLOVES?
(Tenin): SONO TEBUKURO NO NEDAN WA SEN HAPPYAKU EN DESU.	THE PRICE OF THAT PAIR OF GLOVES IS 1800 YEN.
(Brown-san): KORE WA SUKOSHI *TAKA-SUGIMASU.*	THESE ARE A LITTLE TOO EXPENSIVE.
motto yasui	cheaper
motto yasui no	cheaper ones
MOTTO *YASUI NO* WA ARI-MASEN KA.	AREN'T THERE CHEAPER ONES?
sore wa	as for those
hakuraihin desu	(they) are imported goods
kara	because

*sore wa hakuraihin desu kara . . .	*because those are imported goods . . .
takai desu	(they) are expensive
(Tenin): SORE WA HAKURAI-HIN DESU KARA TAKAI DESU.	SINCE THOSE ARE IMPORTED GOODS, THEY ARE EXPENSIVE.
KORE WA NANAHYAKU GO-JUU EN DESU.	THESE ARE 750 YEN.
(Brown-san): SONO IRO WA SUKI DEWA ARIMASEN.	I DON'T LIKE THAT COLOR.
HOKA NO TEBUKURO O *MISE-TE* KUDASAI.	PLEASE SHOW ME OTHER GLOVES.
(Tenin): KORE WA IKAGA DESU KA.	HOW ARE THESE?
taihen ii iro desu	(they) are a very nice color
ga	but
sukoshi	a little
chiisa-sugimasu	too small
(Brown-san): SORE WA TAIHEN II IRO DESU GA SUKOSHI *CHIISA-SUGIMASU.*	THAT IS A VERY NICE COLOR, BUT A LITTLE TOO SMALL.
MOO SUKOSHI *OOKII NO* WA ARIMASEN KA.	AREN'T THERE LARGER ONES?
sore yori	than those
ookii tebukuro wa	larger gloves (nom. case)
*sore yori ookii tebukuro wa . . .	*larger gloves than those . . .

urikiremashita	sold out
kara	because
*urikiremashita kara . . .	*because (they) are sold out . . .

(Tenin): SORE YORI OOKII TEBUKURO WA URIKIREMASHITA KARA ARIMASEN.\ — SINCE THE GLOVES LARGER THAN THOSE ARE SOLD OUT, WE DO NOT HAVE ANY.

sore dewa	in that event
kono	these
shiroi no	white ones
kono shiroi no o	these white ones (obj. case)
kudasai	give me

(Brown-san): SORE DEWA KONO *SHIROI NO* O KUDASAI.\ — IN THAT EVENT, PLEASE GIVE ME THESE WHITE ONES.

(TENIN WA TEBUKURO O KAMI NI TSUTSUMIMASHITA.\) — (THE CLERK WRAPPED THE GLOVES IN PAPER.)

soshite	and
hoteru e	to the hotel
aruite	walking (on foot)
kaerimashita	returned

BROWN-SAN WA TSUGI NI *HONYA DE* SHUUKAN ASAHI *TO IU* ZASSHI O KAIMASHITA.\ SOSHITE HOTERU *E ARUITE KAERIMASHITA*.\ — MR. BROWN NEXT BOUGHT A MAGAZINE CALLED *WEEKLY ASAHI* AT THE BOOKSTORE, AND HE WALKED BACK TO THE HOTEL.

Vocabulary List from the Lesson

irasshaimase	(v.) Welcome! — a form of greeting used when a customer enters a shop, hotel, restaurant, etc. It is also used by a host greeting a guest at home.
kaimono o suru (*ka-i-mo-no*)	(Chi. v.) to shop
kaimono o shitai	want to shop, want to do (some) shopping
Ginza	(n.) name of a street in Tokyo where the famous shopping district lies.
ikimashita	(polite past of *iku,* to go) went
Daimaru	(n.) name of a department store
to iu	called (See I.C. & G.N.)
depaato	(n.) department store
hairu	(v.i.) to enter, to get in (c.v.)
hairimashita	(v.i. polite past of *hairu*) associate the post-position *ni* with this verb: *daigaku* (*heya*, etc.) *ni hairu*—enter (into) a university (room, etc.)
iriguchi	(n.) entrance
tebukuro (*te-bú-ku-ro*)	(n.) gloves
tenin (*ten-in*)	(n.) store clerk
erebeetaa	(n.) elevator
soshite (sooshite)	(conj.) and
ikura (*í-ku-ra*)	how much?
nedan	(n.) price
sen happyaku en	1800 yen
sukoshi (*su-kó-shi*)	a little
taka-sugimasu	to be too expensive (See I.C. & G.N.)
yasui (*ya-su-i*)	(adj.) cheap, inexpensive
no	(n.) one, substituting for a noun (See I.C. & G.N.)
yasui no	cheap one
hakuraihin	(n.) imported goods

miseru	(v.t.) to show (n.c.v.)
misete kudasai	("te" + *kudasai*) please show me
ikaga desu ka	How is it? How are they? How about it? How are you? (Idiomatic—learn as a phrase.)
chiisa-sugimasu	to be too small, too little
moo sukoshi ookii	a little larger, bigger
moo sukoshi ookii no	a little larger one
urikiremashita	(polite past of *urikireru*) to be sold out
kudasai	(v.) give me
sore dewa	in that case, in that event
tsutsumimashita	(polite past of *tsutsumu,* to wrap) wrapped
honya (*hón-ya*)	(n.) bookstore
de	(p.p.) at, in (postposition indicating place of action. See I.C. & G.N.)
Shuukan Asahi	(n.) name of a Japanese weekly magazine, *Weekly Asahi.*
aruite kaerimashita	(polite past of *aruite kaeru,* to walk home, to return on foot) walked home (See I.C. & G.N.)

Additional Vocabulary

mono (*mo-nó*)	(n.) (concrete) thing
shinamono	(n.) merchandise
uru	(v.t.) to sell (c.v.)
warui	(adj.) bad
nagai (*na-gá-i*)	(adj.) long
mijikai (*mi-ji-ka-i*)	(adj.) short
ie (*i-é*)	(n.) house
ashi (*a-shí*)	(o.) leg, legs, foot, feet
toru	(v.t.) to take (c.v.)
sentaku (*sen-ta-ku*)	(n.) wash, *sentaku suru* (Chi. v.)
ryokan	(n.) Japanese inn

hyakkaten
yunyuuhin (*yu-nyuu-hin*) (n.) imported goods

Important Construction and Grammar Notes

TENSES: The Japanese verb tenses, in the polite forms, are formed by adding the various VERB SUFFIXES to the second base of the *yodan* verbs, and to the stem of the *ichidan* verbs. The irregular verb *suru* is handled like a *yodan* verb.

1. *masu:* the polite present as well as the polite definite future ending.
2. *masen:* the NEGATIVE polite present as well as the polite definite future ending.
3. *mashita:* the polite past ending.
4. *masen deshita:* the NEGATIVE polite past ending.

Therefore:

1. *kakimasu:* (I) write, (I) will write, (I) shall write, (I) am going to write.
2. *kakimasen:* (I) do not write, (I) will not write, (I) shall not write, (I) am not going to write.
3. *kakimashita:* (I) wrote, (I) have written.
4. *kakimasen deshita:* (I) did not write, (I) have not written.

This is an example using the verb *kaku,* a *yodan* or conjugating verb. Practice using *ichidan* verbs and the irregular verb *suru* (to do). For derivation of bases and stems, consult Chapter 8, page 113.

TO IU: As used in this lesson, **to iu** can be translated "called," in the sense of "something *called* something" or "something *named* something."

1. department store called Daimaru—*Daimaru to iu depaato.*
2. a man called Brown—*Brown to iu hito.*
3. a city called Chicago—*Chicago to iu machi.*

TO is often equivalent to the English quotation mark, or "that" of an indirect quotation. **To** is placed immediately after the quotational portion of the sentence to identify this.

1. Sensei ga "Kore wa Eigo no hon desu" **to** iimashita.
   (The teacher said, "This is an English book.")
2. Sensei ga kore wa Eigo no hon desu **to** iimashita.
   (The teacher said that this is an English book.)

. . . TO OMOIMASU (OMOU): As explained above, **to** was used with the verb iimasu to indicate quotation. In the same way, **to** can be used with other verbs of exclamation to indicate the quoted portion. Study the following examples.

1. The student shouted "Help!"
   Student wa, "help," *to* shouted.
2. The boy cried, "I want to go home."
   Boy wa, "I want to go home," *to* cried.
3. Mother called, "Dinner is ready!"
   Mother wa, "Dinner is ready," *to* called.

Similarly, *to* is used with *omoimasu* (to think) to point out what has been thought—the content of what the subject thought. For example:

1. I think "I would like to do some shopping tomorrow."
   What I think is included within the quotation marks, so *to* follows this portion.
   Ashita kaimono o shitai **to** *omoimasu.* (Subject "I" is understood.)
2. I think "this is an imported item."
   "This is an imported item" I think.
   Kore wa hakuraihin da **to** *omoimasu.*
4. I think the shoes are on the 5th floor.
   Kutsu wa go-kai ni aru **to** *omoimasu.*

Note: In the following examples, NI is used after the indirect object. Follow the word order explained below where quotational *to* construction is used.

"Speaker *WA* individual (or group) spoken to *NI* quotation *TO* verb of expression"

1. Sensei *WA* seito *NI* ashita shiken (exam) ga arimasu *TO* iimashita.
   (The teacher said to the students that there would be an exam tomorrow.)

2. Brown-san *WA* tenin *NI* motto ookii no o misete kudasai *TO* iimashita. (Brown said to the clerk, "Please show me a bigger one.")

The usage of *NI* to indicate indirect object may be more clearly explained in the following examples.

1. Please give this book to me. ("book" is the direct object and "me" is the indirect object.)
   Watakushi **ni** kono hon **o** kudasai.
2. I will send this magazine to my Japanese friend. ("this magazine" is the direct object, "my Japanese friend" is the indirect object.)
   Nihon no tomodachi **ni** kono zasshi **o** okurimasu.

NO: This has been used earlier (see p. 38) as a postposition. Here it is used as a nominalizer (adjective taking a noun construction). **No** used in this way can often be interpreted as "one" or the "thing," and it is often similar to the English "give me the large *one*" when the object referred to is understood by the context of the sentence. A corollary to this is that **no** is used to avoid frequent use of the noun (or object) in question.

1. Kuroi **no** o kudasai.
   (Give me a black *one*.)
2. Yasui **no** ga arimasen ka.
   (Aren't there (any) cheap *ones?*)
3. Kono tebukuro no uchi de kuroi **no** ga suki desu.
   (Among these gloves, I like the black *ones*—instead of repeating "gloves.")

However, remember that the Japanese equivalent of "this one" and "that one" are *kono* and *sono* respectively.

DE: An additional use of **de**, a postposition, is to designate the place of action. It is used after a noun to indicate where the action takes place.

1. *Gakkoo de* benkyoo o suru—to study at school.
   (shows where the action of STUDYING is done.)
2. *Koojoo de* shigoto o suru—to work in a factory.
   (shows where the WORK will be done)
3. *Daimaru de* kaimono o shimashita. I did (some) shopping at Daimaru.
   (indicates where the SHOPPING was conducted.)

When mere location is indicated and NO action is involved, *ni* is used:

[illegible]

[illegible] he school.
[illegible] tory?
3. *Kono heya no naka ni* nani ga arimasu ka. What is in this room?

REVIEW OF DE, NI, AND E: Because of similarity in the meanings of **de, ni,** and **e,** the importance of having a clear definition of the function of postpositions rather than giving simple English equivalents to postpositions is repeated here.

1. *Watakushi wa kyonen DAIMARU DE shigoto o shimashita.*
   I last year at Daimaru worked.

(This sentence indicates WHERE I worked—place of action.)

2. *Daimaru to iu depaato wa GINZA NI arimasu.*
   Daimaru called a department store in the Ginza is located.

(In this sentence *ni* also indicates WHERE, but no action is specified. *Ni* specifies where it—the department store—is located.)

3. *Watakushi wa ashita DAIMARU E ikimasu.*
   I tomorrow to Daimaru go.

(In this sentence *e* indicates WHERE I am going—showing the direction of movement.)

If *ni* is to be represented by a dot (•) indicating a specific place, *e* may be an arrow (→) showing the direction toward which the action is moving; *de* will be a larger dot (○) where some sort of action takes place.

CONJUNCTION SOSHITE: The conjunction **soshite**, meaning "and," is used to join two clauses. It may also be used to combine sentences.

1. Boku wa sakuban benkyoo o shimashita. *Soshite* eiga e ikimashita.
   (Last night I did some studying, and I went to the movies.)

In Japanese, two clauses joined by *soshite,* though actually connected in thought, are treated as two independent sentences.

2. Boku wa kyoo machi e ikitai desu. *Soshite* kaimono ga shitai desu.
   (I want to go to town today, and do some shopping.)
3. Anata wa kinoo san-ji ni uchi e kaerimashita ka. *Soshite* nani o shimashita ka.
   (Did you go home yesterday at three o'clock? And what did you do?)

Soshite ("and") has some "and then" connotation.

When connecting two nouns, or substantives, use *to* explained below.

TO: **To** is used to connect two nouns, or substantives.

1. *Anata to watakushi*—you and I
2. *Yoi hon to warui hon*—good books and bad books
3. *Machi to inaka*—town and country

Unlike English, this conjunction CANNOT be used to join adjectives or sentences.

SUGIRU: The verb **sugiru** in itself means "to pass," "to exceed," etc. When combined with a true adjective minus its final *i,* **sugiru** expresses "excessiveness" or "over abundance" of a certain quality:

1. aka*i* aka-**sugiru**—to be too red
2. furu*i* furu-**sugiru**—to be too old
3. too*i* too-**sugiru**—to be too far

Therefore:

1. Kono iro wa *aka*-**sugimasu**—This color is excessively red.
2. Kono ie wa *furu*-**sugimasu**—This house is too old.
3. Ano gakkoo wa *too*-**sugimasu**—That school is too far.

The negative form is handled in the same manner as any verb, as explained above in "TENSES." Therefore:

1. ***aka*-sugimasen**—not too red
2. ***yo*-sugimasen**—not too good

VERB + SUGIRU: When combined with the second base of the *yodan* verbs, or the second base of *suru,* or the stem of the *ichidan* verbs, *sugiru* expresses the idea of "too much," or "overdoing" certain activity. Therefore:

1. *tabe-sugimashita*—(I) overate; ate too much.
2. *yomi-sugimashita*—(I) over-read; read too much.
3. *benkyoo o shi-sugimashita*—(I) overstudied; studied too much.
4. *aruki-sugimashita*—(I) over-walked; walked too much.
5. *shigoto o shi-sugimashita*—(I) overworked; worked too much.

As part of your lesson, practice with other verbs and adjectives. Also practice with various tenses.

ARUITE IKU: This is a new construction embodying a "te" form of the verb + a full verb. So far, you have not learned that a "te" verb, for example, **aruite**, has any meaning other than that it is the "te" form of a certain verb. You have learned that when this form is combined with *kudasai,* a polite request form is obtained. You have learned, too, that "te" verb + "*imasu*" is the progressive action form.

Aruite iku is another form. *Aruite,* here, means "walk and . . . ." *Aruite iku* is "to walk and go," or "to go on foot."
Similarly:

1. *aruite kuru*—to come on foot
2. *aruite kaeru*—to return on foot
   etc.

De was introduced in the sense of "by," "by means of," or as *de,* used to show "by what means" or "with what" (see page 116). Hence, you say:

1. *Kisha de ikimashita.* (I) went by train.
2. *Jidoosha de ikimashita.* (I) went by automobile, or by means of an automobile.

However, compare the following:

1. *Aruite ikimashita.*
2. Boku wa *ashi de arukimasu.* Soshite *te de ji* o kakimasu.
   I walk by means of (my) feet, and I write words by means of (my) hands.

YA: Denotes stores and shops used as a suffix after a noun.

1. *hon***ya**—bookstore
2. *sentaku***ya**—laundry
3. *yado***ya**—inn

This suffix cannot be universally employed. *Ten* is sometimes used.

GA: This is a connective used to introduce ideas contrary to expectation.

1. Kore wa takai shinamono desu **ga** kaimasu.
   (These are expensive goods *but* (I) will buy them.)
2. Gakkoo wa tooi desu **ga** aruite ikimasu.
   (The school is far *but* I will walk there.)

GA has another usage which is closer to the English conjunction "and," introducing another clause of equal weight.

1. Kore wa hon desu **ga** sore wa zasshi desu.

Fluency Drill

Kaimasu.
Kaimashita.
Depaato de kaimashita.
Ookii depaato de kaimashita.
Kore o ookii depaato de kaimashita.
Kono tokei o ookii depaato de kaimashita.
Kono tokei o Daimaru to iu ookii depaato de kaimashita.
Kono yasui tokei o Daimaru to iu ookii depaato de kaimashita.
Hakuraihin no tokei o Daimaru to iu ookii depaato de kaimashita.

(I) will buy.
I bought it.
I bought it at the department store.
I bought it at a large department store.
I bought this at a large department store.
I bought this watch at a large department store.
I bought this watch at a large department store called Daimaru.
I bought this cheap watch at a large department store called Daimaru.
I bought an imported watch at a large department store called Daimaru.

Substitution Drill

(Place)		*(Verb)*
GAKKOO		YOMIMASU
KOOEN		TABEMASU
DEPAATO	DE	KAKIMASU
HOTERU		SHIGOTO SHIMASU
etc.		etc.

(*Adj*. minus "i")		
TAKA		
YASU		SUGIMASU
TOO	+	SUGIMASEN (DESHITA)
MIJIKA		SUGIMASHITA
etc.		

(2nd Base of Verb)		
TABE		SUGIMASU
YOMI	+	SUGIMASEN (DESHITA)
BENKYOO SHI		SUGIMASHITA
etc.		

Exercises

Translate into Japanese:

I

Since I wanted to buy the book, I bought it.
Since I didn't go to school yesterday, I will go today.
Since these are imported goods, they are expensive.
Since I overate, I will not eat.
Since I got off, I will walk.

II

I entered the department store called Daimaru.
I go to a school called Tokyo University.
A man named Brown is teaching English at my school.
That bookstore is selling an American magazine called *Life*.

III

I did (some) shopping at the department store.
Please study in this room.
I will eat at the inn.
I got off on the second floor.
I bought the book at the bookstore.

IV

I studied well and played.
I got off the elevator and walked.
This notebook is 300 yen and it is not good.
I entered the room and sat down.
I bought this and wrapped it.

V

I studied Japanese but I don't understand it well.
This newspaper is 10 yen but that magazine is 50 yen.
This is good but it is too expensive.
I like this but it is too big.

VI

The price is a little too high.

The gloves are a little too small.

It is too red.

The school is too far.

I overslept this morning.

VII

In that event, please give me these.

In that case, I'll go to the store.

How are these hats?

How are these imported goods?

VIII

Use the following verbs in sentences with the various tenses specified: (Start from the top and go down the column.)

I will	buy	do	go in	wrap	stay	sell	understand
I won't	"	"	"	"	"	"	"
I want to	"	"	"	"	"	"	"
I don't want to	"	"	"	"	"	"	"
You (imperative)	"	"	"	"	"	"	"
Please	"	"	"	"	"	"	"
I am	buying	doing	going in	wrapping	staying	selling	understanding
I am not	"	"	"	"	"	"	"
I	bought	did	went in	wrapped	stayed	sold	understood
I didn't	buy	do	go in	wrap	stay	sell	understand
I intend to	"	"	"	"	"	"	"
I	over-bought	over-did			over-stayed	over-sold	

Answer in Japanese:

1. Anata wa kaimono o shitai desu ka.
2. Nani o kaitai desu ka.

3. Daimaru to iu ookii depaato e ikimasu ka.
4. Kono chikaku ni arimasu ka.
5. Amerika de ichiban ookii depaato no namae o oshiete kudasai.
6. Daimaru ni erebeetaa ga arimasu ka.
7. Nangai de booshi o utte imasu ka. (Answer: 2nd floor)

Note: You are a customer in a store. Respond to the following statements and questions presented to you by the clerk.

8. Donna iro no booshi o kaitai desu ka.
9. Kuroi no wa arimasen ga shiroi no wa ikaga desu ka.
10. Kono booshi wa ikaga desu ka. (Answer: It is good, but it is too small.)
11. Kore wa hakuraihin desu kara nedan wa sukoshi takai desu.
12. Kore wa sen en desu. Taka-sugimasu ka.
13. Kono aoi booshi wa roppyaku en desu.
14. Kore wa ikaga desu ka. (Answer: It is good, but show me another one.)
15. Hoka no iro wa urikiremashita kara asatte kite kudasai.

Fill in the blanks with suitable postpositions and give the reason why:

1. Tanaka-san wa heya no naka ___ hon o yonde imasu.
2. Anata wa kotoshi fune ___ Nihon ___ ikimasu ka.
3. Anata no ushiro ___ seito ga benkyoo shite imasu.
4. Honya ___ kono jibiki ___ kaimashita.
5. John-san wa furoba ___ ikimashita.
6. Sensei wa shokudoo ___ hiruhan ___ tabete imasu.
7. Brown-san no ryokan ___ Ginza no chikaku ___ arimasu.
8. Kono machi ___ depaato ___ arimasu ka.
9. Watakushi wa Doyoobi no go-zen kooba ___ shigoto o shimashita.
10. Tookyoo eki no mae ___ basu ___ orimashita.
11. Brown-san wa hikooki ___ Nihon ___ ikimashita.
12. Watakushi wa hoteru ___ chooshoku ___ tabetai desu.
13. Daimaru ___ kono booshi ___ kaimashita.
14. Anata wa basu ___ gakkoo ___ ikimasu ka.
15. Tanaka-san wa depaato ___ ikimashita. Soshite soko ___ Nihongo ___ jibiki ___ kaimashita.
16. Anata ___ kono hakuraihin ___ suki desu ka.

17. Watakushi wa gakkoo ____ kono nooto-bukku ____ kaimashita.
18. Watakushi wa hachi-ji ____ depaato ____ shigoto ____ shimasu.
19. Teeburu no ue ____ zasshi ____ arimasen.
20. Hachi-kai ____ erebeetaa ____ norimashita.

You are in a department store and you are seeking the following information:

How do you ask these questions?

1. You want to know what floor the shoes are on.
2. You want to know how much these shoes are.
3. These are too small, so you want to see some others.
4. You don't like brown shoes, so you ask to see black ones.
5. These black shoes are too expensive, so you want to see cheaper ones.
6. You want to know why these shoes are so expensive.
7. Foreign shoes are usually expensive; you want to know if they have any Japanese-made (Nihonsei) shoes.
8. If they are sold out, when will some be available.
9. You want to know if you can have shoes made here (*atsuraeru*—to make to order).
10. These are just right, so you want to know how much they are.
11. You want to know if there is a department store nearby.
12. Please have them wrapped.

Useful Expressions

Apologies (O-wabi)

GOMEN NASAI or GOMEN KUDASAI — "I'm sorry," "I beg your pardon."
It is also used (aside from ordinary situations where such apologies are required) when:

(a) passing in front of another person.
(b) upon entering the house, shop, etc., and announcing your presence.
(c) leaving your seat at a meeting, etc.

(d) going ahead of a person.
(e) making an impolite remark.

SHITSUREI SHIMASHITA—(ITASHIMASHITA)*	"I'm sorry" (for having committed a breach of etiquette, a blunder, a discourteous act). For example, "I have kept you waiting. *Shitsurei shimashita.*" "I gave you the wrong amount of change. *Shitsurei shimashita.*"
SHITSUREI SHIMASU—(ITASHIMASU)*	"Please excuse me" (for the breach of etiquette, or blunder I am about to commit). This explanation may not be so difficult to imagine if you consider a situation such as: "I won't be able to attend the meeting, so *komban shitsurei shimasu,*" or "I must leave now, so *shitsurei shimasu.*" The circumstances listed under *gomen nasai* above will be applicable here also.
SUMIMASEN—SUMIMASEN DESHITA—(past)	This is the more common way of saying, "I'm sorry," "excuse me"—used for apologizing only.

* *Itashimashita* may be used in place of *shimashita*. The former is the humble form of *shimashita*. The humble form is explained in Chapter 19.

CHAPTER 11

GORAKU—ENTERTAINMENT

3rd BASE OF THE VERB	+	**KOTO GA DEKIRU**	=	CAN DO . . . ABLE TO . . . *(potential)*
ABRUPT PAST OF THE VERB	+	**KOTO GA ARU**	=	HAVE THE EXPERIENCE OF . . . HAVE YOU EVER . . .(?)
2nd BASE OF THE VERB	+	**NI IKU** **NI KURU** **NI KAERU**	=	GO COME FOR THE PURPOSE OF . . . RETURN

BROWN-SAN WA AMERIKAJIN NO GAKUSEI DE TANAKA-SAN WA BROWN-SAN NO TOMODACHI DESU.\	MR. BROWN IS AN AMERICAN STUDENT AND MR. TANAKA IS MR. BROWN'S FRIEND.
ame ga futte iru	it is raining
node	because
kembutsu	sightseeing
kembutsu suru	to do the sights
suru koto ga dekimasen	cannot do
AME GA FUTTE IRU NODE MACHI O KEMBUTSU *SURU KOTO GA DEKIMASEN.*	SINCE IT IS RAINING, WE CANNOT DO SIGHTSEEING IN THE CITY.

FUTARI WA EIGA *KA* SHIBAI NI IKU TSUMORI DESU.	TOGETHER THEY INTEND TO GO TO THE MOVIES OR (TO) A PLAY.
(Brown-san): KYOO WA TENKI GA WARUI KARA EIGA E IKIMASEN KA.	SINCE THE WEATHER IS BAD TODAY, WON'T YOU GO TO THE MOVIES?
(Tanaka-san): SORE WA TAIHEN II KANGAE DESU. SASSOKU *IKIMASHOO.*	THAT IS AN EXCELLENT IDEA. LET US GO IMMEDIATELY.
FUTARI WA TAKUSHII O YOBIMASHITA. SOSHITE TAKUSHII NI NORIMASHITA.	THE TWO CALLED A TAXI AND GOT INTO THE TAXI.

TAKUSHII NO NAKA DE: — IN THE TAXI:

Nihon no shibai o mita koto ga arimasu ka	(a) Japanese play (obj. case) have you ever seen?
(Tanaka-san): ANATA WA NIHON NO SHIBAI O *MITA KOTO GA ARIMASU KA.*	HAVE YOU EVER SEEN A JAPANESE PLAY?
Amerika dewa Nihon no shibai o miru koto ga dekimasen node mita koto ga arimasen	in America (place of action) Japanese play (obj. case) cannot see because have not seen
(Brown-san): AMERIKA DEWA NIHON NO SHIBAI O MIRU	WE CANNOT SEE JAPANESE PLAYS IN AMERICA, SO I

KOTO GA DEKIMASEN NODE MADA MITA KOTO GA ARIMASEN.\	HAVE NOT SEEN (ONE) YET.
(Tanaka-san): KABUKI YA ODORI WA IKAGA DESU KA.	HOW ABOUT KABUKI AND DANCES AND THE LIKE?
(Brown-san): ODORI WA MITA KOTO GA ARIMASU GA KABUKI WA MITA KOTO GA ARIMASEN.\	I'VE SEEN ODORI DANCES, BUT I HAVEN'T EVER SEEN KABUKI.
(Tanaka-san): ANATA WA KABUKI O MITAI DESU KA.	DO YOU WANT TO SEE KABUKI?

mi ni	(in order) to see
ikitai desu	want to go

(Brown-san): EE, ZEHI ICHIDO *MI NI IKITAI DESU.*\	YES, I WANT TO GO TO SEE (IT) ONCE BY ALL MEANS.
(Tanaka-san): ODORI WA IKAGA DESU KA.	HOW ABOUT DANCES?
(Brown-san): ODORI WA MITAKU (WA) ARIMASEN.\	I DO NOT WANT TO SEE DANCES.

shibai o	a play (obj. case)
mi ni	(in order) to see
iku tsumori desu	intend to go
kara	because
*shibai o mi ni iku tsumori desu kara . . .	*since I intend to go to see a play . . .

issho ni	together
ikimasen ka	shall we not go

(Tanaka-san): WATAKUSHI WA MYOOBAN SHIBAI O *MI NI IKU TSUMORI DESU* KARA, *ISSHO NI IKIMASEN KA.*

SINCE I INTEND TO GO SEE A PLAY TOMORROW NIGHT, WON'T YOU GO WITH ME?

tomodachi no uchi e	to a friend's home
asobi ni ikimasu	go to visit
kara	because
iku koto ga dekimasen	cannot go

(Brown-san): ARIGATOO GOZAIMASU GA MYOOBAN WA TOMODACHI NO UCHI E *ASOBI NI IKIMASU* KARA, *IKU KOTO GA DEKIMASEN.*

THANK YOU, BUT SINCE I AM GOING TO MY FRIEND'S HOME FOR A VISIT TOMORROW NIGHT, I WON'T BE ABLE TO GO.

RAISHUU NO GETSUYOO NO BAN WA HIMA DESU KARA, ISSHO NI *IKIMASHOO.*

SINCE NEXT MONDAY NIGHT IS FREE, LET'S GO TOGETHER.

(Tanaka-san): EE, DEWA ISSHO NI IKIMASHOO.

YES, THEN LET US GO TOGETHER.

RAISHUU NO SHIBAI WA TAIHEN YOI SOO DESU.

I HEAR NEXT WEEK'S PLAY WILL BE VERY GOOD.

TAKUSHII WA OOSAKA DE

THE TAXI STOPPED IN FRONT

ICHIBAN OOKII SHOOCHIKU-ZA TO IU EIGAKAN NO MAE NI TOMARIMASHITA.\	OF THE LARGEST THEATER IN OSAKA, CALLED SHOO-CHIKU-ZA.
FUTARI WA TAKUSHII KARA ORIMASHITA.\	THE TWO GOT OUT OF THE TAXI.

kippu uriba e	to (the) ticket office
ni-mai no kippu o	two tickets (obj.)
kai ni	(in order) to buy
ikimashita	went

KIPPU URIBA E NI-MAI NO KIPPU O *KAI NI IKIMASHITA.*\	THEY WENT TO THE TICKET OFFICE TO BUY TWO TICK-ETS.

Vocabulary List from the Lesson

de	(used conjunctively to combine two sentences; see p. 246) . . . and . . .
ame (*á-me*)	(n.) rain
ame ga furu	it will rain, it rains
ame ga furimasu	(polite form of the above)
ame ga futte imasu	it is raining
ame ga furimashita	it rained
. . . koto ga dekiru	(known as the "can do" or potential form of "to be able to," "can"; it is preceded by the abrupt present form of a verb. See I.C. & G.N.)
iku koto ga dekiru	to be able to go, can go
iku koto ga dekimasen	cannot go, not able to go

tomodachi (*to-mo-da-chi*) — (n.) friend

shibai (*shi-ba-i*) — (n.) play

tenki — (n.) weather; *tenki ga ii (warui)*—weather is good (bad)

kangae — (n.) an idea

sassoku — immediately, right away

ikimashoo — (v.) let us go (polite probable future form of *iku*; See I.C. & G.N.)

sassoku ikimashoo — let's go right away

yobimashita — (pol. past form of *yobu*) called

mita — (abrupt past form of *miru*) saw

. . . koto ga arimasu — (past experience form) This form, combined with the abrupt past form of a verb expresses past experience. Do not confuse with "*. . . koto ga dekiru*" form. (See I.C. & G.N.)

mita koto ga arimasu — I have seen (in effect, "I have the experience of having seen," see I.C. & G.N.

mada (*má-da*) — still, yet

mada itta koto ga arimasen — . . . haven't been . . . yet.

Kabuki — (n.) a type of classical Japanese drama

zehi (*zé-hi*) — by all means

odori — (n.) dance

ee — same as *hai*—"yes"

wa — (p.p.) (as used in the lesson "Odori *wa* mita koto ga arimasu ga Kabuki *wa* mita koto ga arimasen." *wa* is USED TO SHOW THOUGHT CONTRAST. *O* is not incorrect, but *wa* is preferable to express the idea "as far as odori is concerned. . . .")

myooban — (n.) tomorrow night (consult and memorize chart in Supplement VI, p. 103)

mi — (stem of *miru*)

. . . ni — when combined with the 2nd base of *yodan* verbs and the stem of *ichidan* verbs, it means: "for the purpose of . . .," in order to . . .," "for . . ." (See I.C. & G.N.)

mi ni — for the purpose of seeing, in order to see (often used with *iku, kuru,* or *kaeru*)

issho (*is-sho*) — (n.) together

issho ni — together

issho desu — (we) are together

issho ni ikimashoo — Let us go together. (See I.C. & G.N.)

asobi ni ikimasu — to go to play, while away time, visit

raishuu — next week (consult and memorize table in Supplement VI)

Getsuyoo no ban — Monday night

hima — (n.) unoccupied time, hence: "free," "open" (in the sense of time)

dewa (*dé-wa*) — then, in that case

. . . soo desu — I hear, it is said (see p. 223 for explanation)

de — in (in the sense of "in all of a certain place, locality, group, category, or classification" when comparing. This form is usually followed by "*ichiban*+adjective," to indicate the superlative degree. This *de* (in) is different from *ni* (in), since *ni* merely shows location of existence. Hence, "something *ga* someplace *ni* arimasu." It also differs with *de* (at), which shows location of action. Do not confuse these usages.)

Shoochiku-za — name of a theater

eigakan	a motion picture theater
-kan	(suffix) denotes a building, *toshokan* —library.
uriba	(n.) place of sale, sales room

Additional Vocabulary

gekijoo	(n.) legitimate theater
baa	(n.) cocktail bar
hanami	(n.) flower viewing
kissaten	(n.) tea house (a place to sit and relax and drink tea while listening to records or other music)
ongaku	(n.) music
ongakukai	(n.) concert
yamanobori	(n.) mountain climbing
Gimbura	(n.) a term applied to a popular pastime in Tokyo: "to walk around the Ginza district with no particular purpose." In Osaka, the term is *Shimbura.* Kobe and Yokohama have similar expressions. "*Gimbura suru,*" "*Gimbura ni iku.*"
haikingu	(n.) hiking
booto nori	(n.) boat ride
itsu	when (?)
hidoi	(adj.) severe, harsh
hidoku	(adverbial form of *hidoi*) severely, harshly
ame ga hidoku futte imasu	It is raining severely/hard. It is pouring.
ame ga sukoshi futte imasu	It is raining a little.
yuki (*yú-ki*)	(n.) snow
yuki ga furu	(it) snows, will snow

Important Construction and Grammar Notes

POLITE AND ABRUPT FORMS: The rigid class-stratification in past Japanese society is manifested in different degrees of politeness or abruptness in Japanese speech. The differentiation is usually demonstrated in the verb endings and personal pronouns. The **masu** and **desu** form of ending emphasized throughout this book is the ordinary polite form which is most widely used. This form is polite enough to be used in almost any social situation by students of the language without creating ill-feeling.

The ABRUPT FORM is used among intimates where there is no need to maintain formality. Depending upon the circumstances, this form can be either intimate or impolite. It is considered impolite to use the abrupt form when addressing a stranger, or someone of higher status. The root form (or dictionary form) of the verb is the abrupt (plain) present.

There is another form (which we will call the SUPER POLITE, or HONORIFIC FORM for lack of a better term) generally used among more educated people, women, or attendants (hotel maids, clerks, waitresses, etc.) speaking to their patrons to show respect. The humble form of expression is used by the speaker to underrate or humble himself.

These two forms are explained in Chapter 19 in greater detail.

	POLITE	ABRUPT
(Present)	yomi-masu	yomu
(Past)	yomi-mashita	yonda
	desu	da

Note: The meaning is the same in these two forms. The only difference is in the degree of politeness implied.

HOW TO FORM THE ABRUPT PAST OF THE VERB: We have noted that the abrupt present form of a verb is the same as the "infinitive" or the "root" of a verb. On page 51, an explanation on how to form the **"te"** form of the verb was given. Abrupt past is formed by changing the **e** of the "te" verb to an **a**. Hence:

	INFINITIVE (ABRUPT)	"TE" FORM	ABRUPT PAST
1.	kau	katte	kat**ta** (bought)
2.	yomu	yonde	yon**da** (read)

3. taberu	tabete	tabe**ta** (ate)
4. hairu	haitte	hait**ta** (went in)
5. tobu	tonde	ton**da** (jumped)
6. iru	ite	**ita** (was, animate existence)
7. aru	atte	at**ta** (was, inanimate existence)
8. desu	de (de atte)	de at**ta**, datta (was)
9. iku	itte	it**ta** (went)

Compare the following:

	PRESENT			PAST	
	Abrupt	*Polite*		*Abrupt*	*Polite*
read	yomu	yomimasu	read	yonda	yomimashita
play	asobu	asobimasu	played	asonda	asobimashita
see	miru	mimasu	saw	mita	mimashita
eat	taberu	tabemasu	ate	tabeta	tabemashita
do	suru	shimasu	did	shita	shimashita
come	kuru	kimasu	came	kita	kimashita

. . . KOTO GA DEKIRU: This construction, known as the "potential" or "can do" form, should be memorized as a phrase. It follows the abrupt present or the infinitive form of a verb, and it means: "to be able to . . .," "can. . . ."
Conjugation is done by conjugating **dekiru.**

1. *Iku* koto ga deki*masu:* can go, able to go.
2. *Suru* koto ga deki*masen deshita:* was unable to do.

Students should also familiarize themselves with ". . . **koto ga dekiru**" constructions embodying all the elements of a sentence:

1. Anata wa Eigo o **hanasu koto ga dekimasu** ka.
   Are you able to speak English?
2. Anata wa Nichiyoobi ni eiga e **iku koto ga dekimasu ka.**
   Can you go to the movies on Sunday?

Also note that in answering ". . . *koto ga dekimasu ka*" construction questions, often all the elements preceding *dekimasu* are left out:

(Q) Anata wa kore o *suru koto ga dekimasu* ka. Can you do this?
(ans.) *Hai, dekimasu.* Yes, I can.
(ans.) *Iie, dekimasen.* No, I can't.

. . . KOTO GA ARU: This is the "experience" construction. When combined with ABRUPT PAST form of a verb, it expresses PAST EXPERIENCE. Do not confuse this with ". . . *koto ga dekiru*" construction (potential).

1. Mita **koto ga arimasu.**
   I have seen . . . (but in effect, "I've had the experience of seeing.")
2. Yonda **koto ga arimasu.**
   I have read . . . (but in effect, "I've had the experience of reading.")
3. Anata wa Nihon e itta **koto ga arimasu ka.**
   Have you been to Japan? (but in effect, "Have you had the experience of going to Japan?")

The negative is formed in the usual manner: *arimasu—arimasen.*

It should be noted that the . . . *koto ga arimasu* construction has an additional connotation: "Did you *ever* do," or "have you *ever* done so-and-so?"

1. *Anata wa Nihon no eiga o mita koto ga arimasu ka.*
   Have you EVER seen a Japanese movie?
2. *Hai, mita koto ga arimasu.* *Iie, mita koto ga arimasen.*
   Yes, I have seen (one). No, I have NEVER seen (one).

Bear in mind that since this form already expresses past experience by the use of the past abrupt form of the verb, be careful NOT to make the final verb past. The verb endings should be either *arimasu* or *arimasen.*

See the pattern at the beginning of this chapter.

. . . NI: When combined with the 2nd base of the *yodan* verbs, the stem of the *ichidan* verbs followed by *iku* (to go), *kuru* (to come), *kaeru* (to return), or other verbs of motion, it means "to go, to come, to return FOR THE PURPOSE OF, IN ORDER TO, or FOR." The first verb indicates the PURPOSE for which you GO, COME, or RETURN. See the pattern at the beginning of this lesson.

1. *asobi* **ni** *iku*	to go for a visit (*yodan* verb)
2. *tabe* **ni** *iku*	to go to eat (*ichidan* verb)
3. *benkyoo o shi* **ni** *iku*	to go to study (Chinese verb)

With Chinese verbs, there are two possibilities in deriving condensed constructions utilizing **ni**. For instance:

1. *Shi* **ni** *ikimashita*—("went to do," but the question is, "went to do what?")
   Benkyoo o shi **ni** *ikimashita.*
   Hence, it is more explicit to say:
2. *Benkyoo* **ni** *ikimashita.* (He) went to study.
3. *Kaimono* **ni** *ikimashita.* (He) went shopping.
4. *Shigoto* **ni** *ikimashita.* (He) went to work.

. . . MASHOO: The second base of the *yodan* verb, the stem of the *ichidan* verb + . . . **mashoo,** a verb suffix, gives the probable future form. However, in actual usage, this means "Let us. . . ." showing intention of the first person.

2nd BASE VERB + MASHOO	"Let's . . .!"
iki**mashoo**	Let's go! *(yodan)*
tabe**mashoo**	Let's eat! *(ichidan)*
kaimono o shi**mashoo**	Let's shop! (Chinese)

When this form is used in a question, it has the meaning of "Shall we . . .?" indicating a simple question in the future.

iki**mashoo ka**	Shall we go?
tabe**mashoo ka**	Shall we eat?
kaimono o shi**mashoo ka**	Shall we shop?

PROBABLE FUTURE: The actual probable future is expressed by the form:

2nd BASE VERB + MASU + DESHOO

Deshoo is the probable future form of *desu* and it denotes the idea of "perhaps," "probably," or "may."

1. Ikimasu deshoo. (He) probably will go.
2. Tabemasu deshoo. (He) probably will eat.
3. Kaimono o shimasu deshoo. (He) probably will shop.

The more common form of this construction is:

ABRUPT VERB + DESHOO

1. Iku deshoo.
2. Taberu deshoo.
3. Kaimono o suru deshoo.

These actual probable future forms are NEVER used in the "let us. . . ." sense.

NOUN ADJECTIVE + DESHOO	= Perhaps, probably, I think.

In this usage, *deshoo* also indicates probability or uncertainty. It is read with a falling tone.

Ano kata wa *Nihonjin deshoo.* That person is *probably* a Japanese.

Kore wa *anata no deshoo.* This is yours, *I think.*

Roshiya-go wa *muzukashii deshoo.* Russian language is *probably* difficult.

Imagoro Tookyoo wa *atsui deshoo. Perhaps* Tokyo is hot about now.

When the *deshoo* is read with a rising tone in the above sentences, it will assume the meaning of "don't you think that . . . ?" "don't you suppose that . . . ?" as if the speaker is asking for confirmation.

PAST TENSE AND PAST EXPERIENCE: A distinction must be made between the ORDINARY past and the PAST EXPERIENCE past. The latter is ordinarily used to describe unusual or special experience one enjoyed in the past.

1. *Kinoo kooen e ikimashita.* (I) went to the park yesterday.
2. *Nikkoo e itta koto ga arimasu.* (I) have been to Nikko.

THE VERB "KURU": This verb, together with *suru,* belongs to the irregular group, i.e., it does not conjugate according to any definite rule. Therefore, the four bases of this verb must be memorized as follows:

	KO
KURU	KI
	KURU
	KURE

Different suffixes (*masu, tai, tsumori,* etc.) are therefore attached to their respective bases as in other conjugating verbs.

KA: You have already learned that **ka** is equivalent to the English question mark (?). When used as a conjunction, it is equivalent to the English "or":

1. kore *ka* are—this OR that
2. kyoo *ka* asu—today OR tomorrow
   The above could also be translated: "either this OR that"; "either today OR tomorrow."

Fluency Drill

Ikimasu.
Kai ni ikimasu.
Hon o kai ni ikimasu.
Nihongo no hon o kai ni ikimasu.
Depaato e Nihongo no hon o kai ni ikimasu.
Gakusei wa depaato e Nihongo no hon o kai ni ikimashita.
Ame ga futte iru node takushii de Nihongo no hon o kai ni ikimashita..

(I) will go.
I will go to buy.
I will go to buy a book.
I will go to buy a Japanese book.
I will go to the department store to buy a Japanese book.
The student went to department store to buy a Japanese book.
Because it is raining (I) went by taxi to buy a Japanese book.

Substitution Drill

(Abrupt Past Verb)
ITTA
TABETA
MITA } + KOTO GA ARU
SHITA
etc.

(3rd Base Verb)
IKU
YOMU } + KOTO GA DEKIRU
MIRU
etc.

(2nd Base Verb)

ASOBI TORI KAI MI (n.c.v.) etc.	NI	IKU KURU KAERU

Exercises

1. Can you come tomorrow?	Ashita kuru koto ga dekimasu ka.
2. Yes, I can come.	Hai, kuru koto ga dekimasu (or, just *dekimasu*).
3. Can you read Japanese?	Anata wa Nihongo o yomu koto ga dekimasu ka.
4. Yes, I can read a little.	Hai, sukoshi yomu koto ga dekimasu.
5. Can you speak English?	Anata wa Eigo o hanasu koto ga dekimasu ka.
6. No, I cannot (speak).	Iie, dekimasen.
7. Can you do this?	Anata wa kore o suru koto ga dekimasu ka.
8. No, I cannot do this work.	Iie, kono shigoto o suru koto ga dekimasen.
9. Can you go to Kabuki with me?	Anata wa watakushi to issho ni Kabuki ni iku koto ga dekimasu ka.
10. Yes, I can go with you next week.	Hai, raishuu issho ni iku koto ga dekimasu.
11. Have you ever been to Japan?	Nihon e itta koto ga arimasu ka.
12. No, I have never been to Japan.	Iie, Nihon e itta koto ga arimasen.
13. Have you ever eaten *sashimi* (raw fish)?	Sashimi o tabeta koto ga arimasu ka.
14. Yes, I have eaten it twice.	Hai, ni-do tabeta koto ga arimasu.
15. Have you ever seen a Japanese movie?	Nihon no eiga o mita koto ga arimasu ka.
16. No, I have never seen (one) yet.	Iie, mada mita koto ga arimasen.
17. Have you ever studied Japanese?	Nihongo o benkyoo shita koto ga arimasu ka.

18. Yes, I have studied it.	Hai, benkyoo shita koto ga arimasu.
19. I am going to buy a ticket.	Kippu o kai ni ikimasu.
20. I am going to see Kabuki.	Kabuki o mi ni ikimasu.
21. I am going to study.	Benkyoo o shi ni ikimasu.
22. I am coming to buy this.	Kore o kai ni kimasu.
23. I am coming to watch your television.	Anata no uchi no terebi o mi ni kimasu.
24. I am coming to study Japanese.	Nihongo o benkyoo shi ni kimasu.
25. I am returning (home) to eat.	Tabe ni kaerimasu.
26. I am returning (home) to write a letter.	Tegami o kaki ni kaerimasu.
27. Because it is raining hard, we cannot do the sights (sightsee).	Hidoku ame ga futte iru kara kembutsu suru koto ga dekimasen.
28. Because I want to see the Gion Festival, I will go to Kyoto next week.	Gion Matsuri o mitai kara raishuu Kyooto e ikimasu.
29. Because I saw this movie, I do not want to go.	Kono eiga o mita node ikitaku arimasen.
30. Because I am going home to eat lunch, I cannot do this.	Chuushoku o tabe ni kaeru kara kore o suru koto ga dekimasen.

Translate into Japanese:

1. Have you ever been in an airplane? No, I have never been in an airplane.
2. I want to see a Japanese play, so let's go on Saturday night.

   Note: "So" in English, as used here, signifies the reason of the case for the statement which follows it. Therefore, *kara* is applicable here.
3. Because it is snowing hard, we cannot go (to) flower viewing in Nara.
4. I went to the department store with Mr. Tanaka to buy a kimono.
5. Have you ever eaten sukiyaki at Suehiro's? No, I haven't (eaten it), but I hear it is very delicious.
6. I do not want to go by streetcar, so please call a taxi immediately.
7. Can you read Japanese? No, I cannot, but I can speak a little.
8. I would like to go mountain climbing but I cannot go this week.
9. Please tell me the name of the largest theater in Tokyo *(de ichiban ookii)*. I hear the Kokusai Gekijoo is the largest, but it is far from here.
10. Let's go to a coffee house to listen to some music. That's a good idea.

Answer in Japanese:

1. Anata no uchi kara gakkoo made aruite iku koto ga dekimasu ka. Naze desu ka.
2. Anata wa Nihon e itta koto ga arimasu ka. Ikitai desu ka. Itsu iku tsumori desu ka.
3. Anata wa sukiyaki o tabeta koto ga arimasu ka. Doko de tabemashita ka.
4. Nichiyoobi ni tomodachi to issho ni yamanobori ni ikimasu ka.
5. Washington no hito-bito (people) wa Ichigatsu ni sakura (cherry blossoms) no hanami ni ikimasu ka. Itsu ikimasu ka.
6. Myooban tomodachi no uchi e asobi ni iku tsumori desu ka. Doko e ikimasu ka.
7. Kono chihoo dewa fuyu ni yuki ga hidoku furimasu ka.
8. Itsu Nihon e Nihongo o benkyoo shi ni ikimasu ka. Fune de ikitai desu ka.
9. Anata wa naze gakkoo de Nihongo o benkyoo shite imasu ka. Nihon e iku tsumori desu ka.
10. Anata wa kotoshi atarashii jidoosha o kau koto ga dekimasu ka. Naze desu ka.
11. Anata wa mainichi chuushoku o tabe ni kaerimasu ka. Naze desu ka.
12. Anata wa Nihongo o kaku koto ga dekimasu ka. Nihon no shimbun o yomu koto ga dekimasu ka. Fude (brush) de kaku koto ga dekimasu ka.
13. Anata wa kissaten e ongaku o kiki ni itta koto ga arimasu ka. Kiki ni ikitai desu ka.
14. Doko de booto ni noru koto ga dekimasu ka. Anata wa soko e itta koto ga arimasu ka.
15. Koko de ichiban ookii eigakan no namae wa nan desu ka. Anata wa soko e tabitabi eiga o mi ni ikimasu ka. Naze desu ka.

Give the negative of the following:

(affirmative) Gakusei wa hon o yomimasu.

(negative) Gakusei wa hon o yomimasen.

1. Sensei wa Nihon e ikimasu.
2. Tanaka-san wa kaerimashita.
3. Watakushi wa benkyoo shimasu.
4. Anata wa shigoto o shimashita.
5. Ano kata o mita koto ga arimasu.

6. Booto ni notta koto ga arimasu.
7. Nihongo o hanasu koto ga dekimasu.
8. Kanji o kaku koto ga dekimasu.
9. Kono shibai wa taihen omoshiroi desu.
10. Kono Nihon no eiga wa nagai desu.
11. Sensei wa san-nin imasu.
12. Watakushi wa fune de Nihon e ikitai desu.
13. Sono jitensha wa watakushi no desu.
14. Kono shibai no kippu wa Brown-san no desu.
15. Watakushi wa sashimi o tabetai desu.
16. Nihon e hon o kai ni ikitai desu.
17. Ashita anata no ie e hanashi ni ikitai desu.
18. Tegami o kaite imasu.
19. San Francisco wa Tookyoo yori ookii desu.
20. Kyoo wa kinoo yori atsui desu.

Useful Expressions

Temperature (Ondo)

1. ATSUI — hot
2. SAMUI — cold
3. ATATAKAI — warm
4. SUZUSHII — cool
5. MUSHIATSUI — sultry

Note: The above expressions are used to describe CLIMATIC condition.
Kyoo wa *atsui (samui, atatakai, suzushii)* hi desu.
In addition, the following show the difference in warmth as can be perceived by one's touch.

1. ATSUI — hot — (ATSUI OCHA hot tea)
2. TSUMETAI — cold — (TSUMETAI TENUGUI cold towel)
3. NURUI — lukewarm — (used for liquid only)

CHAPTER 12

YUUBINKYOKU—POST OFFICE

NOUN **ADJ.** + **NARA** **VERB**	=	IF *(conditional clause)*
VERB + **NOUN**	=	. . . who . . . . which . . . . that . . . . *(relative clause)* . . . where . . . . etc.
1st BASE OF VERB + **NAKEREBA NARIMASEN**	=	MUST . . . .

Beikoku e okuru — send to America
miyage — gift
*Beikoku e okuru miyage . . . — *gift which (I) will send to America . . .

KINOO *BEIKOKU E OKURU MIYAGE* O KATTA NODE, SORE O YUUBINKYOKU E *MOTTE IKIMASHITA.*↘

SINCE I BOUGHT A PRESENT YESTERDAY WHICH I AM GOING TO SEND TO THE UNITED STATES, I TOOK (IT) TO THE POST OFFICE.

(Watakushi): KONO KOZUTSUMI

I WANT TO SEND THIS PACK-

O BEIKOKU E OKURITAI DESU GA, IKURA KAKARIMASU KA.	AGE TO THE UNITED STATES, BUT HOW MUCH WILL IT COST?
(Kyokuin): KOZUTSUMI WA KOKO DEWA TORIATSUKAI-MASEN. TSUGI NO MADO NI MOTTE ITTE KUDASAI.	(Postal Clerk): WE DO NOT HANDLE PACKAGES HERE. TAKE IT TO THE NEXT WIN-DOW, PLEASE.
(Watakushi): AA, SOO DESU KA. SHITSUREI SHIMASHITA.	OH, IS THAT SO? EXCUSE ME!
SORE DEWA NIJUU EN KITTE O GO-MAI TO HAGAKI O JUU-MAI KUDASAI.	IN THAT CASE, PLEASE GIVE ME FIVE 20-YEN STAMPS, AND TEN POST CARDS.
Beikoku e iku	go to America
fune	ship
*Beikoku e iku fune . . .	*ship which goes to America . . .
BEIKOKU E IKU FUNE WA IK-KAGETSU NI NAMBEN DEMA-SU KA.	HOW MANY TIMES A MONTH DO SHIPS WHICH GO TO THE UNITED STATES LEAVE?
fune no bin	ship's convenience
fune no bin ga ii	ship's convenience is good
*fune no bin ga ii kara . . .	*because the ship's convenience is good . . .
Beikoku-yuki	America bound
Beikoku-yuki no yuubin wa	as for American bound mail (nom. case)
ikkagetsu ni	in one month
san-shi-hen	three or four times
*ikkagetsu ni san-shi-hen . . .	*three or four times a month . . .
demasu	depart

(Kyokuin): KONO GORO WA FUNE NO BIN GA II KARA, BEIKOKU-YUKI NO YUUBIN WA IKKAGETSU NI SAN-SHI-HEN DEMASU. KEREDOMO TAITEI NO HITO WA KOOKUU-BIN O TSUKAIMASU.	SINCE THE SHIP ACCOMMODATIONS ARE GOOD NOWADAYS, MAIL FOR AMERICA LEAVES THREE OR FOUR TIMES A MONTH. HOWEVER, MOST PEOPLE USE AIRMAIL.
(Watakushi): SOO DESU KA.	IS THAT SO?

amari	too
amari takaku arimasen	not too expensive
nara	if
*amari takaku arimasen nara . . .	*if it is not too expensive . . .
kookuubin de	by airmail
okurimashoo	I shall send

AMARI TAKAKU ARIMASEN NARA KOOKUUBIN DE OKURIMASHOO.	IF IT IS NOT TOO EXPENSIVE, I SHALL SEND IT BY AIR MAIL.
WATAKUSHI WA SOKO DE GO-HYAKU EN KITTE O KAIMASHITA. SOSHITE KOZUTSUMI NI HARIMASHITA. SORE KARA AKAI EMPITSU DE "KOOKUU-BIN" TO KAKIMASHITA.	I BOUGHT A 500-YEN POSTAGE STAMP THERE AND PLACED IT ON THE PACKAGE. AND THEN, WITH A RED PENCIL I WROTE "AIR MAIL."
TSUGI NO MADOGUCHI NI *MOTTE IKIMASHITA.*	I TOOK IT TO THE NEXT WINDOW.

(Watakushi): KORE O O-NEGAI SHIMASU.\	PLEASE TAKE CARE OF THIS.
kakitome ni shimasu	money order to make it . . . .
(Kyokuin): KAKITOME *NI SHIMASU* KA, FUTSUU *NI SHIMASU* KA.	ARE YOU GOING TO MAKE IT REGISTERED OR REGULAR?
daiji na mono nara *daiji na mono nara . . .	valuable thing if *if it is a valuable thing . . .
DAIJI NA MONO NARA KAKITOME NO HOO GA II DESHOO.\	IF IT IS A VALUABLE THING, REGISTERED MAIL IS PROBABLY BETTER.
Ginza de katta kimono *Ginza de katta kimono . . .	bought on Ginza kimono *kimono which (I) bought on Ginza . . .
(Watakushi): KORE WA *KINOO GINZA DE KATTA KIMONO* DESU.\	THIS IS A KIMONO WHICH I BOUGHT ON THE GINZA YESTERDAY.
AMARI TAKAI KIMONO DEWA ARIMASEN KARA, FUTSUU DE KEKKOO DESU.\	SINCE IT IS NOT A VERY EXPENSIVE KIMONO, REGULAR (POSTAGE) IS ALL RIGHT.
KAKARI NO HITO WA KOZUTSUMI O HAKARI NI KAKEMASHITA.\	THE MAN IN CHARGE PUT THE PACKAGE ON THE SCALE (WEIGHED THE PACKAGE)

MEKATA WA CHOODO NI-KIRO ARIMASHITA.	THE WEIGHT WAS EXACTLY TWO KILOGRAMS (AS FOR THE WEIGHT, THERE WERE EXACTLY TWO KILOGRAMS).
futsuu yuubin	ordinary mail
nara	if
*futsuu yuubin nara	*if it is ordinary mail . . .
moo hyaku gojuu en	150 yen more
haranakereba narimasen	must place (attach)
(Kyokuin): *FUTSUU YUUBIN NARA,* MOO HYAKU GOJUU EN KITTE O *HARANAKEREBA NARIMASEN.* KORE DAKE DESU KA.	IF IT IS REGULAR MAIL, YOU MUST PLACE (ATTACH) 150 YEN MORE POSTAGE. IS THIS ALL?
(Watakushi): KONO TEGAMI O SOKUTATSU DE DASHITAI DESU GA, DOKO E MOTTE *IKANAKEREBA NARIMASEN* KA.	I WANT TO SEND THIS LETTER BY SPECIAL DELIVERY. WHERE MUST I TAKE IT?
(Kyokuin): KOKO DE OKURU KOTO GA DEKIMASU. FUUTOO NO OMOTE NI ATENA O HAKKIRI KAITE KUDASAI.	IT IS POSSIBLE TO SEND IT FROM HERE. PLEASE WRITE THE ADDRESSEE'S NAME DISTINCTLY ON THE FACE OF THE ENVELOPE.

tomodachi to	with a friend
roku-ji ni	at 6 o'clock
yuushoku o	dinner (obj. case)
taberu	eat
yakusoku	promise
*tomodachi to roku-ji ni yuushoku o taberu yakusoku . . .	*promise to eat dinner at 6 o'clock with a friend . . .

WATAKUSHI WA TOMODACHI TO ROKU-JI NI *YUUSHOKU O TABERU YAKUSOKU* O SHITE IMASHITA.\	I HAD PROMISED TO HAVE SUPPER WITH MY FRIEND AT SIX O'CLOCK.
YUUBINKYOKU NO TOKEI WA MOO GO-JI GO-FUN SUGI O SASHITE IMASHITA.\	THE POST OFFICE CLOCK WAS ALREADY POINTING TO FIVE AFTER FIVE.
DENSHA DE YONJUU-GO-FUN KARA ICHI JIKAN KAKARU NODE, ISOIDE YUUBINKYO-KU O DEMASHITA.\	SINCE IT TAKES FROM FORTY-FIVE MINUTES TO ONE HOUR ON A STREETCAR, I LEFT THE POST OFFICE HURRIEDLY.

omote de	in front (place of action)
matte ita	was waiting
matte ita takushii	taxi which was waiting
*omote de matte ita takushii . . .	*taxi which was waiting in front . . .
takushii ni	into a taxi
tobi-norimashita	jumped on

SOSHITE *OMOTE DE MATTE ITA TAKUSHII* NI *TOBI-NORI-MASHITA.*\	AND I JUMPED INTO THE TAXI WHICH WAS WAITING IN FRONT.

Vocabulary List from the Lesson

okuru	(v.t.) to send
miyage	(n.) gift, present, souvenir
okuru miyage	(relative clause construction) "to send gift," or a gift to be sent, a gift WHICH is to be sent. (See I.C. & G.N.)
kyokuin	(n.) postal clerk
motte	("te" form of *motsu*. See I.C. & G.N.)
motte iku (or) **motte . . . iku**	"to hold and go," or "to take"
kozutsumi (*ko-zú-tsu-mi*)	(n.) package
kakarimasu	(polite form of *kakaru*) to cost, require
toriatsukaimasu	(polite form of *toriatsukau*) to handle
aa	(interjection) oh!
kitte (*kit-te*)	(n.) postage stamp
hagaki	(n.) postcard
iku fune	(relative clause construction) the boat WHICH goes
ikkagetsu	(n.) one month
demasu	(polite form of *deru*) to go out, to leave
kono goro	nowadays
bin	(n.) opportunity, occasion, accommodation
san-shi-hen	three or four times (See I.C. & G.N.)
keredomo	(conj.) but, however, nevertheless
taitei (*ta-i-te-i*)	(n.) the majority, most
taitei no hito	most people
yuubin (*yuu-bin*)	(n.) mail
kookuuyuubin (*koo-kuu-yuu-bin*)	(n.) airmail
kookuubin	contraction of *kookuuyuubin*
tsukaimasu	(polite form of *tsukau*) to use
sore dewa (or) **dewa**	then, in that case, in that event

mo — also, too (See I.C. & G.N.)
okurimashoo — (polite indefinite future form) shall send
harimashita — (v.t.) placed (from *haru*—to place; in the sense of "to stick," "to paste")
madoguchi — (n.) window, in the sense of "stamp window" or "stamp counter"
kakitome — registered mail (from *kakitome yuubin*)
o-negai shimasu — (idio.) Please—It means, literally, "I would like to ask a favor of you," "I would like to make a request," "Will you please take care of this."
futsuu — (n.) the usual, ordinary, regular
futsuu ni suru — to make (it) regular
daiji — (n.) important
daiji na mono — an important, valuable, or precious thing (See I.C. & G.N.)
nara — if (See I.C. & G.N.)
amari — too, very (See I.C. & G.N.)
kekkoo — (n.) good, fine. When used as a quasi adjective use with *na*—*kekkoo na shinamono* (See I.C. & G.N.)
kakari — (n.) charge, responsibility
kakari no hito — the person in charge
hakari — (n.) scale
kakemashita — (pol. past of *kakeru*) hung; placed
hakari ni kakeru — to weigh (literally, it means "to hang on the scale")
mekata — (n.) weight
choodo — exactly
kiro — abbreviation of kilogram; standard of weight used in Japan, equivalent to 2.2 pounds.
ni-kiro — two kilograms
moo — more

. . . **nakereba narimasen**	must . . .
haranakereba narimasen	must place (See I.C. & G.N.)
dake	only
sokutatsu	(n.) from *sokutatsu yuubin*—special delivery
fuutoo (*fuu-too*)	(n.) envelope
omote	(n.) the surface, or the face side
atena	(n.) addressee
hakkiri	(adv.) plainly, distinctly
dashimashita	(pol. past of *dasu*) sent, mailed
yuushoku	(n.) same as *yuuhan*—evening meal
taberu	(v.t.) to eat (n.c.v.)
yakusoku	(n.) promise
yakusoku o suru	(Chi. v.) to promise
yakusoku o shite imashita	. . . had promised
tokei	(n.) watch, clock
moo	already
sashite	("te" form of *sasu*—to point)
isoide	("te" form of *isogu*—to hurry) "hurried out . . ." or "hurriedly" (function here is adverbial)
tobi-norimashita	(v.) jumped on (See I.C. & G.N.)

Additional Vocabulary

isogashii (*i-so-ga-shii*)	(adj.) busy
muzukashii (*mu-zu-ka-shii*)	(adj.) difficult
wasureru	(v.t.) to forget (n.c.v.)
dooshite	(adv.) why?
anna	(adj. pro.) that kind of . . .
konna	(adj. pro.) this kind of . . .
sonna	(adj. pro.) that kind of . . .
hikui (*hi-kú-i*)	(adj.) low
itsugoro	about when?
chikagoro	recently

ura (*u-rá*)	(n.) back side, opposite of *omote*
fuu o suru	(Chi. v.) to seal (an envelope)
taisetsu	(n.) important, valuable, same as *daiji; taisetsu na kozutsumi.*
kawase	(n.) money order
yuubinbako, posuto	(n.) mailbox
dempoo	(n.) telegram, wire, telegraphic message
dempoo o utsu	to send a telegram (*utsu*—to wire, hit)
benri (*bén-ri*)	(n.) convenience
benri na	(adj.) convenient
baka	(n.) idiot, fool
baka na	(adj.) brainless, senseless, foolish

Important Construction and Grammar Notes

MOTSU: **Motsu** (to hold) is used to express possession, ownership, by using the "te" form of *motsu—motte* + *iru.* Hence:

1. Boku wa empitsu o *motte imasu.* I have (possess) a pencil.
2. Anata wa jidoosha o *motte imasu* ka. Do you have (own) an automobile?

When the "te" form of *motsu* is combined with **iku**, it means "take" (along).

1. Eigo no hon o *motte ikimasu.* (He) will take the English book.
2. Tegami o *motte ikimashita.* (He) took (along with him) a letter.

When combined with **kuru**, it means "bring":

1. Mizu o *motte kinasai.* Bring (me) water.
2. Empitsu o *motte kite* kudasai. Please bring (me) a pencil.

When used with **kaeru**, it means "to take home":

1. Brown-san wa rajio (radio) o *motte kaerimashita.* Mr. Brown took the radio home.

2. Dare ga watakushi no jibiki o *motte kaetta* ka. Who took my dictionary home?

Note: It has been explained that *motsu* signifies POSSESSION and OWNERSHIP. Therefore, it has a meaning equivalent to "have" in English. However, "have" is used more widely than for simply showing possession, e.g.,
1. I have a two-week vacation.
2. I have an appointment.
3. I have a language class in the morning.
4. Mr. Tanaka has two sons.

The "have" in the above sentences does not indicate MATERIAL ownership, so *motsu* cannot be used. Instead, "ni-shuukan no yasumi *ga arimasu*," etc., is the correct translation (see p. 80).

SAN-SHI-HEN: **Hen** is equivalent to *do,* a numeral classifier for "times." Hence, *shi-hen* is "four times." The "h" in *hen* is changed to "p" or "b" after certain sounds: ip*pen,* ni-hen, sam*ben,* shi-hen, go-hen, rop*pen,* shichi-hen, hachi-hen, kyuu-hen, jip*pen* (or) jup*pen.* **Kai** is also used as classifier to indicate frequency of occurrence. *San-shi* expresses the idea of *samben kara shi-hen made,* or *samben ka shi-hen.* It is equivalent to the English "three or four times." Similarly:

1. ichi-ni-hen (ichi-ni-kai)—once or twice
2. ni-samben (ni-san-kai)—two or three times
3. namben (nan-kai)—how many times?

DAIJI NA MONO: You have learned in an earlier lesson that the post-position **no** is used after certain nouns or substantives to obtain adjective forms. Therefore:

1. *Eigo no hon*—an English language book
2. *chikaku no ie*—a nearby house
3. *migi no hito*—the person on the right

In some cases, *na* is used:

1. daiji **na** mono—a valuable thing
2. baka **na** hito—a foolish person
3. benri **na** densha—a convenient street car
4. kirei **na** hana—a beautiful (or a pretty) flower

Now, what is the criteria for using *no* or *na*? The rule which will be given is not infallible, but it is a good guide to follow.

THE RULE: When it is a concrete noun, use *no*. For abstract nouns, use *na*. Such words as convenient, beauty, foolish, etc., are abstract, hence:

1. benri *na*
2. kirei *na*
3. baka *na*

RELATIVE CLAUSES: A relative clause construction is one of the most important constructions in the Japanese language.

At first it may be a little difficult to recognize relative clauses, since there are no relative pronouns to identify them, but CONSTRUCTION IDENTIFICATION is fairly simple.

(A) Remember that in English the relative clause follows the word it modifies, and it is usually preceded by relative pronouns (who, which, where, that, etc.), for example, "the movie WHICH I SAW" or "the man TO WHOM I TALKED," etc., but in Japanese the rule that "the modifier always PRECEDES the word it modifies" holds true in this case also.

(B) Reduced to its simplest form, a relative clause contains just two elements, namely, a VERB and a NOUN. The verb is usually in the abrupt form, but not necessarily so.

VERB + NOUN

1. katta	kitte	—the "purchased postage stamp," or the "postage stamp which I purchased"
2. iku	fune	—the "to go ships," or "ships which go"
3. hanashite iru	hito	—the "speaking person," or the "person who is speaking"

4. **okuru** miyage—the "to send gift," or the "gift which I am going to send"
5. **okuritai** miyage—the "want to send gift," or the "gift which I want to send"
6. **aruite kaeru** hito —the "walk home person," or the "person who is walking home"

(C) Now let us add an OBJECT. The form is:

OBJECT O + VERB + NOUN

1. *Nihongo o* hanashite iru hito—The man who is speaking Japanese. . . .
2. *Hon o* yonde iru gakusei—The student who is reading a book. . . .

(D) BASIC FORM plus Location. The form is:

LOCATION + VERB + NOUN

1. *Yuubinkyoku de* katta kitte—The postage stamps which I bought at the Post Office. . . .
2. *Beikoku e* iku fune—The ships which go to the United States. . . .
3. *Kado de* hanashite iru hito—The man who is talking on the corner. . . .
4. *Tsukue no ue ni* aru hon—The book which is on the table. . . .

(E) BASIC FORM plus LOCATION plus OBJECT. The form is:

LOCATION + OBJECT O + VERB + NOUN

1. *Kado de Nihongo* o hanashite iru hito—The man who is speaking Japanese on the corner. . . .

The relative position of the "object" and "location" may be interchanged:

Nihongo o kado de. . . .

(F) BASIC FORM plus TIME. The form is:

TIME + VERB + NOUN

1. *Kinoo* katta kitte—The postage stamps which I bought yesterday. . . .

(G) BASIC FORM plus TIME plus LOCATION plus OBJECT. The form is:

TIME + LOCATION + OBJECT + VERB + NOUN

1. *Kinoo kado de Nihongo* o hanashite ita hito—The person who was speaking Japanese on the corner yesterday . . .

The relative position of "time," "location," and "object" does not follow a hard and fast rule. Any combination such as LOCATION, TIME, OBJECT: OBJECT, TIME, LOCATION, etc., is possible. However, in the beginning, learning the order described above may be helpful.

HOW USED: A relative clause may be used nominatively, objectively, or predicatively. The entire clause is treated as a single word, and all the rules concerning postpositions apply to the clauses. Hence, if used nominatively, a relative clause takes a nominative postposition; used objectively, the objective postposition, etc.:

1. *Kado de hanashite ita hito* **o** mimashita. (obj.) (I) saw the person who was speaking on the corner.
2. *Kado de hanashite iru hito* **wa** Brown-san desu. (nom.)
   The person who is speaking on the corner is Mr. Brown.
3. Brown-san wa *kado de hanashite iru hito desu.* (pred.)
   Mr. Brown is the person who is speaking on the corner.

Relative Clause Summary

The word order required in relative clause construction may be summarized as follows:

PATTERNS

1.					NOUN
2.				VERB +	NOUN
3.			OBJECT	VERB +	NOUN
4.		LOCATION	OBJECT	VERB +	NOUN
5.	TIME	LOCATION	OBJECT	VERB +	NOUN
	(when)	(where)	(what)		
1.					hito
2.				hanashite iru	hito
3.			Nihongo o	hanashite iru	hito
4.		kado de	Nihongo o	hanashite iru	hito
5.	ima	kado de	Nihongo o	hanashite iru	hito

TRANSLATIONS

1. The person
2. The person who is speaking
3. The person who is speaking Japanese
4. The person who is speaking Japanese on the corner
5. The person who is speaking Japanese on the corner now

Of course, there are variations of the above mentioned patterns, as follows:

PATTERNS

	TIME	LOCATION	VERB	NOUN
1.				NOUN
2.			VERB	NOUN
3.		LOCATION	VERB	NOUN
4.	TIME	LOCATION	VERB	NOUN
	(when)	(where)		
1.				kitte
2.			katta	kitte
3.		yuubinkyoku de	katta	kitte
4.	kinoo	yuubinkyoku de	katta	kitte

TRANSLATIONS

1. The stamp
2. The stamp which I bought
3. The stamp which I bought at the post office
4. The stamp which I bought at the post office yesterday

NARA: **Nara** is a CONDITIONAL POSTPOSITIVE PARTICLE meaning "if." It is a contraction of *naraba*.

At this point recall the explanation of subordinate clauses given on page 135, when *kara* was discussed. The same rule applies with *nara*.

1. SUBORDINATE CLAUSE *kara* + principal clause
   Ashita wa Nichiyoobi desu **kara** gakkoo e ikimasen.
   (because . . .)
2. SUBORDINATE CLAUSE *nara* + principal clause
   Ashita (ga) Nichiyoobi *nara* yamanobori ni ikimasu.
   (if . . . .)

(a) when used with a SUBSTANTIVE, it takes the form:
    Doyoobi nara (if it is Saturday)
(b) when used with a VERB: *yuku no nara* or *yuku nara* (if you go)
(c) with an ADJECTIVE: *muzukashii nara* (if it is difficult)

THE NEGATIVE OF NARA:

	AFFIRMATIVE	NEGATIVE
1.	substantive + nara	substantive + de nai nara* (This is a contraction of *de arimasen nara.*)
2.	arimasu nara (aru nara)	arimasen nara (nai nara)
3.	imasu nara (iru nara)	imasen nara (inai nara)
4.	kakimasu nara (kaku nara)	kakimasen nara (kakanai nara**)
5.	tabemasu nara (taberu nara)	tabemasen nara (tabenai nara)

Note: **nai* is the abrupt form of *arimasen.*
***nai* as abrupt negative suffix is explained on p. 309.

AMARI (or ANMARI): **Amari** is used in the same sense as **sugiru**, only less emphatic. This is used with an affirmative verb to mean "too much . . ." or "so much . . ." expressing that something is in excess.

1. Sono empitsu wa *amari* takai desu: That pencil is too expensive.
2. Sono empitsu wa *taka-sugimasu:* That pencil is too expensive.

Amari + a negative verb has the meaning of "not so . . .," "not too much . . .," "not very much. . . ."

1. Nihongo wa *amari* muzukashiku wa arimasen: Japanese is not so difficult.
2. Shibai niwa *amari* ikitaku arimasen: I do not want very much to go to a play.

Amari and *sugiru* are often combined:

1. Sono empitsu wa *amari taka-sugimasu:* That pencil is too expensive.

When it is desired to express a situation which is quite in excess such as "This is *really* too difficult," or "I am *really* tired" ANMARI + NIMO can be used.

1. Kore wa *amari nimo* muzukashii desu.
2. Watakushi wa *anmari nimo* tsukaremashita node yasumimashoo.

Or, it can be used in the following pattern:

ANMARI NIMO . . . . . . SUGIRU

1. Kore wa *anmari nimo* muzukashi*sugimasu.*
2. Watakushi wa *anmari nimo* tsukare*sugimashita* node yasumimashoo.

NOUN + NI SURU: This construction is used to indicate the meaning "make it Noun" or "decide on Noun." Study the following English expressions:

1. "What will *it be*?" (at a restaurant)—Nani ***ni shimasu*** ka.
   "*Make it* chocolate ice cream." —Chokoreeto aisu kuriimu *ni shimasu.*
   ("I'll *decide on* chocolate.")
2. "Which one will *it be*?" —Dore ***ni shimasu*** ka.
   "*Make it* this red one." —Akai no ***ni shimasu.***
   ("I'll decide on this red one.")
3. "What day will *it be*?" —Nan-nichi ***ni shimasu*** ka.

. . . NAKEREBA NARIMASEN: This is the "MUST" form. It is attached to the first base of the *yodan* verbs and the stem of *ichidan* verbs.

KA + *nakereba narimasen* ("must" form of ***iku.***)
ki
I ku
ke
ko

MI + NAKEREBA NARIMASEN ("must" form of ***miru***)

1. **ika**nakereba narimasen: must go
2. **ori**nakereba narimasen: must get off
3. **shi**nakereba narimasen: must do
4. **ko**nakereba narimasen: must come

The PAST of the "MUST" form is formed by adding the past tense of *desu, deshita.*

1. ikanakereba narimasen **deshita:** had to go
2. orinakereba narimasen **deshita:** had to get off
3. shinakereba narimasen **deshita:** had to do
4. konakereba narimasen **deshita:** had to come

The abrupt form of this is *konakereba* **naranakatta.** (see p. 309)
The negative of this, "don't have to . . . ," will be explained later. (see p. 403)

MO AND DAKE: **Mo** means "also" and **dake** means "only." They are similar in that they restrict, or limit, the noun with which they are used. The postposition **mo** replaces nominative and objective postpositions (**wa, ga,** and **o**).

Study the following examples carefully and note the subtle difference in meaning:

1. Watakushi **mo** Kinyoobi ni gakkoo e iku.	I, *also,* will go to school on Friday. (indicates that others will go)
2. Watakushi **wa** Kinyoobi ni **mo** gakkoo e iku.	I will go to school on Friday *also.* (in addition to other days)
3. Watakushi **wa** Kinyoobi ni gakkoo e **mo** iku.	I will *also* go to school on Friday. (in addition to other places)

DAKE also has the following restrictions on the noun it is used with. *Dake* replaces the nominative and objective postpositions.

1. Watakushi **dake** Kinyoobi ni gakkoo e iku.	*Only* I will go to school on Friday.
2. Watakushi wa Kinyoobi ni **dake** gakkoo e iku.	I go to school *only* on Friday.
3. Watakushi wa Kinyoobi ni gak-koo e **dake** iku.	I go *only* to school on Friday (and nowhere else).

DAKE: **Shika** is used only with negative verbs, and it means "only." The verb meaning is changed to positive.

Dake means "only" or "just," but it is used with affirmative verbs, or negative verbs in the usual manner with the usual meaning. Postposition **ga** may be used to emphasize the subject.

1. . . . dake (ga) arimasu: there is only. . . .
2. . . . dake (ga) arimasen: only . . . there isn't

(a) Kono heya no naka niwa hon *dake* (ga) *arimasu:*
There are only books in this room.

(b) Kono heya no naka niwa hon *dake* (ga) *arimasen:*
Only books are not in this room.

As explained above both SHIKA. . . . MASEN and DAKE mean "only." However there is a nuance in their usage which can be explained as follows:

SHIKA . . . MASEN, used with a negative verb, has a negative connotation. The emphasis is on the negative aspect of the expression while DAKE stresses the positive. In this connection, it might be appropriate to introduce BAKARI which means "just," "nothing but . . ." in the sense of "at the exclusion of all others."

Ano hito wa Nihongo **shika hanashimasen.**	He speaks nothing but Japanese (because he cannot speak any other language).
Ano hito wa Nihongo **dake** hanashimasu.	He speaks only Japanese (although he can speak other languages).
Ano hito wa Nihongo **bakari** hanashimasu.	He speaks just Japanese (excluding other languages he may be able to speak).

TOBI-NORIMASHITA: Such a compound verb is common in Japanese to make the expression more vivid. This example is a combination of two verbs—*tobu* (jump) + *noru* (go on): jump aboard, jump on, jump on board. The meaning of a compound verb is derived from the combination of each verb.

2ND BASE	+	VERB			
ugoki	+	*hajimeru*	(move	begin	—begin to move)
kai	+	*aruku*	(buy	walk	—go around buying)
nori	+	*kaeru*	(ride	change	—transfer trains, buses, etc.)

SECOND BASE OF THE VERB (or CONTINUATIVE BASE): As demonstrated above, the second base of the verb is often the base to which another verb, or other words, are attached to form compound words. Remember that for *ichidan* verbs (n.c.v.), the stem is used. Thus, this base is called *renyookei,* or "continuative base."

hanasu (speak) + au (meet)—hana**shi**-au (discuss)
hataraku (work) + sugiru (exceed)—hatara**ki**-sugiru (overwork)
taberu (eat)+ owaru (end)—ta**be**-owaru (finish eating)
yomu (read) + nikui (difficult)—yo**mi**-nikui (hard to read)
tsukau (use) + yasui (easy)—tsuk**ai**-yasui (easy to use)

Fluency Drill

I

tabete ita hito

chooshoku *o* tabete ita hito

hoteru *de* chooshoku *o* tabete ita hito

kesa hoteru *de* chooshoku *o* tabete ita hito

kesa ku-ji *ni* hoteru *de* chooshoku *o* tabete ita hito

kesa ku-ji *ni* Amerikajin *no* tomodachi *to* hoteru *de* chooshoku *o* tabete ita hito

Note: (a) In this exercise, note the postpositions.
(b) The word order need not conform to the examples given here. *Time, location,* etc., can be interchanged with the proper postpositions.

the man who was eating

the man who was eating breakfast

the man who was eating breakfast at the hotel

the man who was eating breakfast at the hotel this morning

the man who was eating breakfast at the hotel this morning at 9:00

the man who was eating breakfast at the hotel this morning at 9:00 with an American friend

II

yonda hon

yonda Eigo no hon

kinoo yonda Eigo no hon

Kinoo yonda Eigo no hon wa muzukashii deshita.

Kinoo gakkoo de yonda Eigo no hon wa muzukashii deshita.

Kinoo gakkoo no toshokan de yonda Eigo no hon wa muzukashii deshita.

the book which (I) read . . .

the English book which I read . . .

the English book which I read yesterday . . .

The English book which I read yesterday was difficult.

The English book which I read yesterday at school was difficult.

The English book which I read yesterday at the school's library was difficult.

Substitution Drill

(Noun)		
DOYOOBI ANATA NIHONJIN etc.	+	NARA
(3rd Base of Verb)		
HATARAKU TABERU BENKYOO SURU etc.	+	NARA
(Adj.)		
TAKAI TABETAI ISOGASHIKU NAI etc.	+	NARA
(Abrupt Past)		*(Noun)*
MITA UTTA MOTTE KITA etc.	+	EIGA HON JIDOOSHA
(1st Base of Verb)		
IKA YOMA KAWA SHI KO etc.	+	NAKEREBA NARIMASEN (DESHITA)

Exercises

1. If it is Sunday I will go. — Nichiyoobi nara ikimasu.
2. If I were you I wouldn't buy (it). — Watakushi ga anata nara kaimasen.
3. If it is a Cadillac it is expensive. — Cadillac nara takai desu.
4. If it is tomorrow I cannot go. — Ashita nara watakushi wa iku koto ga dekimasen.

5. If you are going I will not go. — Anata ga iku nara watakushi wa ikimasen.
6. If you are (going to) buy (it) I will not sell (it). — Anata ga kau nara watakushi wa urimasen.
7. If it is raining, we will not (go) sightseeing. — Ame ga futte iru nara kembutsu shimasen.
8. If it is easy, I can read it. — Yasashii nara yomu koto ga dekimasu.
9. If it is hot, open the window. — Atsui nara mado o akenasai.
10. If it is cold, close the door. — Samui nara to o shimenasai.
11. If you want to see Kabuki, go in the morning. — Kabuki o mitai nara asa ikinasai.
12. If you want to buy a radio, this store is cheap. — Rajio o kaitai nara kono mise wa yasui desu.
13. The movie which I saw was old. — Watakushi ga mita eiga wa furui deshita.
14. The car which I bought is good. — Watakushi ga katta jidoosha wa yoi desu.
15. The man who is teaching Japanese is Mr. Ito. — Nihongo o oshiete iru hito wa Itoo-san desu.
16. The stores which are in the Ginza are expensive. — Ginza ni aru mise wa takai desu.
17. The student who came here is Jiro. — Koko ni kita gakusei wa Jiroo desu.
18. I must study tonight. — Komban benkyoo shinakereba narimasen.
19. I must write a letter. — Tegami o kakanakereba narimasen.
20. I must send this package. — Kono kozutsumi o okuranakereba narimasen.
21. I must go to buy a magazine. — Zasshi o kai ni ikanakereba narimasen.
22. I must go to teach Japanese. — Nihongo o oshie ni ikanakereba narimasen.
23. I must take this dictionary home. — Kono jibiki o motte kaeranakereba narimasen.
24. Only the teacher came. — Sensei dake kimashita.
25. I want to read this book only. — Kono hon dake o yomitai desu.
26. I will go only to the bookstore. — Honya e dake ikimasu.
27. I saw only a child. — Kodomo dake o mimashita.

Translate into Japanese:

I

The student who bought the car came.

Mr. Brown, who is speaking, is an English teacher.

The book which I want to buy is sold out.

The present which I am going to send is this.

This is the book which I must read by tomorrow. (*asu made ni . . .*)

The person who is walking is an American student.

The teacher who went to see the play did not come to school today.

The foreign student who went to the concert was unable to eat supper.

The man who is working at the factory now is Mr. Jones.

The day before yesterday I bought a present at Daimaru which I am going to send to California.

II

I have a red hat.

I brought my textbook to my class.

I don't want to take the magazine home.

Please bring my Japanese dictionary today.

He did not bring the gift.

III

The train leaves at 10:15 p.m.

The airplane left for New York yesterday.

I want to leave the class immediately.

The bus does not leave in the morning.

IV

I go to school four or five times a week.

The train leaves the station three or four times a day.

Does the train leave for New York once a month?

Most people go to the theater once a week.

Note: "Number of times in a specified period of time" construction, such as "once a week" or "twice a year" is expressed by *(period)* NI *(frequency)* —*isshuukan NI ichi-do, ichi-nen NI ni-do.*

V

I, too, will go hiking tomorrow.
The teacher does not like Kabuki either.
I also wanted to go to the concert.
I don't like this department store either.
The teacher and the student also went to see the play.

VI

Give me one more.
I placed an additional five-cent stamp on the special delivery letter.
Please handle one more package.
Has he gone to the post office already? (*moo*—already)
I have already sent the gift.

VII

I studied Japanese, but my Japanese is still poor.
I like ice cream, but I am unable to eat it.
The students went to the concert; however, I stayed at home.
The stamp was $1.20; however, I had only one dollar bill.
I like to go hiking; however, it is raining today.

VIII

If it is Saturday, I can go to the Post Office.
If it is too big, I cannot send it today.
If you leave, I will leave too.
If the weather is bad, the airplane will not leave this afternoon.
If it costs 35¢, I will not buy it because it is too expensive.

IX

This book is a very valuable book.
He speaks poor Japanese.
The airplane is a convenient thing.
She is a very beautiful woman.
An automobile is a more convenient thing than a bicycle.

X

It isn't too far.

This merchandise isn't very cheap.

Since registered mail is not too expensive, please send it by registered mail.

Since Nara is not too convenient, I like Osaka better.

Since it is not raining too much, let's go mountain climbing.

XI

You must study Japanese tonight.

You must place an eight-cent stamp on regular mail.

I must send this special delivery letter immediately.

You must write the addressee's name distinctly on the letter.

Since it is raining, I must stay at home.

Since today is Monday, I must go to school.

XII

Is that all?

Is it only you?

Is it today only?

I want to study Japanese only.

Shall we teach only the foreign students?

Only my book is not on the table.

Answer in Japanese: (Some questions are based on the story in the main text.)

1. Kono hito wa nani o kaimashita ka.
2. Doko e motte ikimashita ka.
3. Kono kozutsumi o doko e okuritai no desu ka.
4. Kakari no hito wa kozutsumi o sugu ni toriatsukaimashita ka. (*sugu ni*—immediately)
5. Sore kara doko e motte ikimashita ka.
6. Tsugi no mado de nani o kaimashita ka.
7. Kyoto kara Hiroshima e iku kisha wa doko kara demasu ka.
8. Beikoku-yuki no fune wa ikkagetsu ni nan-do deru to iimashita ka.
9. Minna wa doko de kitte o kaimasu ka.

10. Futsuu yuubin to kookuubin dewa dochira ga takai desu ka.
11. Daiji na mono wa nan de okurimasu ka.
12. Yuubinkyoku dewa kozutsumi o nani ni kakemasu ka.
13. America dewa futsuu yuubin ni ikura no kitte o haranakereba narimasen ka.
14. Fuutoo no omote ni nani o kakimasu ka.
15. Tomodachi to yakusoku o shita koto ga arimasu ka. Donna yakusoku desu ka.
16. Anata no tokei wa nan-ji desu ka.
17. Omoi kozutsumi nara kookuubin no hoo ga yasui deshoo ka.
18. Atena wa fuutoo no omote ni kakimasu ka, ura ni kakimasu ka.
19. Kono ookii kozutsumi wa yuubinbako ni ireru koto ga dekimasen (*ireru*—"to put in"). Doko e motte ikanakereba narimasen ka.
20. Koko kara Tookyoo made futsuubin nara ikkagetsu gurai kakarimasu ka. Nan-nichi gurai kakarimasu ka.

Useful Expressions

Feelings (Kimochi)

TSUKAREMASHITA.	I'm tired. (n.c.v. *tsukareru*)
ATAMA GA ITAI DESU.	I have a headache (literally, "head is painful"). Therefore, if you wish to say, "I have a stomach ache," the expression is *onaka ga itai desu.*
ONAKA GA SUKIMASHITA.	I am hungry (literally, "the stomach is empty").
ONAKA GA IPPAI DESU.	I am not hungry ("the stomach is full").
KIBUN GA II DESU.	I feel well (used when you feel well physically). For example, a sick person after a good night's rest will say, *"Kesa wa kibun ga ii desu."*
KIBUN GA WARUI DESU.	I don't feel well (due to internal physical conditions).
KIMOCHI GA WARUI DESU.	I don't feel good (because of some EXTERNAL cause, such as seeing a gruesome sight, shock, fright, etc.).
KIMOCHI GA II DESU.	I feel good (because it is cool, after a refreshing bath, etc., due to EXTERNAL reasons).

CHAPTER 13

SUKIYAKI O TABE NI IKU— GOING OUT FOR SUKIYAKI

VERB	+	**KOTO NI SURU**	=	DECIDE TO. . . .
NOUN	+	**NI SURU**	=	DECIDE ON. . . .

"TE" FORM OF THE VERB	+	**KARA**	=	AFTER. . . .

"TE" FORM OF THE VERB	**(WA) IKEMASEN. . . .**	=	MUST NOT. . . . DON'T HAVE TO. . . . NEED NOT. . . .

yuubinkyoku o	Post Office
dete kara	after leaving
*yuubinkyoku o dete kara . . .	*after leaving the Post Office . . .
isoide itta	hurriedly went
node	because
*isoide itta node . . .	*because (I) went in a hurry . . .
choodo roku-ji ni	exactly at 6 o'clock
yakusoku shita	promised
tokoro	place
*yakusoku shita tokoro de . . .	*at the promised place . . .
tomodachi ni	with (my) friend
aimashita	met
*choodo roku-ji ni tomodachi ni aimashita	*met my friend at exactly 6 o'clock

WATAKUSHI WA YUUBIN-KYOKU O *DETE KARA* ISOIDE	AFTER LEAVING THE POST OFFICE, SINCE I WENT IN A

ITTA NODE, CHOODO ROKU-JI NI YAKUSOKU SHITA TOKORO DE TOMODACHI NI AIMASHITA. — HURRY, I MET MY FRIEND IN (or AT) THE PROMISED PLACE AT EXACTLY SIX O'CLOCK.

(Watakushi): YAA, CHOODO MA NI AIMASHITA. WATAKUSHI WA ONAKA GA SUKIMASHITA. ANATA WA IKAGA DESU KA. — AH, I MADE IT JUST ON TIME! I'M HUNGRY! HOW ABOUT YOU?

watakushi mo	I, too
taihen	very much
onaka ga sukimashita	am hungry

(Tomodachi): WATAKUSHI MO TAIHEN ONAKA GA SUKIMASHITA. *NANI-KA* OISHII MONO GA TABETAI DESU NEE. — I'M VERY HUNGRY, TOO. I WANT TO EAT SOMETHING GOOD!

(Watakushi): YOOSHOKU O TABEMASHOO KA, WASHOKU O TABEMASHOO KA. — SHALL WE EAT WESTERN FOOD OR JAPANESE FOOD?

(Tomodachi): WASHOKU NO HOO GA SUKI DESU. — I LIKE JAPANESE FOOD BETTER.

kono atari ni aru	located in this neighborhood
ii ryooriya	good eating place
*kono atari ni aru ii ryooriya . . .	*good eating place in this neighborhood . . .
shitte imasu ka	do you know?

KONO ATARI NI ARU II RYOO- — DO YOU KNOW OF A GOOD

RIYA O SHITTE IMASU KA.	EATING PLACE LOCATED AROUND HERE?
(Watakushi): SUEHIRO NO SUKIYAKI WA TAIHEN OISHII *SOO DESU* KARA *SUEHIRO NI SHIMASHOO.*	SINCE IT IS SAID THAT SUKIYAKI AT SUEHIRO'S IS VERY DELICIOUS, LET US DECIDE ON SUEHIRO'S.
(Tomodachi): SENGETSU KOOBE DE SUKIYAKI O TABEMASHITA GA TAIHEN OISHII DESHITA.	LAST MONTH I HAD SUKIYAKI IN KOBE, AND IT WAS VERY DELICIOUS.
SUEHIRO NO SUSHI WA DOO DESU KA.	HOW IS SUEHIRO'S SUSHI?

(o)sushi mo	sushi too
naka naka	very
oishii soo desu	I hear (it) is delicious

(Watakushi): (O)SUSHI MO NAKA NAKA OISHII *SOO DESU.*	I HEAR SUSHI IS QUITE DELICIOUS ALSO.

gohan o	meal (obj. case)
tabete kara	after eating
*gohan o tabete kara . . .	*after eating the meal . . .
eiga o	movie (obj. case)
mi ni ikimashoo	let's go to see

GOHAN O *TABETE KARA* EIGA O MI NI IKIMASHOO.	AFTER EATING DINNER, LET'S GO TO SEE A MOVIE.

Suehiro to iu ryooriya wa	eating place called Suehiro
watakushi-tachi ga	we
tatte	were standing (and)
hanashite ita	were talking

tokoro kara	from the place where (rel. cl.)
*watakushi-tachi ga tatte hanashite ita tokoro kara . . .	*from the place where we were standing and talking . . .
*chikakatta node . . .	*because (it) was near . . .
SUEHIRO TO IU RYOORIYA WA WATAKUSHI-TACHI GA *TATTE* HANASHITE ITA TOKORO KARA CHIKAKATTA NODE ARUITE IKIMASHITA.	SINCE THE EATING PLACE CALLED SUEHIRO WAS NEAR (FROM) WHERE WE WERE STANDING AND TALKING, WE WALKED THERE.
Suehiro ni	into Suehiro
haitte	entered (and)
*Suehiro ni haitte . . .	*entered Suehiro and . . .
zashiki ni	to a room
agaru	go up
to	when
*zashiki ni agaru to . . .	*when we went up and into the room . . .
jochuu ga	maid (nom. case)
sugu ni	immediately
ocha to kondatehyoo o	tea and a menu (obj. case)
motte kimashita	brought
SUEHIRO NI *HAITTE,* ZASHIKI NI AGARU TO JOCHUU GA SUGU (NI) OCHA TO KONDATEHYOO O MOTTE KIMASHITA.	WHEN WE ENTERED SUEHIRO'S AND WENT INTO THE ROOM, THE WAITRESS IMMEDIATELY BROUGHT TEA AND A MENU.
(Watakushi): ANATA GA CHUUMON O . . .	WILL YOU DO THE ORDERING?
(Tomodachi): *NANI NI SHIMASU KA.*	WHAT SHALL WE DECIDE ON?

(Watakushi): SUKIYAKI GA II DESU NE. SUKIYAKI NI SHITE KUDASAI.	SUKIYAKI IS FINE. PLEASE MAKE IT SUKIYAKI.
(Tomodachi): SUKIYAKI O NI-NIN MAE KUDASAI. SORE KARA GOHAN O TAKU-SAN KUDASAI. SORE DAKE DESU.	PLEASE GIVE US TWO ORDERS OF SUKIYAKI. AND THEN GIVE US LOTS OF RICE. THAT WILL BE ALL.
JOCHUU WA NIKU YA YASAI YA TOOFU NO HAITTA OOKII SARA O MOTTE KIMASHITA.	THE WAITRESS BROUGHT A LARGE PLATE WHICH CONTAINED SUCH THINGS AS MEAT, VEGETABLES, SOYBEAN CAKES, ETC.
naifu to fooku o	knife and fork (obj. case)
tsukatte wa ikemasen	don't use
(Watakushi): NAIFU TO FOOKU O *TSUKATTE WA IKEMASEN.* HASHI DE TABERU KOTO GA DEKIMASU KA.	DON'T USE A KNIFE AND FORK. CAN YOU EAT WITH CHOPSTICKS?
(Tomodachi): IIE, DEKIMASEN. *TSUKAIKATA* O OSHIETE KUDASAI.	NO, I CANNOT. PLEASE SHOW ME (HOW) TO USE THEM.

niku ya yasai o	meat and vegetables (obj. case)
nimasu	cook
kara	because
*niku ya yasai o nimasu kara . . .	*because I will cook the meat and vegetables . . .
anata wa	you
ryoori no shikata o	cooking method (obj. case)
mite inasai	watch
*anata wa ryoori no shikata o mite inasai . . .	*you watch how (I) cook . . .

(Watakushi): *OSHIETE AGEMASHOO.* — I SHALL SHOW YOU.

DEWA WATAKUSHI GA NIKU YA YASAI O NIMASU KARA ANATA WA *RYOORI NO SHIKATA* O MITE INASAI. — THEN, SINCE I AM GOING TO COOK THE MEAT AND VEGETABLES, YOU WATCH (HOW) I COOK.

(Tomodachi): NAKA NAKA II NIOI GA SHIMASU, NE. — IT CERTAINLY SMELLS GOOD, DOESN'T IT?

ICHIJIKAN ATO DE: — ONE HOUR LATER:

(Watakushi): TAIHEN OISHIKATTA NODE ZUIBUN TAKUSAN TABEMASHITA. — SINCE IT WAS VERY DELICIOUS, I CERTAINLY ATE A LOT!

dezaato wa	as for dessert
nani ni shimasu ka	what to decide on

DEZAATO WA *NANI NI SHIMASU KA.* — WHAT SHALL WE HAVE FOR DESSERT?

(Tomodachi): MOO ONAKA GA — I AM FULL ALREADY.

IPPAI DESU. KAERIMASHOO.	LET'S GO HOME.
CHOTTO, IKURA DESU KA.	OH, SAY, HOW MUCH IS IT?

gochisoo shimasu	(I) will treat (you)
kara	because
*gochisoo shimasu kara . . .	*because I will treat you . . .
haratte wa ikemasen	(you) must not pay

(Watakushi): WATAKUSHI GA GOCHISOO SHIMASU KARA ANATA WA *HARATTE WA IKEMASEN.*	SINCE I AM GOING TO TREAT YOU, YOU MUST NOT PAY.
(Jochuu): (O)KANJOO WA CHOODO NI-SEN KYU-UHYAKU EN DESU.	THE (AMOUNT OF THE) CHECK IS EXACTLY 2900 YEN.
WATAKUSHI WA SEN EN-SATSU O SAN-MAI DASHI-MASHITA.	I TOOK OUT THREE 1000 YEN BILLS.
(Watakushi): OTSURI WA IRIMASEN.	I DON'T WANT THE CHANGE. (KEEP THE CHANGE.)
(Jochuu): ARIGATOO GOZAI-MASHITA.	THANK YOU.

ryooriya o	restaurant
dete kara	after leaving
*ryooriya o dete kara . . .	*after leaving the restaurant . . .
eiga o	movies (obj. case)

mi ni iku	go to see
koto ni shimashita	decided

RYOORIYA O *DETE KARA* EIGA O MI NI *IKU KOTO NI SHIMASHITA.*	AFTER LEAVING THE RESTAURANT WE DECIDED TO GO TO SEE A MOVIE.

Vocabulary List from the Lesson

deru	(n.c.v.) to go out, to leave, (place) *O deru.* (Associate postposition *o* when leaving a place.)
dete kara	*after* (I) leave, after leaving (See I.C. & G.N.)
au	(v.i.) to meet
aimashita	(pol. past of *au*) met
. . . ni aimashita	met (somebody) (This takes the postposition *NI* to indicate the person whom one meets. *Sensei NI aimashita.*)
yaa	(interj.) oh!
ma ni au	(v.i.) to be on time (takes the postposition *NI* for "to be on time *for* a class, train, etc." *Kurasu NI ma ni au.*)
onaka ga sukimashita	(I am) hungry.
nani-ka	something (See I.C. & G.N.)
gochisoo	(n.) good thing to eat, delicious food
nee	(interj.) isn't it?
yooshoku	(n.) western food
washoku	(n.) Japanese food; *Nihonshoku* is also used.
kono atari	(n.) around here, hereabouts
ryooriya	(n.) eating place, restaurant
shiru	(v.t.) to know (c.v.) see p. 113

shitte iru	(v.t.) The verb *shiru* is always in the progressive when used in the affirmative sense.
shirimasen	(v.t.) do not know
sukiyaki	(n.) name of a Japanese dish
oishii	(adj.) delicious
oishikatta	was delicious (See I.C. & G.N.)
(o)sushi	(n.) name of a Japanese dish (*o* is added for politeness)
naka naka	quite, very (same as *taihen*)
. . . tachi	(suffix) denoting plural (human beings)
zashiki	(n.) Japanese-style room with *tatami* mats
to	when, if (See I.C. & G.N.)
jochuu	(n.) waitress, or maid
sugu (ni)	(adv.) immediately
(o)cha	(n.) green tea
kondatehyoo	(n.) a menu; *menyu* is used also.
chuumon	(n.) the ordering
chuumon o suru	(Chi. v.) to order
mae	(n.) an order
ninin mae	two orders, or ". . . for two"
sore kara	(conj.) and, then, and then
gohan	(n.) cooked rice; meal (in general)
niku	(n.) meat
yasai	(n.) vegetable
toofu	(n.) soybean cake
ya	(conj.) and (See I.C. & G.N.)
(o)chawan	(n.) rice bowl
(o)hashi	(n.) chopsticks
tsukau	(v.t.) to use
tsukaikata	method of using, way to use, how to use (See I.C. & G.N.)
oshiete ageru	(v.t.) to show (you, him, her, etc.—NEVER me—See I.C. & G.N.)
nimasu	(polite form of *niru*) boil, cook

ryoori (n.) cooking
ryoori no shikata how to cook (See I.C. & G.N.)
nioi (n.) smell
nioi ga suru (v.i.) to smell
zuibun extremely, very (syn: *taihen*)
onaka (n.) stomach
onaka ga ippai (idio.) lit., stomach is full, I am full
chotto I say! Hey! Look here! (Used to call attention.)
gochisoo (n.) treat, feast
gochisoo suru (Chi. v.) to entertain at dinner, treat someone
harau (v.t.) to pay
. . . te wa ikemasen must not, don't . . . (See I.C. & G.N.)
haratte wa ikemasen must not pay, don't pay
dashimashita (past tense of *dasu*) produced, submitted
(o)tsuri (n.) change (monetary)
iru (v.i.) to need (note that this verb, though it ends in *iru* and therefore should be a non-conjugating verb, is an exception. It conjugates as *ira, iri, iru, ire, ire*. See p. 113.)
irimasen (negative of *iru*) do not need

Additional Vocabulary

tabemono (n.) things to eat (from *taberu mono*)
(o)kane (n.) money
kudamono (n.) fruit
ringo (n.) apple
suika (n.) watermelon
budoo (n.) grapes
mikan (n.) orange

biiru	(n.) beer
sake	(n.) Japanese rice-wine
booi-san	(n.) waiter (from "boy-san")
pan	(n.) bread
bataa	(n.) butter
sakana	(n.) fish
mizu	(n.) water
koohii	(n.) coffee
koocha	(n.) black tea
gyuunyuu, miruku	(n.) milk
maagarin	(n.) margarine
sampo	(n.) a stroll
sampo o suru	(Chi. v.) to take a walk
kasu	(v.t.) to lend
nomu	(v.t.) to drink
shokuji	(n.) meal
shokuji o suru	(Chi. v.) to have one's meal, to eat
tempura	(n.) popular Japanese dish of deep-fried shrimp, vegetables, etc.
chippu	(n.) tip

Important Construction and Grammar Notes

KARA: There are three main usages of **kara**:

1. *Kara* after "te" form of the verb:

Kara following the "te" form of the verbs *(te* or *de)* means "after," "since," or "after . . . ing."

a. Yuuhan o **tabete kara** ongakukai e ikimasu.
After eating dinner I will go to a concert.

b. Boku wa Nihongo o *benkyoo* **shite kara** nemasu.
I will go to bed *after studying* Japanese.

The following two usages of *kara* have already been discussed:

2. *Kara* after statements:

When *kara* follows a statement (or a verb or adjective) it means "because" or "since."

a. Kono kisha wa Chicago-yuki desu **kara** Seattle niwa ikimasen.
b. Ima shokuji o shimasu **kara** ato de (later) ano kata ni aimasu.

Note the similarity of the Japanese construction, but the great difference in meaning in the following examples. Sentences numbered (1) are verb + *kara*=because; (2) are . . . *te* + *kara*=after.

1. shita kara
2. shite kara

1. tabeta kara
2. tabete kara

1. deta kara
2. dete kara

3. *Kara* after nouns:
In this case *kara* means "from."

a. Nihon *kara* kita kisen wa ookii desu.	The steamer which came from Japan is large.
b. Sengetsu *kara* ame ga furimasen.	It has not rained since last month.

Distinguish the difference in the meaning of the following:

1. Kinyoobi kara —from Friday (*kara* following a noun)
2. Kinyoobi desu kara—because it is Friday (*kara* following a verb)

SOO DESU: This is attached to the abrupt present and past tense of verbs and adjectives, and gives the meaning, "it is said that. . . . ," "I hear that . . .," and "I understand that. . . ."

1. Beikoku no tomodachi wa Nihon e *iku soo desu.*	I hear that my American friend is going to Japan.
2. Itoo-san wa uchi e *kaetta soo desu.*	I hear that Mr. Ito went home.
3. Hawai wa taihen atsui *soo desu.*	I hear Hawaii is very hot.
4. Kore wa amari oishikunai *soo desu.*	I understand that this is not so tasty.

This expression is used when the speaker has received the information second hand.

NANI-KA: **Nani** is "what." **Nani** + **ka** is "something." Similarly:

1. dare	*dare-ka*	"somebody"
2. itsu	*itsu-ka*	"sometime"
3. dore	*dore-ka*	"one of several"
4. dochira	*dochira-ka*	"one of the two"
5. doko	*doko-ka*	"somewhere"
6. nani	*nani-ka*	"something"

When *ka* is replaced with *mo*, note the change in meaning:

1. dare	*dare-mo*	"no one"—used with negative verb only
2. itsu	*itsu-mo*	"always"
3. dore	*dore-mo*	"all"
4. dochira	*dochira-mo*	"both"
5. doko	*doko-mo*	"everywhere"
6. nani	*nani-mo*	"nothing"—used with negative verb only

(See page 366 for further explanation.)

"TE" FORM OF THE VERB USED AS A CONNECTIVE: We have seen the following usages of *"te" verbs:*

1. "te" verb + *kudasai* —"please. . . ."
2. "te" verb + *imasu* —progressive form ". . . ing"
3. "te" verb + *kara* —"after. . . ."

The fourth usage is that of a connective, in which the "te" verb takes the same tense as the final verb, as follows:

Ginza e *itte* kudamono o kai-mashita.	I went to the Ginza and bought (some) fruit.

The above sentence is actually two sentences which have been combined with *soshite.*

Ginza e ikimashita. *Soshite* kudamono o kaimashita.

By using the "te" construction in the first sentence, repetition of the conjunction *soshite* can be avoided and a compound sentence is formed.

A variation of this is the "te" verb used in the sense of *kara* (because).

1. Onaka ga *suite* matsu koto ga dekimasen deshita.
   Because I was hungry (I) could not wait.
2. Ame ga *futte* doko e mo iku koto ga dekimasen deshita.
   Because it rained (I) was not able to go anywhere.

YA: The conjunction **ya** is used in the same way and has the same meaning as **to.** However, **ya** is used when you select a few samples from a longer list instead of giving the complete series, while **to** is used where all the nouns in the series are mentioned.

1. Kudamonoya dewa, ringo **ya** ichigo **ya** mikan o utte imasu.
   (Here, besides apples *(ringo)*, strawberries *(ichigo)*, and oranges *(mikan)*, there are many other kinds of fruit *(kudamono)* which are not all listed.)

(VERB) + ATO DE: This means "after." Used with the abrupt past tense of the verb, it refers to the time after some action has already taken place.

1. Tegami o *kaita* **ato de,** sampo o shi ni ikimashoo.
   After I've written the letters, let's go for a walk.
2. Ryooriya de shokuji o *shita* **ato de** biiru o nomi ni ikimashita.
   After I had my meal at the restaurant, I went to drink beer.

Used after a noun, the *NOUN + NO ATO DE* pattern is used.

1. Kurasu **no ato de** kimashita. (He) came after class.
2. Shigoto **no ato de** kite kudasai. Please come after work.

NEGATIVE IMPERATIVE: "Must not," "don't," and "not to be allowed" can be expressed by the "te" verb followed by **wa ikemasen.**

1. Sono furui ichigo o *tabete* **wa ikemasen.** — Don't eat those old strawberries.
2. Kono suika o *totte* **wa ikemasen.** — You must not take this watermelon.

"TE" VERB + WA IKEMASEN	= "... must not ..."

KATA: The expression "how to + verb (walk, open, etc.)" is rendered into Japanese by the addition of **kata** to the second base of *yodan* verb and to the stem of the *ichidan* verb.

1. Nihongo no *kakikata* o oshiete kudasai. — Show me *how to write* Japanese.
2. Anata no benkyoo no *shikata* ga warui desu. — Your *method of studying* is poor.

2nd BASE OF THE VERB + KATA	= "how to ..."

PAST TENSE OF ADJECTIVES: One way of forming the past tense of adjectives is by adding the past tense of *desu* (**deshita**) to adjectives.

1. takai *deshita* —(was expensive)
2. furui *deshita* —(was old)

However, this form of expression is not as common as the following. Another method of forming the past is by adding **katta** to the stem of the true adjectives (adjectives without the final "i"). This is the abrupt (or plain) past.

1. taka-*katta*
2. furu-*katta*
3. ooki-*katta*

Note that the "katta" ending, like other abrupt endings of verbs, viz., *taberu-tabeta,* etc., may be used to complete a statement.

Eiga wa omoshirokatta.

However, this has a harsh, abrupt ring to the statement. So, in order to soften this, **desu** is added.

Eiga wa omoshirokatta **desu.**

There is no difference in meaning between:

(a) *Eiga wa omoshiroi* **deshita.**
(b) *Eiga wa omoshiro***katta desu.**

Although the first sentence (a) is grammatically conceivable and it is occasionally used, the second form (b) is used much more frequently.

ADJ. (minus "i") + KATTA taka + katta	= "was—"

In this same way the past of the desiderative can be formed:

1. tabetai — tabeta*katta* (wanted to eat)
2. ikitai — ikita*katta* (wanted to go)

AGERU (YARU): This means "to give." When the person giving something away is in a lower social position, **ageru** is used. **Yaru** is used when the person to whom something is given is on very intimate terms with the giver, or when the giver is superior (see p. 311 for detailed explanation of this). This can be used when the *first person* gives away to a *second* or *third person.*

Kono kirei na hana o anata (sensei) ni *agemasu.*
(I) shall give these beautiful flowers to you (teacher).

Agemasu can also be used when a *second person* gives to a *third person*; or between *third persons.*

1. Anata wa sono kirei na hana o sensei ni *agemasu* ka.
   Are you going to give those beautiful flowers to the teacher?
2. Brown-san wa sensei ni kirei na hana o *agemashita.*
   Mr. Brown gave the teacher the beautiful flowers.

In these examples note the usage of *ni* after the INDIRECT OBJECT. **Ageru** is not used when the receiver is the first person, i.e., this verb is never used in the sense of "give to me."

OSHIETE AGERU: Here, used with a "te" verb, **ageru** means that you want to do something as a favor to someone else. The meaning is "for the benefit of . . ."

1. Ongakukai no kippu o katte *agemasu.*	I will buy a concert ticket for you (for your benefit).
2. Okane o kashite *agemasu.*	I will lend some money to you (as a favor to you).

TO: Used with the root form of the verb, it constitutes a subordinate clause, making this the condition of the following principal clause. It can be translated as "when." **To** also has a meaning of "if." The rule "SUBORDINATE CLAUSE + **to,** PRINCIPAL CLAUSE" is applicable.

1. Hachi-ji no kisha ni noru **to** go-ji ni Hiroshima ni tsukimasu.	When/if you get on the eight o'clock train, you will arrive in Hiroshima at five o'clock.
2. Koocha o nomu **to** gohan o taberu koto ga dekimasen.	When/if I drink tea, I cannot eat (my) meal.

In addition, **to** is used to indicate one action preceding another, or one action becoming the base of, or setting the stage for another.

Uchi e kaeru **to** sugu benkyoo shimasu.	When I return home, I study immediately.
Natsu ni naru **to** atsuku narimasu.	When it becomes summer, it becomes hot.

. . . KOTO NI SURU: This means literally "to make a situation," but in usage, it means "to decide." This is used with a root form of a verb.

3rd BASE VERB	+	KOTO NI SURU	=	" to decide . . ."

1. Ashita kara mainichi *sampo o suru* **koto ni shimasu.**
   I will (decide to) take a walk everyday from tomorrow (on).
2. Rainen Nihon e *iku* **koto ni shimashita.**
   We have decided to go to Japan next year.
3. Natsuyasumi niwa doko e mo *ikanai* **koto ni shimashita.**
   We have decided not to go anywhere during summer vacation.

When used with a noun, it follows the following pattern:

NOUN + NI SURU

1. *Dore* **ni shimasu** ka.	Which will it be?
Akai *no* **ni shimasu.**	I will decide on the red one.
2. *Nichiyoobi* **ni shimashoo.**	Let's make it Sunday. (Let's decide the date as Sunday.)

Substitution Drill

("te" Verb)

TABETE
MITE
KAITE
YONDE
SHITE
KITE
etc. } + KARA

("te" Verb)

SHIMETE
ORITE
NONDE
TSUKATTE
SHITE
KITE
etc. } + (WA) IKEMASEN

Exercises

1. After I eat I will study.	Tabete kara benkyoo shimasu.
2. After I see a movie I will go home.	Eiga o mite kara kaerimasu.
3. After I write a letter, I will go.	Tegami o kaite kara ikimasu.
4. After I read a magazine, I will come.	Zasshi o yonde kara kimasu.
5. After I do this, I will go to buy a book.	Kore o shite kara hon o kai ni ikimasu.
6. After I come, you go home.	Watakushi ga kite kara kaerinasai.

First give the affirmative, then the negative (7–13):

7. Close the window.	Mado o shimenasai. Mado o shimete wa ikemasen.
8. Get off at the next corner.	Tsugi no kado de orinasai. Tsugi no kado de orite wa ikemasen.
9. Drink some coffee.	Koohii o nominasai. Koohii o nonde wa ikemasen.
10. Use my automobile.	Watakushi no jidoosha o tsukainasai. Watakushi no jidoosha o tsukatte wa ikemasen.
11. Do this work.	Kono shigoto o shinasai. Kono shigoto o shite wa ikemasen.
12. Come at six o'clock.	Roku-ji ni kinasai. Roku-ji ni kite wa ikemasen.
13. Get on at the next corner.	Tsugi no kado de norinasai. Tsugi no kado de notte wa ikemasen.
14. I entered the house and sat down.	Ie ni haitte koshikakemashita.
15. I stood up and read the book.	Tatte hon o yomimashita.
16. I bought a book and took it to the Post Office.	Hon o katte yuubinkyoku e motte ikimashita.
17. I sold my old car and bought a new one.	Furui jidoosha o utte atarashii no o kaimashita.

18. I used chopsticks and ate sukiyaki.	Hashi o tsukatte sukiyaki o tabemashita.
19. I met the teacher and talked one hour.	Sensei ni atte ichi jikan hanashimashita.
20. I had dinner and took a walk.	Shokuji o shite sampo o shimashita.
21. I paid the bill and left the restaurant.	Kanjoo o haratte ryooriya o demashita.
22. If I go to Japan, I will see a Kabuki play.	Nihon e iku to Kabuki o mimasu.
23. If you eat this, you will get well.	Kore o taberu to yoku narimasu.
24. If you cook this you can eat it.	Kore o ryoori suru to taberu koto ga dekimasu.
25. If you order now, it will come next week.	Ima chuumon suru to raishuu kimasu.
26. If you get off here, the hotel is near.	Koko de oriru to hoteru wa sugu chikaku desu.
27. I want to go to Japan sometime.	Itsu-ka Nihon e ikitai desu.
28. Please come sometime.	Itsu-ka kite kudasai.
29. Let us go somewhere.	Doko-ka e ikimashoo.
30. I want to go somewhere.	Doko-ka e ikitai desu.
31. Somebody came.	Dare-ka kimashita.
32. Somebody forgot (his) book.	Dare-ka hon o wasuremashita.
33. There is something in the bag.	Kaban no naka ni nani ka arimasu.
34. Give me something.	Nani-ka kudasai.

Translate into Japanese:

1. Because I am very hungry, let's go someplace to eat.
2. I wanted to go, but because I had (there was) an engagement (promise), I was not able to go.

   Note: (a) First notice that this sentence is composed of two subordinates and one principal clause.
   (b) (subordinate) BUT (subordinate) BECAUSE (principal clause)
   (c) ____ *ga* ____ *kara* (or) *te* (principal clause).

3. The strawberries which I bought at the fruit shop were delicious.

4. Please lend me (some) money. I will lend you 5,000 yen.

   Note: The second part of this sentence must be interpreted to mean that "I will give you the favor of. . . ." *(kashite ageru).*

5. Because my friend did not have (any) money, I treated him.
6. After eating dinner, if it is not raining, let's take a walk.

   Note: Use *te* + *kara* or *ta* + *ato de.*

7. If you go to Kyoto, be sure *(zehi)* to go to a Japanese restaurant called "Tenichi" and have (eat) tempura.

   (a) ____ *to* ____ *itte* ____.
8. Waiter, please bring me a cup *(ippai)* of black tea. Later, give me bread and butter. (give me—*kudasai*)
9. Last night he drank too much beer and sake, so he was not in time for work. (drank too much—*nomi* + *sugiru*; for work—*shigoto NI*)
10. The man whom I met at the coffee house said he had been to the United States. (Use past experience construction for this.)

Answer in Japanese:

1. Anata wa sukiyaki ka tempura o tabeta koto ga arimasu ka. Doko de tabemashita ka.
2. Anata wa Nihongo o benkyoo shite kara Nihon e iku tsumori desu ka.
3. Anata wa kesa gakkoo e aruite kimashita ka. Aruite kaerimasu ka.
4. Shokuji no kanjoo wa kyuuhyaku gojuu en deshita. Watakushi wa sen en-satsu o dashimashita. Otsuri wa ikura desu ka.
5. Anata wa asa shichi-ji ni okiru to hachi-ji no kurasu ni ma ni aimasu ka. Isoganakereba narimasen ka.
6. Yooshoku to washoku dewa dochira ga suki desu ka. Anata wa itsu-mo washoku o tabemasu ka.
7. Amerikajin wa naifu (knife) to fooku (fork) de tabemasu ga Nihonjin wa nan de tabemasu ka. Anata wa (o)hashi no tsukaikata o shitte imasu ka.
8. Anatagata wa ima kanji (Chinese written characters) no kakikata o naratte imasu ka. Nani o benkyoo shite imasu ka.
9. Anata wa maiban nan-ji ni shokuji o shimasu ka. Shokuji o shita ato de sampo o shimasu ka.
10. Anata no uchi no chikaku ni aru suupaa-maaketto (supermarket) de toofu ya yasai ya niku o kau koto ga dekimasu ka.

The following are answers to questions. Form the questions:

1. Kesa hachi-ji no kurasu ni ma ni aimashita.
2. Iie, Tookyoo-yuki no kisha ni ma ni aimasen deshita.
3. Suehiro no sukiyaki wa oishikatta desu.
4. Ano ryooriya no (o)sushi wa amari oishikunai soo desu.
5. Asa ku-ji goro sensei no uchi e iku to dare-mo imasen.
6. Heya no naka ni dare-mo imasen.
7. Washoku no hoo ga suki desu.
8. Hai, hashi de taberu koto ga dekimasu.
9. Iie, toofu o tabeta koto wa arimasen.
10. Sukiyaki no ryoori no shikata o shirimasen.
11. Gohan o tabete kara gakkoo e ikanakereba narimasen.
12. Kesa okite kara sampo o shimashita.
13. Kinoo depaato de Tanaka-san ni aimashita.
14. Biiru wa ippon nihyaku en desu.
15. Watakushi wa hikooki de Nihon e kimashita.
16. Kono jibiki o gakkoo de kaimashita.
17. Ashita Kabuki o mi ni ikitai desu.
18. Teikoku hoteru made densha de jippun kakarimasu.
19. Juugo-fun shika kakarimasen.
20. Chikatetsu no hoo ga hayai desu.

You want to tell the waitress:

1. to bring some tea.
2. to bring some more toofu.
3. to show you the menu.
4. that you haven't ordered yet.
5. that you are hungry, so please hurry.
6. that you want 3 orders of sukiyaki.
7. that you want the check.
8. that the meal was good.
9. whether you can order coffee and cake here.
10. that you want her to show you how to use chopsticks.

The following conversation takes place between you and your guest. Translate:

You: What would you like to eat—Japanese food or Western food?
Guest: I like Japanese food better.
You: Have you ever eaten sukiyaki at Suehiro's?
Guest: No, never.
You: Shall I order?
Guest: Please order (for me). I would like to eat sukiyaki.
You: Shall I order some sake too?
Guest: No, thank you (*kekkoo desu*).
You: Would you like to eat with chopsticks?
Guest: I would like to *use them and try* (*tsukatte mitai**).
Please teach me how to use them.
What is this white thing?
You: That is called "tofu." Do you like it?
Guest: I like it very much.
You: *How about* some more tea? (. . . *wa ikaga desu ka*)
Guest: Thank you. Give me some.
You: How about some more rice?
Guest: No thank you. I am full.
It was very delicious.
You: Please eat a lot. How about some dessert?
Guest: I cannot eat anymore.
You: Shall we take a little walk?
Guest: That's a good idea.

* **Note:** In the English expression "eat and see . . .," "read and see . . .," and "do and see . . .," "see" is used in the sense of "try out" with the purpose of "finding out." The Japanese equivalent of this is *"te" verb + MIRU,* meaning "to experiment" or "to try experimentally."

1. Sashimi o *tabete miru.*—Eat raw fish and see (try out).
2. Kono hon o *yonde minasai.*—Read this book and see.
3. Kono shigoto o *shite mimashita.*—I did this work and tried.

Useful Expressions

Taste (Aji)

When *tabemono* (food) is good, it is *oishii*. When it is not so savory, it is *mazui*. The following expressions are used to describe taste *(aji)*.

AMAI	sweet	Satoo (sugar) wa *amai* desu.
KARAI	hot or peppery	Kono karee-raisu wa *karai* desu.
NIGAI	bitter	Kono kusuri (medicine) wa *nigai* desu.
SUI	sour	Remon (lemon) wa *sui* (or *suppai*) desu.
SHIOKARAI	salty	Kono sakana wa *shiokarai* desu.
MIZUKUSAI MIZUPPOI	refers to a taste which lacks sufficient seasoning.	

Note: The suffix *sugiru* is added to the adjective to indicate excess (see page 157).

KARA-SUGIRU	too hot, or too salty
AMA-SUGIRU	too sweet

CHAPTER 14

NIHON—JAPAN

NOUN + NI NARU **ADVERB + NARU**	=	BECOME . . . .
3rd BASE of VERB + NO NI / TAME	=	IN ORDER TO . . . .

KORE WA NIHON NO CHIZU DESU.\	THIS IS A MAP OF JAPAN.
Nihon no chiri o benkyoo suru toki ni *Nihon no chiri o benkyoo suru toki ni . . .	Japan's geography (obj. case) study when *when (one) studies (the) geography of Japan . . .
NIHON NO CHIRI O BENKYOO SURU *TOKI NI* CHIZU O TSUKAIMASU.\	WHEN YOU STUDY THE GEOGRAPHY OF JAPAN, YOU USE A MAP.
Eikoku ni nita kuni *Eikoku ni nita kuni . . .	resembles England country *a country which resembles England (rel. cl.) . . . .
NIHON WA EIKOKU *NI NITA* CHIISAI KUNI DESU.\	JAPAN IS A SMALL COUNTRY RESEMBLING ENGLAND.

Nihon wa	as for Japan
takusan no shima kara	from (by) many islands
naritatte imasu	made up of

NIHON WA TAKUSAN NO SHIMA KARA *NARITATTE IMASU.*

JAPAN IS COMPOSED OF MANY ISLANDS.

KONO UCHI DE ICHIBAN OOKII SHIMA WA HONSHUU TO IIMASU.

AMONG THESE, THE LARGEST ISLAND IS CALLED HONSHU.

yama ga takusan	many mountains
atte	there are and . . .
*yama ga takusan atte . . .	*there are many mountains and . . .
noogyoo ni tekisuru	suited for agriculture
heiya	plain
*noogyoo ni tekisuru heiya . . .	*plain suited for agriculture (rel. cl.) . . .

HONSHUU NIWA YAMA GA TAKUSAN *ATTE* NOOGYOO NI TEKISURU HEIYA GA SUKUNAI DESU.

BECAUSE THERE ARE MANY MOUNTAINS ON HONSHU, THERE ARE FEW PLAINS SUITED FOR AGRICULTURE.

KYUUSHUU TO SHIKOKU WA HONSHUU NO MINAMI NI ARIMASU GA HOKKAIDOO WA KITA NI ARIMASU.

KYUSHU AND SHIKOKU ARE IN (TO) THE SOUTH OF HONSHU, BUT HOKKAIDO IS IN (TO) THE NORTH.

kanari atatakai kara	because it is fairly warm
noogyoo ni tekishite imasu	suited for farming
ga	but (however)
Hokkaidoo wa	Hokkaido (nom. case)
naka naka samukute . . .	very cold and . . .

KYUUSHUU TO SHIKOKU WA KANARI ATATAKAI KARA NOOGYOO NI TEKISHITE IMASU GA HOKKAIDOO WA NAKA NAKA *SAMUKUTE,* FUYU NI WA YUKI GA TAKUSAN FURIMASU KARA NOOGYOO NI TEKISHITE IMASEN.↘	KYUSHU AND SHIKOKU ARE FAIRLY WARM, SO THEY ARE SUITED FOR FARMING, BUT SINCE HOKKAIDO IS VERY COLD, AND IN THE WINTER IT SNOWS CONSIDERABLY, IT IS NOT SUITABLE FOR AGRICULTURE.
Tookyoo wa	Tokyo (nom. case)
Nihon no shufu	Japan's capital
de	is and . . .
*Tookyoo wa Nihon no shufu de . . .	*Tokyo is Japan's capital and . . .
TOOKYOO WA NIHON NO SHUFU *DE,* HONSHUU NI ARIMASU.↘	TOKYO IS THE CAPITAL OF JAPAN, AND IT IS ON HONSHU.
TOOKYOO WA SENSOO NO MAE MADE WA SEKAI DE SAMBAMME NO TOKAI DESHITA GA SENGO SEKAI-ICHI NO DAITOKAI *NI NARIMASHITA.*↘	TOKYO WAS THE THIRD LARGEST CITY IN THE WORLD BEFORE THE WAR, BUT IT BECAME THE LARGEST CITY IN THE WORLD AFTER THE WAR.
rippa na	magnificent
gekijoo ga	theaters (nom. case)
ari . . .	there are and . . .
*rippa na gekijoo ga ari . . .	*there are magnificent theaters and . . .
London no yoo na	like (similar to) London (mod.)
tokai desu	is a city

*London no yoo na tokai desu	*(it) is a city like London
MODAN NA GINKOO YA KAISHA NO TATEMONO YA RIPPA NA GEKIJOO GA *ARI,* NEW YORK YA LONDON *NO YOO NA* TOKAI DESU.	THERE ARE MANY MODERN BANK AND COMPANY BUILDINGS, MAGNIFICENT THEATERS, AND IT IS A CITY LIKE NEW YORK OR LONDON.
NIHON NIWA AMARI GENRYOO GA NAI NODE IRO-IRO NA SEIHIN O YUSHUTSU *SHI,* BEIKOKU YA CANADA KARA GENRYOO O YUNYUU SHINAKEREBA NARIMASEN.	BECAUSE JAPAN DOES NOT HAVE MUCH RAW MATERIAL SHE EXPORTS MANUFACTURED GOODS AND MUST IMPORT RAW MATERIALS FROM THE UNITED STATES, CANADA, ETC.
koogyookoku ni naru	to become an industrial nation
tame ni	in order to
*koogyookoku ni naru tame ni . . .	*in order to become an industrial nation . . . .
genryoo o	raw materials (obj. case)
yunyuu shite imasu	(they) are importing
NIHON WA KOOGYOOKOKU *NI NARU TAME NI* GENRYOO O YUNYUU SHITE IMASU.	JAPAN, IN ORDER TO BECOME AN INDUSTRIAL NATION, IS IMPORTING RAW MATERIALS.
OOSAKA WA NIBAMME NO TOKAI DE KOOGYOO NO CHUUSHINCHI DESU.	OSAKA IS THE SECOND (LARGEST) CITY AND IT IS THE CENTER OF MANUFACTURING.

Oosaka no chikaku ni ari . . .	(Kyoto) is near Osaka and . . . .
mukashi no miyako de . . .	(it) is an ancient capital and . . . .
rekishiteki meisho desu	(it) is a famous historical site

KYOOTO WA OOSAKA NO CHIKAKU NI ARI, MUKASHI NO MIYAKO DE, *REKISHITEKI* MEISHO DESU.

KYOTO IS (LOCATED) NEAR OSAKA: IT IS AN ANCIENT CAPITAL, AND A FAMOUS HISTORICAL PLACE.

Nihon ni wa	in Japan
keshiki no yoi tokoro ga takusan	many scenic spots
aru node	because there are
*Nihon ni wa keshiki no yoi tokoro ga takusan aru node . . .	*because there are many scenic spots in Japan . . .
haru ni naru to	when it becomes spring
kembutsu suru hito ga oozei	many people who sightsee (nom. case)

NIHON NI WA KESHIKI NO YOI TOKORO GA TAKUSAN ARU NODE, HARU *NI NARU* TO KEMBUTSU SURU HITO GA OOZEI GAIKOKU KARA KIMASU.

SINCE THERE ARE MANY (GOOD) SCENIC SPOTS IN JAPAN, IN THE SPRING (WHEN IT BECOMES SPRING) MANY PEOPLE COME FROM FOREIGN COUNTRIES TO SIGHTSEE.

TAIHEIYOO SENSOO NI MAKETA NODE SENGO NIHONJIN WA TAIHEN KOMARIMASHITA.

SINCE (JAPAN) LOST THE PACIFIC WAR, THE JAPANESE WERE IN GREAT DISTRESS (WERE GREATLY TROUBLED) DURING (THE) POSTWAR (YEARS).

keredomo	however
Nihon kokumin wa	Japanese people (nom. case)
heiwa	peace
heiwa na kuni o	peaceful country (obj. case)
tsukuru tame ni	in order to make
*heiwa na kuni o tsukuru tame ni . . .	*in order to make a peaceful nation . . .
isshookenmei	with all their might
hataraite imasu	are working

KEREDOMO NIHON KOKUMIN WA HEIWA NA KUNI O TSUKURU TAME NI ISSHOOKENMEI HATARAITE IMASU.

HOWEVER, THE JAPANESE PEOPLE ARE WORKING WITH ALL THEIR MIGHT IN ORDER TO CREATE A PEACEFUL NATION.

Vocabulary

chizu	(n.) map
chiri	(n.) geography
toki ni	when (See I.C. & G.N.)
Eikoku	(n.) England
niru	(v.i.) to resemble (n.c.v.) when it resembles something: *object NI niru.*
(ni) nita	(abrupt past of *niru*)
kuni	(n.) country
shima	(n.) island
naritatsu	(v.i.) composed of . . .
naritatte	("te" form of *naritatsu*)
Honshuu	(n.) the main island of Japan
yama	(n.) mountain
heiya	(n.) plain

sukunai	(adj.) few (in number)
minami	(n.) south
kita	(n.) north
kanari	fairly
atatakai	(adj.) warm
noogyoo	(n.) agriculture
tekisuru	(v.i.) to be appropriate, to be suitable (takes the postposition *ni* to express "suitable FOR something") *Kono seihin wa yushutsu NI tekishimasen.*
samui	(adj.) cold
fuyu	(n.) winter
takusan	(with verb) a lot, considerably
shufu	(n.) capital
de	(contraction of *desu* used connectively) "... is ... and" (See I.C. & G.N.)
sensoo	(n.) war
sengo	(n.) postwar (same as *sensoo no ato*)
sambamme	(n.) third (in order)
daitokai	(n.) large metropolis
modan	(n.) modern
ginkoo	(n.) bank
kaisha	(n.) firm, company
rippa	(n.) magnificent (*rippa na* is a quasi adj.)
yoo na	like (*yoo na* + noun, See I.C. & G.N.)
mukashi	(n.) olden days
miyako	(n.) capital (used historically)
rekishi	(n.) history
rekishiteki	historical
meisho	(n.) famed place
iro-iro	(n.) various (used as *iro-iro na* to modify)
yushutsu suru	(Chi. v.) to export

genryoo	(n.) raw material
tame ni	in order to (See I.C. & G.N.)
nai	(abrupt form of *arimasen*)
yunyuu suru	(Chi. v.) to import
seihin	(n.) manufactured goods
koogyoo	(n.) manufacturing industry
chuushinchi	(n.) center
keshiki	(n.) scenery
haru	(n.) spring
gaikoku	(n.) foreign country
oozei	many (use only with humans—*oozei no hito*)
Taiheiyoo	(n.) Pacific Ocean
Taiheiyoo sensoo	(n.) Pacific war; the Japanese refer to World War II by this term.
makeru	(v.i.) to lose—when you lose in a competition, race, game, bet, etc., use "... *ni makeru*" (n.c.v.)
maketa	(abrupt past of *makeru*) lost
komaru	(v.i.) to be troubled, inconvenienced
kokumin	(n.) people of a country, nationals
... **no ni (tame ni)**	in order to ... (See I.C. & G.N.)
isshookemmei (ni)	(adv.) with all one's might

Additional Vocabulary

kawa	(n.) river
minato	(n.) harbor
mizuumi	(n.) lake
Taiseiyoo	(n.) Atlantic Ocean
Nihonkai	(n.) Japan Sea
umi	(n.) ocean
hashi	(n.) bridge
mura	(n.) village

higashi	(n.) east
nishi	(n.) west
natsu	(n.) summer
aki	(n.) autumn
onsen	(n.) hot spring
hyakushoo o suru	(Chi. v.) to farm
booeki	(n.) trade
booeki o suru	(Chi. v.) to trade
shoogyoo	(n.) commerce
gaikoku booeki	(n.) foreign trade
gaikokujin	(n.) foreigner
jinkoo	(n.) population
Kankoku	(n.) Korea
Chuugoku	(n.) China
Taiwan	(n.) Formosa
. . . **yoo ni**	like (followed by a verb, see I.C. & G.N.)
Yooroppa	(n.) Europe
Indo	(n.) India
katsu	(v.i.) to win (in competition—associate with . . . *ni katsu*)

Important Construction and Grammar Notes

NOUN + NI NARU	= to become (the noun) . . .

1. gunjin **ni** naru. . . . — to become a soldier (winter, large city, etc.) is expressed by the above formula. Note that "a soldier, winter, and large city" are nouns; therefore, these must be followed by *NI* when used with *NARU*. These nouns are the goal of "becoming" *(naru)*.

gunjin **ni** naritai. . . .	(I) wish to become a soldier.
gunjin **ni** narimashita.	(I) became a soldier.

2. fuyu **ni** naru to . . .	when it becomes winter
3. Nagoya wa daitokai **ni** narimashita.	Nagoya became a large city.

ADVERBIAL FORM OF THE ADJECTIVE (. . . KU) + NARU

1. taka**ku** naru . . .	to become expensive (cold, few, etc.). First, change the true adjective to an adverb (taka*i*—taka*ku*; samu*i*—samu*ku*) and use *NARU.* In this construction *ni* IS NOT NECESSARY.
2. Kodomo ga ooki**ku** naru.	A child becomes big.

Keep in mind that *ni* is not used after the adverbial form of the adjective.

. . . TAKU NARU: The desiderative suffix **tai,** meaning "want to . . .," has the adjectival ending **ai.** Therefore, ". . . **tai**" can be handled like any adjective.

1. It can modify a noun:
   yomi*tai* hon (want to read—book)
   mi*tai* eiga (want to see—movies)
   shi*tai* shigoto (want to do—work)
2. Negative is formed by . . . *ku arimasen* (adj. is aka*ku arimasen*).
   iki*taku arimasen* or iki*taku*+*nai*
   tabe*taku arimasen* or tabe*taku*+*nai*
3. Abrupt past is *katta* (adj. is aka*katta*)
   kaita*katta* (wanted to buy)
   urita*katta* (wanted to sell)
   arukita*katta* (wanted to walk)
4. Similarly, . . . *ku naru* construction, explained above, is applicable to *tai,* with the literal meaning "become so that you want to. . . ." and "get the urge to . . .", or "feel like . . ."
   nomi*taku naru* (get the urge to drink)
   naki*taku naru* (feel like crying)
   sumi*taku naru* (get the feeling of wanting to live)

COMPOUND SENTENCE: There are two methods by which simple sentences can be joined, and a compound sentence formed.

1. By means of the "te" form of the verbs, or the adjectives:
   a. *Ano kata wa chooshoku o* **tabete,** *gakkoo e ikimasu.*
   This sentence is equivalent to two simple sentences connected with *soshite: Ano kata wa chooshoku o tabemasu.* **Soshite** *gakkoo e ikimasu.*
2. By using the second base of the *yodan* verb (c.v.) or the stem of *ichidan* verb (n.c.v.):

a. Hokkaidoo dewa yuki ga takusan **furi,** taihen samui tokoro desu.	It snows a lot in Hokkaido *and* it is a very cold place.
b. Boku wa gohan o **tabe,** isoide eiga e ikimashita.	I ate (my) meal *and* I hurried to see the movie.

3. *De* can also be used as a conjunction. *De* is a contraction of *desu,* and when used in this way, it has the meaning of "and" as well as "is."
   a. Kono kaisha wa booeki gaisha **de,** Taiwan kara banana o yunyuu shimasu.
   This company is a trading company *and* imports bananas from Taiwan.
   b. John-san wa gaikokujin **de** watakushi wa Nihonjin desu.
   John is a foreigner *and* I am a Japanese.

. . . TOKI (NI). **Toki ni** pinpoints the time when something happens, and it is another connective for a subordinate clause. It means "when . . . ," "time. . . ." This is used AFTER the subordinate clause followed by a principal clause.

Subordinate Clause + TOKI (NIWA), Principal Clause = When. . . .

1. Indo e iku *toki (niwa),* hikooki de ikimasu.
   When I go to India, I will go by plane.
2. Kyonen Indo e itta *toki (niwa)* hikooki de ikimashita.
   When I went to India last year, I went by plane.
3. Chooshoku o taberu *toki (ni),* watakushi o yonde kudasai.
   When you eat breakfast, please call me.

. . . NO YOO NA; . . . NO YOO NI; . . . NO YOO DESU: These three expressions mean "like," or "similar to," but their usage is different.

1. NOUN + NO YOO NA + NOUN

a. Tookyoo wa New York	NO YOO NA	tokai desu.
(Tokyo is a New York-like		city.)
b. Kyoo wa natsu	NO YOO NA	hi desu.
(Today is a summer-like		day.)

2. NOUN + NO YOO NI + VERB

a. Watakushi wa sensei	NO YOO NI	Nihongo o hanashitai desu.
(I	like a teacher	want to speak Japanese.)
b. Kono mizuumi wa takusan ame ga furu to . . . umi	NO YOO NI	narimasu.
(This lake, when it rains hard . . .	like an ocean	becomes.)

3. NOUN + NO YOO DESU

a. Kono yama wa Fujisan	NO YOO DESU.
(This mountain is like Mt. Fuji.)	
b. Hokkaido wa America	NO YOO DESU.
(Hokkaido is like America.)	

. . . NO NI (TAME NI): This expression is used after a root form of the verb and as a conjunction of a subordinate clause. The meaning is "in order to. . . ," "for the purpose of. . . ," showing the purpose, or aim.

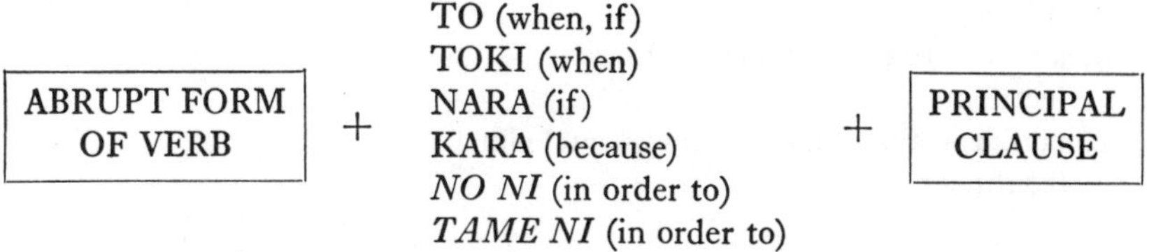

ABRUPT FORM OF VERB
+
TO (when, if)
TOKI (when)
NARA (if)
KARA (because)
NO NI (in order to)
TAME NI (in order to)
+
PRINCIPAL CLAUSE

1. Nihon kara tokei ya toranjisutaa rajio o yunyuu suru **no ni** ginkoo kara okane o karimasu.
   (*In order to* import watches and transistor radios, etc. from Japan, (I) will borrow money from the bank.)
2. Nihongo o benkyoo suru **no ni** kono jibiki o tsukaimasu.
   (*In order to* study Japanese, (I) use this dictionary.)

Compare this construction with *2nd BASE + NI* used with IKU, KURU, or KAERU (explained on p. 176) which has similar meaning of "in order to," but is more limited in its usage.

. . . NO NI has another usage. It has the concessive meaning of "although," "whereas," or "in spite of the fact that . . ."

Used with a Verb:

1. Ame ga *futte iru no ni* shigoto e ikimashita.	Although it is raining, he went to work.
2. Shigoto ga *aru no ni* sensei wa kimasen.	Although there is some work, the teacher won't come.

Used with an Adjective:

1. *Atsui no ni* mado o akemasen.	Although it is hot, he will not open the window.
2. *Muzukashii no ni* yomu koto ga dekimashita.	Although it was difficult, I was able to read it.

With a Noun + NA NO NI:

1. *Nihonjin na no ni* Nihongo o hanashimasen.	In spite of the fact that he is a Japanese, he doesn't speak Japanese.
2. *Nichiyoobi na no ni* shigoto o shimasu.	Even though it is Sunday, he works.

NOUN + TEKI: This combination gives the meaning of "from the standpoint of . . ." and is often used as an adjective.

a. rekishi + **teki** = historical (from the standpoint of history)
(history)

b. keizai + **teki** = economical
(economy)

c. tairiku + **teki** kikoo = continental climate
(continent)

TAME (NI): This expression has three different usages.

I. When used with THIRD BASE of the YODAN VERB (c.v.), it means "in order to . . ." and forms a subordinate clause. When used in this way, it has the same meaning as NO NI explained above. *Ni* is optional.

3rd BASE OF VERB	+	TAME (NI)	=	"in order to . . ."

1. Nihongo o benkyoo *suru tame ni* toshokan e ikimasu.	I will go to the library (in order) to study Japanese.
2. Hako o *tsukuru tame ni* ki o kaimashita.	I bought some wood (in order) to make a box.
3. Tegami o *dasu tame ni* kitte ga irimasu.	You need stamps (in order) to send a letter.

II. *Tame (ni)* may be used with a verb, adjective, or noun to mean "because . . ." This has the same function as *kara* and *node* giving the reason.

VERB ADJECTIVE NOUN NO	+	TAME (NI)	=	"because . . ."

Verb

1. Yuki ga *futte iru tame* (ni) samui desu.	Because it is snowing it is cold.
2. Kore o *katta tame* (ni) okane ga arimasen.	Because I bought this I don't have any money.

Adjective

1. Atama ga *itai tame* (ni) kyoo shigoto o yasumimasu.	Because I have a headache I will not go to work today.
2. *Osoi tame* (ni) takushii de ikimasu.	Because it is late I will go by taxi.

Noun

1. *Byooki no tame* (ni) ikemasen deshita.	Because of illness I was not able to go.
2. *Yasumi no tame* (ni) mise wa shimatte imasu.	Because it is a holiday the stores are closed.

III. Used with a noun, it means "for the sake of . . .," "in behalf of. . . ."

NOUN + NO TAME (NI)	= "for the sake of . . ."

1. Kono kooen wa *kodomo no tame* desu. — This park is for children.
2. *Gakkoo no tame ni* hataraite kudasai. — Please work for (the sake of) your school.

Note that the use of *Noun + no tame (ni)* has two meanings of "for the sake of . . . ," as well as "because . . . ," so that the differentiation will have to be made from the context.

Fluency Drill

I

Takaku naru.
Jidoosha wa takaku naru.
Atarashii jidoosha wa takaku naru.
Atarashii jidoosha wa sukoshi takaku naru.
Rainen kara atarashii jidoosha wa sukoshi takaku naru.

(A car) will be expensive.
A car will be expensive.
A new car will be expensive.
A new car will be a little expensive.
From next year a new car will be a little expensive.

II

Sensei ni naru.
Brown-san wa sensei ni naru.
Brown-san wa daigaku no sensei ni naru.
Brown-san wa daigaku no eigo no sensei ni naru.
Brown-san wa daigaku o dete kara eigo no sensei ni naru.
Brown-san wa rainen daigaku o dete kara eigo no sensei ni naritai.

become a teacher
Mr. Brown will be a teacher.
Mr. Brown will be a university teacher.
Mr. Brown will be a university English teacher.
Mr. Brown, after graduating (from) college, will be an English teacher.
Mr. Brown, after graduating (from) college next year, would like to be an English teacher.

Substitution Drill

WATAKUSHI WA	*(3rd Base Verb)* IKU KAU SURU TSUKURU etc.	+	TAME NI. . . .
	(Adverb) TAKAKU MUZUKASHIKU SAMUKU TOOKU etc.	+	NARU
	(Noun) FUYU RIPPA DAITOKAI CHUUSHINCHI etc.	+	NI NARU

Exercises

1. In order to send this package, please give me money.	Kono kozutsumi o okuru no ni okane o kudasai.
2. In order to buy a magazine, please give me money.	Zasshi o kau no ni okane o kudasai.

3. In order to make a cake, please give me money.	Keeki o tsukuru no ni okane o kudasai.
4. In order to go home by taxi, please give me money.	Takushii de kaeru no ni okane o kudasai.
5. In order to pay the bill, please give me money.	Kanjoo o harau no ni okane o kudasai.
6. Although it is expensive, he bought it.	Takai no ni kaimashita.
7. Although it is cold, he doesn't wear an overcoat.	Samui no ni oobaa o kimasen.
8. Although he can speak Japanese, he doesn't speak it.	Nihongo o hanasu koto ga dekiru no ni hanashimasen.
9. Although he is a child, he smokes (*tabako o suu*).	Kodomo na no ni tabako o suimasu.
10. Although it is a holiday, he works.	Yasumi na no ni hatarakimasu.
11. The automobile will be expensive next year.	Rainen jidoosha wa takaku narimasu.
12. The Japanese language will become difficult.	Nihongo wa muzukashiku narimasu.
13. The building has become old.	Tatemono wa furuku narimashita.
14. It has become hot.	Atsuku narimashita.
15. My work has become busy.	Watakushi no shigoto wa isogashiku narimashita.
16. It will be winter.	Fuyu ni narimasu.
17. I will be a teacher.	Sensei ni narimasu.
18. This boy will be eight.	Kono otoko no ko wa yattsu ni narimasu.
19. This town became a capital.	Kono machi wa shufu ni narimashita.
20. Mr. Tanaka became my friend.	Tanaka-san wa watakushi no tomodachi ni narimashita.
21. Japan is like England.	Nihon wa Eikoku no yoo desu.
22. This building is like a bank.	Kono tatemono wa ginkoo no yoo desu.
23. Today is like winter.	Kyoo wa fuyu no yoo desu.
24. Americans are like Englishmen.	Americajin wa Eikokujin no yoo desu.

25. I want to be like my teacher.	Sensei no yoo ni naritai.
26. I want to speak like my teacher.	Sensei no yoo ni hanashitai.
27. Jiro walks like Taro.	Jiroo wa Taroo no yoo ni arukimasu.
28. Tokyo has become like New York.	Tookyoo wa New York no yoo ni narimashita.
29. This train runs like a plane.	Kono kisha wa hikooki no yoo ni hashirimasu.
30. Brown writes kanji like a Japanese.	Brown wa Nihonjin no yoo ni kanji o kakimasu.
31. If I go to Japan, I will go by ship.	Nihon e iku nara fune de ikimasu.
32. When I go to Japan, I will go by ship.	Nihon e iku toki wa fune de ikimasu.
33. Because I am going to Japan, I will buy a camera in Japan.	Nihon e iku kara Nihon de camera o kaimasu.
34. In order to go to Japan I bought a ship ticket.	Nihon e iku no ni fune no kippu o kaimashita.

Translate into Japanese:

1. When / If / Because / In order to } (we) win this war, (we) must be an industrial country.

   Note: "must be" is expressed as follows (see p. 202):
   NARU—NA ra + nakereba narimasen (1st base)
   ri
   ru
   re

2. Before the war, Manchuria was an agricultural country, but after the war, (it) became an industrial country.
3. American people are made up of (composed of) many races *(jinshu)* who came from many foreign countries.
4. It doesn't rain much in this area *(chihoo)*, so the land is not suited to farming. The people who are in this area are in great trouble.

   Note: *komatte imasu*—the progressive form can be used to indicate the STATE OF BEING. Here, it indicates the distressed state or condition the people are in. (See p. 293)

5. Detroit is the automobile manufacturing center and *(de)* Chicago is the commercial center.
6. (a) Japan is like England. (. . . no yoo desu)
   (b) Japan is a country like England. (. . . no yoo na kuni desu)
   (c) Japan will be like England. (. . . no yoo ni narimasu)
7. In order for Japan to import many raw materials from foreign countries, (she) must export manufactured goods.

   Note: In analyzing this sentence:
   In order . . . from foreign countries = subordinate clause connected with *no ni*
   she must . . . manufactured goods = principal clause
8. Japan lost the war and America won. The world is now (at) peace.

   Note: Translate this into one sentence and without using conjunctions. First use the "*te* form" as a conjunctive; next, use the second base or the stem; lastly, alternate the two forms.
9. If you want to go to Japan (and) if you work hard (with all your effort), you can go next spring.

   Note: first subordinate clause— . . . *tai nara*
10. South Korea's population is greater than North Korea's, but (its) raw materials are fewer than the North's.

Answer in Japanese:

1. Naze Honshuu wa noogyoo ni tekisuru heiya ga sukunai desu ka.
2. Nihon no yottsu no ookii shima o kita kara itte kudasai.
3. Nihon no koogyoo no chuushinchi wa kita Kyuushuu ni arimasu ka. Doko ni arimasu ka.
4. Anata wa fuyu ni naru to sukii (ski) o shi ni ikimasu ka. Kono chihoo ni sukii o suru no ni yoi yama ga arimasu ka.
5. New York wa Kyooto no yoo na tokai desu ka. Doo chigaimasu ka.

   Note: *doo*—how? *chigaimasu*—from *chigau*—differ
6. Nihon e kembutsu shi ni iku no ni itsu ga ichiban yoi kisetsu (season) desu ka. Fuyu wa yoi kisetsu desu ka. Naze desu ka.
7. Eikoku wa Indo ya Chuugoku no yoo na kuni desu ka. Doo chigaimasu ka.
8. Anata wa Nihonjin no yoo ni Nihongo o hanasu koto ga dekimasu ka. Naze desu ka. Nihonjin no yoo ni Nihongo o hanashitai to omoimasu ka.

9. Chizu o mite kudasai. Yokohama kara Taiwan e iku toki ni Taiheiyoo o watarimasu ka. Nagasaki kara Kankoku e wataru toki wa, dono umi o watarimasu ka.

   Note: *watarimasu*—from *wataru* (to cross, to go over)
   The usage of the postposition *o* is not as the object of a verb here, but to indicate the action taking place in space, covering space. It is used with verbs of movement, e.g., *Hikooki wa ima Fujisan no ue* **o** *tonde imasu.* (see p. 291 below)

10. Nikkoo wa rekishiteki meisho desu ka. Keizaiteki ni daiji na tokoro (important place) desu ka. Oosaka wa donna tokoro desu ka.

    Note: Nikkoo is located about 120 miles north of Tokyo, and has a mausoleum built in 1632 dedicated to Tokugawa Ieyasu.

Combine the following sentences, using the connectives indicated:

1. I got up. I went to school. (use "te")
2. I go to school. I study in the library. (use "te")
3. Japan is small. The U.S. is large. ("te")
4. Winter is cold. Summer is hot. ("te")
5. Tokyo is the capital. It is the largest city. ("de")
6. I am a teacher. You are a student. ("de")
7. Japan exports manufactured goods. (She) imports raw materials. (2nd base)
8. He won. I lost. (2nd base)
9. He became a teacher. He became rich. (2nd base)
10. Kyoto is in Yamato. It is an old city. It has many temples (*tera*). (2nd base, "te")
11. My high school is in Tokyo. It is a large school. It has many students. ("te")
12. I get up. I wash my face. I eat breakfast. ("te," 2nd base)
13. I go home. I rest a little. I study. (2nd base, "te")
14. He is a Japanese. He cannot speak Japanese. (use "but")
15. Japan is a small country. She is an industrial nation. (use "but")
16. It becomes summer. It becomes hot. (use "when")
17. He doesn't have any money. He is troubled. (use "because")
18. The center of town is far. We will go by car. (use "because")
19. Farming is difficult. I don't want to farm. (use "because")

20. It is a large city. There will be banks. (use "if")
21. It is cold. Close the window. (use "if")
22. I go to school. I need money. (use "no ni," make the first sentence the reason for the second.)
23. I will study Japanese. I will buy a dictionary. (use "no ni")
24. I will eat lunch. Please give me some money. (use "no ni")
25. I will send this package to Japan. I must take it to the post office. (use "no ni")

Supplement IX

Shinrui (Family Relations)

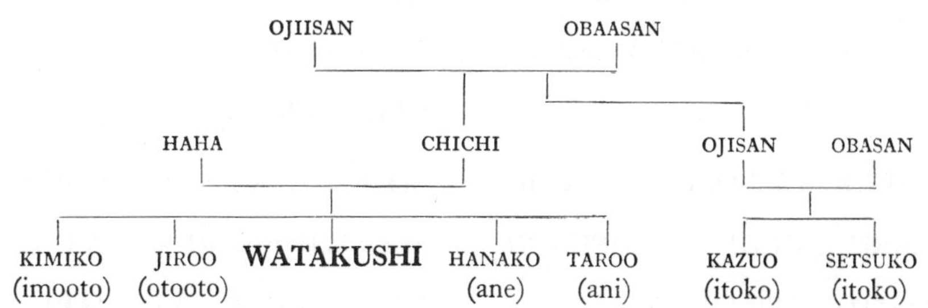

KONO ZU O GORAN NASAI.	LOOK AT THIS DIAGRAM.
WATAKUSHI NIWA KYOODAI GA YONIN IMASU.	I HAVE FOUR BROTHERS AND SISTERS.
WATAKUSHI NO ANI NO NAMAE WA TAROO DE, DAIGAKU NO SANNENSEI DESU.	MY OLDER BROTHER'S NAME IS TARO, AND (HE IS) A THIRD YEAR STUDENT (AT A) COLLEGE.
WATAKUSHI NO ANE NO HANAKO WA KOOTOOGAKKOO NO NINENSEI DESU.	MY OLDER SISTER, HANAKO, IS (A) SECOND YEAR HIGH SCHOOL STUDENT.
WATAKUSHI WA CHUUGAKKOO NO SANNENSEI DESU.	I AM A THIRD YEAR JUNIOR HIGH SCHOOL STUDENT.
JIROO WA WATAKUSHI NO OTOOTO DE, IMA SHOOGAK-	JIRO IS MY YOUNGER BROTHER AND (HE IS) NOW AT-

KOO E ITTE IMASU.	TENDING ELEMENTARY SCHOOL.
KIMIKO WA KYONEN UMARETA BAKARI DE MADA AKAMBOO DESU.	KIMIKO WAS BORN JUST LAST YEAR AND (SHE IS) STILL A BABY.
CHICHI WA SARARII-MAN DE MARUNOUCHI *NO* KAISHA NI TSUTOMETE IMASU.	MY FATHER IS A SALARIED MAN WHO WORKS IN A COMPANY (WHICH IS) IN MARUNOUCHI.
HAHA WA ICHINICHIJUU UCHI NI IMASU.	MY MOTHER IS AT HOME ALL DAY LONG.
KAZUO-SAN NO OTOOSAN TO WATAKUSHI NO CHICHI WA KYOODAI DESU KARA KAZUO-SAN TO SETSUKO-SAN WA WATAKUSHI NO ITOKO DESU.	KAZUO'S FATHER AND MY FATHER ARE BROTHERS, SO KAZUO AND SETSUKO ARE MY COUSINS.
KAZUO-SAN NO OTOOSAN TO OKAASAN WA WATAKUSHI NO OJI TO OBA NI NARIMASU.	KAZUO'S FATHER AND MOTHER ARE (BECOME) MY UNCLE AND AUNT.
SETSUKO-SAN WA KAZUO-SAN YORI MITTSU TOSHIUE DE NEESAN DESU.	SETSUKO IS THREE YEARS OLDER THAN KAZUO, SO (SHE IS HIS) OLDER SISTER.
KAZUO-SAN WA WATAKUSHI	KAZUO IS TWO YEARS

YORI FUTATSU TOSHISHITA DESU.	YOUNGER THAN I.
WATAKUSHI NO OJIISAN WA HACHIJUU-GO-SAI DE TOSHI-YORI DESU. OBAASAN WA GO-NEN MAE NI NAKUNARI-MASHITA.	MY GRANDFATHER IS 85 YEARS OLD, AND (HE IS A) VERY OLD MAN. GRAND-MOTHER DIED FIVE YEARS AGO.

Vocabulary and Notes

	PLAIN	HONORIFIC
family	KAZOKU	GO-KAZOKU
father	CHICHI	OTOOSAN
mother	HAHA	OKAASAN
grandfather	SOFU	OJIISAN
grandmother	SOBO	OBAASAN
elder brother	ANI	(O)NIISAN
elder sister	ANE	(O)NEESAN
younger brother	OTOOTO	OTOOTOSAN
younger sister	IMOOTO	IMOOTOSAN
uncle	OJI	OJISAN
aunt	OBA	OBASAN
brothers and sisters	KYOODAI	GO-KYOODAI
son	MUSUKO	MUSUKOSAN, (O)BOTCHAN*
daughter	MUSUME	MUSUMESAN, OJOOSAN*
baby	AKAMBOO	AKACHAN*
husband	SHUJIN	GO-SHUJIN
wife	KANAI	OKUSAN
grandchild	MAGO	(O)MAGOSAN

* These are affectionate terms.
Botchan is used for boys up to about 10 years old.

Although the honorific form is NOT used when referring to members of your own family when talking about them to a third party, note that this form is used when addressing them directly. For example:

(a) *Watakushi no chichi to haha to ani wa Tookyoo ni sunde imasu.*
Here you are talking about your family to someone else.

(b) *Otoosan, okaasan, niisan, Jiroo, o-yasumi nasai.*
Father, mother, (older) brother, and Jiro, goodnight!

In this example (b) you are addressing them, so you indicate respect to your elders by using the honorific SAN. SAN is added when addressing relatives who are older than you are. Jiro, who is your younger brother, does not rate a SAN.

"NO" USED IN RELATIVE CLAUSE: **No,** as used in *Marunouchi no kaisha,* or *Tokyo no ani,* is used to show the existence of the object in that particular locale. Therefore, **no** has the meanings of *ni aru* in the former, and *ni iru* in the latter.

(a) *Marunouchi no kaisha—Marunouchi ni aru kaisha*
A company which is located in Marunouchi

(b) *Tokyo no ani—Tokyo ni iru ani*
My brother who is in Tokyo

THE SCHOOL SYSTEM IN JAPAN is established after the American system.

SHOOGAKKOO —grade school, six years
CHUUGAKKOO —junior high school, three years
KOOTOOGAKKOO—senior high school, three years
DAIGAKU —university, four years
DAIGAKUIN —graduate school

CHAPTER 15

ABRAHAM LINCOLN

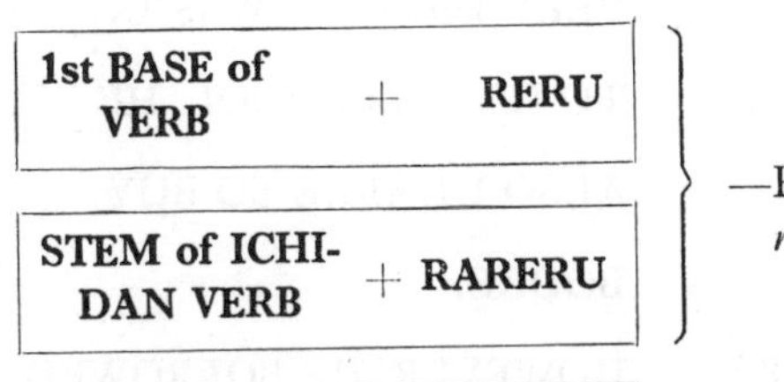

1st BASE of VERB + RERU
STEM of ICHI-DAN VERB + RARERU
4th BASE of VERB + RU

—PASSIVE VOICE *(the subject receiving the action of a verb)*

—CAN *(potential form)*

ABRAHAM LINCOLN WA IMA KARA HYAKU ROKUJUU-SAN NEN GURAI MAE AMERICA GASSHUUKOKU KENTUCKY-SHUU HARDING-GUN NI UMAREMASHITA.

ABRAHAM LINCOLN WAS BORN IN THE COUNTY OF HARDING, STATE OF KENTUCKY, UNITED STATES OF AMERICA ABOUT ONE HUNDRED AND SIXTY-THREE YEARS AGO (FROM NOW).

Lincoln wa	as for Lincoln (nom. case)
kodomo no toki kara	from when (he) was a child
gakumon ga suki deshita ga	liked studies but. . .
*Lincoln wa kodomo no toki kara gakumon ga suki deshita ga . . .	*Lincoln, from his childhood, liked his studies but. . .
uchi ga	(his) home (nom. case)
hijoo ni bimboo deshita	was very poor

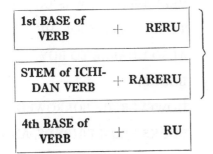

node	so
gakkoo e	to school
ikemasen deshita	was not able to go

LINCOLN WA KODOMO NO	FROM HIS CHILDHOOD,
TOKI KARA GAKUMON GA	LINCOLN LIKED (TO) STUDY,
SUKI DESHITA GA UCHI GA	BUT SINCE (HIS) HOME WAS
HIJOO NI BIMBOO DESHITA	VERY POOR HE WAS UNABLE
NODE, GAKKOO E *IKEMASEN*	TO GO TO SCHOOL. HE WAS
DESHITA.\ HON MO *KAEMA-*	ALSO UNABLE TO BUY
SEN DESHITA.\	BOOKS.
SHIKASHI, TOMODACHI KARA	HOWEVER, HE BORROWED
HON O KARITE *HITORI DE*	BOOKS FROM FRIENDS, AND
ISSHOOKEMMEI NI BENKYOO	HE STUDIED WELL (HARD)
SHIMASHITA.\	BY HIMSELF.
LINCOLN WA WAKAI TOKI	WHEN LINCOLN WAS YOUNG
IRO-IRO NA SHIGOTO O	HE DID A VARIETY OF WORK.
SHIMASHITA.\	

hyakushoo o shitari	at one time (he) farmed
hito ni yatowarete	hired by someone
hataraitari	at another time he worked
*hito ni yatowarete hataraitari . . .	*at another time he was hired by someone and worked . . .
shoonin ni nattari shimashita	at another time he became a merchant

ARU TOKI WA HYAKUSHOO O	AT ONE TIME HE FARMED,
SHITARI, HITO NI YATOWARE-	AT ANOTHER TIME HE WAS
TE *HATARAITARI,* SHOONIN	HIRED BY SOMEONE, AND HE
NI *NATTARI SHIMASHITA*.\	ALSO BECAME A MERCHANT.

jibun de	by himself
hooritsu o	law (obj. case)
benkyoo shi . . .	studied and . . .
*jibun de hooritsu o benkyoo shi . . .	*he studied law by himself and . . .
nijuu-hassai no toki	when he was 28 years old
Springfield e utsutte	moved to Springfield
*nijuu-hassai no toki Springfield e utsutte . . .	*he moved to Springfield when he was 28 years old and . . .
bengoshi ni narimashita	became an attorney

LINCOLN WA JIBUN DE HOO-RITSU O BENKYOO SHI, NI-JUU-HASSAI NO TOKI SPRING-FIELD E UTSUTTE BENGOSHI NI NARIMASHITA.\

LINCOLN STUDIED LAW BY HIMSELF, AND WHEN HE WAS 28 YEARS OLD, HE MOVED TO SPRINGFIELD AND BE-CAME AN ATTORNEY.

dan dan	gradually
yuumei ni natte	became famous (and)
*dan dan yuumei ni natte . . .	(He) gradually became famous and . . .
tootoo	finally
sen happyaku rokujuu-nen ni	in 1860 (specific time)
America Gasshuukoku no	United States of America's
daitooryoo ni	to the presidency
erabaremashita	was elected (passive)

DAN-DAN YUUMEI NI NATTE, TOOTOO SEN HAPPYAKU ROKUJUU-NEN NI (WA) AMERICA GASSHUUKOKU NO DAITOORYOO NI *ERABARE-MASHITA*.\

GRADUALLY HE BECAME FAMOUS, AND FINALLY IN 1860 HE WAS ELECTED PRESI-DENT OF THE UNITED STATES OF AMERICA. (ELECT-ED TO THE PRESIDENCY).

LINCOLN GA DAITOORYOO NI NATTE IRU TOKI YUUMEI NA

DURING THE TIME LINCOLN WAS PRESIDENT HE MADE

"DOREI KAIHOO NO SENGEN" O SHIMASHITA.	THE FAMOUS "DECLARATION TO EMANCIPATE THE SLAVES."
minami no shuu ni totte	for the southern states
dorei wa	as for the slaves (nom. case)
keizaiteki ni	from the standpoint of economy
hitsuyoo deshita kara	because (they) were necessary
SHIKASHI MINAMI NO SHUU *NI TOTTE,* DOREI WA KEIZAITEKI NI HITSUYOO DESHITA KARA KONO SENGEN NI HANTAI SHIMASHITA.	HOWEVER, FOR THE SOUTHERN STATES, THE SLAVES WERE NECESSARY ECONOMICALLY, SO THEY OPPOSED THIS PROCLAMATION.
SONO TAME, SEN-HAPPYAKU ROKUJUU-ICHI-NEN NI NAMBOKU SENSOO GA OKOTTE, MINAMI NO SHUU TO KITA NO SHUU GA TATAKAIMASHITA.	DUE TO THIS, THE CIVIL WAR STARTED (BROKE OUT) IN 1861 AND THE SOUTHERN STATES AND THE NORTHERN STATES FOUGHT.
KITA NO SHUU DEWA KOOGYOO GA SAKAN DE MINAMI WA NOOGYOOKOKU DESHITA.	IN THE NORTHERN STATES, INDUSTRIES WERE FLOURISHING, AND THE SOUTH WAS AN AGRICULTURAL COUNTRY.
kono sensoo wa	as for this war (nom. case)
yonenkan	four years
tsuzukimashita	continued
ga	but (conj.)

*kono sensoo wa yonenkan tsuzukimashita ga . . .	*This war continued for four years but . . .
tootoo	finally
kita no shuu ga katte	northern states won (and)
minami no shuu ga makemashita	southern states lost

KONO SENSOO WA YONENKAN TSUZUKIMASHITA GA TOO-TOO KITA NO SHUU GA KAT-TE, MINAMI NO SHUU GA MAKEMASHITA.	THIS WAR LASTED FOUR YEARS, BUT FINALLY THE NORTHERN STATES WON AND THE SOUTHERN STATES LOST.
KONO SENSOOCHUU KITA NO HITOTACHI MO MINAMI NO HITOTACHI MO TAIHEN KOMARIMASHITA.	DURING THIS WAR THE NORTHERN PEOPLE AND THE SOUTHERN PEOPLE WERE GREATLY TROUBLED.

hajime no uchi wa	at the beginning
minami no shuu no hitotachi ni	by the people of the southern states (agent of action)
yoku omowaremasen deshita	was not well thought of

DESU KARA, LINCOLN WA HAJIME NO UCHI WA MINAMI NO SHUU NO HITOTACHI NI (WA) YOKU *OMOWAREMASEN* DESHITA.	FOR THIS REASON, IN THE BEGINNING LINCOLN WAS NOT WELL THOUGHT OF BY THE PEOPLE OF THE SOUTH-ERN STATES.
MATA, ARU HITOTACHI KARA (WA) WARUKU *IWAREMASHI-TA.*	AGAIN (FURTHERMORE), HE WAS ILL-SPOKEN OF BY SOME PEOPLE (NOT WELL SPOKEN OF).

SEN-HAPPYAKU ROKUJUU-GO-NEN SHIGATSU JUUYOKKA NO BAN FORD-ZA DE SHIBAI O MITE ITA TOKI JOHN BOOTH TO IU MONO NI PISUTORU DE ATAMA O *UTAREMASHITA*.

(ON THE) NIGHT OF APRIL 14, 1865, WHEN (HE) WAS WATCHING A PLAY AT THE FORD THEATER, HE WAS SHOT (IN THE) HEAD WITH A PISTOL BY A FELLOW CALLED JOHN BOOTH.

chikaku no ie e	to the nearby house
okurarete	was sent and (passive)
*chikaku no ie e okurarete . . .	*(he) was sent to a nearby house and . . .
isha no teate o ukemashita	doctor's care received
keredomo	however . . .
*isha no teate o ukemashita keredomo . . .	*(he) received the doctor's care but . . .

LINCOLN WA SUGU (NI) CHIKAKU NO IE E *OKURARE-TE*, ISHA NO TEATE O UKE-MASHITA KEREDOMO, YOKU-ASA SHICHI-JI HAN NI NAKU-NARIMASHITA.

LINCOLN WAS SENT (TAKEN) TO A NEARBY HOUSE IMMEDIATELY AND RECEIVED DOCTOR'S TREATMENT, BUT HE PASSED AWAY AT 7:30 ON THE FOLLOWING MORNING.

Vocabulary List from the Lesson

Amerika Gasshuukoku	(n.) U.S.A.
gun	(n.) county
umareru	(v.i.) to be born (n.c.v.)
umaremashita	(polite past of *umareru*) was born *Tookyoo* (place) *de umaremashita.*

kodomo (n.) child
gakumon (n.) studies
hijoo ni (adv.) very; same meaning as *taihen*
bimboo (n.) poor (in the sense of material wealth)
ikemasen (n.) cannot go; negative potential form of *iku* (See I.C. & G.N.)
shikashi (conj.) however, but, nevertheless
tomodachi (n.) friend
wakai (adj.) young
ikka (n.) a family
yatou (v.t.) to hire
yatowareru (passive form of *yatou*) to be hired (See I.C. & G.N.)
yatowarete ("te" form of *yatowareru* used connectively) . . . was hired and . . .
hataraku (v.i.) to work
hataraitari (alternate action form of *hataraku*—See I.C. & G.N.)
mata (conj.) again
shoonin (n.) businessman, tradesman
shoobai (n.) business; *shoobai suru*—to do business
nijuuhassai (n.) *nijuuhachi*—28; *sai* is the classifier used to count age of animate beings. *Hassai* is the phonetic change.
jibun de by oneself
hooritsu (n.) law
utsuru (v.i.) to move (location)
bengoshi (n.) attorney, lawyer
dan-dan gradually
yuumei (n.) famous; *yuumei na* (adj.)
tootoo finally
daitooryoo (n.) president, or presidency (of a nation)
erabareru (passive form of *erabu*—to elect), to be elected (See I.C. & G.N.)

okoru	(v.i.) to start, to break out
okotte	("te" form of *okoru,* used connectively) . . . broke out and . . .
tatakau	(v.i.) to battle, to engage in war, to fight (in the sense of "to battle" or "engage in war," postposition *to* is used after the object one fights "against." *Beikoku to tatakau.*)
dorei	(n.) slaves
kaihoo	(n.) emancipation
sengen	(n.) proclamation; *sengen suru* (Chi. v.)—to proclaim
. . . **ni totte**	for . . . (used in the sense of "*as far as* the southern states *are concerned. . . .*")
hitsuyoo	(n.) necessary
hantai suru	(Chi. v.) to oppose (takes the postposition *ni* when used to oppose something: *sono hanashi NI hantai suru*).
tsuzuku	(v.i.) to continue, to last, to extend
sakan	(n.) flourishing, thriving
sensoochuu	(n.) during the war. Suffix *chuu* (or *juu*) means "during the period," e.g., *natsujuu*—during the summer; *ichinichijuu*—throughout the entire day. Learn which suffix to use by association.
hajime	(n.) the beginning, the lead, the first
hajime ni	in the beginning
. . . **tachi**	(suffix) denotes plural; usually Japanese nouns do not have number, but pronouns such as *watakushi, ano kata, kono hito, sono hito, anata, ano onna no hito,* etc., are singular. In order to show plural of such words, *tachi* is added. (*ra:* less polite)

omowareru	(passive form of *omou*—to think) to be thought of
omowaremasen deshita	(polite neg. past) was not well thought of
iwareru	(passive form of *iu*—to say) to be spoken of
iwaremashita	(polite past of *iwareru*)
aru toki	one time, once upon a time, once
. . . -za	(suffix) denotes a theatre
mono ni	(p.p.) Here *ni* is used to introduce an "agent of action," or that which acted upon the subject. (See I.C. & G.N.)
atama	(n.) head
utareru	(passive form of *utsu*—to shoot, hit, strike, administer a blow) to be hit—See I.C. & G.N.
utaremashita	(polite past of *utareru*) was shot
mono	(n.) a person, a fellow
sugu (ni)	(adv.) at once, immediately, promptly
okurareru	(passive form of *okuru*—to send) to be sent
okurarete	("te" form, used connectively) . . . was sent and . . .
isha	(n.) doctor
teate	(n.) treatment
teate o suru	(Chi. v.) to give treatment
teate o ukeru	to receive treatment, to be treated (medically)
teate o ukemashita	(polite past) received treatment
yokuasa	(n.) following morning. (*Yoku* is a prefix meaning "following." *yokuban, yokujitsu, yokunen,* etc.)
nakunaru	(v.i.) to pass away (in the sense of "to die"; it is used only in connection with the death of a human being.)
nakunarimashita	(polite past of *nakunaru*) died

Additional Vocabulary

byooin	(n.) hospital
byooki	(n.) illness
kusuri	(n.) medicine
senkyo	(n.) election
senkyo suru	(Chi. v.) to elect
seiji	(n.) politics
seijika	(n.) politician; *ka* indicates the person
seijiteki	(adj.) political
seijigaku	(n.) political science; *gaku* shows study
shikaru	(v.) to scold
shinu	(v.) to die

Important Construction and Grammar Notes

PASSIVE VOICE: The verb is in the ACTIVE VOICE when the subject does the acting. Conversely, when the subject is acted upon, the verb is in the PASSIVE VOICE.

The Japanese passive voice is formed by adding *reru* to the first, or the negative base of the *yodan* verb (c.v.), and *rareru* to the stem of the *ichidan* verb (n.c.v.):

erabu	era*ba-reru*	(was elected)
miru	mi-*rareru*	(was seen)

The passive forms of the irregular verbs *suru* and *kuru* are:

sa-reru　　*ko-rareru*

Therefore:

1st BASE of C.V. + *RERU*	=	PASSIVE
STEM of N.C.V. + *RARERU*		

The resulting passive verbs are conjugated as non-conjugating *(eru)* verbs:

erabareru
erabaremasu
erabaremashita
erabaremasen deshita
erabareta
etc.

Note the active and passive voice in the following examples:

1. Booth ga Lincoln o uchimashita.	Booth shot Lincoln. (active)
2. Lincoln wa Booth **ni** pisutoru de utaremashita.	Lincoln was shot with a pistol by Booth.

. . . NI: This has the meaning of "by . . ." **Ni** as used here is often referred to as the postposition which introduces the "agent of action" or that which acts upon the subject.

1. Lincoln wa pisutoru **de** *utaremashita.*	Lincoln was shot *with* a pistol.

In this example **de** introduces the instrument used in this act. Make the distinction between this and the "agent" of action given below (see below for more examples of this).

2. Lincoln wa *Booth* **ni** pistoru **de** *utaremashita.*	Lincoln was shot with a pistol *by* Booth.
3. Watakushi wa *sensei* **ni** *shikarareta.*	I was scolded *by* the teacher.

The following passive patterns should be memorized:

1.	*SUBJECT* who	WA	*VERB* what happened
	Doroboo (The robber	WA	utaremashita. was shot.)

2.

SUBJECT	WA	*AGENT*	NI	*VERB*
who		by whom		what happened

Doroboo	WA	junsa	NI	utaremashita.
(The robber		by the police		was shot.)

3.

SUBJECT	WA	*AGENT*	NI	*INSTRUMENT*	DE	*VERB*
who		by whom		with what		what happened

Doroboo	WA	junsa	NI	pisutoru	DE	utaremashita.
(The robber		by the police		with a pistol		was shot.)

4.

SUBJECT	WA	*AGENT*	NI	*INSTRUMENT*	DE	*OBJECT*	O	*VERB*
who		by whom		with what		what		what happened

Doroboo	*WA*	junsa	*NI*	pisutoru	*DE*	ashi	*O*	utaremashita.
(The robber		by the police		with a pistol		(in) the leg		was shot.)

Note: (a) The "agent" and the "instrument" can be interchanged. The basic rule that the subject should come at the beginning and the object next to the verb should be adhered to.

(b) *DO NOT* use passive form unless it is desired to emphasize the subject as the recipient of the action. Notice the difference in the following expressions:

i. The horse kicked me. (In this sentence, "the horse" is the subject and "me" is the object.)—*Uma wa watakushi o kerimashita.*

ii. I was kicked by a horse—*Watakushi wa uma ni kerarem ashita.* (This places emphasis on the subject receiving the kicking).

Do not confuse "agent of action" with "by means of" or "with." Study the following examples:

1. Dare ga Lincoln o pisutoru *de* uchimashita ka.	Who shot Lincoln with a pistol?
2. Booth to iu mono ga Lincoln o pisutoru *de* uchimashita.	A fellow called Booth shot Lincoln with a pistol.
3. Lincoln wa dare *ni* pisutoru *de* utaremashita ka.	By whom was Lincoln shot with a pistol?
4. Booth to iu mono *ni* Lincoln wa pisutoru *de* utaremashita.	Lincoln was shot with a pistol by a fellow called Booth.

5. Dare ga uchimashita ka. — Who shot (Lincoln)?
6. Booth ga uchimashita. — Booth did.
7. Dare ga utaremashita ka. — Who was shot?
8. Lincoln ga utaremashita. — Lincoln was shot.
9. Nan *de* utaremashita ka. — With what was (he) shot?
10. Pisutoru *de* utaremashita. — (He) was shot with a pistol.
11. Dare *ni* utaremashita ka. — By whom was (he) shot?
12. Booth *ni* utaremashita. — (He) was shot by Booth.

ANOTHER USAGE OF PASSIVE FORM: This form is also used to indicate a situation where an action is indirectly inflicted on the subject, the indirect result of an act done by some other person's action. Unlike the normal usage where a transitive verb is used and the action is directly inflicted on the subject, in this example the intransitive verb is used, and the subject is suffering the consequence of this action.

A similar expression in English is "The motor went dead *on me,* and I was stuck." "The workers walked out *on me,* so I closed shop," etc.

1. *Benkyoochuu Tanaka-san ni* **korarete** *komarimashita.*
   During (my) study Mr. Tanaka came and I was distressed.
   (meaning I suffered the consequence of his visit).
2. *Ichiban isogashii toki ni (watakushi wa) jochuu ni* **derarete** *komatta.*
   (During) the busiest time, the maid walked out on me, and I was in trouble.

POTENTIAL FORM (the short form): In Chapter 10 one form of the potential form was introduced.

The 4th base of the *yodan* verb (c.v.) is the short potential form meaning "to be able." The short potential form of **hanasu** (to speak) is as follows:

1.
sa
shi
shi
hana su
SE . . . *hanasemasu* or *hanaseru* (can speak)

Hanaseru means "to be speakable" or "to be able to be spoken"; *kakeru,* "to be able to be written." In translation, however, *Nihongo ga hanaseru—*

"Japanese language is speakable," *kanji ga kakeru*—"Kanji is writeable" should be "I *can speak* Japanese" and "I *can write* kanji."

2.
ka
ki
ka ku
KE . . . *kakemasu* or *kakeru* (can write)

The resulting verbs are handled as non-conjugating verbs: *hanaseru, hanasemasu,* etc. With *ichidan* verbs (n.c.v.), *rareru* is added to the stem.

1. mi + *rareru*—mirareru (can see)
2. tabe + *rareru*—taberareru (can eat)

Note that this form is the same as the passive form. Therefore, the meaning must be determined by the context.

Thus:

4th BASE of C.V.	+	RU (MASU)	= CAN . . . (Potential)
STEM of N.C.V.	+	RARERU	

GA FOR O: With potential forms constructed by verb conjugation, the objective postposition **o** of the **koto ga dekiru** form changes to **ga** or **wa.**

1. Anata wa gohan **o** taberu koto ga dekimasu ka.	Are you able to eat cooked rice?
Anata wa gohan **ga** taberaremasu ka.	Are you able to eat cooked rice?
2. Anata wa hon **o** yomu koto ga dekimasu ka.	Can you read a book?
Anata wa hon **ga** yomemasu ka.	Can you read a book?

. . . TARI, . . . TARI SURU: This construction is usually used in pairs to express alternate action when it is desired to show the subject "sometimes does (did) . . ., at another time does (did) . . .," "at one time (I) did . . . and then (I) did . . .," "now . . . then." The two verbs ending in **tari** must always be followed by some form of **suru** which determines the tense of the whole sentence. Sometimes, one **tari** is used, but in this case other parallel acts are implied though not enumerated. The order of the action in this use is not important.

1. *Watakushi wa gakusei no toki sara o arat*tari *gareeji de hatarai*tari *shimashita.* (When I was a student, at one time I washed dishes, and at another time worked in a garage.)
2. *Nichiyoobi ni tegami o kai*tari *terebi o mi*tari *shimashita.* (On Sunday I did such things as writing letters and watching T.V.)

Here the main idea is that these actions were done on Sunday, with no attempt to show in what order they were done.

When the order of action is consecutive, i.e., when the intent is to indicate the second action following the completion of the first act, use the "te" form (see p. 224).

1. Chooshoku o *tabete* gakkoo e ikimashita.
2. Nihon e *itte* Nihongo o benkyoo shimasu.

HOW TO FORM ALTERNATE ACTION:

1. First, form the abrupt past (simply change the "e" of the "te" verb to "a").
2. Add *ri* to the abrupt past.
3. Use it in pairs and complete the construction by using some form of the verb *suru*.

yomu	— yon*de*	— yon*da*	— yond*ari*
taberu	— tabe*te*	— tabe*ta*	— tabe*tari*
suru	— shi*te*	— shi*ta*	— shi*tari*

Fluency Drill

In this drill, pay close attention to the use of the postposition. The word order of different parts need not be so definite—most of them are movable.

Doroboo *wa* utareta.
Doroboo *wa* ashi *o* utareta.

Doroboo *wa* junsa *ni* ashi *o* utareta.
Doroboo *wa* junsa *ni* pisutoru *de* ashi *o* utareta.
Doroboo *wa* sakuban junsa *ni* pisutoru *de* ashi *o* utareta.
Doroboo *wa* ie *no* mae *de* sakuban junsa *ni* pisutoru *de* ashi *o* utareta.
Doroboo *wa* ie *no* mae *de* sakuban ku-ji goro junsa *ni* pisutoru *de* ashi *o* utareta.

The robber was shot.
The robber was shot in the leg.
The robber was shot in the leg by the police.
The robber was shot in the leg with a pistol by the police.
The robber was shot in the leg with a pistol by the police last night.
The robber was shot in the leg in front of the house with a pistol by the police last night.
The robber was shot in the leg in front of the house with a pistol by the police last night about 9 o'clock.

Substitution Drill

(1st Base Verb)
UTA
KAKA
OKURA } + RERU
DASA
etc.

(Stem of N.C.V.)
MI
TABE } + RARERU
SHIRABE **
etc.

(4th Base Verb)
KAKE
ARUKE
HANASE } + RU
YOME
etc.

** *shiraberu*—to investigate

Exercises

1. The boy was scolded.	Otoko no ko wa shikarareta.
2. The boy was scolded by the teacher.	Otoko no ko wa sensei ni shikarareta.
3. The girl (*onna no ko*) was kicked.	Onna no ko wa kerareta.
4. The girl was kicked by a horse.	Onna no ko wa uma ni kerareta.
5. Jiro was elected.	Jiroo wa erabareta.
6. Jiro was elected by the students.	Jiroo wa seito ni erabareta.
7. I was seen.	Watakushi wa mirareta.
8. I was seen by the principal (*koochoo*).	Watakushi wa koochoo ni mirareta.
9. The cow (*ushi*) was sold.	Ushi wa urareta.
10. The cow was sold by the farmer.	Ushi wa hyakushoo ni urareta.

Say the following 5 sentences 2 ways—the long form (. . . *koto ga dekimasu*), and the short form (4th base + *ru*).

11. I can speak Japanese.	Nihongo o hanasu koto ga dekimasu. Nihongo ga hanasemasu.
12. I can write kanji.	Kanji o kaku koto ga dekimasu. Kanji ga kakemasu.
13. He can buy a car.	Ano kata wa jidoosha o kau koto ga dekimasu. Ano kata wa jidoosha ga kaemasu.
14. I cannot wait.	Matsu koto ga dekimasen. Matemasen.
15. You cannot eat this.	Anata wa kore o taberu koto ga dekimasen. Anata wa kore ga taberaremasen.
16. Last night I watched T.V. and read books.	Sakuban terebi o mitari hon o yondari shimashita.
17. On Sundays I study and take a walk.	Nichiyoobi ni benkyoo shitari sampo shitari shimasu.
18. People are getting on and off the train.	Hitobito wa kisha ni nottari oritari shite imasu.

19. He is walking back and forth.	Ittari kitari shite imasu.
20. The children are standing and sitting.	Kodomotachi wa tattari koshikaketari shite imasu.
21. The people are drinking and eating.	Hitobito wa nondari tabetari shite imasu.

Combine the following sentences, using *te,* and the 2nd base.

22. The northern states won. The southern states lost.	Kita no shuu wa katte (kachi) minami no shuu wa makemashita.
23. He became a lawyer. He became famous.	Ano kata wa bengoshi ni natte (nari) yuumei ni narimashita.
24. I received treatment. I went home by taxi.	Teate o ukete (uke) ie e takushii de kaerimashita.
25. He studied political science. He became a politician.	Seijigaku o benkyoo shite (shi) seijika ni narimashita.
26. Mr. Brown got up early, (and) ate breakfast. He went sightseeing.	Brown-san wa hayaku okite, chooshoku o tabe, kembutsu ni dekakemashita.
27. The boy came at 7 o'clock. He went home at 10 o'clock.	Otoko no ko wa shichi-ji ni kite, juu-ji ni kaerimashita.

Translate into Japanese:

1. I was born in the city of Los Angeles, California, on July 4, 1930.

   Note: In translating date, address, and other similar data, start from the general to more specific, e.g., 1930, July, 4, hour, minute, second.

2. Because I began studying Japanese two months ago, I cannot read kanji yet, but (I) can speak a little.

   Note: Use the long and short potential forms in translating this.

3. My money was stolen and I was not able to buy the ticket. I was extremely troubled.

   Note: The passive form is used to indicate the subject indirectly suffering the result.

4. Throughout the summer vacation, I occasionally read, and at other times I wrote a book.

   Note: summer vacation—*natsuyasumi*

5. First I was scolded by my teacher. After I came home I was struck on the head by my brother.
6. The Pacific War broke out on December 7, 1941, and continued for four years. During this war, both the American people and the Japanese people were distressed.

   Note: both—*mo . . . mo . . .* (see p. 96).

7. In America, the President is elected by the people of 50 states once every four years.
8. The following day I went to the hospital in the town to receive treatment from the doctor.

   Note: hospital (which is) in the town—"in the town" (relative clause) modifies "hospital," so:

   a. *machi ni aru byooin*

   or

   b. *machi no byooin*—*no* takes the place of *ni aru* in a relative clause. *Tokyo no tomodachi*—this means "a friend who is in Tokyo."

9. I did not want to be sent to Formosa, but I was chosen by my company.

   Note: "did not want to be sent"

   to send—okuru
   to be sent—oku*rareru*
   want to be sent—okurare*tai*
   do not want to be sent—okurareta*kunai*
   did not want to be sent—okuraretaku*nakatta*

10. In the beginning, Japan imported many manufactured goods, but now Japan is an exporter. For Japan, foreign trade is necessary.

    Note: exporter—*yushutsukoku*

Answer in Japanese:

1. Lincoln wa naze kodomo no toki gakkoo e ikemasen deshita ka.
2. Ima America de daigaku e iku no ni takusan okane ga irimasu ka. Bengoshi ni naru no ni nan-nen gakkoo e ikanakereba narimasen ka.
3. Anata wa jidoosha ni hikareta koto ga arimasu ka.

   Note: *hiku*—"to run over"

4. Amerika no daitooryoo wa dare ni erabaremasu ka. Amerikajin wa mainen daitooryoo o erabimasu ka.

5. Naze Namboku Sensoo ga okorimashita ka.
   Dochira ga katte, dochira ga makemashita ka.
6. Anata wa maiban rajio o kiitari terebi o mitari shimasu ka.
   Taitei nani o shimasu ka.
7. Kodomo no toki *kara* nakunaru toki *made* Lincoln ni tsuite hanashite kudasai.

   Note: *kara . . . made*—"from . . . up to (until)"
   . . . ni tsuite—"concerning, about"

8. Naze John Booth to iu mono wa daitooryoo o pisutoru de uchimashita ka.
   Lincoln ga utareta toki nani o shite imashita ka.
9. Gakusei ga tabi-tabi eiga (movie) e ittari asondari suru to yoi gakusha (scholar) ni naru koto ga dekimasu ka.
10. "Dorei o kaihoo suru sengen" wa keizaiteki ni daiji na sengen deshita ka.
    Seijiteki ni daiji deshita ka.

Put appropriate postpositions and conjunctions in the blanks:

1. Watakushi ______ gakkoo ______ sensei ______ shikararemashita.
2. Gakusei ______ sensei no hanashi ______ hantai shimashita.
3. Ano kata wa hokubu ______ umarete dan-dan yuumei ______ bengoshi ______ narimashita.
4. Ano seijika wa daitooryoo ______ erabaremashita ______ sono shigoto ______ tekishite imasen.
5. Kyoo wa natsu ______ yoo ______ hi desu.
6. Haru ______ naru ______ atatakaku narimasu.
7. Anata ______ otoosan ______ dare ______ yatowarete imasu ka.
8. Anata ______ uchi ______ hachi-ji ______ itta toki dare ______ imasen deshita.
9. Watakushi wa ie ______ isha ______ teate ______ uketa ato de byooin ______ okuraremashita.
10. Yokohama ______ fune ______ notte, higashi no hoo ______ Taiheiyoo ______ wataru ______ San Francisco ______ tsukimasu.
11. Watakushi ______ gakkoo ______ ikemasen deshita ______ tomodachi ______ hon ______ karite benkyoo shimashita.
12. Eki no mae ______ aru kippu uriba ______ kippu ______ ni-mai katte hoomu (platform) no hoo ______ ikimashita.

Compose sentences using the following verbs in "alternate action" construction. Note the verb tense required.

	(a)	(b)
1.	(a) hon o yomimasu	(b) tegami o kakimasu
2.	(a) akeru	(b) shimeru
3.	(a) terebi o mimashita	(b) rajio o kikimashita
4.	(a) biiru (beer) o nonda	(b) (o)sushi o tabeta
5.	(a) hashitte imasu	(b) tonde imasu (*tobu*—jump)
6.	(a) naite iru (*náku*—cry)	(b) waratte iru (*warau*—laugh)
7.	(a) shikararemashita	(b) homeraremashita (*homeru*—praise)
8.	(a) tatsu	(b) koshikakeru
9.	(a) tabeta	(b) nonda

CHAPTER 16

TEISHAJOO—STATION

NOUN O + VERB (of movement)	= THROUGH . . .
	(action in space)

"TE" VERB + { **ARIMASU** or **IMASU** } = CONDITION *(state of being)*

Brown-san wa	as for Mr. Brown (nom. case)
Nihon ni kite kara	after coming to Japan
isogashikute	being busy and
*Brown-san wa Nihon ni kite kara isogashikute . . .	*Mr. Brown, after coming to Japan, being busy . . .
kembutsu suru	to do the sights
kembutsu suru hima	time to go sightseeing (rel. cl.)
*kembutsu suru hima ga arimasen	*no time to go sightseeing

BROWN-SAN WA NIHON NI KITE KARA ISOGASHIKUTE KEMBUTSU SURU HIMA GA ARIMASEN DESHITA.

SINCE MR. BROWN CAME TO JAPAN, HE HAS BEEN BUSY AND HAD NO TIME TO GO SIGHTSEEING.

ashita kara	from tomorrow
natsuyasumi ga	summer vacation (nom. case)
hajimaru	begins
node	because
*ashita kara natsuyasumi ga hajimaru node . . .	*because summer vacation begins (from) tomorrow . . .

Kyooto kembutsu ni dekakeru	for (the purpose of) Kyoto sightseeing to depart
dekakeru tsumori	intend to depart
*Kyooto kembutsu ni dekakeru tsumori desu	*intend to go Kyoto sightseeing
ASHITA KARA NATSUYASUMI GA HAJIMARU NODE KYOOTO KEMBUTSU NI DEKAKERU TSUMORI DESU.	BECAUSE SUMMER VACATION BEGINS TOMORROW, HE IS PLANNING TO GO SIGHTSEEING IN KYOTO.
eki no annaijo de	at the station's information desk
tazunete imasu	is asking
IMA EKI NO ANNAIJO DE TAZUNETE IMASU.	HE IS NOW ASKING AT THE STATION'S INFORMATION DESK.
(Brown): KOBE MADE NO NITOO NO KIPPU WA DOKO DE KAEMASU KA.	WHERE CAN I BUY A SECOND CLASS TICKET TO KOBE?
(Clerk): GO-BAN NO MADOGUCHI DESU.	NUMBER FIVE WINDOW.
(Brown): TSUGI NO KOOBEYUKI WA NAN-JI NI DEMASU KA.	WHAT TIME DOES THE NEXT KOBE-BOUND TRAIN LEAVE?
(Clerk): JUUNI-JI NIJUU-GOFUN NI DEMASU.	IT WILL LEAVE AT 12:25.

(Brown): SORE WA KYUUKOO DESU KA, TOKKYUU DESU KA.	IS THAT AN EXPRESS OR SUPER EXPRESS?
(Clerk): KYUUKOO DESU.	IT IS (AN) EXPRESS.
(Brown): KOOBE NI NAN-JI NI TSUKIMASU KA.	AT WHAT TIME DOES IT ARRIVE IN KOBE?
(Clerk): ASU NO ASA NO ROKU-JI YONJIPPUN NI TSUKIMASU GA, SAN-NO-MIYA NIWA ROKU-JI SANJIPPUN NI TSUKIMASU.	IT ARRIVES AT 6:40 TOMORROW MORNING, BUT IT ARRIVES AT SAN-NO-MIYA AT 6:30.

chikagoro wa	nowadays
kisha ga	train (nom. case)
konde imasu	is crowded (state of being)
kara	because
*chikagoro wa kisha ga konde imasu kara . . .	*because the trains are crowded nowadays . . .
kippu ga	tickets
kaenai	cannot buy (potential)
kamo shiremasen	may
*kippu ga kaenai kamo shiremasen	*may not be able to buy tickets

SHIKASHI CHIKAGORO WA KISHA GA TAIHEN *KONDE IMASU* KARA KIPPU GA KAENAI *KAMO SHIREMASEN*.	HOWEVER, SINCE THE TRAINS ARE VERY CROWDED NOWADAYS, YOU MAY NOT BE ABLE TO BUY A TICKET.
(Brown): KONO KISHA NI SHIMBASHI KARA NOREMASU KA.	CAN YOU RIDE ON THIS TRAIN FROM SHIMBASHI?

keredomo	however
tsugi no	next (quasi adj.)
futsuu ressha nara	if it is regular train
*keredomo tsugi no futsuu ressha nara . . .	*however, if it is the next regular train . . .
Shimbashi eki kara	from Shimbashi station
demo	even
noremasu	can get on
*Shimbashi eki kara demo noremasu.	*(You) can get on even from Shimbashi station.

(Clerk): IIE, KYUUKOO WA SHIMBASHI NIWA TOMARIMASEN. KEREDOMO TSUGI NO FUTSUU RESSHA NARA SHIMBASHI EKI KARA DEMO NOREMASU.

NO, THE EXPRESS DOES NOT STOP AT SHIMBASHI, BUT IF IT IS THE NEXT REGULAR TRAIN, IT CAN BE BOARDED EVEN FROM SHIMBASHI STATION.

(Brown): FUTSUU RESSHA NIWA NORITAKU ARIMASEN. TSUGI NO TOKKYUU WA HIKONE *O TOORIMASU* KA.

I DON'T WANT TO TAKE AN ORDINARY TRAIN. DOES THE NEXT SPECIAL EXPRESS TRAIN PASS (THROUGH) HIKONE?

Hikone o	Hikone (action in space)
toorimasu	passes

(Clerk): HAI, HIKONE *O TOORIMASU* GA TOMARIMASEN.

YES, IT PASSES HIKONE, BUT DOESN'T STOP (THERE).

(Brown): KOOBE MADE NITOO ICHI-MAI.

ONE SECOND CLASS TO KOBE.

(Clerk): KATAMICHI DESU KA OOFUKU DESU KA.	IS IT ONE WAY OR ROUND TRIP?
(Brown): KATAMICHI O O-NEGAI SHIMASU.	I WOULD LIKE ONE WAY.
(Clerk): SEN NIHYAKU EN DESU.	IT IS 1200 YEN.
(Brown): KYUUKOO-KEN TO SHINDAI-KEN MO KUDASAI.	GIVE ME ALSO AN EXPRESS AND A SLEEPER TICKET.
(Clerk): SHINDAI WA UE DE II DESU KA. SHITA WA MOO URIKIREMASHITA.	WILL THE UPPER BERTH BE ALL RIGHT? THE LOWERS ARE ALREADY SOLD OUT.
(Brown): SORE DEWA SHIKA-TA GA ARIMASEN KARA UE DE II DESU.	IN THAT CASE, SINCE IT CAN-NOT BE HELPED, THE UPPER WILL BE ALL RIGHT.
KOOBE-YUKI WA NAMBAN-SEN DESU KA.	KOBE TRAINS ARE ON WHAT TRACK NUMBER?
(Clerk): ROKU-BAN-SEN DESU. MADA JIKAN GA ARIMASU *YO.*	IT IS TRACK NUMBER SIX. THERE IS STILL TIME.

(Brown): AKABOO-SAN, KONO TORANKU DAKE AZUKETE, TESAGE KABAN WA KISHA NO NAKA E *MOCHI-KONDE KUDASAI.*	REDCAP, PLEASE CHECK ONLY THIS TRUNK, AND TAKE THE SUITCASE INTO THE TRAIN.

(Redcap): KASHIKOMARIMASHITA. SORE DEWA CHOTTO KIPPU O KASHITE KUDASAI. TORANKU O AZUKE NI IKIMASU KARA**. . . .

CERTAINLY. IN THAT CASE, WILL YOU LEND ME THE TICKET FOR A MOMENT, SINCE I AM GOING TO CHECK THE TRUNK.

ANATA NO ZASEKI WA NAMBAN DESU KA.

WHAT IS YOUR SEAT NUMBER?

(Brown): HACHI-GOO-SHA NO NIJUU-ICHI-BAN DESU.

IT IS NO. 21 OF CAR NO. 8.

watakushi no kisha wa	my train (nom. case)
moo	already
kite imashita	has come (state of being)
node	because (so)
*watakushi no kisha wa moo kite imashita node . . .	*my train was already in, so . . .
ooisogi de	in a great hurry
kaidan o	stairs (action in space)
hashitte agarimashita	ran and climbed

WATAKUSHI NO KISHA WA MOO *KITE IMASHITA* NODE OOISOGI DE KAIDAN *O HASHITTE AGARIMASHITA*. MINNA WA MOO *NARANDE IMASHITA*.

MY TRAIN WAS ALREADY IN, SO I RAN UP THE STAIRS IN GREAT HASTE. THEY WERE ALL ALREADY LINED UP.

***kara* construction here, giving the reason, shows an afterthought. This pattern is used quite frequently in conversation—see p. 389 below.

Vocabulary List from the Lesson

isogashii	(adj.) busy
isogashikute	("te" form of *isogashii*) busy and . . .
hima	(n.) free time (away from one's main preoccupation.)
kembutsu suru hima	time to do sightseeing; *verb* + *hima* means "time to *verb*"; *Shimbun o yomu hima* (time to read newspaper); *terebi o miru hima* (time to watch T.V.).
natsuyasumi	(n.) summer vacation
hajimaru	(v.i.) to begin (*hajimeru*—v.t.)
dekakeru	(v.i.) to leave (for a destination)
annaijo	(n.) information place, information desk.
tazuneru	(v.t.) to ask (use the postposition *NI* after the person to whom you are inquiring. *Sensei NI tazunenasai.*)
tazunete imasu	(prog. form) asking
ni-too	(n.) second class (*too,* a suffix indicating "class" or "grade," *san-too*—3rd class)
. . . **-ban**	classifier for "number" Used after the numeral to indicate room number, telephone number, etc. *namban*—what number?
kyuukoo	(n.) express train
tokkyuu	(n.) super express train
tsuku	(v.i.) to reach (*NI* is used after the "place" where one arrives at. *N.Y. NI tsuku.*)
San-no-Miya	(n.) name of the station before Kobe.
shikashi	(conj.) however, but

komu	(v.i.) to be crowded (in reference to a "state" or "condition," use the progressive form—See I.C. & G.N.)
konde imasu	("te" + *imasu,* state of being) is crowded
. . . kamo shiremasen	a form of expressing probability, doubt, or guess; maybe, possibly, probably, etc. (See I.C. & G.N.)
Shimbashi	(n.) name of a place near Tokyo.
noreru	(v.—potential form of *noru*—to ride, to get on) can get on
noremasu	(polite form of *noreru*)
futsuu	(n.) ordinary
ressha	(n.) train
demo	even (used after the noun it limits)
tooru	(v.i.) to pass through (use the post-position *O* after the area that is gone through. *Tonneru O tooru.*)
katamichi	(n.) one way
oofuku	(n.) round trip
o-negai shimasu	(idio.) "Please take care of this." "I would like to make this request."
. . . -sen	railroad, streetcar line, track
namban-sen	what number line, what track (?)
shindai	(n.) bed, or sleeper on a train
shindai-ken	(n.) sleeper ticket; *ken* is a suffix meaning "ticket." *Tokkyuu-ken* —special express train ticket.
shikata ga arimasen	(idio.) "It cannot be helped."
ryoohoo	(n.) both, both sides
ii desu	all right, sufficient

akaboo	(n.) redcap
tesage kaban	(n.) suitcase, handbag
toranku	(n.) trunk
azukeru	(v.t.) to check (to put something in someone's care . . . *o* . . . *ni azukeru*)
azuke ni ikimasu	go (in order) to check
mochi-komu	(v.t.) to take in, to take into . . ., carry in
mochi-konde kudasai	("te" of *mochi-komu* + *kudasai*) please take in . . .
kashikomarimashita	(idio.) certainly; "yes, I will accept (your request)"
chotto	(n.) a short space of time, a moment, a fraction of time
chotto no aida	(n.) for the duration of a short time, a short space of time, a moment
zaseki	(n.) seat
kasu	(v.t.) to lend (. . . *o* . . . *ni* kasu)
kashite kudasai	("te" of *kasu* + *kudasai*) please lend me
kaidan	(n.) stairs
narabu	(v.i.) to stand in line
narande imashita	("te" + imasu, state of being) were lined up (See I.C. & G.N.)

Additional Vocabulary

jikanhyoo	(n.) time table
shuppatsu jikan	(n.) time of departure
toochaku jikan	(n.) time of arrival
kaisatsu guchi	(n.) ticket gate
tonneru	(n.) tunnel
tekkyoo	(n.) bridge (made of steel)

tenimotsu toriatsukaijo	(n.) hand baggage department
hoomu	(n.) platform
nori-kaeru	(v.t.) to transfer, to change (a train, bus, etc.)
machiaishitsu	(n.) waiting room
okureru	(n.c.v.) to be late (use *ni* to specify what you are late for—*kurasu ni okureru*)
shokudoo-sha	(n.) dining car
shindai-sha	(n.) sleeper, pullman
gesha suru	(Chi. v.) to get off the train
Shinkansen	This fast, modern train links Tokyo and Osaka. The trains average 100 miles an hour on this line. *Shinkansen de Oosaka e iku.*

Important Construction and Grammar Notes

"O" USED AS "THROUGH": Another usage of **O** is:

NOUN + O + VERB OF MOTION

In this situation **o** signifies that the action occurred in space, that the movement was carried out along a certain length of area. Therefore, the verb used here will be one indicating movement covering space, such as *tobu* (fly), *tooru* (pass through), *wataru* (cross), *noboru* (climb), *magaru* (turn), etc.

sakamichi **o noboru**—climb an inclined road
hoteru no mae **o tooru**—pass in front of the hotel
kono michi **o ikinasai**—go on this road

Contrast this **o** with **de** showing specific place of action. If we were to indicate **de** by a circle ○ showing the locale where the action took place, action in space **o** could be represented by an arrow → signifying the ground covered by the movement of this action.

. . . KAMO SHIREMASEN: When **kamo** is immediately followed by the negative of **shireru** (to be known), or **wakaru** (to understand, or to be known), the combined form expresses probability, doubt, or conjecture. It may be translated "may," "maybe," "perhaps," "possibly," etc.

I. AS USED WITH NOUNS:

1. Ano hito wa *gunjin kamo shiremasen.*	Maybe he is a soldier. (Lit., whether he is a soldier, it cannot be known.)

II. AS USED WITH VERBS:

1. Asu *kuru kamo shiremasen.*	He may come tomorrow (pres. tense).
2. Gakkoo e *itta kamo shiremasen.*	Perhaps (he) went to school (past tense).
3. Uchi e *konai* kamo shiremasen.*	Possibly (he) won't come (to my) home (pres. neg.).
4. Kono inu wa mizu o *nomitai kamo shiremasen.*	This dog may want to drink (some) water (desiderative form).
5. Komban kaisha e *ikanakereba naranai* kamo shiremasen.*	I may have to go to the company tonight ("must" form).

**nai* is an abrupt negative suffix attached to the first base of *yodan* verbs. See p. 309 for further explanation.

III. AS USED WITH ADJECTIVES:

1. Eki wa *tooi kamo shiremasen.*	The station may be far.
2. Kore wa *oishikunai kamo shiremasen.*	This may not taste good.

In summary:

ADJECTIVE VERB NOUN	+ KAMO SHIREMASEN	=	maybe . . ., possibly . . .

***Note**: When there are two verbs in a sentence, i.e., one verb for the subordinate clause and another the principal, the first verb is given in an abrupt form and the final one in a polite form.

1. Nihon e *iku* hikooki de iki*masu*.
2. Katamichi kippu o *kau* nara oofuku kippu o kai*masu*.

STATE OF BEING, or the expression showing that something is (or was) in a certain condition, such as "the door was open," "the light is on," "the toy is broken," etc., indicates that the subject is in a certain condition, or a certain status has come about. "The door is in the state of having been opened," or "the book is in a torn condition" is expressed by the following constructions:

a. *transitive verb* + arimasu*
b. *intransitive verb + imasu*

Note that Japanese, unlike English, has transitive and intransitive forms of the same verb. For example, the verbs "to open," "to turn on (a light)," and "to break" have the following two forms:

to open	***akeru*** (transitive)—open something
	aku (intransitive)—"something" opens
to turn on	***tsukeru*** (transitive)—turn on something
	tsuku (intransitive)—"something" goes on
to break	***kowasu*** (transitive)—break something
	kowareru (intransitive)—"something" breaks

Usually, ***eru*** and ***su*** ending verbs are transitive. However, as in the last example, between *su* and ***eru***, ***su*** indicates the transitive verb ending. It must also be noted that some verbs are used only as transitive (***kaku, yomu,*** etc.) and some only as intransitive (***iku, neru,*** etc.).

Therefore using the "state of being" patterns given above, these 3 verbs can be expressed as follows:

a.	To wa *akete arimashita.* To wa *aite imashita.*	The door was open. (The door was in the state of having been opened.)
b.	Denki wa *tsukete arimasu.* Denki wa *tsuite imasu.*	The light is on. (The light is in the state of having been turned on.)
c.	Omocha wa *kowashite arimasu.* Omocha wa *kowarete imasu.*	The toy is broken. (The toy is in the state of having been broken.)

There is, however, difference in usage. When a *transitive verb + arimasu* form is used, the meaning implied is that the condition was intentionally

* See above p. 52 for explanation of transitive and intransitive verb.

brought about by the subject. "The door was left open for me (when I got home last night)," in contrast to "The door was open last night. Who forgot to close it?" The former sentence implies that some member of the family purposely left the door open for you, so the *transitive verb + arimasu (akete + arimashita)* is used, while the second sentence indicates the door was left open due to someone's negligence, so that *intransitive verb + imasu (aite + imashita)* must be used.

In this construction, though a transitive verb is used, the object of the verb is now the subject of the state of being that exists now. Therefore, it takes the nominative postposition *wa* or *ga*.

1. Tokei *o* naosu. Repair a watch.
   Tokei *wa* naoshite arimasu. The watch is repaired.
2. Jidoosha *o* tomeru. Stop a car.
   Jidoosha *ga* tomete aru. The car is stopped (parked).

Unintentional state of being construction is the same as the progressive form. The distinction must be made according to context.

In summary, one can say:

TRANSITIVE VERB + ARU *(naoshite aru)* INTRANSITIVE VERB + IRU *(naotte iru)*	}	STATE OF BEING
TRANSITIVE VERB + IRU *(naoshite iru)* INTRANSITIVE VERB + IRU *(naotte iru)*	}	PROGRESSIVE

TRANSITIVE AND INTRANSITIVE VERBS: The following is a list of some commonly used transitive verbs with their counterpart intransitive verbs. In using the transitive verb, bear in mind that this requires an object as "some action (transitive verb) is done to something or somebody (object)," while the intransitive verb implies "something happens (intransitive verb)."

TRANSITIVE	INTRANSITIVE
akeru—(open something)	aku—(open)
shimeru—(close something)	shimaru—(close)
waru—(break something)	wareru—(break)
tomeru—(stop something)	tomaru—(stop)
hajimeru—(begin something)	hajimaru—(begin)
ageru—(raise something)	agaru—(go up, rise)
tsuzukeru—(continue something)	tsuzuku—(continue)
ugokasu—(move something)	ugoku—(move)
dasu—(send, put out something)	deru—(go out)
okosu—(wake someone)	okiru—(get up)
otosu—(drop something)	ochiru—(drop, fall)
kakusu—(hide something)	kakureru—(hide)
naosu—(fix something)	naoru—(get better)
kowasu—(damage something)	kowareru—(break)
tsukeru—(attach something) (turn on something)	tsuku—(attach, go on)

Fluency Drill

Kippu o kaimashita.
Kisha no kippu o kaimashita.
Madoguchi de kisha no kippu o kaimashita.
Ni-ban no madoguchi de Kyooto-yuki no kisha no kippu o kaimashita.
Ni-ban no madoguchi de kisha no kippu to shindai-ken o kaimashita.
Ni-ban no madoguchi de kisha no kippu to shindai-ken o ni-mai kaimashita.
Kinoo ni-ban no madoguchi de kisha no kippu to shindai-ken o ni-mai sen go-hyaku en de kaimashita.

(I) bought a ticket.
(I) bought a train ticket.
At the window (I) bought a train ticket.
At window #2 (I) bought a train ticket for Kyoto.
At window #2 (I) bought a train ticket and pullman tickets.

At window #2 (I) bought a train ticket and two pullman tickets.
Yesterday at the window #2 (I) bought a train ticket and two pullman tickets for 1,500 yen.

Substitution Drill

("Te" Form of Transitive Verb)

AKETE NAOSHITE TABETE etc.	+	ARU

("Te" Form of Intransitive Verb)

HAJIMATTE NAOTTE KOWARETE etc.	+	IRU

Exercises

1. The door opens at 9:00.	To wa ku-ji ni akimasu.
2. I will open the door at 9:00.	Ku-ji ni to o akemasu.
3. The door is open.	To wa aite imasu. To wa akete arimasu.
4. The toy broke.	Omocha wa kowaremashita.
5. I broke the toy.	Omocha o kowashimashita.
6. The toy is broken.	Omocha wa kowarete imasu. Omocha wa kowashite arimasu.
7. The street car stops in front of the hotel.	Densha wa hoteru no mae de tomarimasu.
8. Please stop the car in front of the hotel.	Hoteru no mae de kuruma o tomete kudasai.
9. A car is stopped in front of the hotel.	Hoteru no mae ni kuruma ga tomatte imasu. Hoteru no mae ni kuruma ga tomete arimasu.

10. The class (*jugyoo*) begins at 8:00.	Jugyoo wa hachi-ji ni hajimarimasu.
11. The teacher begins the class at 8:00.	Sensei wa hachi-ji ni jugyoo o hajimemasu.
12. The class has begun (is in session).	Jugyoo wa hajimatte imasu.
13. I get up at 7:30 a.m.	Shichi-ji han ni okimasu.
14. The landlady (*obasan*) will wake the students.	Obasan wa gakusei o okoshimasu.
15. The students are up.	Gakusei wa okite imasu.
16. I write my name in Japanese.	Nihongo de namae o kakimasu.
17. I am writing my name in Japanese.	Nihongo de namae o kaite imasu.
18. My name is written in Japanese.	Nihongo de namae ga kaite arimasu.
19. It may be cold.	Samui kamo shiremasen.
20. It may not be far.	Tookunai kamo shiremasen.
21. He may not be a student.	Gakusei de nai kamo shiremasen.
22. He may be a Japanese.	Ano kata wa Nihonjin kamo shiremasen.
23. It may rain.	Ame ga furu kamo wakarimasen.
24. He may come.	Ano hito wa kuru kamo wakarimasen.
25. He may not come.	Ano hito wa konai kamo wakarimasen.
26. He may not go to Japan.	Ano hito wa Nihon e ikanai kamo wakarimasen.
27. I may go shopping.	Kaimono ni iku kamo wakarimasen.
28. I have time to watch T.V.	Terebi o miru hima ga arimasu.
29. I have time to play golf.	Gorufu o suru hima ga arimasu.
30. I do not have time to take a walk.	Sampo o suru hima ga arimasen.
31. I do not have time to read newspapers.	Shimbun o yomu hima ga arimasen.
32. I do not have time to shop.	Kaimono o suru hima ga arimasen.

Translate into Japanese:

1. If you buy a round trip ticket, it is cheaper.

   Note: cheaper—*motto yasui*

2. Because the eight o'clock Osaka-bound train is crowded, let's take the next train.

   Note: The verb "to take" has many uses in English. You *take* a vacation, a walk, a nap, a girl out, etc. In Japanese, *toru* simply means "to take something," so "to take a train or a cab"—*ni noru* is used.

3. The pullman tickets are sold out, so let's go by special express.

4. How many hours will it take by express train from here to Kobe?

   How many hours will it take by ordinary train?

5. The express is faster than the ordinary train. The special express is the fastest, but it doesn't stop at Atami.

6. Because I was late for (my) Japanese language class, I was scolded by my teacher.

7. The departure time of this plane is 6:15 a.m. and the arrival time at Haneda airport is noon.

   Note: noon—*shoogo;* airport—*hikoojoo*

8. You cannot take on your suitcase and trunk. You must check (them) after you buy the tickets.

9. a. Mr. Brown may be waiting *(matsu)* in the waiting room.

   b. This may be the dining car.

   c. The train may be late.

10. In order to go to Kobe, you must transfer at Osaka.

11. a. It is cloudy in the mountains.

    b. It is clear in the town.

    Note: (a) *kumoru* (v.i.) to become cloudy
    hareru (v.i.) to become clear
    (b) In these sentences "cloudy" and "clear" are referring to the state of condition.
    (c) "In the mountains" is expressed as *yama no hoo, hoo* showing "in the general direction of. . . ."

    c. The train is stopped at the railroad station.

    d. Your name is not written on this trunk.

    e. When I went to the bank it was already closed.

Imagine that you are a conductor of a train and the following questions are asked. How would you answer them in Japanese?

1. Kyuukoo to futsuu ressha dewa dochira ga hayai desu ka.
2. Tsugi no Kyooto-yuki no kisha wa nan-ji ni dete, nan-ji ni Kyooto ni tsukimasu ka.
3. Kono ressha ni shindai-sha to shokudoo-sha ga arimasu ka.
4. Kono ookii toranku o kisha no naka e mochi-konde mo ii desu ka.

   Note: *"te" verb + mo ii desu*—"It's all right if you . . .," "you may. . . ." (*Eigo o hanashite mo ii desu*—You may speak English.)
5. Kono kisha wa Nagoya ni tomarimasu ka. Nampunkan tomarimasu ka.
6. Hiroshima e iku no ni Oosaka de nori-kaenakereba narimasen ka.
7. Oosaka kara hachi-ji ni deru Hiroshima-yuki no kisha wa futsuu desu ka.
8. Futsuu nara noritaku arimasen kara tsugi no kyuukoo wa nan-ji desu ka.
9. Sono kyuukoo wa konde imasu ka. Kyuukoo-ken o kau koto ga dekimasu ka.
10. Oofuku kippu to katamichi kippu dewa dochira ga yasui desu ka.
11. Hachi-ji no Hiroshima-yuki no kisha wa nan-ji ni Hiroshima ni tsukimasu ka. Nan jikan kakarimasu ka.
12. Oosaka kara Hiroshima made hikooki de ikeba ikura desu ka.
13. Oosaka-eki kara hikoojoo made basu ga arimasu ka.
14. Tsugi no eki de (o)bentoo (box lunch) o kau koto ga dekimasu ka.
15. Kono kippu de tochuu gesha suru koto ga dekimasu ka.

    Note: *tochuu*—on the way, along the way
    tochuu gesha—get off the train before you reach the destination

You want to get the following information. How do you ask:

1. Whether there is a seat on the 9 o'clock train to Osaka.
2. Whether it is an ordinary train, express train, or special express.
3. What track the train leaves from.
4. How much a one-way ticket to Osaka is; how much a round-trip ticket costs.
5. At what ticket window you can buy a super express ticket to Osaka.
6. Whether you can get on this train from Yokohama, and how long this train stops there.

7. Whether you will have time to get off at Nagoya to buy lunch.
8. How much faster the special express train is than the express train.
9. The arrival time of this train in Osaka.
10. Whether this train has a pullman attached to it.
11. How much luggage you can carry on the train.
12. Whether there is a hotel near the Osaka station; how far it is from the station.
13. Whether you can get off the train at Nagoya and go on to Osaka the following morning with the ticket you have.
14. Whether there is a redcap because you have some luggage which you cannot carry yourself.

Useful Expressions

Feelings (Kimochi)

1. sabishii—lonely
   tanoshii—pleasant, delightful
   ureshii—happy
   kanashii—sad
   omoshiroi—interesting, funny, amusing

These expressions are all adjectives; therefore, the following adjectival endings are possible:

a. Watakushi wa sabishiku**nai** (arimasen) desu.
b. Kinoo wa taihen tanoshi**katta** desu.
c. Rainen Nihon e iku node ure**shii** desu.
d. Watakushi wa kanashi**ku** narimasu.
e. Tanaka-san wa omoshir**oi** hito desu.

The suffix *garu* can be added to adjectives without the "i," making them verbs. It is used in describing a person other than one's self to mean "to feel," "to get the feeling of . . .," "to feel a certain way."

sabishi + *garu*—feel lonely
tanoshi + *garu*—feel happy
ureshi + *garu*—feel happy

II. ai suru—to love
yorokobu—to be glad, rejoice, be happy
okoru—to be angry
naku—to cry
warau—to laugh
odoroku—to be surprised, astonished

These are conjugating verbs with the following common suffixes attached to different bases:

a. Haha wa taihen yoroko*bimashita.*
b. Watakushi wa okorita*kunai* desu.
c. Sensei ni wara*waremashita.*
d. Watakushi wa anata o ai *shite* imasu.

III. shimpai suru—to worry
anshin suru—to feel relieved (from worry)
gakkari suru—to be discouraged, disappointed

These verbs are Chinese verbs so they *all* conjugate by changing *suru.*

a. Chichi wa *shimpai shimashita* ga watakushi o miru to *anshin shimashita.*
b. Doozo *anshin shite kudasai.*
c. Shiken (examination) ni ochita (to fail) node *gakkari shimashita.*

CHAPTER 17

MOMOTARO

"TE" FORM OF VERB	+	AGERU / MORAU / KURERU	=	EXCHANGE OF FAVORS *(to do for you, for me, etc.)*
5th BASE of VERB	+	TO SURU	=	TRY TO. . . . ABOUT TO. . . .

KONO HANASHI WA YUUMEI NA NIHON NO KODOMO NO HANASHI DESU.	THIS IS A FAMOUS JAPANESE CHILDREN'S STORY.
NIHON NO KODOMO WA MINNA KONO HANASHI O SHITTE IMASU.	ALL THE JAPANESE CHILDREN KNOW THIS STORY.
1. MUKASHI, MUKASHI ARU TOKORO NI OJIISAN TO OBAASAN GA SUNDE IMASHITA.	LONG, LONG AGO AT A CERTAIN PLACE, THERE LIVED AN OLD MAN AND AN OLD WOMAN.
kodomo ga nai	there was no child
node	because
*kodomo ga nai node . . .	*because (they) did not have any children . . .
futari de	together

sabishiku	in loneliness
kurashite imashita	(they) were living

2. KODOMO GA NAI NODE FUTARI DE SABISHIKU KURASHITE IMASHITA. — HAVING NO CHILDREN, THEY LIVED TOGETHER IN LONELINESS.

3. MAINICHI OJIISAN WA YAMA E TAKIGI O TORI NI, OBAASAN WA KAWA E SENTAKU NI IKIMASHITA. — EVERY DAY THE OLD MAN (WENT) TO THE MOUNTAIN TO GATHER FIREWOOD, AND THE OLD WOMAN WENT TO THE RIVER TO WASH.

obaasan ga	old woman (nom. case)
kawa de	at the river
sentaku o shite iru to	when (she) was washing
*obaasan ga kawa de sentaku o shite iru to . . .	*when the old woman was washing at the river . . .
kawakami kara	from upstream
ookina momo ga	large peach (nom. case)
nagarete kimashita	came floating

4. ARU HI, OBAASAN GA KAWA DE SENTAKU O SHITE IRU TO, KAWAKAMI KARA OOKINA MOMO GA NAGARETE KIMASHITA. — ONE DAY WHEN THE OLD WOMAN WAS WASHING AT THE RIVER, A BIG PEACH CAME FLOATING FROM UPSTREAM.

5. OBAASAN WA SONO MOMO O HIROTTE, UCHI E KAERIMASHITA. — THE OLD WOMAN PICKED UP THAT PEACH AND TOOK IT HOME.

ojiisan ga	old man (nom. case)
yama kara	from the mountain
kaette kara	after returning
*ojiisan ga yama kara kaette kara . . .	*after the old man returned from the mountain . . .
obaasan ga	old woman (nom. case)
hoochoo de	with a knife
sono momo o	that peach
kiroo to suru to	tried to cut
*obaasan ga hoochoo de sono momo o kiroo to suru to . . .	*when the old woman tried to cut that peach with a knife . . .

6. OJIISAN GA YAMA KARA KAETTE KARA OBAASAN GA HOOCHOO DE SONO MOMO O *KIROO TO SURU* TO MOMO GA FUTATSU NI WARETE, NAKA KARA OOKINA OTOKO NO KO GA UMAREMASHITA.	AFTER THE OLD MAN RETURNED FROM THE MOUNTAIN, THE OLD WOMAN TRIED TO CUT THE PEACH WITH A KITCHEN KNIFE. THE PEACH SPLIT IN TWO, AND A BIG BOY WAS BORN FROM THE INSIDE.
7. OJIISAN TO OBAASAN WA TAISOO YOROKONDE, SONO KO NI MOMOTAROO TO IU NA O TSUKEMASHITA.	THE OLD MAN AND THE OLD WOMAN WERE OVERJOYED, AND NAMED THE CHILD "MOMOTARO."

daiji ni	carefully
sodateraremashita	was reared (passive)

8. MOMOTAROO WA DAIJI NI SODATERAREMASHITA.	MOMOTARO WAS BROUGHT UP WITH GREAT CARE.

9. MOMOTAROO WA DANDAN OOKIKU NATTE, TAISOO TSUYOKU NARIMASHITA.

HE GREW UP GRADUALLY, AND BECAME VERY STRONG.

hito o koroshitari	sometimes (they) killed people
mono o nusundari	sometimes (they) stole things
shita node	because (they) did (these things)

10. CHOODO SONO KORO ONI-GA-SHIMA KARA TOKIDOKI ONI GA KITE, HITO O KOROSHITARI MONO O NUSUNDARI SHITA NODE

JUST ABOUT THEN, OGRES CAME FROM OGRE ISLAND FROM TIME TO TIME, AND SOMETIMES KILLED PEOPLE AND STOLE THINGS,

11. HITOBITO WA KANEMOCHI MO BIMBOONIN MO, OTONA MO KODOMO MO MINNA TAISOO KOMATTE IMASHITA.

SO THE PEOPLE, RICH AS WELL AS POOR, GROWNUPS AS WELL AS CHILDREN, WERE ALL GREATLY DISTRESSED.

soko de	whereupon
Momotaroo wa	Momotaro (nom. case)
oni o	ogres (obj. case)
seibatsu shiyoo to omotte	thinking of conquering

12. SOKO DE MOMOTAROO WA ONI O SEIBATSU *SHIYOO TO OMOTTE,* OJIISAN TO OBAASAN NI HANASHIMASHITA.

THEREUPON, MOMOTARO, THINKING OF CONQUERING THE OGRES, TALKED TO THE OLD MAN AND THE OLD WOMAN.

futari wa	two (nom. case)
taihen yorokonde	to be very happy and
*futari wa taihen yorokonde . . .	*two were very happy and . . .
obaasan wa	old woman (nom. case)
Momotaroo ni	to Momotaro
kibidango o	dumpling (obj. case)
koshiraete yarimashita	made and gave (to him)

13. FUTARI WA TAIHEN YOROKONDE, OBAASAN WA MOMOTAROO NI KIBIDANGO O *KOSHIRAETE YARIMASHITA*. — THE TWO WERE VERY PLEASED, AND THE OLD WOMAN MADE SOME "KIBIDANGO" FOR HIM.

14. MOMOTAROO GA SASSOKU SHITAKU O SHITE SUKOSHI YUKU TO, — MOMOTARO MADE IMMEDIATE PREPARATIONS AND WHEN HE WENT A SHORT DISTANCE,

15. INU GA KITE . . . — A DOG CAME AND . . .

tsuzuku—to be continued

Vocabulary List from the Lesson

hanashi	(n.)	story, *hanashi o suru* (Chi. v.)—to tell a story
mukashi	(n.)	long time ago
aru		certain; *aru* + noun, *aru hito*—a certain person
aru tokoro ni		at a certain place
futari de		by two, together
kurasu	(v.)	to live, earn one's living, spend one's time (distinguish between *sumu*—to reside)

kurashite imashita	(past progressive) was living
aru hi	one day
takigi	(n.) firewood
toru	(v.t.) to take, gather
tori ni	in order to gather
sentaku (mono)	(n.) washing
sentaku o suru	(Chi. v.) to wash (clothing)
sentaku ni	(same as *sentaku o shi ni*) for the purpose of washing
kawakami	(n.) upstream
ookina	(adj.) same as *ookii*. (Other true adjectives, besides *ookii* and *chiisai,* do not appear in this form. Hence, *chiisana* is all right, but don't use this for other form adjectives.)
nagareru	(v.i.) to flow
nagarete kimashita	came floating
hirou	(v.t.) to pick up, find, gather
hirotte	("te" form of *hirou,* used conjunctively)—picked up and . . .
hoochoo	(n.) kitchen knife
kiru	(v.t.) to cut (though it has an "iru" ending, it is a conjugating verb)
kiroo to suru	try to cut (See I.C. & G.N.)
wareru	(v.i.) . . . *ga wareru:* to split, crack, break
warete	("te" form of *wareru*). broke and . . .
otoko	(n.) male, man
otoko no ko	(n.) a boy
taisoo	very, very much
taisoo yorokonde	rejoiced very much and. . . . were overjoyed and
tsukeru	(v.t.) to attach, to put
na o tsukeru	(idio.) to name; literally, to attach a name, give a name
daiji	(n.) a matter of great importance, grave, serious

daiji ni	(adv.) with great care
sodateru	(v.t.) to raise, rear, bring up
sodateraremashita	(past passive of *sodateru*) was brought up
dan-dan	gradually, by degrees, step by step, little by little, increasingly, more and more
tsuyoi	(adj.) strong
tsuyoku	(adverbial form of *tsuyoi*)
choodo	exactly, just
oni	(n.) ogre
Oni-ga-Shima	(n.) Ogre Island
korosu	(v.t.) to kill
koroshitari	(alternate action form of *korosu;* see p. 275)
nusumu	(v.t.) to steal
nusundari	(alternate action form of *nusumu;* see p. 275)
hito	(n.) a person, people
hitobito	(n.) people (plural)
bimboonin	(n.) same as *bimboo na hito*—a poor person, opposite of *kanemochi*——rich man
otona	(n.) an adult, a fully grown person as contrasted with *kodomo*—child
komaru	(v.i.) to be inconvenienced, to be troubled, to be distressed
komatte imashita	(state of being form of *komaru,* see p. 293)
soko de	thereupon
seibatsu suru	(Chi. v., archaic) to exterminate, conquer, subjugate
seibatsu shiyoo to omotte	thinking of exterminating, wanting to subjugate (See I.C. & G.N.)
kibidango	(n.) a kind of dumpling

yaru	(v.t.) *ni yaru,* or *ni. . . . o yaru*—to give to . . . (See I.C. & G.N.)
yarimashita	(pol. past of *yaru*) gave
shitaku	(n.) preparation
shitaku o suru	(Chi. v.) to prepare

Important Construction and Grammar Notes

"NAI," THE ABRUPT NEGATIVE SUFFIX: This can be derived by changing the . . . **masen** endings to . . . **nai,** and the . . . **masen deshita** endings to . . . **nakatta.** The abrupt negative endings are attached to the first or the negative base of the *yodan* verbs. With *ichidan* verbs, use the stem. The bases for **suru** and **kuru** are **shi** . . . and **ko**. . . . Hence:

	POLITE NEGATIVE	ABRUPT NEGATIVE
1. yomu	yomi*masen*	yoma*nai* (1st base + **nai**)
2. taberu	tabe*masen*	tabe*nai* (stem + **nai**)
3. suru	shi*masen*	shi*nai*
4. kuru	ki*masen*	ko*nai*
1. yomu	yomi*masen deshita*	yoma*nakatta* (1st base + **nakatta**)
2. taberu	tabe*masen deshita*	tabe*nakatta* (stem + **nakatta**)
3. suru	shi*masen deshita*	shi*nakatta*
4. kuru	ki*masen deshita*	ko*nakatta*

There is no difference in meaning between the two—just the difference in the degree of politeness intended.

With the verb *aru, nai* is its opposite. *Aru ka nai ka* . . . : "whether there is, or whether there is not. . . ."

Note that the first base of double vowel ending verbs will be *wa* instead of a single *a,* as in the case of most *yodan* verbs (c.v.).

```
             WA+NAI=kawanai                 WA+NAI=arawanai
             i                              i
kau=KA+u                      arau=ARA+u
             e                              e
             o                              o
```

USE OF 5th BASE TO MEAN "TRIED TO . . .," "ABOUT TO. . . ."—5th base of the verb can be used to give the following different meanings:

I. The abrupt future of the *yodan* verbs is what would be the 5th base with the long final vowel.

iku	**ikoo**	(let us go)
kaeru	kae**roo**	(let us go home)

With the *ichidan* verbs (n.c.v.), the stem plus **yoo**:

taberu	tabe**yoo**	(let us eat)
neru	ne**yoo**	(let us sleep)
miru	mi**yoo**	(let us look)

The abrupt future of *suru—shiyoo;* of *kuru—koyoo.*

II. When **to omou** is added to the abrupt future of a verb, the combination expresses the idea: "thinking of doing something . . .," "with the intention of. . . ."

5th BASE OF VERB + TO OMOU

1. Watakushi wa kaimono o *shiyoo to omotte* depaato e ikimashita.	Thinking of doing some shopping, I went to a department store.
2. Watakushi wa Chicago e *ikoo to omotte* kisha ni norimashita.	Thinking of going to Chicago, I boarded a train.

III. When **to suru** is added to the abrupt future of a verb, the combination expresses the idea that the act is attempted: "tried to. . . ."

5th BASE OF VERB + TO SURU

1. *Kiroo to shita.*	He tried to cut (it).
2. Doroboo wa uchi e *hairoo to shimashita.*	The thief tried to enter the house.
3. Otoko no ko wa *okashi o toroo* to shimashita.	The boy tried to take the candy.

IV. 5th base of the verb + **to suru** also has the meaning of an act about to be done: "just about to. . . ." Often this usage can be interpreted as the same as "tried to. . . ." mentioned above. The distinction between "tried to. . ." and "about to. . . ." must be made from context.

1. Uchi o *deyoo to suru* to tomodachi ga kimashita.	When I was just about to leave the house, a friend came.
2. Denwa o *shiyoo to shita* toki ni, Brown-san ga kimashita.	When I was just about to telephone, Mr. Brown came.

AGERU (YARU), MORAU (ITADAKU), KURERU (KUDASARU):

I. AGERU, "to give," is used when (1) the recipient is equal to, or (2) superior in social status to the giver, or (3) when expression of courtesy is felt necessary toward the receiver (see diagram below). Also, in common usage, *ageru* (and *itadaku,* explained in the next section) is used merely to make the entire statement more polite. *YARU* also has the same meaning, but the giving is done to someone equal to or lower in social status than the giver—to hand *down* to someone, or to animals or inanimate things.

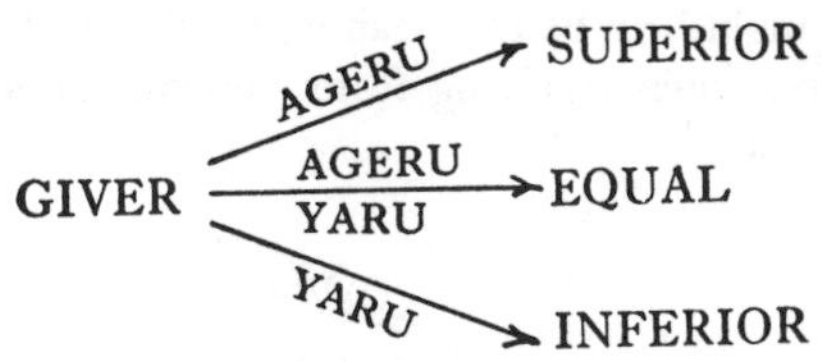

. . . OBJECT (what) O (to whom) NI < AGERU / YARU

1.	Watakushi wa	kono jibiki	O	sensei	NI	AGEMASU.
2.	Sensei wa	hookokusho	O	koochoo	NI	AGEMASHITA.
	(The teacher	report		to the principal		gave.)
3.		Kono sakana	O	neko	NI	YARU.

In sentence 1, jibiki is the direct object, sensei is the indirect object; therefore, note the postpositions NI and O. This word order can be reversed.

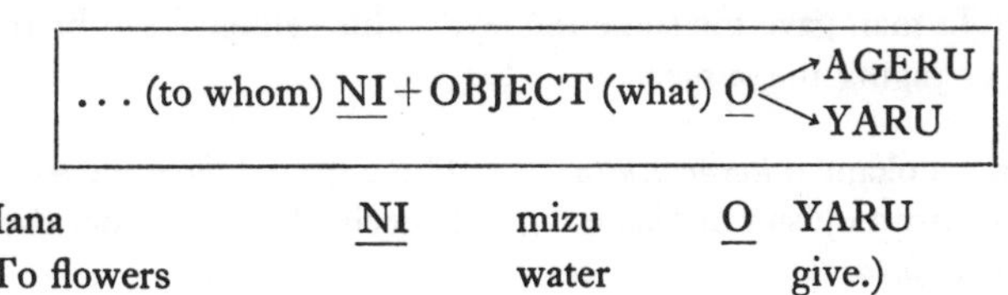

4.	Hana	NI	mizu	O	YARU
	(To flowers		water		give.)

II. MORAU (ITADAKU), "to receive." When (1) something is received from someone equal to or (2) superior to the receiver in social status, or (3) to express the feeling of gratitude in receiving something, ITADAKU is used. MORAU, as shown in the diagram, is used between equals, or when the subject receives from an inferior.

1. Watakushi wa Kurisumasu (Christmas) ni Suzuki-san kara (ni) rekoodo (record) o *itadakimashita.*
2. Anata wa otootosan kara (ni) nani o *moraimashita* ka.

III. KURERU means "give," but the recipient is in the *first person only.* "Gives to me" might be a better meaning for this verb. *KUDASARU* is the more polite form, when receiving from someone superior in status to you (see diagram below).

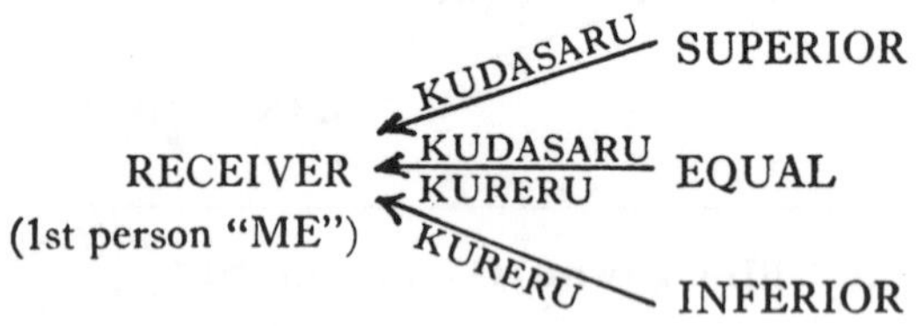

1. Sensei wa jibiki o *kudasaimashita* (see below).	(The) teacher gave me a dictionary.
2. Otooto wa Kabuki no kippu o *kuremashita.*	My brother gave me a Kabuki ticket.

Since *kureru* is used only when the first person is the recipient, it is not necessary to translate "me."

"The old man gave me some money." This sentence can be translated as follows, changing the subject:

1. Ojiisan wa okane o *kuremashita.*	The old man gave me some money.
2. Watakushi wa ojiisan ni okane o *moraimashita.*	I received money from the old man.

Kudasaru is the polite form of *kureru,* and is used in the same way. This verb conjugates as follows:

```
              ra
              *RI + MASU
kudasa  +     ru
              re
```

*However, in speaking, the "*r*" in *kudasarimasu* is dropped, and it is now pronounced *kudasaimasu.*

EXCHANGE OF FAVORS: When a favor is done for another, or when the subject receives a favor, the following formula is used:

```
                ⎧AGERU (YARU)
                ⎪     or
"TE" VERB  +    ⎨MORAU (ITADAKU)
                ⎪     or
                ⎩KURERU (KUDASARU)
```

1. I will wait for you.
2. Dad bought the car for me.
3. Mr. Tanaka had a letter translated by my teacher.

These expressions indicate an act where a favor was exchanged:

1. I will do you the favor of waiting.
2. Dad did me the favor of buying a car.
3. Mr. Tanaka received a favor from my teacher by having a letter translated.

1. Watakushi wa *matte agemasu.*
2. Chichi wa jidoosha o *katte kuremashita.*
   Watakushi wa chichi ni jidoosha o *katte moraimashita.*
   (I, from my father, received the favor of car-buying.)
3. Tanaka-san wa sensei ni tegami o *yakushite moraimashita.* (*yakusu*—to translate)

Fluency Drill

I

Akete arimasu.

Mado ga akete arimasu.

Ni-kai no mado ga akete arimasu.

Ni-kai no ookii mado ga akete arimasu.

Atsui kara ni-kai no ookii mado ga akete arimasu.

Kyoo wa atsui kara ni-kai no ookii mado ga akete arimasu.

Senshuu kara atsui node ni-kai no ookii mado ga akete arimasu.

Senshuu no Kinyoo kara atsui node ni-kai no ookii mado ga akete arimasu.

Senshuu no Kinyoo kara atsui node ni-kai no ookii mado ga anata no tame ni akete arimasu.

Note: . . .*no tame ni*—for (the sake of) . . .

It is open.

The window is open.

The upstairs window is open.

The large upstairs window is open.

Because it is hot, the large upstairs window is open.

Because it is hot today, the large upstairs window is open.

Because it has been hot since last week, the large upstairs window is open.

Because it has been hot since Friday of last week, the large upstairs window is open.

Because it has been hot since Friday of last week, the large upstairs window is open for you.

II

Yonde agemasu.

Hon o yonde agemasu.

Anata ni kono hon o yonde agemasu.

Komban anata ni kono hon o yonde agemasu.

Watakushi wa komban anata ni kono hon o yonde agemasu.

(I) will read (for you).
(I) will read a book (for you).
(I) will read this book for you.
(I) will read this book for you tonight.
I will read this book for you tonight.

III

Katte kuremasu.
Terebi o katte kuremasu.
Chichi wa terebi o katte kuremasu.
Chichi wa Kurisumasu ni terebi o katte kuremasu.

(He) will buy (for me)
(He) will buy a T.V. (for me).
My father will buy a T.V. (for me).
My father will buy a T.V. (for me) on Christmas.

IV

Katte moraimasu.
Terebi o katte moraimasu.
Ano hito wa terebi o katte moraimasu.
Ano hito wa otoosan ni terebi o katte moraimasu.
Ano hito wa otoosan ni, Kurisumasu ni terebi o katte moraimasu.

(He) will receive (the favor of) buying.
(He) will receive (the favor of) buying a T.V. set.
He will receive (the favor of) buying a T.V. set.
He will receive (the favor of) buying a T.V. set from his father.
He will receive (the favor) of buying a T.V. set from his father on Christmas.
(He will have his father buy a T.V. set for him on Christmas.)

Substitution Drill

("Te" Verb)

YONDE KAITE KATTE KITE etc.	+	AGERU MORAU KURERU

(5th Base Verb)

IKOO HANASOO HAIROO TABEYOO etc.	+	TO SURU

Exercises

Practice translating English to Japanese, Japanese to English:

In the following 15 sentences, interpret them as exchange of favor construction:

1. I will read this letter (for you).	Kono tegami o yonde agemasu.
2. I will do the work (for you).	Shigoto o shite agemasu.
3. I will write the kanji (for you).	Kanji o kaite agemasu.
4. I will send this package (for you).	Kono kozutsumi o okutte agemasu.
5. I will buy a dictionary (for you).	Jibiki o katte agemasu.
6. I had him read the letter (for me).	Ano hito ni tegami o yonde moratta. Ano hito wa tegami o yonde kureta.
7. I had him do the work (for me).	Ano hito ni shigoto o shite moratta. Ano hito wa shigoto o shite kureta.
8. I had him write the kanji (for me).	Ano hito ni kanji o kaite moratta. Ano hito wa kanji o kaite kureta.
9. I had him send the package (for me).	Ano hito ni kozutsumi o okutte moratta. Ano hito wa kozutsumi o okutte kureta.

10. I had him buy a dictionary (for me).	Ano hito ni jibiki o katte moratta. Ano hito wa jibiki o katte kureta.
11. He read the letter (for me).	Ano hito ni tegami o yonde moratta. Ano hito wa tegami o yonde kureta.
12. He will do the work (for me).	Ano hito ni shigoto o shite morau. Ano hito wa shigoto o shite kureru.
13. He will write the kanji (for me).	Ano hito ni kanji o kaite morau. Ano hito wa kanji o kaite kureru.
14. He will send this package (for me).	Ano hito ni kozutsumi o okutte morau. Ano hito wa kozutsumi o okutte kureru.
15. He will buy a dictionary (for me).	Ano hito ni jibiki o katte morau. Ano hito wa jibiki o katte kureru.
16. I am thinking of going to Japan.	Nihon e ikoo to omotte imasu.
17. I am thinking of selling my car.	Kuruma o uroo to omotte imasu.
18. I am thinking of writing a book.	Hon o kakoo to omotte imasu.
19. I have thought of becoming a teacher.	Sensei ni naroo to omoimashita.
20. I have thought of quitting my job.	Shigoto o yameyoo to omoimashita.
21. The dog tried to eat the meat.	Inu wa niku o tabeyoo to shita.
22. The man tried to enter the house.	Otoko no hito wa ie ni hairoo to shita.
23. I tried to read his letter.	Ano kata no tegami o yomoo to shita.
24. The thief tried to sell the car.	Doroboo wa kuruma o uroo to shita.
25. The policeman was about to shoot the thief.	Junsa wa doroboo o utoo to shita.
26. When I was about to leave the house . . .	Ie o deyoo to shita toki . . .
27. When I was about to eat supper . . .	Bangohan o tabeyoo to shita toki . . .
28. When I was about to get on the train . . .	Kisha ni noroo to shita toki . . .
29. When I was about to get off the streetcar . . .	Densha o oriyoo to shita toki . . .

30. When I was about to show my ticket . . . | Kippu o miseyoo to shita toki . . .

Translate into Japanese:

1. Because my parents moved to Tokyo, I am living with my older sister, and I am lonesome. (In the principal clause consider "lonesome" as an adverb so this sentence should be translated as follows: ". . . I, with my older sister, am lonesomely living.")
2. The train ticket which you picked up was the one I lost.
3. When I tried to buy a new car, my father opposed me.
4. This puppy was weak when he was born, but (it) gradually became strong.
5. In America both the rich and the poor can enter college if (they) study hard.
6. Because the teacher's wallet (*saifu*) was stolen, (he) is in trouble.
7. Have you ever eaten "kibidango?" No, I have never eaten it, but I would like to eat it once.
8. Why did Momotaro leave the old man and the old lady's home? He thought of exterminating the ogres.
9. When I was just about to (go to) sleep, the telephone rang *(naru)*.
10. Use the abrupt form:

    a. do not cut
    b. did not cut
    c. want to cut
    d. wanted to cut

Answer in Japanese:

1. Jibun no kotoba de, Momotaroo no hanashi o shite kudasai:

   Note: (a) *jibun*—oneself, himself *jibun no kotoba*—one's own words
   jibun no shigoto—one's own work
   Ano otoko no ko wa *jibun de* tabemasu.
   (That boy eats by himself.)
   (b) *hanashi*—(noun) a story
   hanashi o suru—to tell a story
2. Naze ojiisan to obaasan wa sabishiku kurashite imashita ka.
3. Ojiisan no shigoto wa nan deshita ka. Obaasan no shigoto mo onaji deshita ka.
4. Anata ga ima sunde iru tokoro wa gakkoo no chikaku desu ka.
5. Anata wa jibun de sentaku o shimasu ka. Sentakuya e motte ikimasu ka.
6. Oni-ga-Shima ni sunde ita oni wa donna warui koto o shimashita ka.
7. Momotaroo ga oni o seibatsu shi ni iku to ojiisan to obaasan ni hanashita toki, futari wa hantai shimashita ka. Naze hantai shimasen deshita ka.

8. Anata wa doko *de* umarete, doko *ni* sunde imasu ka. Doko *e* Nihongo o benkyoo shi ni ikimasu ka.
9. Anata wa eiga e iku toki, itsu mo hitori de ikimasu ka. Tomodachi to ikimasu ka.

   Note: *hitori de*—literally by one person or alone
   tomodachi to—*to* means "together with," e.g.,
   "I will go to Japan *with* my father."
   Watakushi wa *chichi to* Nihon e ikimasu.
10. Naze ojiisan to obaasan wa kono otoko no ko ni Momotaroo to iu namae o tsukemashita ka.

I. Make the (a) *abrupt negative,* (b) *abrupt negative past,* (c) *polite negative past,* of the following:

Example: (O)kane o yarimasu.
(a) (O)kane o yara*nai.*
(b) (O)kane o yara*nakatta.*
(c) (O)kane o yari*masen deshita.*

1. Watakushi wa washoku o tabetai desu.
2. Gogo sampo ni dekakemashita.
3. Kyooto de futsuka tomaru tsumori desu.
4. Hyaku en de kono jibiki ga kaemasu.
5. Ano hito wa Nihongo o hanasu koto ga dekiru.
6. Sakuban shibai e iku koto ga dekita.
7. Gakkoo made sambyaku en kakatta.
8. Kyooto wa tooi desu.
9. Kurisumasu ni rajio o katte kureta.
10. Tookyoo de Kabuki o miru koto ga dekimashita.
11. Nihongo ga kaite arimasu.
12. Watakushi wa gunjin ni naritai.

II. Make the *past* of the following, and the *negative past* wherever possible:

1. Hayaku okite sampo o shimasu.
2. Koohii (coffee) o nomitai.
3. Kono tokei wa takai desu.
4. Nan-ji ni dekakemasu ka.
5. Maiban benkyoo shimasen.
6. Amai (sweet) mono o tabetaku naru.

7. (O)kane ga nai kara asobanai.
8. Kono hana o motte kaeru.

Miscellaneous Useful Expressions

The following super polite expressions #1–6 will be explained later on p. 344 so here commit to memory as idiomatic expressions.

1. OMEDETOO (gozaimasu) —Congratulations!
   SOTSUGYOO, OMEDETOO —Graduation congratulations!
   GO-KEKKON, OMEDETOO —Wedding congratulations!
2. MATA IRASSHAI—Come again.
   DOOZO MATA IRASHITE KUDASAI (more polite)
3. YOKU IRASSHAIMASHITA—Welcome! I'm happy you came.
4. MATA O-ME NI KAKARIMASU—I'll see you again.
   ASHITA O-ME NI KAKARIMASU—I'll see you tomorrow.
   DEWA MATA (o-me ni kakarimasu)—I'll see you again.
5. O-KI O TSUKETE ITTE IRASSHAI—(literally, "be careful and go")
   Take care of yourself.
   O-GENKI DE ITTE IRASSHAI—(Literally, "in fine spirits, go")
   Both of these expressions are used as a parting comment wishing safe return, or in the same sense as "Bon Voyage!"

   Note: KI O TSUKERU—to be careful, to pay attention
   KI O TSUKETE KUDASAI—Please be careful.
   KI O TSUKENASAI—Be careful!
   ABUNAI (desu)—It's dangerous, look out!
6. O-MATASE ITASHIMASHITA—Sorry, I made you wait!
7. DAME DESU—no good, bad. This expression has wide usage, expressing general disapproval.
   ANO HITO WA DAME DESU.
   KONO MONO WA DAME DESU.
   ASHITA WA DAME DESU.
8. DOCHIRA DEMO KEKKOO DESU.—Either one is all right.
   DOCHIRA DEMO KAMAIMASEN.—Either one is all right.

CHAPTER 18

MOMOTARO (*continued*)

4th BASE OF VERB + BA	= IF. . . . *(conditional form)*

1. "MOMOTAROO-SAN, MOMOTAROO-SAN, DOKO E IRASSHAIMASU KA."	"MOMOTARO, WHERE ARE YOU GOING?"
2. "ONI-GA-SHIMA E ONI O SEIBATSU NI. . . ."	"TO OGRE ISLAND TO CONQUER THE OGRES."
3. "(O)KOSHI NI TSUKETA MONO WA NAN DESU KA."	"THAT THING WHICH IS ATTACHED TO YOUR WAIST, WHAT IS IT?"
4. "NIHON-ICHI NO KIBIDANGO."	"THE BEST KIBIDANGO IN JAPAN."
5. "HITOTSU KUDASAREBA (O)TOMO SHIMASHOO."	"IF YOU GIVE ME ONE, I WILL ACCOMPANY YOU."
6. MOMOTAROO WA INU NI KIBIDANGO O HITOTSU YARIMASHITA.	MOMOTARO GAVE ONE KIBIDANGO TO THE DOG.

INU WA YOROKONDE KERAI NI NARIMASHITA.	THE DOG HAPPILY BECAME (HIS) FOLLOWER.
7. SOREKARA MOMOTAROO TO INU GA SUKOSHI IKU TO SARU NI AIMASHITA. SARU WA INU TO ONAJI KOTO O KIKIMASHITA. SOOSHITE SARU MO KERAI NI NARIMASHITA.	AFTER THAT, WHEN MOMOTARO AND THE DOG WENT A LITTLE (WAY) THEY MET A MONKEY. THE MONKEY ASKED THE SAME THING AS THE DOG. AND THE MONKEY BECAME A FOLLOWER ALSO.
8. TSUGI NI KIJI MO KIBIDANGO O MORATTE KERAI NI NARIMASHITA. MOMOTAROO WA INU, SARU, KIJI O TSURETE ONI-GA-SHIMA NI TSUKIMASHITA.	NEXT, A PHEASANT, AFTER RECEIVING THE KIBIDANGO, BECAME HIS FOLLOWER, TOO. MOMOTARO ACCOMPANIED BY A DOG, A MONKEY, AND A PHEASANT, ARRIVED AT OGRE ISLAND.

Momotaroo ga	Momotaro (nom. case)
kuru no o	coming (obj. case)
mite	seeing
*Momotaroo ga kuru no o mite . . .	*seeing Momotaro come . . .
mon o	gate (obj. case)
shimemashita	closed
node	so
*mon o shimemashita node . . .	*because they closed the gate. . . .
naka ni	inside
hairu koto ga dekimasen deshita	was not able to enter

9. ONITACHI WA MOMOTAROO GA KURU *NO O* MITE, MON O SHIMEMASHITA NODE NAKA NI HAIRU KOTO GA DEKIMASEN DESHITA.	THE OGRES, UPON SEEING THE COMING OF MOMOTARO, CLOSED THE GATE SO (THEY) WERE UNABLE TO GO INSIDE.

soko de	whereupon
kiji wa	pheasant (nom. case)
tonde itte	went flying
*soko de kiji wa tonde itte . . .	*whereupon the pheasant went flying and . . .
teki no yoosu o	enemy's condition (obj. case)
shirabemashita	examined
*teki no yoosu o shirabemashita	*he examined the enemy's condition

10. SOKO DE KIJI WA TONDE ITTE TEKI NO YOOSU O SHIRABEMASHITA.	WHEREUPON, THE PHEASANT FLEW IN AND OBSERVED THE ENEMY'S CONDITION.

saru wa	monkey (nom. case)
mon o nobotte	climbed the gate
*saru wa mon o nobotte . . .	*monkey climbed the gate and . . .
naka e	inside
hairi	entered and . . .
*naka e hairi . . .	*(he) entered inside and . . .
mon o	gate
akemashita	opened

SARU WA MON O NOBOTTE NAKA E HAIRI MON O AKEMASHITA.	THE MONKEY CLIMBED THE GATE, WENT INSIDE, AND OPENED THE GATE.
11. MOMOTAROO TO INU WA	MOMOTARO, TOGETHER

ISSHO NI SEME-KOMIMA-SHITA. KIJI WA TOBI-MA-WATTE ONI NO ME O TSUTSUKIMASHITA. SARU WA ONI O HIKKAKIMA-SHITA.	WITH THE DOG, ATTACKED. THE PHEASANT FLEW AROUND AND PECKED (AT) THE OGRES' EYES. THE MON-KEY SCRATCHED THE OGRES.
12. INU WA ONI NI KAMI-TSUKIMASHITA. MOMO-TAROO WA ONI NO TAI-SHOO TO TATAKAIMASHI-TA.	THE DOG BIT THE OGRES. MOMOTARO FOUGHT WITH THE LEADER OF THE OGRES.

Momotaroo wa	Momotaro (nom. case)
taihen tsuyoi node	because (he) was very strong
oni no taishoo wa	leader of the ogres
tootoo	finally
koosan shimashita	surrendered

13. MOMOTAROO WA TAIHEN TSUYOI NODE ONI NO TAISHOO WA TOOTOO KOOSAN SHIMASHITA.	MOMOTARO WAS SO STRONG THAT THE LEADER OF THE OGRES FINALLY SURREN-DERED.

moo	anymore
kesshite	never
warui koto o shimasen	will not do bad things
kara	because
*moo kesshite warui koto o shimasen kara . . .	*because (we) will never do any more bad things . . .
yurushite kudasai	please pardon us

14. ONI NO TAISHOO WA "MOO KESSHITE WARUI KOTO O SHIMASEN KARA YURUSHITE KUDASAI" TO ITTE IRO-IRO NA TAKARAMONO O DASHITE TANOMIMASHITA. MOMOTAROO WA ONI O YURUSHITE YARIMASHITA.

THE LEADER PLEADED, "PLEASE FORGIVE ME, FOR I WILL NEVER DO ANYTHING WRONG AGAIN," AND PRODUCED VARIOUS TREASURES. MOMOTARO FORGAVE THE OGRES.

inu ga	dog (nom. case)
sono kuruma o	the cart (obj. case)
hiki	pulled
*inu ga sono kuruma o hiki . . .	*the dog pulled the cart and . . .
saru ga	monkey (nom. case)
ato o	behind (obj. case)
oshite	pushed
*saru ga ato o oshite . . .	*the monkey pushed (from behind) and . . .
kiji wa	pheasant (nom. case)
tsuna o	rope (obj. case)
hikimashita	pulled

15. TAKARAMONO O TAKUSAN KURUMA NI TSUNDE DEKAKEMASHITA. INU GA SONO KURUMA O HIKI, SARU GA ATO O OSHITE, KIJI WA TSUNA O HIKIMASHITA.

(THEY) LOADED MANY TREASURES ON THE CART AND STARTED OFF. THE DOG PULLED THE CART, THE MONKEY PUSHED (IT) AND THE PHEASANT PULLED THE ROPE.

ojiisan to obaasan wa	old man and old woman (nom. case)
Momotaroo no rusuchuu	during Momotaro's absence
shimpai shimashita	worried
*ojiisan to obaasan wa Momotaroo no rusuchuu taihen shimpai shimashita ga . . .	*the old man and old woman were greatly worried during Momotaro's absence but . . .
Momotaroo ga	Momotaro (nom. case)
kaette kuru no o	his return (obj. case)
miru to	when (they) saw
*Momotaroo ga kaette kuru no o miru to . . .	*when they saw Momotaro coming home . . .
taihen yorokobimashita	greatly rejoiced

16. OJIISAN TO OBAASAN WA MOMOTAROO NO RUSUCHUU TAIHEN SHIMPAI SHIMASHITA GA MOMOTAROO GA KAETTE KURU *NO O* MIRU TO TAIHEN YOROKOBIMASHITA.	THE OLD MAN AND OLD WOMAN WERE VERY WORRIED DURING MOMOTARO'S ABSENCE, BUT WHEN (THEY) SAW MOMOTARO'S RETURN THEY WERE VERY HAPPY.
17. SOREKARA MINNA KOOFUKU NI KURASHIMASHITA.	AFTER THAT EVERYONE LIVED HAPPILY.

Vocabulary from the Lesson

irassharu (v.i.) to go, to come, superpolite form (see page 358)

irasshaimasu (v.i.) superpolite, present form of *irassharu.* Corrupt form of *irasshari* + *masu.*

koshi (n.) waist

(o)koshi (n.) *o* is the honorific prefix.

mono (n.) (concrete) thing

Nihon-ichi (n.) number one in Japan; the best in Japan, equivalent to *Nihon de ichiban.* Also, *sekai-ichi no dai-tokai* (largest city in the world); *Tookyoo-ichi no gekijoo* (the best theater in Tokyo)

kudasareba (conditional form of *kudasaru*—give me) if you give me (See I.C. & G.N.)

(o)tomo suru (Chi. v.) to accompany

kerai (n.) follower, servant

saru (n.) monkey

onaji (n.) same (used as an adjective—*onaji hito,* same person; *onaji toki,* same time)

koto (n.) (abstract) thing

sorekara and then

sukoshi few (in quantity)

kiji (n.) pheasant

tsureru (tsurete) (v.t.) to take (someone) along (. . . *e tsurete iku,* to take someone to; . . . *o tsurete iku,* to take someone; . . . *tsurete kaeru,* to take someone home.)

mon (n.) gate

sokode whereupon

tobu (v.i.) to fly

teki (n.) enemy

yoosu (n.) condition, appearance

shiraberu (v.t.) to investigate, research

shirabemashita (pol. past of *shiraberu*) investigated

noboru (v.t.) to climb

nobotte ("te" form of *noboru* used connectively) . . . climbed and . . .

semeru (v.t.) to attack

seme-komu (v.t.) to attack and enter

seme-komimashita (pol. past of *semekomu*)

mawaru (v.i.) to turn, to go around

me (n.) eyes

tsutsuku (v.t.) to peck

tsutsukimashita (pol. past of *tsuttsuku*) pecked

hikkaku (v.t.) to scratch (maliciously)

hikkakimashita (pol. past of *hikkaku*) scratched

kami-tsuku (v.t.) to bite, causing harm (usually by animals, *kamu*—to bite)

kami-tsukimashita (pol. past of *kamitsuku*) bit

taishoo (n.) leader, head, or general

koosan suru (Chi. v.) to surrender

kesshite (adv.) never . . . (always used with negative verb)

yurusu (v.t.) to forgive, . . . *o yurusu,* to forgive someone.

yurushite kudasai ("te" form of *yurusu* + *kudasai*) please forgive me

dasu (v.t.) to put out, produce

dashite ("te" form of *dasu* used connectively) produced and . . .

tanomu (v.t.) to request (someone) *ni* (about) *o tanomu*

tanomimashita (pol. past of *tanomu*)

kuruma (n.) general term for vehicle—car, cart, etc.

tsumu (v.t.) to load, (vehicle) *ni* (object) *o tsumu*

tsunde ("te" form of *tsumu* used connectively) loaded and . . .

dekakeru (v.i.) to leave for, *sampo ni dekakeru*

dekakemashita (pol. past of *dekakeru*) started (for)

hiku (v.t.) to pull

hiki	(2nd base of *hiku* used connectively) . . . pulled and . . .
osu	(v.t.) to push
oshite	("te" form of *osu* used connectively) . . . pushed and . . .
tsuna	(n.) rope
rusu	(n.) absence
rusuchuu	(n.) during the absence
koofuku	(n.) happiness
koofuku ni	(adv.) happily

Important Construction and Grammar Notes

"BA" AS A CONDITIONAL FORM: So far, we have covered several ways of expressing "IF" (or conditional form). Let us review them:

1. Nihon e *iku to,* Nihongo o hanashimasu.

   "Root form of the verb + *to*"—this form has a double meaning of "IF" or "WHEN." This is used *only* with the present tense (root form of the verb).

2. Nihon e iku *nara,* hikooki de ikimasu.

   Nara can be used with a noun, verb, or adjective to express "IF." This form of making the conditional can be used with the past tense of the verb to form the past conditional.

Sono shigoto o *shita nara* kore o shite wa ikemasen.	If you *did* this work, don't do this.
Kesa kusuri o *nonda nara* yoku narimasu.	If you took (drank) medicine this morning, you will get well.
Kyonen hon o *kaita nara* kotoshi mo kakimasu ka.	If you wrote a book last year will you write one this year too?

3. The third and most common way of forming a conditional is:

4th BASE OF YODAN VERB	+	BA	=	IF + (verb) . . .

or

STEM OF ICHIDAN VERB + REBA	= IF + (verb) . . .

dasu = DA sa
shi
su
SE + *BA* = *daseba*
so

yomu = YO ma
mi
mu
ME + *BA* = *yomeba*
mo

For *ichidan* verbs, the rule is as follows:

dekakeru	dekake (stem) + REBA	= *dekakereba*
miru	mi (stem) + REBA	= *mireba*

Examples:

1. Ima *kaeba* yasui desu.	If (you) buy now it is cheap.
2. Ame ga *fureba* yasumimasu.	If it rains I will stay away.
3. Kore o *tabereba* byooki ni narimasu.	If you eat this you will be sick.
4. Shigoto o *sureba* jidoosha ga kaemasu.	If you work you will be able to buy a car.

"TARA" AS CONDITIONAL FORM: The fourth method of constructing a conditional is:

ABRUPT PAST OF VERB (. . . ta) + RA

The formation of "abrupt past" was already explained (see p. 174).

1. Kore o *tabetara* byooki ni narimasu.
2. Kyooto ni *tsuitara* denwa shite kudasai.

Some ways in which this construction can be used are:

a. Aside from the ordinary function as a conditional, this form also introduces the past tense into conditional form.

Kesa Tanaka-san ga *kitara* gogo wa kimasen.	If Tanaka came this morning, he will not come in the afternoon.
Kinoo *shitara* kyoo wa ii deshoo.	If you did it yesterday, it's all right today.

b. The *tara* form also has an additional use of "WHEN" in the past tense.

Kesa sensei no uchi e *ittara* dare mo imasen deshita.	This morning when I went to the teacher's house there wasn't anyone (there).
Sakuban aisukuriimu o *tabetara* onaka ga itaku natta.	When I ate some ice cream last night I got a stomach ache.

c. This form is also used to express subjunctive mood where a present condition is contrary to fact, or wishes.

Ima Nihon e *ittara* sakura o miru koto ga dekimasu.	If I were to go to Japan now, I could see the cherry blossoms.
Chichi ga *itara* watakushi wa shigoto o shinakute mo ii.	If my father were here, I wouldn't have to work.

Whether . . . *tara* is used in the sense of a, b, or c as explained above, will have to be determined by context.

NEGATIVE CONDITIONAL: "If you do not . . ." is expressed as follows:

1. First, form the abrupt negative of the verb.
   a. 1st BASE OF VERB + NAI (*Nai* is the abrupt negative suffix)

RA + *NAI* = *uranai*
ri
uru=U ru
re
ro

b. STEM OF
NON-CONJ. + NAI ORI (RU)—ORI + NAI = *orinai*
VERB

2. Next, add the conditional suffixes, using the rules given above.
   a. URANAI + TO
   b. URANAI + NARA
   c. URANA (I) + KEREBA = *uranakereba*
   (In forming a "BA" negative conditional, the final "I" is dropped, and "*KEREBA*" is added.)
   d. URANA + KATTARA = *uranakattara*
   (abrupt past of *ai*-ending words is *katta* without the *i*)

Mada *uranakattara* watakushi ga kaimasu.	If he had not sold it yet, I would buy (it).

EXAMPLES:

a. Benkyoo *shinai to* chichi ni shikararemasu.	If I do not study I will be scolded by father.
b. Anata ga *ikanai nara* watakushi mo ikimasen.	If you are not going, I won't go either.
c. Hayaku ok*inakereba* osoku narimasu.	If you do not get up early, you will be late.
d. Ima ka*wanakattara* takaku narimasu.	If you do not buy now, it will become expensive.

"IF" (CONDITIONAL) OF ADJECTIVES: The Japanese adjectives have the attributes of a verb in that they conjugate like a verb as explained below.

1. In forming the conditional of adjectives, we have already discussed the use of *NARA* (see p. 200).

a. Atsui *nara* mado o akenasai. If it is hot, open the window.
b. Yasui *nara* kaimasu. If it is cheap, I will buy it.

2. The second method is by the addition of *KEREBA* to adjectives without the last "i."

a. Taka*kereba* kaemasen. If it is expensive, I cannot buy it.
b. Too*kereba* takushi de ikimasu. If it is far, I will go by taxi.
c. Muzukashi*kereba* wakarimasen. If it is difficult, I can't understand.

3. *KATTARA* can also be used to make a conditional following the rule explained for *kereba.*

a. Isogashi*kattara* ii desu. If you are busy, it's all right (don't bother).
b. Too*kattara* ikemasen. If it is far, I can't go.

FORMATION OF PAST OF ADJECTIVES: *Adjective + deshita* is the pattern introduced earlier to make the past tense of adjectives.

muzukashii *deshita*—was difficult
yasui *deshita*—was cheap

1. The *NEGATIVE* of these are:
muzukashi*ku arimasen deshita*
yasu*ku arimasen deshita*

2. The *PAST* of adjectives is formed by the addition of *KATTA:*
muzukashi-*katta*
yasu-*katta*

3. The *PAST NEGATIVES* are:
muzukashi*ku-nakatta*
yasu*ku-nakatta*

The *katta* ending is abrupt, so *desu* is often added to give the polite ending. This pattern is used more commonly than the one mentioned above.

a. Shiken wa muzukashi-*katta desu.* The examination was difficult.
b. Eiga wa omoshiroku-*nakatta desu.* The movie was not good.

DESIDERATIVE "TAI": The *ai* ending of a desiderative is the same as the true adjective ending. Therefore, all the rules mentioned above with reference to the formation of conditional, negative, etc., are equally applicable. The *yodan* (c.v.) verb *yomu,* and *ichidan* (n.c.v.) verb *taberu* are given below for contrast.

1. *Conditional of "tai"*
   yomi*tai nara*—if you want to read
   tabe*tai nara*—if you want to eat
   yomi*ta-kereba*—if you want to read
   tabe*ta-kereba*—if you want to eat
   yomi*ta-kattara*—if you want to read
   tabe*ta-kattara*—if you want to eat

2. *Negative conditional of "tai"*
   yomi*takunai nara*—if you do not want to read
   tabe*takunai nara*—if you do not want to eat
   yomi*taku-nakereba*—if you do not want to read
   tabe*taku-nakereba*—if you do not want to eat
   yomi*taku-nakattara*—if you do not want to read
   tabe*taku-nakattara*—if you do not want to eat

3. *Past of "tai"*
   yomitai *deshita*—wanted to read
   tabetai *deshita*—wanted to eat
   yomi*ta-katta*—wanted to read
   tabe*ta-katta*—wanted to eat

4. *Negative past of "tai"*
   yomitaku *arimasen deshita*—I did not want to read.
   tabetaku *arimasen deshita*—I did not want to eat.
   yomi*taku-nakatta*—I did not want to read.
   tabe*taku-nakatta*—I did not want to eat.

NO WA, NO O: When a verb is used as the subject of a sentence, **no** is used as a nominalizer, followed by a nominative postposition **wa**. The function of **no** in this case (and also in the following **no o**) is that it serves as a noun following the relative clause construction.

1. "Smoking is bad for your health."
   In analyzing this sentence, "smoking," a gerund, is the subject of this sentence. "Smoking" in Japanese is *tabako o nomu.* Therefore, in order to use this verbal phrase as a subject, it must be first nominalized as follows:

Tabako o nomu *no*—(this *no* may be interpreted as "the *act* of smoking.")

Therefore:

Tabako o nomu *NO WA* karada ni yoku arimasen.

2. "It is difficult to write kanji."
The subject here is "it," but the true subject is "to write kanji" (is difficult). Therefore:

   Kanji o kaku *NO WA* muzukashii desu.

3. "I saw a robber enter a house."
What did I see? The expression "a robber enter a house," therefore, is the object of "saw." "A robber enter a house" is *Doroboo ga ie ni hairu.* Now, let us put these parts into the formula:

   SUBJECT WA + OBJECT O + VERB

   Watakushi wa doroboo ga ie ni hairu *NO O* mimashita.

4. "I did not know that John went to Japan."
John ga Nihon e itta *NO O* shirimasen deshita.
(The *fact* that John went to Japan, (I) didn't know.)

Fluency Drill

I

Mimashita.
Otoko no ko o mimashita.
Otoko no ko ga toru no o mimashita.
Otoko no ko ga hon o toru no o mimashita.
Otoko no ko ga sensei no hon o toru no o mimashita.
Otoko no ko ga sensei no Nihongo no hon o toru no o mimashita.

(I) saw.
(I) saw a boy.

(I) saw a boy take

(I) saw a boy take a book.

(I) saw a boy take the teacher's book.

(I) saw a boy take the teacher's Japanese book.

II

Watakushi wa suki desu.

Watakushi wa okiru no ga suki desu.

Watakushi wa asa okiru no ga suki desu.

Watakushi wa asa hayaku okiru no ga suki desu.

Watakushi wa asa hayaku roku-ji goro okiru no ga suki desu.

Watakushi wa asa hayaku okite sampo suru no ga suki desu.

Watakushi wa asa hayaku okite kooen no naka o sampo suru no ga suki desu.

I like.

I like to get up.

I like to get up in the morning.

I like to get up early in the morning.

I like to get up early about 6 o'clock in the morning.

I like to get up early in the morning and take a walk.

I like to get up early in the morning and take a walk in the park.

Substitution Drill

(4th Base Verb)

YOME		
KAKE		
IKE	+	BA
KAE		
etc.		

(Stem of N.C.V.)

MI DE TABE NE etc.	} +	REBA

Exercises

Translate the following 29 sentences using four different "conditional" constructions and then complete each sentence.

1. If you learn Japanese. . . .
   a. Nihongo o narau to. . . .
   b. Nihongo o narau nara. . . .
   c. Nihongo o naraeba. . . .
   d. Nihongo o narattara. . . .
2. If you get up at 8 o'clock. . . .
3. If you speak French. . . .
4. If you ask (request) him. . . .
5. If you leave home now. . . .
6. If you close the window. . . .
7. If you stand on the chair. . . .
8. If you want to learn Japanese. . . .
   a. Nihongo o naraitai nara. . . .
   b. Nihongo o naraitakereba. . . .
   c. Nihongo o naraitakattara. . . .
9. If you want to go. . . .
10. If you do not buy now. . . .
    a. Ima kawanai to. . . .
    b. Ima kawanai nara. . . .
    c. Ima kawanakattara. . . .
11. If you do not study tonight. . . .
12. If the class does not begin at 9:00. . . .

13. If you do not run fast . . .
14. If you do not tell the teacher . . .
15. If you cannot come at 9:00 . . .
    a. Ku-ji ni kuru koto ga dekinai to . . .
    b. Ku-ji ni kuru koto ga dekinai nara . . .
    c. Ku-ji ni kuru koto ga dekinakereba . . .
    d. Ku-ji ni kuru koto ga dekinakattara . . .
16. If you cannot speak Japanese . . .
17. If you cannot live in Tokyo . .
18. If you do not want to go . . .
    a. Ikitakunai to . . .
    b. Ikitakunai nara . . .
    c. Ikitakunakereba . . .
    d. Ikitakunakattara . . .
19. If you do not want to buy my car . . .
20. If you do not want to study tonight . . .
21. If you do not want to bring your dog . . .
22. If the room is hot . . .
    a. Heya ga atsui to . . .
    b. Heya ga atsui nara . . .
    c. Heya ga atsukereba . . .
    d. Heya ga atsukattara . . .
23. If the teacher's house is far . . .
24. If the book is difficult . . .
25. If the car is expensive . . .
26. If the car is not old . . .
    a. Kuruma ga furukunai to . . .
    b. Kuruma ga furukunai nara . . .
    c. Kuruma ga furukunakereba . . .
    d. Kuruma ga furukunakattara . . .
27. If the room is not cold . . .
28. If the movie is not interesting . . .
29. If the story is not long . . .
30. The examination was difficult. Shiken wa muzukashikatta (desu).
31. The movie was interesting. Eiga wa omoshirokatta (desu).
32. The road was bad. Michi ga warukatta (desu).

33. The room was not expensive.	Heya wa takakunakatta (desu).
34. The movie was not long.	Eiga wa nagakunakatta (desu).
35. The necktie was not blue.	Nekutai wa aokunakatta (desu).
36. I like to walk.	Aruku no ga suki desu.
37. I like to climb mountains.	Yama o noboru no ga suki desu.
38. I do not like to work.	Shigoto o suru no ga kirai desu.
39. I do not like to go to school.	Gakkoo e iku no ga kirai desu.
40. I saw him take (it).	Toru no o mimashita.
41. I saw him leave.	Dekakeru no o mimashita.
42. I saw the boy eat (it).	Otoko no ko ga taberu no o mimashita.
43. It is easy to speak Japanese.	Nihongo o hanasu no wa yasashii desu.
44. It is your work to load these books.	Kono hon o tsumu no wa anata no shigoto desu.
45. It is expensive to go by airplane.	Hikooki de iku no wa takai desu.
46. It is fun to climb Mt. Fuji.	Fujisan ni noboru no wa omoshiroi desu.
47. It is difficult to write kanji.	Kanji o kaku no wa muzukashii desu.
48. Walking is good for your health.	Aruku no wa kenkoo ni ii desu.
49. Using chopsticks is difficult.	Hashi o tsukau no wa muzukashii desu.
50. Learning kanji is not easy.	Kanji o narau no wa yasashiku arimasen.

Translate into Japanese:

1. I waited for him 15 minutes, so I was late for work. (exchange of favor)
   He did not wait for me, so I was late for work. (exchange of favor)
2. If you meet the principal in Tokyo, please give him my regards.

   Note: Please give him my regards—*yoroshiku itte kudasai.*
3. The children had (some) dumplings made (for them) by (their) mother, and they happily started out.

   Note: Children received the favor of . . .
4. I saw the teachers and students eating lunch in the dining room (*shokudoo*).

   Note: "Lunch" can be either *chuushoku* or (*o*)*bentoo.* (*O*)*bentoo* is used for a packed lunch, picnic lunch, etc.

5. It is difficult to speak Japanese like a person born in Japan.

   Note: (a) (speak) like . . .—*no yoo ni* + verb
   (b) The subject of this sentence is "to speak Japanese . . . born in Japan."

6. The enemy country finally surrendered after it had continued fighting hard for five years.

   Note: "to continue fighting" is a COMPOUND VERB, a combination of two verbs—"continue" and "fighting."
   The formula in this case is:

   2nd BASE
   of the + *tsuzukeru*—*tatakai-tsuzukeru*
   VERB

   "continue raining"—*ame ga furi-tsuzukeru*
   "continue studying"—*benkyoo shi-tsuzukeru*

7. The old man takes a walk every morning accompanied by his dog (taking along his dog).
8. I did not know (that) (the fact) you were bitten by a dog.

   Note: . . . *koto* o shirimasen deshita.

9. When I went to your home during your absence, there was a car stopped in front of the house.

   Note: Use 3 different ways of forming a "when" clause.

10. Because my boy's return was late, I was very worried, but when he telephoned I was relieved.

    Note: my boy—*watakushi no musuko* (son)
    Quite often, *uchi no* is used in the sense of "belonging to the family or household," e.g., *uchi no jidoosha,* or *uchi no jochuu* (our maid).

Translate into English:

First, form the *past tense* of the following sentences, and translate.
Second, form the *negative* and translate. (Some are already in the negative form.)
Third, form the *past negative* and translate.

1. Ie no mae ni inu ga imasu.
2. Watakushi wa daigaku o dete kara sensei ni naritai.
3. Nihongo ga hanasenai.
4. Watakushi wa kurasu ni rajio o motte kimasen.

5. Kono eiga o Nihon de miru.
6. Sensei wa Amerika kara hikooki de kimasu.
7. Koko no sushi wa oishii desu.
8. Fude de kanji o kaku no wa muzukashii.
9. Tookyoo no fuyu wa atatakakunai.
10. Heya no denki wa tsuite imasen.
11. Kono inu wa sakana o taberu.
12. Mado ga aite inai.
13. Brown-san wa maiban Nihongo no benkyoo shimasu.
14. Brown-san wa komban shigoto o suru.
15. Gakusei wa aruite gakkoo e kuru.
16. Ima atarashii ootobai ga kaenai.
17. Chichi ni kuruma o katte morau.
18. Kodomo ni omocha o katte ageru.
19. Daigaku o dete kara sensei ni naru.
20. Natsuyasumichuu ni hon o yondari sampo o shitari suru tsumori desu.

Answer in Japanese:

1. Momotaroo no kerai wa nan-nin imashita ka. Ichiban hajime (first) ni kita no wa dare deshita ka.
2. Onitachi wa Momotaroo ga kuru no o miru to doo shimashita ka. Sugu ni koosan shimashita ka.
3. Kiji wa donna daiji na shigoto o shimashita ka.
4. Dare ga mon o nobotte mon o akemashita ka.
5. Anata wa saru ni hikkakareta koto ga arimasu ka.
   Anata wa inu ni kamitsukareta koto ga arimasu ka.
6. Oni wa koosan shita toki donna yakusoku o shimashita ka.
7. Ojiisan wa naze Momotaroo no rusuchuu shimpai shimashita ka.
8. Sekai-ichi no takai tatemono wa doko ni arimasu ka.
   Oosaka wa Nihon-ichi no daitokai desu ka.
9. Anata wa shiken o ukeru mae ni kesshite shimpai shimasen ka.
   Itsu anshin shimasu ka.
10. Anata wa tomodachi to chuushoku o taberu toki itsu-mo gochisoo shite moraimasu ka. Gochisoo shite agemasu ka.

Use the proper postpositions in the blank spaces: (Know why you are using the particular postposition.)

1. Watakushi wa Nihon ni ita toki Fujisan ___ noborimashita.
2. Otoko no ko wa sensei ___ shikarareta.
3. Kono taipuraitaa ___ tomodachi ___ azukemasu.
4. Nara-yuki no kisha wa Kyooto ___ nori-kaenakereba narimasen.
5. Otoko no ko wa Nihongo no kurasu ___ okuremashita.
6. Watakushi wa tanjoobi (birthday) ___ chichi ___ atarashii jidoosha ___ katte moraimashita.
7. Anata wa sakuban hitori ___ (alone) eiga ___ ikimashita ka. Tomodachi ___ ikimashita ka.
8. Anata wa Nihon ___ Tanaka-san ___ aimashita ka.
9. Sensei wa seito ___ yurushite yarimashita.
10. Tookyoo ___ ichiban ookii hoteru no mae ___ takushii ___ tomarimashita.
11. Asa hayaku okiru no ___ muzukashii desu.
12. Akaboo wa jidoosha ___ toranku ___ tsumimashita.
13. Lincoln wa Booth ___ pisutoru ___ atama ___ utaremashita.
14. Kono kisha wa nan-ji ___ Kyooto ___ tsukimasu ka.
15. Tookyoo wa sekai ___ ichiban ookii tokai ___ narimashita.
16. Amerika wa Doitsu ___ yonenkan tatakaimashita.
17. Teki ___ hikooki wa machi no ue ___ tobi-mawarimashita.
18. Gekijoo no mae ___ watakushi ___ sensei to Tanaka-san ___ aimashita
19. Otoko no ko wa inu ___ ashi ___ kami-tsukaremashita.

ANSWER:
1. O
2. NI
3. O, NI
4. DE
5. NI
6. NI, KARA (NI), O
7. DE, E, TO
8. DE, NI
9. O
10. DE, DE, WA
11. WA
12. NI, O
13. NI, DE, O
14. NI, NI
15. DE, NI
16. TO
17. NO, O
18. DE, WA, NI
19. NI, O

POLITE AND ABRUPT FORMS

Study this chart which gives the polite and the abrupt, the affirmative and negative forms.

	PRESENT	PAST	PRESENT NEGATIVE (do not. . . .)	PAST NEGATIVE (did not. . . .)
YODAN VERB read	(Polite) yomimasu (Abrupt) yomu	yomimashita yonda	yomimasen yomanai	yomimasen deshita yomanakatta
play	(Polite) asobimasu (Abrupt) asobu	asobimashita asonda	asobimasen asobanai	asobimasen deshita asobanakatta
buy	(Polite) kaimasu (Abrupt) kau	kaimashita katta	kaimasen kawanai	kaimasen deshita kawanakatta
ICHIDAN VERB see	(Polite) mimasu (Abrupt) miru	mimashita mita	mimasen minai	mimasen deshita minakatta
eat	(Polite) tabemasu (Abrupt) taberu	tabemashita tabeta	tabemasen tabenai	tabemasen deshita tabenakatta
IRREG. VERB come	(Polite) kimasu (Aprupt) kuru	kimashita kita	kimasen konai	kimasen deshita konakatta
do	(Polite) shimasu (Abrupt) suru	shimashita shita	shimasen shinai	shimasen deshita shinakatta
ADJECTIVE large	(Polite) ookii desu (Abrupt) ookii	ookii deshita ookikatta	ookiku arimasen ookikunai	ookiku arimasen deshita ookikunakatta
cold	(Polite) samui desu (Abrupt) samui	samui deshita samukatta	samuku arimasen samukunai	samuku arimasen deshita samukunakatta
DESIDERATIVE want to see	(Polite) mitai desu (Abrupt) mitai	mitai deshita mitakatta	mitaku arimasen mitakunai	mitaku arimasen deshita mitakunakatta

CHAPTER 19

SUPERPOLITE AND HUMBLE FORMS*

SUPERPOLITE AND HUMBLE FORMS	ORDINARY FORM
1. (a) SORE WA NAN *DE GOZAIMASU* KA.	Sore wa nan desu ka.
(b) KORE WA TAIWAN KARA KITA TAKE NO FUDE *DE GOZAIMASU.*	Kore wa Taiwan kara kita take no fude desu.
2. (a) WATAKUSHI NO PEN GA SOKO *NI GOZAIMASU KA.*	Watakushi no pen ga soko ni arimasu ka.
(b) HAI, *GOZAIMASU.*	Hai, arimasu.
3. (a) JIBIKI MO SOKO *NI GOZAIMASU* KA.	Jibiki mo soko ni arimasu ka.
(b) IIE, *GOZAIMASEN.*	Iie, arimasen.

* In order to gain proficiency in the use of this form of expression, try converting the ordinary forms on the right side into the Superpolite and Humble Forms.

4. (a) KONO HON WA *OMOSHIROO GOZAIMASU KA.*	Kono hon wa omoshiroi desu ka.
(b) IIE, AMARI *OMOSHIROO GOZAIMASEN.*	Iie, amari omoshiroku arimasen.
5. (a) NAZE KORE WA SONNA NI *TAKOO GOZAIMASU* KA.	Naze kore wa sonna ni takai desu ka.
(b) KORE WA *ATARASHUU GOZAIMASU* KARA, SUKOSHI *TAKOO GOZAIMASU.*	Kore wa atarashii desu kara sukoshi takai desu.
6. (a) WATAKUSHI NO NOOTO GA *O-WAKARI NI NARIMASHITA* KA.**	Watakushi no nooto ga wakarimashita ka.
(b) WAKARIYASUKU *KAITE GOZAIMASHITA* KARA, YOKU WAKARIMASHITA.	Wakariyasuku kaite arimashita kara, yoku wakarimashita.
7. (a) OKUSAMA WA DOCHIRA E *O-DEKAKE NI NARIMASHITA* KA.**	Okusama wa dochira e dekakemashita ka.

** The honorific prefixes, "O" and "GO," are hyphenated in this chapter to emphasize their usage in superpolite expressions.

	(b) KYOO WA KAIMONO NI *IRASSHARU* TO *OSSHATTE IMASHITA.*	Kyoo wa kaimono ni iku to itte imashita.
8.	(a) ANATA NO O-TOMODACHI WA MADA NEW YORK NI *IRASSHAIMASU* KA.	Anata no o-tomodachi wa mada New York ni imasu ka.
	(b) HAI, TANAKA-SAMA WA NEW YORK DE HATARAITE *IRASSHAIMASU.*	Hai, Tanaka-san wa New York de hataraite imasu.
9.	(a) OKUDA-SAMA WA MOO OKITE *IRASSHAIMASU* KA.	Okuda-san wa moo okite imasu ka.
	(b) OKUDA-SAMA WA MADA *NETE IRASSHARU* YOO DESU.	Okuda-san wa mada nete iru yoo desu.
10.	(a) GO-SHUJIN WA DOCHIRA E *OIDE NI NARIMASHITA* KA.	Go-shujin wa dochira e ikimashita ka.
	(b) GO-SHUJIN WA SAKUJITSU HIKOOKI DE CHICAGO E *O-TACHI NI NARIMASHITA.*	Go-shujin wa kinoo hikooki de Chicago e tachimashita.

SORE DEWA KONO TEGAMI O *O-WATASHI KUDASAIMASEN* KA.	Sore dewa kono tegami o watashite kudasaimasen ka.
11. (a) KYOO DOCHIRA E *OIDE NI NARIMASHITA* KA.	Kyoo dochira e ikimashita ka.
(b) KYOO WATAKUSHI WA AOYAMA NO HOO E *MAIRIMASHITA.*	Kyoo watakushi wa Aoyama no hoo e ikimashita.
12. (a) GO-SHUJIN WA ITSU KAETTE *IRASSHAIMASU* KA.	Go-shujin wa itsu kaette kimasu ka.
(b) SHUJIN GA SAKUBAN *KAETTE MAIRIMASHITA* KARA CHOTTO UCHI MADE *OIDE KUDASAIMASEN* KA.	Shujin ga sakuban kaette kimashita kara chotto uchi made kite kudasaimasen ka.
13. (a) KYOO OKUSAMA WA DOCHIRA E *OIDE DE GOZAIMASU* KA.	Kyoo okusan wa dochira e ikimasu ka.
(b) KYOO WA DOCHIRA E MO *MAIRIMASEN.*	Kyoo wa dochira e mo ikimasen.
14. (a) DOOSHITE SONO YOO NA KOTO O MAINICHI *NASAIMASU* KA.	Dooshite sonna koto o mainichi shimasu ka.

(b) HAYAKU KONO SHIGOTO O OETAI KARA MAINICHI *ITASHIMASU.*	Hayaku kono shigoto o oetai kara mainichi shimasu.
15. (a) BROWN-SAN WA DONATA TO GO-ISSHO NI KONO SHIGOTO O *NASAIMASHITA* KA.	Brown-san wa dare to issho ni kono shigoto o shimashita ka. (With whom did Mr. Brown do this work?)
(b) ANO KATA WA ANNA MUZUKASHII KOTO O HITORI DE *NASAIMASHITA.*	Ano kata wa anna muzukashii koto o hitori de shimashita. (He did such a difficult thing alone.)
16. (a) DENWA O SURU JIKAN *GA GOZAIMASU* KA.	Denwa o suru jikan ga arimasu ka. (Is there time to telephone?)
(b) IIE, HAYAKU KISHA NI *O-NORINASAI.*	Iie, hayaku kisha ni norinasai.
17. (a) HAYAKU KONO SHIGOTO O SHITE *ITADAKITAI* DESU GA . . .	Hayaku kono shigoto o shite moraitai desu ga . . .
(b) GO-TSUGOO GA YOROSHIKEREBA KOMBAN ITASHIMASHOO.	Tsugoo ga yokereba komban shimashoo.

18. (a) TANAKA-SAN WA O-HITORI DE KONO SHIGOTO O *NASARU* KOTO GA DEKIMASU *KASHIRA.*	Tanaka-san wa hitori de kono shigoto o suru koto ga dekimasu kashira. (I wonder if Mr. Tanaka can do this work alone.)
(b) O-TETSUDAI *ITASHIMASU* KARA *GO-ANSHIN KUDASAI.*	Tetsudaimasu kara anshin shite kudasai.
19. (a) ANO KATA NO JI O *GORAN NI NATTA KOTO GA GOZAIMASU* KA.	Ano kata no ji o mita koto ga arimasu ka. (Have you ever seen his writing?)
(b) IIE, MADA ICHIDO MO *HAIKEN SHITA KOTO WA GOZAIMASEN.*	Iie, mada ichido mo mita koto wa arimasen.
20. (a) KYOOTO KARA KITA KONO TEGAMI O *GORAN NI NARIMASHITA* KA.	Kyooto kara kita kono tegami o mimashita ka.
(b) HAI, SAKUJITSU *HAIKEN ITASHIMASHITA.*	Hai, sakujitsu mimashita.
21. (a) NAKAJIMA-SAN O *GOZONJI DE IRASSHAIMASU* KA.	Nakajima-san o shitte imasu ka.

	(b) IIE, YOKU WA *ZONJI-MASEN* GA KYOOTO NO IMOOTO GA *ZONJI-AGETE* IRU SOO DESU.	Iie, yoku shirimasen ga Kyooto no imooto ga shitte iru soo desu.
22.	(a) KOMBAN TSUGOO GA YOROSHII NODE, UCHI MADE *IRASHITE ITA-DAKITAI* TO *ZONJI-MASU.*	Komban tsugoo ga yoi kara, uchi made kite hoshii to omoimasu.
	(b) *GO-ZONJI* NO TOORI HAHA GA BYOOKI *DE GOZAIMASU* KARA *MAI-REMASEN.*	Shitte iru toori, haha ga byooki desu kara ikemasen. (As you know, mother is sick, so I won't be able to go.)
23.	(a) KONO SHUKUDAI WA DOO SHITARA *YORO-SHUU GOZAIMASU* KA.	Kono shukudai wa doo shitara ii desu ka. (How should I do this homework?)
	(b) SENSEI NO *OSSHATTA* TOORI NI SHINASAI.	Sensei no itta toori ni shinasai. (Do as your teacher tells you.)
24.	(a) WATAKUSHI NO PEN O *O-TSUKAI NI NARI-MASEN* KA.	Watakushi no pen o tsukaimasen ka. (Won't you use my pen?)
	(b) SORE DEWA CHOTTO MANNENHITSU O *HAI-SHAKU ITASHIMASU.*	Sore dewa chotto mannenhitsu o karimasu.

25. (a) DONATA-SAMA *DE IRASSHAIMASU KA.*	Dare desu ka.
(b) WATAKUSHI WA TANAKA TO *MOOSHIMASU.*	Watakushi wa Tanaka to iimasu.
26. (a) DOKO DE *O-MACHI ITASHIMASHOO* KA.	Doko de machimashoo ka.
(b) DOOZO KOCHIRA E *IRASHITE* KUDASAI.	Doozo kochira e kite kudasai.
27. (a) KYOOTO E *MAIRIMASU* GA NANI-KA GO-YOO *GA GOZAIMASU* KA.	Kyooto e ikimasu ga nani-ka yoo ga arimasu ka.
(b) KYOOTO E *IRASSHATTARA* ANI NO UCHI E *OIDE NASAI.*	Kyooto e ittara ani no uchi e ikinasai.
28. (a) IMA KOOGI O NASATTE *IRASSHARU* O-KATA WA DONATA-SAMA *DE GOZAIMASU* KA.	Ima koogi o shite iru kata wa dare desu ka. (Who is the person who is lecturing now?)
(b) ANO KATA WA DAIGAKU KYOOJU NO TANAKA-SAN *DE GOZAIMASU.*	Ano kata wa daigaku kyooju no Tanaka-san desu.
29. (a) GO-RYOOSHIN WA O-GENKI *DE IRASSHAIMASU* KA.	Ryooshin wa genki desu ka. (Are both of your parents well?)

(b) OKAGESAMA DE GENKI *DE GOZAIMASU.*	Okagesama de genki desu.
30. (a) MOO HIRUGOHAN O *MESHIAGARIMASHITA* KA.	Moo hirugohan o tabemashita ka.
(b) IIE, MADA DE GOZAI-MASU. CHUUSHOKU NI CHUUKA RYOORI O *ITADAKITAI DESU.*	Iie, mada desu. Chuushoku ni chuu-ka ryoori o tabetai desu.

Vocabulary from the Lesson

okusama	(n.) honorific term used for someone else's wife. For one's own wife use *tsuma* or *kanai.*
. . . -sama	(suf.) more polite form of *san.*
(go)shujin	(n.) master (of a house, shop, etc.), husband; *go* is added to refer to someone else's husband or master.
tatsu	(v.i.) In addition to "stand," it also means to "depart, leave." Use postposition *o* to show where it departs from—*Kyooto o tatsu.*
o-tachi ni narimashita	(superpolite form of *tatsu*) departed.
dooshite	same as *naze.*
oeru	(v.t.) to finish, complete (*Owaru* is the intransitive verb.)
tetsudau	(v.t.) to help, to lend a hand
o-tetsudai itashimasu	(superpolite form of *tetsudau*—See I.C. & G.N.)

toori "exactly as. . . ." (usually used with a verb, *hanashita toori*—"exactly as I said")

koogi (n.) lecture. However, when used as a Chinese verb, *koogi suru,* it means "to lecture."

(go)ryooshin (n.) both parents. *Go* is added to refer to someone else's parents.

okagesama de . . . (idio.) thanks to your consideration . . .

tsugoo (n.) convenience, conditions

tsugoo ga ii "to be convenient"; this expression is used when referring to the convenience of one's schedule; *benri ga ii,* which also means "convenient," is with reference to the physical convenience.

ryoori (n.) cooking; *Chuuka ryoori*—Chinese food. *Ryoori suru*—to cook. *ryoorinin*—a cook. *ryooriya*—a (Japanese) restaurant.

Important Construction and Grammar Notes

SUPERPOLITE (HONORIFIC) AND HUMBLE FORMS have already been referred to in Chapter 10, p. 165. Here we will go into greater detail as to how to form this superpolite style of expression. Remember, however, that this is *not* archaic, or too formal, or no longer in use. A foreigner in Japan can get along quite well by speaking in the ordinary polite form emphasized throughout this book. On the other hand, he will have great difficulty in comprehending if he is not familiar with this form, since it is widely used among educated people, or by those in business catering to customers.

The honorific form is used to indicate respect or social grace by using more polite forms, or it may be used in speaking to a superior, either in age or in social status. This is not a hard and fast rule, since one often hears this style used where the sense of superior and inferior does not exist, e.g., a considerate mother talking to her own child, probably in the hope of instilling some manners. The humble form is used only of oneself (or, first person) showing humility, with the meaning, "I humbly say (do, etc.). . . ." The use of honorific form goes hand in hand with the use of humble—exalt the others but humble oneself is the principle.

It is not too helpful to attempt to give meaning to these expressions. It is more important to acquire the "feeling" for them. When using this form of expression, note that the kinship terms (*your* father, uncle, etc.) must also conform to the polite usage as explained in the chart on p. 257. The other party is always exalted, but when referring to members of your own family, use the ordinary form.

Therefore, there are three styles to this expression:

1. Honorific: this category can be further differentiated between verbs which are already honorific in form (or "built in" honorific words) and the regular verbs converted into honorific form.
2. Humble.
3. Polite and Humble words.

These are explained below.

The following chart shows the more commonly used verbs with their honorific and humble equivalents. (The numbers below indicate the examples given in the text.)

VERB	PLAIN	HONORIFIC	HUMBLE (for 1st person only)
is, are (to be)	desu	de gozaimasu 1a–b, 22b, 28a, 29a	
there is (are)	aru	ga gozaimasu 2a–b, 3a–b, 16a, 27a, 28b, 29b	
there is (are)	iru	irassharu, 8a	oru
go	iku	irassharu, 1b, 11a, 27b	mairu, 11b, 13b, 27a
come	kuru	irassharu, 22a, 26b	mairu, 22b
do	suru	nasaru, 15a–b asobasu agaru	itasu, 14b, 17b

eat (drink)	taberu (nomu)	meshiagaru, 30a agaru	itadaku, 17a, 30b
see	miru	goran ni naru, 20a	haiken suru, 20b
say, speak	iu	ossharu, 7b, 23b	moosu, mooshiageru, 25b
wear	kiru	o-meshi ni naru	
know	shiru	go-zonji desu, 22b	zonjiru, 22a zonjiageru, 21b
sleep	neru	o-yasumi ni naru	
give	yaru	ageru	sashiageru
receive	morau		itadaku
visit	tazuneru		agaru, ukagau
hear	kiku		ukagau, uketamawaru

Note: 1. Most honorifics are used when referring to someone higher in social status than the speaker, but there are verb forms which are used for "things" as well as "persons." In this usage, they are more for politeness, e.g., *de gozaimasu* (for "things" and "persons"); *ga gozaimasu* (for "things").

2. These verbs, with the exception of *zonjiru, ageru, sashiageru,* and *mooshiageru,* are all *yodan* verbs (c.v.). This includes *mairu. Gozaimasu* is really *masu* attached to the 2nd base of *gozaru,* which is *gozari* + *masu.* However, in ordinary everyday conversation, the "r" has been omitted. Therefore, for the same reason, *irasshaimasu* and *nasaimasu* are more commonly used.

3. *Haiken suru* has the meaning of seeing something with a feeling of respect, or reverence. Therefore, you do not use this when referring to "seeing a movie, or a picture." When it is a special picture, however, you are gratefully acknowledging to the painter the opportunity afforded you. Then *haiken suru* is permissible.

4. *Oide ni naru* has the meaning of "to go" (see sentences 10a, 11a), "to come," or "to be" (same as *imasu*).

Oide de gozaimasu means "to go" (see sentence 13a).
Oide nasai is polite imperative meaning "go!" or "come!" (see sentence 27b).
Oide kudasai is the polite request, "please . . ." (see sentence 12b).

O (GO) . . . NI NARU: With verbs that do not have honorific equivalents, the following formula can be used to form honorific verbs. Remember that it is the verb which changes to express various degrees of politeness.

		2nd BASE		NI NARU (or NASARU)
"O"	+	of	+	NASAI—(Do . . .)
(GO)		VERB (noun form)		KUDASAI—(Please. . . .)

kaku	—**o**-ka*ki*	ni **naru**	(or nasaru)
		kudasai	(or kudasaru)
yomu	—**o**-yo*mi*	ni **naru**	(or nasaru)
		kudasai	
kau	—**o**-ka*i*	ni **naru**	(or nasaru)
		kudasai	
dekakeru	—**o**-deka*ke*	ni **naru**	(non-conjugating verb)
		kudasai	

O-kaki kudasai is more polite than *kaite kudasai.*

FUNCTION OF DOOZO—**Doozo,** meaning "please," is often used with the superpolite request form mentioned above.

1. **Doozo o**-hairi kudasai.	Please come in.
2. **Doozo o**-kake kudasai.	Please sit down.
3. **Doozo o**-machi kudasai.	Please wait.
4. **Doozo** mado o **o**-shime kudasai.	Please close the window.

Compare this form of request with the ordinary polite request discussed in Chapter 4.

It must be remembered that *doozo* alone does not make the polite request sentence, but it is the . . . *2nd base + kudasai* ending which gives this meaning.

In certain situations the use of *doozo* alone will give the full implied meaning. For example, someone knocks on the door and you say just, *"Doozo!"* meaning *"Doozo o-hairi kudasai,"* or you motion to a chair and say to your guest, *"Doozo,"* indicating *"Doozo o-kake kudasai."* In either instance, what *doozo* is referring to is quite clear.

FIRST PERSON HONORIFIC: Following pattern is used to form honorific involving first person.

O +	2nd BASE of Verb	+	SURU (ITASU)	= (I) DO (verb) . . .

	o-*tsukuri* shimasu.	(itashimasu)
Watakushi ga	**o-*yobi* shimasu.**	(„)
	o-*ai* shimasu.	(„)
	o-*tazune* shimasu.	(„)

Itasu is used for humble meaning.

Contrary to the principle that superpolite is used only for others, this pattern is used for *first person only* and gives polite tone to the sentence. Note, however, that this form is not applicable to all verbs. Learn by usage.

Now compare the following:

a. Sensei ga **o-*mukae ni* narimasu.** Teacher will meet (someone).
b. Watakushi ga **o-*mukae* shimasu.**

(a) is used in reference to someone else, while (b) is for first person.

PASSIVE AS HONORIFIC: Some passive forms of verbs can also be used to show the honorific. However, this expression is limited in usage.

1. Koochoo-sensei wa mada *korare-masen.*	(Passive of *kuru* but used as honorific; "The principal has not come yet.")
2. Sensei wa nan to *iwaremashita* ka.	(Passive of *iu;* "What did the teacher say?")
3. Kabuki e *ikaremashita* ka.	(Passive of *iku;* "Did you go to Kabuki?")

HONORIFIC FORMS OF NOUNS: By attaching **o** (and sometimes **go**) to nouns the honorific forms of nouns can be formed.

o + noun	*go + noun*
o-furo —bath	**go**-byooki —illness
o-tearai —toilet	**go**-tsugoo —convenience

o-tegami—letter
o-hashi —chopsticks

go-fuufu —(married) couple
go-chisoo —good food

There is no rule to indicate when one is preferable to the other—only through constant association will the student learn to understand the correct usage. However, in general, *go* is used with Chinese compound words, viz., *go-benkyoo* (studying), *go-shimpai* (worry), *go-annai* (guide), *go-tsugoo* (convenience), etc.

IRASSHARU has the meaning of *iku, kuru,* and *iru*—"to go," "to come," and "is" respectively. The distinction in meaning must be made from the context.

Dochira e **irasshaimasu** ka.	Where are you going?
Kochira e irasshai.	Come here.
Sensei wa doko ni **irasshaimasu** ka.	Where is the teacher?

When *irassharu* is used with the *te* form of the verb—*te* + *irassharu*—this is the same as *te* + *imasu,* the progressive form.

Benkyoo o shite *irasshaimasu.*	He is studying.
Yasunde *irasshaimasu.*	He is resting.

In summary:

iku, kuru	honorific:	*irassharu*
	humble:	*mairu*
iru	honorific:	*irassharu*
	humble:	*oru*

MESU: This is the honorific form having several uses—to wear, to catch a cold.

1. Nani o **o-meshi** ni narimasu ka.—What are you going to wear?
2. Sensei ga kaze o **o-meshi** ni narimashita.—The teacher caught a cold.

HONORIFIC ADJECTIVES can also be constructed by adding *o*.

o-atsui
o-hayai
o-isogashii
o-utsukushii

However, when these expressions are used in a statement, the "i" of the adjective is changed to "o" or "u" and pronounced either **oo** or **uu** depending on the endings as follows:

1. Kyoo wa hontoo ni *atsui* desu.	Today is certainly hot.
Kyoo wa hontoo ni **(o)atsuu gozaimasu.**	(*o-atsui desu* is also used.)
2. Kono shinamono wa *takai desu.*	These goods are expensive.
Kono shinamono wa **(o)takoo gozaimasu.**	(or *o-takai desu.*)
3. Shibai wa *omoshiroi* deshita.	The play was interesting.
Shibai wa **omoshiroo gozaimashita.**	

O and *GO* prefixes are not used with *all* nouns or adjectives. Indiscriminate usage of these may result in ludicrous statements.

DE GOZAIMASU is the honorific form of *desu;* the formula is as follows:

NOUN + DE GOZAIMASU

Kono kata wa watakushi no *sensei* **de gozaimasu.**
Kore wa watakushi no *jibiki* **de gozaimashoo** ka.

GOZAIMASU is the honorific form of ARIMASU, showing existence of something. This is from GOZARU, a conjugating verb, viz.,

	ra				
	RI	+	*MASU*	=	*gozarimasu*
goza	ru				
	re				
	ro				

MASU is added to the second base, but "r" has dropped from conversational usage—thus, GOZA(*r*)IMASU. (The omission of "r" as explained here occurs in other polite verb conjugations, e.g., IRASSHARU, OSSHARU, etc.)

This expression, like DE GOZAIMASU mentioned above, is used for the purpose of politeness, disregarding the status concept.

Sensei no otaku **wa** dochira ni **gozaimasu** ka.
Kono heya ni rajio **ga gozaimasen.**

... TE GOZAIMASU: This form is equivalent to the state of being condition explained in Chapter 16.

"*te*" of transitive verb + gozaimasu / arimasu = state of being

Nihongo ga **kaite gozaimasu.**
Mado ga **akete gozaimasu.**

... KASHIRA used with the root form of the verb, noun, or adjective, expresses the doubt or uncertainty of the speaker. It has the meaning of "I wonder if (whether, how, etc.) . . ."

VERB

Ame ga *furu kashira.*	*I wonder if* it will rain.
Kore wa *taberareru kashira.*	*I wonder if* this is edible.

NOUN

Ano kata wa *Nihonjin kashira.*	*I wonder if* he is a Japanese.
Kore wa *dare no kashira.*	*I wonder* whose this is.

ADJECTIVE

Atsui kashira.	*I wonder if* it is hot.
Muzukashii kashira.	*I wonder if* it is difficult.

Exercises

Use the honorific form in translating the following:

1. (a) What are these?	Kore wa nan de gozaimasu ka.
(b) These are wooden clogs (*geta*).	Kore wa geta de gozaimasu.
2. (a) What is the name of that mountain?	Ano yama no namae wa nan de gozaimasu ka.
(b) That mountain is Mt. Fuji.	Ano yama wa Fujisan de gozaimasu.
3. (a) Where is the public phone?	Kooshuu denwa wa doko ni gozaimasu ka.
(b) The phone is in the room.	Denwa wa heya no naka ni gozaimasu.
4. (a) Do you have American magazines?	Amerika no zasshi ga gozaimasu ka.
(b) Yes we do.	Hai, gozaimasu.
5. (a) Where is Professor Tanaka?	Tanaka-kyooju wa doko ni irasshaimasu ka. . . . doko ni oide ni narimasu ka. . . . doko ni oide de gozaimasu ka.
(b) Professor Tanaka is in the classroom.	Tanaka-kyooju wa kyooshitsu ni irasshaimasu. (or) Kyooshitsu ni oide ni narimasu. Kyooshitsu ni oide de gozaimasu.
6. (a) Who is in the room?	Donata ga heya ni irasshaimasu ka.
(b) Nobody is.	Donata mo irasshaimasen.
7. (a) Are you going to the concert?	Ongakukai ni irasshaimasu ka. . . . ni oide ni narimasu ka. . . . ni oide de gozaimasu ka.
(b) Yes, I am going.	Hai, mairimasu.
8. (a) Are you coming to my house?	Watakushi no uchi e irasshaimasu ka.
(b) No, I cannot come.	Iie, mairemasen.
9. (a) What is Mr. Tanaka's father doing now?	Tanaka-sama no otoosama wa nani o nasatte (shite) irasshaimasu ka.
(b) He is not doing anything, I hear.	Nani-mo nasatte irassharanai soo desu.

10.	(a)	Where is he working now?	Ima doko ni o-tsutome ni natte irasshaimasu ka.
	(b)	He is working (*tsutomeru*) at the university.	Daigaku ni o-tsutome ni natte irasshaimasu.
11.	(a)	Have you eaten lunch yet?	Chuushoku o moo meshiagararemashita ka.
	(b)	No, not yet.	Iie, mada itadakimasen.
12.	(a)	What do you want to eat?	Nani o meshiagaritai desu ka.
	(b)	I want to eat Chinese food.	Chuuka ryoori o itadakitai desu.
13.	(a)	Have you seen Mr. Tanaka's picture?	Tanaka-sama no e o goran ni narimashita ka.
	(b)	Yes, I have.	Hai, haiken shimashita.
14.	(a)	What did the teacher say?	Sensei wa nan to osshaimashita ka.
	(b)	The teacher said that there will be an exam.	Sensei wa shiken ga aru to osshaimashita.
15.	(a)	Did you say that you will not come?	Anata wa konai to osshaimashita ka.
	(b)	Yes, I said so.	Hai, soo mooshimashita.
16.	(a)	What are you going to wear for graduation?	Sotsugyooshiki ni nani o o-meshi ni narimasu ka.
	(b)	I will wear kimono.	Kimono o kimasu.
17.	(a)	Do you know Mr. Tanaka of Nara?	Nara no Tanaka-sama o go-zonji desu ka.
	(b)	Yes, I do know (him).	Hai, zonjiagete imasu.
18.	(a)	Did you know Mr. Tanaka when you were in Japan?	Nihon ni irashita toki Tanaka-sama o go-zonji deshita ka.
	(b)	Yes, I knew him. He was my teacher.	Hai, zonjiagete imashita. Ano kata wa watakushi no sensei de gozaimashita.
19.	(a)	Has he gone to bed?	O-yasumi ni narimashita ka.
	(b)	Yes, he went to bed at 9:00.	Hai, ku-ji ni o-yasumi ni narimashita.
20.	(a)	Has he returned from Hiroshima?	Ano kata wa Hiroshima kara o-kaeri ni narimashita ka.
	(b)	Yes, he returned on the 8 o'clock train.	Hai, hachi-ji no kisha de o-kaeri ni narimashita.

21. (a)	Have you read Mr. Tanaka's book?	Tanaka-sama no hon o o-yomi ni narimashita ka.
(b)	No, I have not read it yet.	Iie, mada yomimasen.
22. (a)	Did he meet the principal in Kyoto?	Ano kata wa Kyooto de koochoo sensei ni o-ai ni narimashita ka.
(b)	Yes, he did.	Hai, o-ai ni narimashita.
23. (a)	Shall I call the doctor?	O-isha o o-yobi itashimashoo ka.
(b)	Yes, please call immediately.	Hai, sugu o-yobi kudasaimase.
24. (a)	Shall I visit your parents?	Anata no go-ryooshin o o-tazune itashimashoo ka.
(b)	Yes, please call on them.	Hai, o-tazune kudasaimase.
25. (a)	Have you ever lived in Osaka?	Anata wa Oosaka ni o-sumi ni natta koto ga arimasu ka.
(b)	No, I have not.	Iie, gozaimasen.

Translate into Japanese, using Honorific and Humble forms:

1. Have you ever been to Japan? No, but I would like to go once.
2. Our mistress went shopping at Daimaru, but she has not come home yet.

   Note: *Uchi* (house) is often used to indicate "our" in the sense of "belonging to the household."

   Uchi no jidoosha wa furui desu, or
   Uchi no ko wa itazura (mischievous) *de komarimasu.*

3. What time shall I call you, and what time do you (want to) eat breakfast?

   Note: *O + YOBI + ITASU* is the correct form for "to call." The humble form is used here because the speaker is in the first person.

   Shokuji o suru means "to have (one's) meal." Remember that *NASARU* is the honorific form of *SURU*.

4. When are you going to read this letter? I would like you to return (it) tomorrow.

   Note: The second sentence is requesting a favor. "Please give me the favor of. . . ." Therefore, *kaeshite itadakitai desu,* or *kaeshite itadakitoo gozaimasu.*

5. There is a television (set) in my room, but (it) is not mine.
6. I would (like) to introduce this person. This person is my teacher.
7. When you go to Tokyo will you meet Professor Tanaka?

Note: *Sensei* is used after a name, not only when referring to a teacher, but also to anyone who is respected because of his special training or esteemed status in his community (doctors, lawyers, politicians, etc.). ***Kyooju*** is reserved for college professors only.

8. Do you know my master (boss) who is living in Kyoto now?
   No, I do not know him at all.

   Note: *Go-zonji desu* is the honorific form for *shitte iru,* so it is used when referring to 2nd (you) or 3rd (he) person. For use by 1st person (I) *zonjiru* is used.

9. What time are you leaving tomorrow morning?
   What time are you returning to the inn? And where are you going?

   Note: "going," though in the progressive form, is used in the future tense, e.g., "I am going to Japan next month."

10. If you do not do exactly as your teacher says, you will be scolded.

   Note: "If you do not do . . ." is negative, conditional of ***nasaru,*** which is *nasa + ra + nakereba.*

Answer in Japanese, using both ordinary and superpolite (or ***humble****) forms.*

1. New York no natsu wa taihen o-atsuu gozaimasu ga Tookyoo wa ikaga de gozaimasu ka.
2. Sakuban (or *yuube*) benkyoo ga owatte kara terebi o goran ni narimashita ka.

   Note: In answering this question do not use *haiken suru,* as explained above in I.C. & G.N.

3. Anata wa konogoro nan-ji ni o-yasumi ni narimasu ka. Hayaku o-yasumi ni naru no ga o-suki desu ka.
4. Anata no otoosan wa ima uchi ni irasshaimasu ka. Nan-ji ni o-shigoto e o-dekake ni narimasu ka.
5. Anata wa ikutsu kanji o go-zonji desu ka. Doko de Nihongo o benkyoo nasaimashita ka.
6. Anata wa rainen no natsu Nihon e irassharu tsumori desu ka.
   Hikooki de ikaremasu ka.
7. America ni yoi Nihongo gakkoo ga gozaimasu ka.
   Sore wa donna gakkoo de gozaimasu ka.
8. Anata no ryooshin no o-namae wa nan to osshaimasu ka.
   Go-ryooshin wa o-genki de irasshaimasu ka.
9. Anata wa ima Eigo o go-benkyoochuu desu ka.

Note: The usage of the suffix *chuu* here is "in the midst of . . ." or "in the process of . . ."

a. Ima shigoto-*chuu* desu (in the midst of work).
b. Denwa wa hanashi-*chuu* deshita (in the midst of conversation, or the line was busy).

10. Anata wa Tookyoo daigaku no kyooju ga kakareta rekishi no hon o o-yomi ni narimashita ka.

Useful Expressions

At the Dinner Table (Shokutaku de)

1. HOST would say: *DOOZO TAKUSAN MESHIAGATTE KUDASAI.*—In persuading the guest to begin the meal, the host would say, "Please eat a lot."
2. GUEST would say: ITADAKIMASU.—A term used when beginning the meal. It has the meaning of "I am most grateful to receive this food."
3. HOST: *O-KAWARI O* (or *MOO SUKOSHI*) *IKAGA DESU KA.* The host, upon seeing that his guest is about ready for a refill on rice, sake, etc., would ask, "How about a refill (or a little more)?"
4. GUEST: *MOO KEKKOO DESU.*
   or
   MOO TAKUSAN DESU.—When the host offers another bowl of rice, sake, etc., and you wish to decline, it means, "I have had sufficient."
5. GUEST: *GOCHISOO SAMA DESHITA.*—"It was a delicious meal."
6. HOST: *O-SOMATSU SAMA DESHITA.*
   or
   O-SOMATSU DESHITA.—When the guest says, "*Gochisoo sama deshita,*" the host replies, "It wasn't much."

SUPPLEMENT X

INTERROGATIVE PRONOUN + KA

Postpositions are normally omitted with the following expressions, except for *doko-ka:*

itsu-ka	—sometime	(Watakushi wa *itsu-ka* Nihon e ikitai desu. I want to go to Japan *sometime.*)
dare-ka	—someone, somebody	(*Dare-ka* kono saifu o otoshimashita. *Someone* dropped this wallet.)
doko-ka	—someplace, somewhere	(*Doko-ka e* hirugohan o tabe ni ikimashoo. Let's go *someplace* to eat lunch.)
nani-ka	—something	(*Nani-ka* tsumetai mono o kudasai. Please give me *something* cool.)
ikura-ka	—some amount	(Ano kata wa *ikura-ka* Nihongo ga wakarimasu. He understands Japanese *somewhat.*)

INTERROGATIVE PRONOUN + DEMO

itsu-demo (itsu-mo)	—always, anytime	(Brown-san wa *itsu-mo* Nihongo o hanashimasu.—Mr. Brown *always* speaks Japanese.)
dare-demo	—anybody, everybody	(Amerika dewa *dare-demo* daigaku e ikemasu. —In Amerika, *anyone* can go to college.)
doko-demo (doko mo)	—anywhere, everywhere	(Nihon niwa *doko-demo* honya ga arimasu. In Japan, there are bookstores *everywhere.*)
nan-demo	—anything everything	(Watakushi no inu wa *nan-demo* tabemasu. My dog eats *anything.*)
ikura-demo	—any amount	(*Ikura-demo* meshiagatte kudasai. Please eat *any amount* [as much as you want.])

INTERROGATIVE PRONOUN + MO + NEGATIVE VERB

Note: Postpositions are not necessary with the following expressions:

*itsu-mo**	—never	(Sensei wa *itsu-mo* uchi ni imasen. The teacher *isn't ever* at home.)

dare-mo	—nobody, no one	(Atsumari ni *dare-mo* kimasen deshita. *No one* came to the meeting.)
*doko-mo**	—nowhere	(Nichiyoobi ni wa *doko-mo* mise ga aite imasen. On Sunday, shops are *not* open *anywhere.*)
nani-mo	—nothing	(Tsukue no naka ni *nani-mo* arimasen. There is *nothing* in the desk.)
ikura-mo	—no great amount	(Okane wa *ikura-mo* kakarimasen. It doesn't cost much money.)

* These words, when used with positive verb endings become:

itsu-mo	+	positive verb	=	always
doko-mo	+	positive verb	=	everywhere

INTERROGATIVE PRONOUN + "TE" VERB + MO

itsu . . . te mo	—whenever, no matter when . . .	(Fujisan wa *itsu mite mo* utsukushii desu. Mt. Fuji is beautiful *no matter when* you see it.)
dare . . . te mo	—whoever, no matter who . . .	(*Dare ga itte mo* au koto ga dekimasen. *No matter who* goes, (you) will not be able to see (him).
doko . . . te mo	—wherever, no matter where . . .	(*Doko de tabete mo* ii desu. *No matter where* I eat, it's all right. It doesn't matter where I eat.)
nani . . . te mo	—whatever, no matter what . . .	(*Nani o tabete mo* oishii desu. *No matter what* I eat, it's delicious.)
ikura . . . te mo	—however much, no matter how much . . .	(*Ikura denwa o shite mo* henji ga arimasen. *No matter how much* I telephone, there's no answer.)

USE OF KA AND DEMO WITH INTERROGATIVE PRONOUNS

Interrogative Pronouns	Int. Pro. + *ka*	Int. Pro. + *demo*	Int. Pro. + *mo* + positive verb	Int. Pro. + *mo* + neg. verb	Int. Pro. + "te" verb + *mo*
itsu (when)	sometime	always, anytime	always	never	whenever (no matter when)
dare (who)	someone, somebody	anybody, everybody	—	nobody, no one	whoever (no matter who)
doko (where)	someplace, somewhere	anywhere, everywhere	everywhere	nowhere	wherever (no matter where)
nani, nan (what)	something	anything, everything *(nan)*	—	nothing *(nani)*	whatever *(nani)* (no matter what)
ikura (how much)	some amount	any amount	any amount	no great amount	however much (no matter how much)

Exercises

Translate into Japanese:

1. Nobody knows about Tanaka's return to Japan.

   Note: about—*no koto*

2. Let us go somewhere to eat something warm.
3. a. This child takes everything home.

   b. He knows everything about Japan, so ask him.

4. a. There are always many students at his house.

   b. Please come anytime.

5. a. There are small shops everywhere in Japan.

   b. I cannot go anywhere nowadays.

   Note: nowadays—*chikagoro, konogoro, imagoro*

6. In America anybody can go to college if he studies hard.

   Note: hard—*yoku,* or *isshookenmei ni*

7. I didn't do anything in class today.
8. I have a feeling that I met him somewhere, sometime.

   Note: have a feeling—*yoo na ki ga suru*

9. Nobody said anything at the meeting *(kai)*.
10. Nobody likes to work without resting.

    Note: without resting, eating, buying, etc.—1st base of verb + *zu (ni)*

Answer in Japanese:

1. Anata wa *itsu-mo* Nihongo o hanashimasu ka.
2. Anata wa *itsu-ka* Nihon e iku tsumori desu ka.
3. Kono gakkoo no chikaku ni *doko-ka* chuushoku o taberu tokoro ga arimasu ka.
4. America dewa *dare-demo* daigaku e iku koto ga dekimasu ka.
5. Anata wa washoku nara *nan-demo* tabemasu ka.
6. Kyoo anata no uchi e Nihon kara *dare-ka* kimasu ka.
7. Nihonjin wa *dare-mo* Eigo o hanashimasen ka.
8. Ichinichijuu *nani-mo* tabenakereba doo narimasu ka.

    Note: *doo narimasu ka*—what will happen? (in the sense of "how will it turn out?")
    doo narimashita ka—what happened?
    doo shimasu ka—what will you do?
    doo shimashita ka—what did you do?

9. Kono chihoo de wa *doko-demo* jidoosha o nagai aida tomeru koto ga dekimasu ka.
10. Anata wa Nichiyoobi ni wa *itsu-mo doko-ka* e ikimasu ka.
12. Anata wa kyonen no natsuyasumi ni *doko-ka* e ikimashita ka.
    Doko-mo ikimasen deshita ka.
13. Anata wa maiasa *nani-mo* tabezu ni gakkoo e kimasu ka.
14. *Ikura-demo* gohan o taberu hito wa doo narimasu ka.
15. Anata wa Tanaka-san ni *itsu-ka doko-ka* de atta koto ga arimasu ka.

CHAPTER 20

DENWA NO KAIWA—TELEPHONE CONVERSATION

FAMILIAR (ABRUPT) FORMS

FIRST BASE of VERB	+	NAI DE / ZU NI	=	WITHOUT . . .
VERB or ADJ.	+	SHI	=	IN ADDITION TO . . .

chuugaku jidai kara	from junior high school time
chuugaku jidai kara no yoi tomodachi	good friends from junior high school days

KIMURA-KUN TO YAMADA-KUN WA CHUUGAKU JIDAI KARA NO YOI TOMODACHI DE ARU.	KIMURA AND YAMADA HAVE BEEN GOOD FRIENDS SINCE JUNIOR HIGH SCHOOL DAYS.

natsuyasumichuu	through the summer vacation
kuni e kaette	returned home and . . .
*Kimura-kun wa natsuyasumichuu kuni e kaette . . .	*Kimura was (returned) home through the summer vacation and . . .

chichi no shigoto o	father's work (obj.)
tetsudatte ita	was helping
*chichi no shigoto o tetsudatte ita ga . . .	*he was helping his father's work, but . . .
aki no gakki ga	fall semester (nom.)
hajimaru shi . . .	will begin, furthermore . . .
yooji ga dekita node	business came up, so . . .
*aki no gakki ga hajimaru shi yooji ga dekita node . . .	*because the fall semester will begin, and furthermore, (some) business came up . . .
itsu-mo yori hayaku	earlier than usual

KIMURA-KUN WA NATSU-YASUMICHUU KUNI E KAETTE CHICHI NO SHIGOTO O TETSUDATTE ITA GA AKI NO GAKKI GA HAJIMARU *SHI* YOOJI GA DEKITA NODE ITSU-MO YORI HAYAKU TOOKYOO E DETE KITA.

KIMURA WAS HOME THROUGH THE SUMMER AND WAS HELPING HIS FATHER (WITH HIS) WORK, BUT THE FALL SEMESTER WILL BEGIN (SOON) AND, FURTHERMORE, (SOME) BUSINESS CAME UP SO HE CAME OUT TO TOKYO EARLIER THAN USUAL.

YAMADA-KUN NO OTOOSAN WA GINKOOIN DE UCHI WA TOOKYOO NO KOOGAI NI ARU.

YAMADA'S FATHER IS A BANKER AND (HIS) HOME IS IN A SUBURB OF TOKYO.

Tookyoo no aru daigaku ni	to a certain university in Tokyo
nyuugaku o kiboo shite	desire entrance and
*Tookyoo no aru daigaku ni nyuugaku o kiboo shite . . .	*(He) wished to enter a certain university in Tokyo and . . .
rainen no sangatsu no	next year's March
nyuugaku shiken	entrance examination
juken jumbichuu	in the midst of preparation for the examination

KARE WA TOOKYOO NO ARU DAIGAKU NI NYUUGAKU O KIBOO SHITE IMA WA RAINEN NO SANGATSU NO NYUUGAKU SHIKEN NO JUKEN JUMBICHUU DE ARU.	HE IS HOPING TO ENTER A CERTAIN UNIVERSITY IN TOKYO AND IS IN THE MIDST OF PREPARATION FOR NEXT MARCH'S ENTRANCE EXAMINATION NOW.
benkyoo bakari	only study
benkyoo bakari shite ita node . . .	because (he) has been only studying . . .
shoo-shoo taikutsu shi	somewhat bored and
kaette kureba ii naa	it would be good if (he) returns
NAGAI AIDA BENKYOO BAKARI SHITE ITA NODE SHOO-SHOO TAIKUTSU SHI, HAYAKU TOMODACHI NO KIMURA-KUN GA KAETTE KUREBA II NAA TO OMOTTE ITA.	BECAUSE HE HAD BEEN JUST STUDYING FOR A LONG TIME, HE WAS SOMEWHAT BORED AND HE WAS THINKING IT WOULD BE NICE IF HIS FRIEND KIMURA WOULD COME HOME SOON.
denwa o kakeru	to telephone
denwa o kakeru tokoro	on the point of telephoning
KIMURA-KUN WA YAMADA-KUN NI DENWA O KAKERU *TOKORO* DE ARU.	KIMURA IS ABOUT TO PHONE YAMADA.
K: MOSHI MOSHI, MITAKA NO	HELLO, I WOULD LIKE TO

YAMADA-SAN NO DENWA BANGOO O SHIRITAI NO DESU GA . . .	KNOW THE TELEPHONE NUMBER OF MR. YAMADA IN MITAKA, BUT. . . .
KOOKANSHU: SHOO-SHOO O-MACHI KUDASAI . . . MOSHI, MOSHI, YAMADA-SAN NO DENWA BANGOO WA MITAKA NO ICHI-ICHI-NI-NANA-BAN DESU.	PLEASE WAIT A LITTLE. . . . HELLO, YAMADA'S TELEPHONE NUMBER IS MITAKA 1127.
K: ARIGATOO.	THANK YOU.
MOSHI, MOSHI, YAMADA-SAN NO OTAKU DESU KA.	HELLO, IS (THIS) MR. YAMADA'S RESIDENCE?
JOCHUU: HAI, SAYOO DE GOZAIMASU.	YES, IT IS.
DONATA-SAMA DE IRASSHAIMASU KA.	WHO IS THIS?
K: KIMURA KENJI DESU. YOSHIO-SAN WA IRASSHAIMASU KA.	THIS IS KENJI KIMURA. IS YOSHIO-SAN IN?
JOCHUU: HAI, IRASSHAIMASU. CHOTTO O-MACHI KUDASAIMASE. O-YOBI ITASHIMASU KARA.	YES, HE IS. PLEASE WAIT AWHILE. I WILL CALL HIM.
K: O-NEGAI ITASHIMASU.	PLEASE DO.

(The English translation of the following portion will be given at the end of this section.)

		FAMILIAR FORM	ORDINARY POLITE FORM
1.	Y:	MOSHI, MOSHI, KIMURA-KUN KA.	Moshi, moshi, Kimura-kun desu ka.
		HISASHIBURI DA NE.	Hisashiburi desu ne.
		KIMI, MADA TOOBUN KAETTE KONAI TO OMOTTE ITA.	Anata wa mada toobun kaette korarenai to omotte imashita.
2.		DOOSHITE SONNA NI HAYAKU KAETTE KITA N' DA.	Dooshite sonna ni hayaku kaette kimashita ka.
3.	K:	TOOKYOO GA KOISHIKU NATTE KAETTE KITA...	Tookyoo ga koishiku natte kaette kimashita.
		KIMI WA ZUTTO BENKYOO KAI.	Anata wa zutto benkyoo desu ka.
4.	Y:	UN, SOO DA YO. KIMI GA KUNI E KAETTE KARA DOKO E MO *IKAZU NI* BENKYOO SA.	Hai, soo desu. Anata ga kuni e kaerarete kara doko e mo ikazu ni benkyoo desu.
		SORE NI KONO ATSUSA DAROO.	Sore ni kono atsusa deshoo.

	SUKKARI KUSATCHATTA.	Sukkari kusatte shimaimashita.
	INAKA WA DOO DATTA.	Inaka wa doo deshita ka.
	ATSUKATTA KA.	Atsukatta desuka.
5. K:	AIKAWARAZU DA.	Aikawarazu desu ka.
	ASA KARA BAN MADE OYAJI NO TETSUDAI SASERARETE SA, BENKYOO NAN-KA SURU HIMA ZENZEN NAKATTA.	Asa kara ban made chichi no tetsudai o saserarete benkyoo nado suru hima ga zenzen arimasen deshita.
6.	SUGOKU ISOGASHII N' DA.	Taihen isogashii no desu.
	TEGAMI O KAKU HIMA GA NAKATTA GURAI DA.	Tegami o kaku hima ga nai gurai deshita.
	DA KARA ZUTTO GOBUSATA SHICHATTA.	Desu kara zutto go-busata shite shimaimashita.
7.	TOOKYOO WA GOTAGOTA SHITE IRU GA YAHARI TOOKYOO NO HOO GA II NE.	Tookyoo wa gota-gota shite imasu ga yahari Tookyoo no hoo ga ii desu ne.
8. Y:	SOO KA NE. KIMI O URA-	Soo desu ka ne. Anata o urayamashi-

	YAMASHIKU OMOTTE ITA N' DA. . . . INAKA NO NOMBIRI SHITA SEIKATSU GA DEKITE SA. .	ku omotte imashita. . . . Inaka no nombiri shita seikatsu ga dekimasu no de . . .
9.	SORE WA SOO TO, KIMI CHOODO II TOKI NI DETE KITE KURETA YO.	Anata wa choodo ii toki ni dete kite kuremashita.
10.	SUUGAKU NO SHUKU-DAI NAN DA GA WAKA-RANAI TOKORO GA TAKUSAN ATTE MAI-TCHATTA.	Suugaku no shukudai desu ga waka-ranai tokoro ga takusan atte maitte shimaimashita.
11.	TESUDATTE KURENAI KAI.	Tetsudatte kuremasen ka.
K:	UN, II YO.	Hai, ii desu.
12. Y:	SOSHITE, TENKI MO II SHI DOKO-KA E IKOO JA NAI KA. ASU NO ASA WA ISOGASHII KAI.	Soshite, tenki mo yoi shi doko-ka e ikoo dewa arimasen ka. Asu no asa wa o-isogashii desu ka.
13. K:	IYA, BETSU NI. ORE MO KIMI O SASOI-DASOO	Iie, betsu ni. Watakushi mo anata o o-sasoi shiyoo to omotte (o)denwa o

TO OMOTTE DENWA SHITA N' DA YO. DOKO E IKOO KA.

shimashita. Doko e ikimashoo ka.

14. Y: ANO NE, HITOMAZU BOKU NO UCHI E KITE KURENAI KAI. CHUU-SHOKU DEMO ISSHO NI TABETE KARA DOKO-KA E DEKAKEYOO.

Ano, hitomazu watakushi no uchi e kite kuremasen ka. Chuushoku demo issho ni tabete kara doko-ka e deka-kemashoo.

15. K: JAMA JA NAI KA. ASU WA DOYOOBI DE MIN-NA IE NI IRU N' DAROO.

Jama dewa arimasen ka. Asu wa do-yoobi de minasan ie ni orareru no deshoo.

16. Y: SONNA SHIMPAI IRAN SA.

Sonna shimpai wa irimasen.

ENRYO *SEZU NI* KOI YO. OFUKURO NI NANI-KA GOCHISOO TSUKUTTE MORAU KARA . . .

Enryo sezu ni kinasai. Haha ni nani-ka gochisoo o tsukutte moraimasu kara . . .

17. K: NAN-JI GORO GA II KAI.

Nan-ji goro ga ii desu ka.

18. Y: SOO DA NE. JUU-JI GORO, DOO DA.

Soo desu ne. Juu-ji goro wa ikaga desu ka.

19. K: ASA NO UCHI CHOTTO

Asa no uchi chotto gakkoo ni yorima-

	GAKKOO NI YORU KARA SUKOSHI OSOKU NARU KAMO SHIRENAI GA....	su kara sukoshi osoku naru kamo shiremasen ga....
20. Y:	JA, MATTE IRU YO. KOKO E KURU MICHI SHITTE IRU DAROO.	Dewa, matte imasu. Koko e kuru michi wa shitte imasu deshoo.
21. K:	UN, SHITTE IRU YO... NI-SAN-KAI ITTA KOTO GA ARU KARA.... MITAKA NO EKI KARA CHIKAKATTA NE.	Hai, shitte imasu. Ni-san-kai itta koto ga arimasu kara.... Mitaka no eki kara chikakatta desu ne.
22. Y:	SOO DA YO. WAKARA-NAKATTARA DENWA KURE YO.... MUKAE NI IKU KARA....	Soo desu. Wakaranakattara denwa kudasai.... Mukae ni ikimasu kara.
K:	JA, MATA.	Dewa, mata.

TRANSLATION

1. Y: Hello, is this Kimura? It's been a long time, hasn't it? I thought you weren't coming home for some time yet.
2. Why did you return so soon?
3. K: I became homesick for Tokyo and came back. Have you been studying all along?

4. Y: Since you went home I've been studying without going anywhere.
And this heat!
I'm completely disgusted.
How was the country?
Was it hot?

5. K: Same as usual. I was made to help my father from morning till night and I did not have any time to study.

6. It was terribly busy . . . didn't have time to write any letters.
Therefore, I have completely neglected to write.

7. Tokyo is confusing, but Tokyo is better after all.

8. Y: Is that right? I was feeling envious of you, being able to live a carefree country life.

9. Incidentally, you returned just in time.

10. About the math homework, there are many points that I do not understand. I'm completely stupefied.

11. Won't you help me?
K: O.K.

12. Y: And since the weather is good, shouldn't we go somewhere?
Are you busy tomorrow morning?

13. K: No, not especially. I, too, telephoned with the intention of asking you out.
Where shall we go?

14. Y: Say, won't you come to my house first? Let's eat lunch together and go someplace.

15. K: Won't I be in the way? Tomorrow is Saturday and probably everybody will be home.

16. Y: There is no need for such concern. Don't hesitate, and come on. I'll have my mother prepare something good.

17. K: What time shall we make it?

18. Y: Let me see. About 10 o'clock, how about it?

19. K: In the morning I'll drop by at school for awhile, so I may be a little late.

20. Y: Then, I'll be waiting. You know the way to get here, don't you?

21. K: Yes, I do, since I've been there two or three times.
It was near Mitaka station, wasn't it?

22. Y: That's right. If you can't figure it out, give me a call.
I'll come after you.
K: Then, I'll see you later.

The above conversation, when carried on between two girl friends, will be as follows. Notice the endings and the use of "emphasizing particles." The tendency is toward the use of milder sounding endings. Also note the intonation mark (——╱) placed at the end of the sentence to indicate the pitch.

1. Y: MOSHI MOSHI, KIMURA-SAN. HISASHIBURI NE. ANATA, MADA TOOBUN KAETTE KONAI TO OMOTTE ITA WA YO.

2. DOOSHITE SONNA NI HAYAKU KAETTE KITA NO.

3. K: TOOKYOO GA KOISHIKU NATTE KAETTE KITA WA. ANATA WA ZUTTO BENKYOO.

4. Y: EE, SOO YO. ANATA GA KUNI E KAETTE KARA DOKO E MO IKANAI DE BENKYOO YO.
SORE NI KONO ATSUSA DESHOO.
SUKKARI IYA NI NATCHATTA WA.
INAKA WA DOO.
ATSUKATTA.

5. K: AIKAWARAZU YO. ASA KARA BAN MADE CHICHI NO TETSUDAI O SASERARETE NE—BENKYOO NANKA SURU HIMA ZENZEN NAKATTA WA. SUGOKU ISOGASHII NO YO. TEGAMI O KAKU HIMA GA NAKATTA GURAI YO. DAKARA ZUTTO GO-BUSATA SHICHATTA WA.

7. TOOKYOO WA GOTA-GOTA SHITE'RU KEDO YAHARI TOOKYOO NO HOO GA II WA.

8. Y: SOO. ANATA O URAYAMASHIKU OMOTTE ITA NO YO.... INAKA NO NOMBIRI SHITA SEIKATSU GA DEKITE.

9. SORE WA SOO TO, ANATA CHOODO II TOKI NI DETE KITE KURETA WA.

10. SUUGAKU NO SHUKUDAI DA KEDO, WAKARANAI TOKORO GA TAKUSAN ATTE NE—KOMATCHATTA NO YO.

11. TETSUDATTE KURENAI.

K: EE, II WA YO.

12. Y: SOSHITE, TENKI MO II SHI DOKO-KA E IKANAI.

ASU NO ASA ISOGASHII.

13. K: IIE, BETSU NI. WATASHI MO ANATA O SASOI DASOO TO OMOTTE DENWA SHITA NO YO. DOKO E IKU NO.

14. Y: ANO NE, HITO MAZU WATASHI NO UCHI E KITE KURENAI.

CHUUSHOKU DEMO ISSHO NI TABETE KARA DOKO-KA E IKANAI.

15. K: JAMA JA NAI. ASU DOYOO DE MINNA UCHI NI IRASSHARU N' DESHOO.

16. Y: SONNA SHIMPAI IRANAI WA YO. ENRYO SHINAI DE KITE YO.

HAHA NI NANI-KA GO-CHISOO TSUKUTTE MORAU KARA. . . .

17. K: NAN-JI GORO GA II.

18. Y: SOO NE. JUU-JI GORO DOO.

19. K: ASA NO UCHI CHOTTO GAKKOO NI YORU KARA SUKOSHI OSOKU NARU KAMO SHIRENAI KEDO.

20. Y: JA, MATTE'RU WA YO. KOKO E KURU MICHI SHITTE IRU WA NE.

21. K: EE, SHITTE IRU WA YO. NI-SAN-KAI ITTA KOTO GA ARU KARA. MITAKA NO EKI KARA CHIKAKATTA WA NE.

22. Y: SOO YO. WAKARANAKATTARA DENWA CHOODAI. MUKAE NI IKU KARA.

K: JA, MATA.

Vocabulary from the Lesson

jidai	(n.) period, era, days. ***Meiji Jidai***—Meiji Period
kuni	(n.) country, place of birth, rural area
tetsudau	(v.t.) help, assist
gakki	(n.) semester, school term (*kongakki*—this semester; *sengakki*—last semester; *raigakki*—next semester)
. . . shi	(conj.) furthermore, in addition to (See I.C. & G.N.)
yooji	(n.) business, errand
yooji ga dekiru	business came up
itsu-mo yori . . .	than always, than usual
koogai	(n.) suburb
nyuugaku	(n.) school entrance
nyuugaku shiken	(n.) entrance examination
nyuugaku suru	(Chi. v.) enter school

kiboo	(n.) hope, desire
kiboo suru	(Chi. v.) hope (for), look forward to
juken suru	(Chi. v.) to take a test
jumbi	(n.) preparation
jumbi suru	(Chi. v.) prepare; . . .*no jumbi suru* —prepare *for*. . . .
juken jumbi	(n.) preparation for an examination
juken jumbichuu	in the midst of preparation for an exam
bakari	(suf.) only, just
taikutsu suru	(Chi. v.) be bored, weary
shoo-shoo	(same as *sukoshi*) little, few
. . . **ba ii naa**	if . . . it would be nice (See I.C. & G.N.)
denwa o kakeru	(same as *denwa o* to telephone *suru*)
. . . **tokoro**	at the time . . ., just when . . ., (See I.C. & G.N.)
hisashiburi	(idio.) after a long time (interval, silence)
toobun	for some time, for a while
koishii	(adj.) long for, love for
koishiku naru	to get a feeling for
un	informal of *hai* (yes)
kusatchatta	(v.) same as *kusatte shimaimashita;* (See I.C. & G.N.) completely disgusted, gloomy, depressed.
inaka	rural area, country
oyaji	(n.) familiar form of father, used by men only.
tetsudai saserarete	(causative, passive form of *suru*) . . . was made to help
nan-ka (nado)	such things as, among other things
sugoi	(adj.) horrible, terrible, tremendous
sugoku	(adv.) terribly, tremendously

gurai	. . . to the extent, to the same degree as . . .
go-busata suru	(Ch. v.) neglect to write, neglect to call
shichatta	(same as *shite shimaimashita*) did it completely
gota-gota	confusion, trouble
gota-gota suru	(Chi. v.) confusing, be upset
urayamashii	(adj.) envious
nombiri suru	(Chi. v.) relax, feel at leisure
seikatsu	(n.) life, existence; *seikatsu suru*— to live
suugaku	(n.) mathematics
mairu	(v. i.) tired, upset
ore	(pro.) I, familiar for *watakushi*, used by men only.
sasou	(v. t.) invite, ask
sasoi-dasu	(compound verb) invite out, ask out
ano ne	(expression used to call attention of the listener) Say!
jama	(n.) hindrance, obstacle, nuisance
jama suru	(Chi. v.) stand in the way, obstruct
enryo	(n.) hestitation, modest
enryo suru	(Chi. v.) refrain from, be modest
yoru	(v. i.) drop by, call at; *place* + *ni yoru*—call at . . .
mukaeru	(v. t.) meet, call
mukae ni iku	go to meet, go to pick up
ofukuro	(n.) familiar form of "mother," used by men only.

Important Construction and Grammar Notes

FAMILIAR (ABRUPT) FORM: Throughout this book the polite form of speech (*masu* and *desu* endings) has been emphasized because this form is polite enough to express respect and courtesy, but not so polite that it is awkwardly out of place. Since Japanese society is a polite one, the language reflecting this is very refined. In the previous chapter the honorific (or superpolite form) was introduced. Formality signifies certain social distance, or lack of intimacy between the speakers. However, there is an area where such formality may be dispensed with and the exchange is conducted on a "familiar," intimate basis, such as between members of the same family, although a mother will often continue to use the polite form, between social superiors talking to inferiors, or among close friends. The same form of familiar speech patterns are not used in all the relations mentioned here. A father, talking to other members of the family, may use the familiar form, but this would not be the same as the form used among male friends. Again, this would differ when female friends are involved. Therefore, great caution must be exercised when using this pattern because it can easily create embarrassing moments for those who are on the receiving side, while the speaker may be innocently unaware of his mistakes. In this chapter, the familiar form used among male friends is introduced first, followed by conversation between female friends.

This lesson is introduced here mainly to familiarize the reader with this form of expression when he hears it, rather than to teach it for general conversational use. The understanding of the underlying "feeling" of familiarity is too difficult to explain and adequately illustrate. Improper usage at an inopportune moment may sound too familiar and abrupt, and often impolite.

CONCLUDING PARTICLES *(shuujoshi)*: The difference between male and female familiar forms is mainly in the usage of "concluding particles," viz., *ne, no, yo, wa,* etc., as explained below.

I. a. *YO* is used to emphasize, to point out.

1. Mada hachi-ji *yo.*
2. Ii *yo.*
3. Ano hito da *yo.*

. . . *NO YO* ending used by women only

1. Wakaranai *no yo.*
2. Asu korarenai *no yo.*

. . . *WA YO* (women only)

1. Moo kaetta *wa yo.*
2. O-kane nai *wa yo.*

b. *YO* used with a verb to command or encourage
   1. Ike *yo.*
   2. Yamenasai *yo.*

c. *YO* used with the 5th base to invite, to coax
   1. Hayaku ikoo *yo.*
   2. Tabeyoo *yo.*

II. a. *WA* is used to emphasize lightly, used more often by women to moderate what has been said so that it will not sound too harsh.
   1. Soo omou *wa.*
   2. Ikitaku nai *wa.*

b. . . . *WA NE* (women only) for mild exclamatory remark
   1. Suteki da *wa ne.* (Isn't it wonderful!)
   2. Yoku irasshaimashita *wa ne.*

III. a. *SA* is used to lightly dismiss a statement or something that is so obvious to the speaker that there is no need to talk further about it.
   1. Kare wa dame *sa.*
   2. Yasashii mono *sa.*

b. *SA,* when used with an interrogative word, restates a question.
   1. Doko e iku no *sa.* (Where are you going, huh?)
   2. Nani *sa* kore. (What is this, anyway?)

c. *SA* is used to emphasize a point in order to call attention.
   1. Da kara *sa* . . . (for this reason. . . .)
   2. Kimi *sa* moo sukoshi ki o tsukero. (YOU should be more careful.)

IV. a. *NE* is used at the end of a statement to demonstrate light exclamation.
   1. Kono heya, ii heya *ne.*
   2. Komatta hito *ne.* (He certainly is a troublesome person.)

b. *NE* is used for light insistence, for light emphasis.
   1. Watakushi wa soo omoimasu *ne.*
   2. Nihonjin o mita toki ureshikatta *ne.*

c. *NE* is used to ask for agreement with you, or when asking for response.
   1. Hachi-ji no kisha desu *ne.*
   2. Hontoo ni irasshai *ne.*

d. *NE* is also used to emphasize, or merely as a pausing word.
   1. Kimi *ne* dekiru kai.
   2. Sore wa *ne* chigau yo.
   3. Kesa *ne* watakushi wa *ne* . . .

v. a. *NO* is used by women to lightly conclude.
1. Tabetaku nai *no.*
2. Ashita yasumi desu *no.*
3. Anata ga warui *no.*
4. Wakaranai *no yo.*
5. Kinoo dashita *no yo.*

b. *NO* is used to ask a question.
1. Kore kimi *no* (?)
2. Kore kureru *no* (?)
3. Mada bangohan taberarenai *no* (?)

vi. a. *ZE* is used by men to call attention in a friendly manner.
1. Kore oishii *ze.*
2. Hayaku kaeroo *ze.*

b. *ZE* is also used to show confidence of the speaker.
1. Ammari ate ni naranai *ze.* (He isn't too reliable.)
2. Kimi ga warui n' da *ze.*

vii. a. *ZO* is used by men to convince someone of something.
1. Omoshiroi *zo.*
2. Nani ka aru *zo.*

b. *ZO* is used to emphasize, to warn, to call attention to something.
1. Kare keikan (police) da *zo.*
2. Koko wa abunai *zo.*

WOMEN'S SPEECH PATTERNS: Some of the characteristic features of the informal and formal speech patterns used by women may be listed as follows:

i. Frequent use of "*te*" form of ending
a. Ano mise wa *takakutte yo.* (emphatic ending)
b. Okusan wa nan to *itte*? (interrogative)
c. Hayaku *irashite.* (request)

ii. Use of "concluding particles" *wa, yo, no, na, ne* (explained above)
a. Ikimasu *wa.*
b. Komban ikenai *no.* Naze desu *no*?
c. Kore wa watakushi *no yo.*
d. Shizuka *ne.*

III. Questions ending with a noun
   a. Dare?
   b. Sore nani?
   c. Hontoo? (Is it true?)

IV. Common use of intonation in expressing one's feeling (examples given on pages 380–382)

ABRUPT ENDINGS: Another feature of the familiar form is the abrupt endings of sentences. The following chart shows these endings.

ABRUPT ENDINGS

	PRESENT	(neg.)	PAST	(neg.)
VERBS				
read	yomu	yomanai	yonda	yomanakatta
write	kaku	kakanai	kaita	kakanakatta
eat	taberu	tabenai	tabeta	tabenakatta
do	suru	shinai	shita	shinakatta
come	kuru	konai	kita	konakatta
there is	aru	nai	atta	nakatta
standing	tatte iru	tatte inai	tatte ita	tatte inakatta
walking	aruite iru	aruite inai	aruite ita	aruite inakatta
ADJECTIVES				
hot	atsui	atsukunai	atsukatta	atsukunakatta
far	tooi	tookunai	tookatta	tookunakatta
big	ookii	ookikunai	ookikatta	ookikunakatta
NOUNS				
(It is) a book	hon da	hon ja nai	hon datta	hon ja nakatta
(He is) a Japanese	Nihonjin da	Nihonjin ja nai	Nihonjin datta	Nihonjin ja nakatta

OMISSION OF POSTPOSITIONS AND USE OF CONTRACTIONS: In the examples given in the text of this chapter, the reader may have noticed the omission of postpositions. The speech tends to become slovenly and imprecise and the postpositions (usually *wa* and *o*) are often ignored.

a. Kimi mita ka.
b. Kimi bangohan tabeta ka.

For the same reason, the contractions of words occur more frequently.

. . . *ja* is the contraction of . . . *de wa.*
. . . *janai* is the contraction of . . . *dewa arimasen.*
. . . *chatta* is the contraction of . . . *te shimatta.*
. . . *n' da* is the contraction of . . . *no desu.*

WORD ORDER: Often the word order, viz., the subordinate clause + principal clause, is reversed (see sentences 8, 16, 21, and 22). However, this is a feature common not only in familiar forms but in all colloquial expressions. The subordinate clause is often attached as if an afterthought. Instead of saying:

a. *Ame ga futte iru kara* ikimasen.
b. *Anata ga iku nara* watakushi mo ikimasu.

In colloquial form one may say:

a. Ikimasen—*ame ga futte iru kara.*
b. Watakushi mo ikimasu—*anata ga iku nara.*

OMISSION OF "DESU KA": In sentences 1 and 12, the questions are asked without **desu ka.** Compare the 3 levels of politeness given in the following examples:

	FAMILIAR		POLITE	SUPERPOLITE
	Men	*Women*		
"Is this Kimura?"	Kimura-kun ka. Kimura-kun kai.	Kimura-san?	Kimura-san desu ka.	Kimura-san de gozaimasu ka.
"What is it?"	Nani ka.	Nani?	Nan desu ka.	Nan de gozaimasu ka.
"Is it expensive?"	Takai ka. Takai kai.	Takai?	Takai desu ka.	Takoo gozaimasu ka.
"Do you want to go?"	Ikitai ka. Ikitai kai	Ikitai?	Ikitai desu ka.	Ikitoo gozaimasu ka.

The question form used by women is given by the rise in intonation at the end of the word.

USAGE OF "DA": **da** is the familiar form of **desu** used more often by men. In sentences 1, 5, 6, and 8, examples of this usage are given.

	FAMILIAR		POLITE	SUPERPOLITE
	Men	*Women*		
"It's been a long time, hasn't it!"	Hisashiburi da ne.	Hisashiburi ne.	Hisashiburi desu ne.	Hisashiburi de gozaimasu ne.
"Telephone!"	Denwa da yo.	O-denwa yo.	O-denwa desu.	O-denwa de gozaimasu.
"This is (the) teacher's"	Sensei no da.	Sensei no yo.	Sensei no desu.	Sensei no de gozaimasu.

Datta is the past form of **da;** its formal equivalent is **deshita.**

	FAMILIAR		POLITE	SUPERPOLITE
	Men	*Women*		
"It was a boy."	Otoko no ko datta (yo).	Otoko no ko datta wa.	Otoko no ko deshita.	Otoko no ko de gozaimashita.
"It was Sunday."	Nichiyoobi datta (yo).	Nichiyoobi datta wa.	Nichiyoobi deshita.	Nichiyoobi de gozaimashita.

... SHI: Used with the root form of verbs as well as adjectives, this form is used to bind two clauses together and mean "in addition to" or "moreover." It is used to describe a situation more fully by saying "not only . . . but also . . ."

VERB:

Kyoo wa ame ga *futte iru shi* shigoto ga takusan *aru shi* doko e mo ikimasen. — It's raining today; moreover, I have lots of work, so I will not go anywhere.

Brown san wa Nihongo ga *hanaseru shi* kanji mo yoku kakeru. — Brown can not only speak Japanese, he can write kanji well.

ADJECTIVE:

Kono jidoosha wa *chiisai shi* yasui kara kaimasu. — This car is small; furthermore, it is cheap, so I'll buy it.

NOUN:

Kyoo wa *Nichiyoobi da shi* ashita wa yasumi da kara yama e ikimasu.	Today is Sunday; moreover, tomorrow is a holiday, so I'll go to the mountains.

. . . CHATTA (. . . TE SHIMATTA): **Shimatta** is the past form of **shimau**, which indicates completion or finality of an action.

tabete *shimau*	eat it *up*
yonde *shimatta*	read it *through*
tsukatte *shimatta*	used it *all up*
utte *shimaimashita*	sold it (and) *now gone*

POLITE	FAMILIAR
yonde *shimatta*	*yonjatta*
tsukatte *shimatta*	*tsukatchatta*
utte *shimatta*	*utchatta*

. . . ZU NI (or . . . NAI DE): These negative suffixes are added to the negative stem of the verb—the first base—and gives the meaning of ". . . without . . ."

1. Nani-mo ka*wazu ni* kaetta. Nani-mo ka*wanai de* kaetta.	I returned *without buying* anything.
2. Chooshoku o tabe*zu ni* itta. Chooshoku o tabe*nai de* itta.	I went *without eating* breakfast.
3. Benkyoo se*zu ni* gakkoo e itta. Benkyoo shi*nai de* gakkoo e itta.	I went to school *without studying*.

Note that in this usage "without . . ." is the subordinate clause which must come first, followed by the principal clause.

. . . BA II NAA: This familiar form is used by men only. Literal translation of this construction is "if . . . it would be nice," expressing a desire, or an aspiration.

Hayaku yasumi ni *nareba ii naa.*	If it becomes vacation soon, it would be nice. (Won't it be wonderful if it becomes vacation soon!)

Jidoosha ga *areba ii naa.*	It would be nice to have a car.
Sensei ga *kureba ii naa.*	I wish the teacher would come.
Shiken ga *yasashikereba ii naa.*	I hope the exam will be easy.

CAUSATIVE FORM: This form of expression is used to show the subject making, or causing, someone to do something. Study the following sentences to understand how and when this expression is used.

1. I made the taxi wait.
2. The mother made the boy eat the fruit.

In the first sentence "I" caused the "taxi" to "wait" and in the second "the mother" caused the "boy" to "eat."

Hence, the causative form of the verb is used.

1st BASE OF YODAN VERB	+	SERU

Causative forms for *matsu, kaku, yomu* are:

ta + SERU—make (someone) wait
chi
ma + tsu
te
to

ka + ka + SERU—make (someone) write
yo + ma + SERU—make (someone) read

For ichidan, or non-conjugating verb, the causative is:

STEM OF ICHIDAN VERB	+	SASERU

tabe + SASERU—make (someone) eat
mi + SASERU—make (someone) see

Let us now consider a situation where passive is combined with the causative—a situation where the subject is made to do something.

1. I am made to wait.
2. The students are made to see . . .

First, form the causative according to the rule given above:

1. mataseru
2. misaseru

Now, make the passive of these non-conjugating verbs, the rule being STEM OF NON-CONJUGATING VERB + RARERU.

1. matase + *rareru*—(I) am made to wait.
2. misase + *rareru*—(I) am made to see.

Study the causative + passive form of the following:

1. *sase* + *rareru*—(I) am made to do. (The first base of *suru* is *sa*. The causative is *sa* + *seru*. When the passive is added to this it becomes *sase* + *rareru*.)
2. *tatase* + *rareru*—(I) am made to stand.
3. *arukase* + *rareru*—(I) am made to walk.
4. *kisase* + *rareru*—(I) am made to wear.

Consider the following:

If	you	do not	want	to be made	to wait. . . .
cond.	pass.	negative	desid.	causative	

This is translated as follows:

matsu
mata*se* (causative)
matase*rare* (caus. + passive)
matasrare*tai* (caus. + pass. + desiderative)
matasrare*takunai* (caus. + pass. + desid. + negative)
matasraretakuna*kereba* (caus. + pass. + desid. + neg. + conditional)

This example amply illustrates the agglutinative nature of Japanese verbs.

Fluency Drill

Tabezu ni itta.
Tabezu ni gakkoo e itta.
Chooshoku o tabezu ni gakkoo e itta.
Chooshoku o tabezu ni gakkoo e aruite itta.
Mainichi chooshoku o tabezu ni gakkoo e aruite iku.
Osoi kara chooshoku o tabezu ni gakkoo e isoide ikinasai.
Osoi nara nani mo tabezu ni gakkoo e basu de isoide ikinasai.

(I) went without eating.
(I) went to school without eating.
(I) went to school without eating breakfast.
(I) walked to school without eating breakfast.
Everyday (I) walk to school without eating breakfast.
Because it's late, hurry to school without eating breakfast.
If it's late, hurry to school by bus without eating anything.

Substitution Drill

(First Base Verb + ZU NI)

KAWAZU NI (kawanai de) MOTAZU NI (motanai de) MIZU NI (minai de) SEZU NI (shinai de)	+ GAKKOO E IKU

Exercises

Translate the following, using polite and informal endings:

1. I went to school without washing my face.	Kao o arawazu ni gakkoo e itta. (arawanai de)
2. I went to school without eating breakfast.	Chooshoku o tabezu ni gakkoo e itta. (tabenai de)
3. I went to school without taking my lunch.	Bentoo o motazu ni gakkoo e itta. (motanai de)
4. I went in without paying any money.	O-kane o harawazu ni hairimashita. (harawanai de)
5. I went in without buying a ticket.	Kippu o kawazu ni hairimashita.
6. I went in without writing my name.	Namae o kakazu ni hairimashita.
7. I worked without resting *(yasumu)*.	Yasumazu ni hatarakimashita.
8. I worked without saying anything.	Nani-mo iwazu ni hatarakimashita.
9. I worked without sleeping.	Nezu ni hatarakimashita.
10. I worked without standing.	Tatazu ni hatarakimashita.
11. Mr. Tanaka speaks English and furthermore he can type.	Tanaka-san wa Eigo o hanasu shi taipu mo uteru.
12. Mr. Tanaka does not speak English, and furthermore, he cannot type.	Tanaka-san wa Eigo o hanasanai shi taipu mo utenai.
13. Today the wind is blowing *(fuku)*, and furthermore, it is cold.	Kyoo wa kaze ga fuite iru shi samui desu.
14. Today the weather is good, and furthermore, it is warm.	Kyoo wa tenki ga ii shi atatakai desu.
15. This room is inexpensive, and furthermore, it is quiet *(shizuka)*.	Kono heya wa yasui shi shizuka desu.
16. This room is expensive, and furthermore, it is noisy *(yakamashii)*.	Kono heya wa takai shi yakamashii desu.

17. He is the eldest son, and furthermore, his brother died last year. — Ano kata wa choonan da shi otooto wa kyonen nakunarimashita.
18. I am alone, and furthermore, I don't have a car. — Watakushi wa hitori da shi jidoosha mo arimasen.
19. He has a big house, and furthermore, he has a house in Japan too. — Ano kata ni wa ookii ie ga aru shi Nihon ni mo ie ga arimasu.
20. The dog ate the meat (up). — Inu wa niku o tabete shimaimashita.
21. I drank the medicine (all up). — Kusuri o nonde shimaimashita.
22. The magazines are completely sold out. — Zasshi wa urikirete shimaimashita.
23. I have completely read all those books. — Sorera no hon o yonde shimaimashita.
24. I loaded all the baggage on the truck. — Torakku ni nimotsu o tsunde shimaimashita.

Give the (a) familiar for men, (b) familiar for women, (c) polite, and (d) formal forms of the following sentences:

25. Where is your home?
    (a) Kimi no uchi doko da.
    (b) Anata no uchi doko.
    (c) Anata no uchi wa doko desu ka.
    (d) Anata no o-uchi wa doko de gozaimasu ka.
26. My home is in Tokyo.
    (a) Ore no uchi Tookyoo da.
    (b) Watashi no uchi Tookyoo yo.
    (c) Watakushi no uchi wa Tookyoo desu.
    (d) Watakushi no uchi wa Tookyoo de gozaimasu.
27. What is this?
    (a) Kore nan dai.
    (b) Kore nani.
    (c) Kore wa nan desu ka.
    (d) Kore wa nan de gozaimasu ka.
28. This is a *sumie* painting.
    (a) Kore sumie da.
    (b) Kore sumie yo.
    (c) Kore wa sumie desu.

(d) Kore wa sumie de gozaimasu.

29. Is this book difficult?

(a) Kono hon muzukashii kai.
(b) Kono hon muzukashii.
(c) Kono hon wa muzukashii desu ka.
(d) Kono hon wa muzukashuu gozaimasu ka.

30. Yes, this book is difficult.

(a) Un, kono hon muzukashii (yo).
(b) Ee, kono hon wa muzukashii wa.
(c) Hai, kono hon wa muzukashii desu.
(d) Hai, kono hon wa muzukashuu gozaimasu.

31. Yes, this book was difficult.

(a) Un, kono hon wa muzukashikatta (yo).
(b) Un, kono hon wa muzukashikatta wa.
(c) Hai, kono hon wa muzukashikatta desu.
(d) Hai, kono hon wa muzukashuu gozaimashita.

32. Was he a teacher?

(a) Kare sensei datta kai.
(b) Ano kata wa sensei datta no.
(c) Ano kata wa sensei deshita ka.
(d) Ano kata wa sensei de gozaimashita ka.

33. No, he was not a teacher.

(a) Iya, sensei ja nakatta.
(b) Iie, sensei ja nakatta wa.
(c) Iie, sensei dewa arimasen deshita.
(d) Iie, sensei dewa gozaimasen deshita.

34. Does he speak Japanese at home?

(a) Kare ie de Nihongo (o) hanasu kai.
(b) Ano kata wa ie de Nihongo (o) hanasu no.
(c) Ano kata wa ie de Nihongo o hanashimasu ka.
(d) Ano o-kata wa ie de Nihongo o o-hanashi ni narimasu ka.

35. No, he does not speak Japanese at home.
   (a) Iya, ie de Nihongo (o) hanasanai.
   (b) Iie, ie de Nihongo (o) hanasanai wa.
   (c) Iie, ie de Nihongo o hanashimasen.
   (d) Iie, ie de Nihongo o o-hanashi ni narimasen.

36. He did not speak Japanese at home.
   (a) Kare ie de Nihongo (o) hanasanakatta (yo).
   (b) Ano kata (wa) ie de (wa) Nihongo (o) hanasanakatta wa.
   (c) Ano kata wa ie de (wa) Nihongo o hanashimasen deshita.
   (d) Ano kata wa ie de (wa) Nihongo o o-hanashi ni narimasen deshita.

37. Where is Mr. Tanaka?
   (a) Tanaka wa doko da (kai).
   (b) Tanaka-san wa doko.
   (c) Tanaka-san wa doko ni imasu ka.
   (d) Tanaka-sama wa doko ni irasshaimasu ka.

38. Mr. Tanaka is in the classroom.
   (a) Tanaka (wa) kyooshitsu ni iru yo.
   (b) Tanaka-san (wa) kyooshitsu ni iru wa (yo).
   (c) Tanaka-san wa kyooshitsu ni imasu.
   (d) Tanaka-sama wa kyooshitsu ni irasshaimasu.

39. Are you coming right away?
   (a) Sugu kuru no ka (kai).
   (b) Sugu kuru?
   (c) Sugu kimasu ka.
   (d) Sugu irasshaimasu ka (oide ni narimasu ka).

40. Yes, I'll go right away.
   (a) Un, sugu iku (yo).
   (b) Ee, sugu iku wa (yo).
   (c) Hai, sugu ikimasu.
   (d) Hai, sugu mairimasu.

41. What are you doing now?
(a) Ima nani shite iru n' da(i).
(b) Ima nani shite iru no.
(c) Ima nani o shite imasu ka.
(d) Ima nani o nasatte irasshaimasu ka.

42. I am studying.
(a) Benkyoo shite iru n' da.
(b) Benkyoo shite iru no yo.
(c) Benkyoo shite imasu.
(d) Benkyoo shite (itashite) orimasu.

43. Isn't that your school?
(a) Are kimi no gakkoo ja nai ka(i).
(b) Are anata no gakkoo ja nai (no).
(c) Are wa anata no gakkoo dewa arimasen ka.
(d) Are wa anata no gakkoo dewa gozaimasen ka.

44. No, it isn't.
(a) Iya, soo ja nai (yo).
(b) Iie, soo ja nai wa (yo).
(c) Iie, soo dewa arimasen.
(d) Iie, soo dewa gozaimasen.

Use the abrupt ending for the following sentences:

45. a. I made (him) sell the car.	Watakushi wa jidoosha o uraseta.
b. He was made to sell the car.	Ano hito wa jidoosha o uraserareta.
46. a. The teacher made the students buy dictionaries.	Sensei wa gakusei ni jibiki o kawaseta.
b. The students were made to buy dictionaries by the teacher.	Gakusei wa sensei ni jibiki o kawaserareta.
47. a. The police made the boy push the car.	Junsa wa otoko no ko ni jidoosha o osaseta.
b. The boy was made to push the car by the police.	Otoko no ko wa junsa ni jidoosha o osaserareta.
48. a. My father made me walk to school.	Chichi wa watakushi o gakkoo made arukaseta.
b. I was made to walk to school.	Watakushi wa gakkoo made arukaserareta.

49. a. The principal made the bad boy remain after class.	Koochoo-sensei wa itazura na otoko no ko o kurasu no ato nokosaseta.
b. The bad boy was made to remain after class by his principal.	Itazura na otoko no ko wa kurasu no ato koochoo-sensei ni nokosaserareta.

Note: In sentences 46a, 47a, *ni* indicates the indirect object. In 46b, 47b, 49b, *ni* shows the agent doing the action.

You are talking to your friend, Mr. Tanaka. First, ask the questions in the polite form, followed by the informal form of questioning.

YOUR QUESTION	MR. TANAKA'S ANSWER
1. What he did during the summer vacation.	Helped his father who is a butcher.
2. Whether he had time to study for the entrance examination.	Not too much, but studied in the evening after the shop closed at 7:00 p.m.
3. If he finished his mathematics problems.	Finished half, very difficult, and thoroughly confused.
4. When does he plan to take the entrance examination.	April 20th, in Tokyo.
5. Whether it was hot where he was during the summer.	Was tremendously hot, so Tokyo is better.
6. When he came back to Tokyo.	Wednesday of last week.
7. Why he hasn't called you sooner.	Had business at school.
8. You haven't been to school for a long time, so you want to know how things are at school.	Same as usual.
9. Whether he would like to go see a movie or something.	There is a movie at Shochiku which he would like to see very much.
10. Where you can meet him.	12:30 in front of the theater.
11. Find out whether he would like to eat before going to see a movie.	There is a Chinese restaurant near the theater, so he wants to eat there first.

12. What time he has to go home tonight.	There is not anything to do tonight, and since tomorrow is a holiday, if he gets home by 10:00 it will be all right.
13. Since he treated you before, you would like to treat him.	It is not necessary—he just received some spending money *(kozukai)* so he feels rich.
14. You want to know how he will get there.	His father is not using the car, so probably he will come in a car.

APPENDIX I

VERB BASES AND SUFFIXES

Following are the various suffixes attached to different bases to obtain the meaning indicated here: the chart on page 410 summarized the following.

I. YODAN VERBS (c.v.) (ARUKU)

A. | ARUKA + |

Add the following endings to the first base:

Plain Negative (pres./fut.)	1. *nai* (doesn't ___, won't ___). Aru*kanai* (I won't walk).
Negative Concessive	2. *nakute mo ii desu* (even if I don't ___, it's all right; I don't have to ___; it doesn't matter if I don't ___). Aru*kanakute mo ii desu* (I don't have to walk).
"must" form	3. *nakereba narimasen* (I must ___; I have to ___). Aru*kanakereba narimasen* (I must walk).
"without" form	4. *zu ni, nai de* (without ___). Aru*kazu ni* (without walking).
Causative	5. *seru* (made to ___) (see page 407)
Passive	6. *reru*
	7. *nakereba* (if ___ not ___). Aru*kanakereba* karada ni warui desu (If I don't walk, it is bad for my health).

B. ARUKI +

Attach the following endings to the second base:

Polite Positive (pres./fut.)	1. *masu* (walk; will walk). Aru*kimasu* (I will walk).
Polite Negative (pres./fut.)	2. *masen* (don't walk; will not walk). Aru*kimasen* (I do not walk).
Polite Positive Probable	3. *mashoo* (probably will ___; let's ___). Aru*kimashoo* (let's walk).
Noun Form	4. Second base often stands alone as a *noun*, example: *odori, asobi.*
Desiderative	5. *tai* (want to ___; will want to ___) Aru*kitai* (I want to walk). *taku wa arimasen* (doesn't want to ___; won't want to ___). Aru*kitaku wa arimasen* (I don't want to walk).
Plain Imperative	6. *nasai* (Walk!). Aru*kinasai.* *"te" verb + wa ikemasen.* Arui*te wa ikemasen* (Don't walk).
	7. *ni* (with IKU, KURU, KAERU to express purpose; "in order to," "for"). Kai *ni* iku (go to buy).
Simultaneous Action	8. *nagara** (while ___; during ___). Aru*kinagara* aisukuriimu o taberu (Eat ice cream while walking).
	9. *nikui* (hard to ___; difficult to ___). Kono kutsu wa aru*kinikui* desu (These shoes are hard to walk in).
	10. *yasui* (easy to ___). Kono pen wa ka*kiyasui* desu (This pen is easy to write with).

* *Nagara* is used to express two actions taking place simultaneously and conducted by the same person. *Watakushi wa itsu-mo rajio o kikinagara benkyoo shimasu. Hon o yominagara aruku.*

Compound Verb

11. It is used with another verb to form compound verb.
aru*ki-mawaru* (walk around)
to*bi-noru* (jump on board)

C. ARUKU +

The following endings are added to the third base:

Purpose

1. *no ni* (expresses purpose—"in order to," "for," in constructions *not* ending in IKU, KURU, KAERU)
Aruku no ni kono kutsu o tsukaimasu. (I use these shoes for walking).

Potential

2. *koto ga dekiru* (can, able to).
Aruku koto ga dekiru (I am able to walk.)

"about to"

3. *tokoro (desu)*—(about to).
Aruku tokoro desu (I am about to walk).

Comparative

4. *hoo ga ii* desu (had better, is better).
Aruku hoo ga ii desu (it is better to walk).

Reasonable Expectation

5. *hazu (desu)*—(ought to, should).
Aruku hazu desu (I should walk).
Kinoo *aruku hazu* deshita (He was supposed to walk yesterday).

"time for"

6. *hima ga aru* (free time).
Kyoo *aruku hima ga arimasu* (I have time to walk today).

Secondhand Information

7. *soo desu* (I hear, I understand).
Ano akamboo wa moo *aruku soo desu.* (The baby already walks, I hear).

Intention

8. *tsumori* (desu)—(I intend to).
Aruku tsumori desu (I intend to walk).
Aruku tsumori dewa arimasen (I don't intend to walk).

Before

9. *mae* (before I walk).
Aruku mae ni sukoshi yasumimasu. (I will rest awhile before walking).

10. *tochuu* (on the way . . .).
Kaeru tochuu . . . (on the way home . . .).

D. | ARUKE + |

Add the following endings to the fourth base:

Present Positive Conditional	1. *ba* (if . . .) Gakkoo made aru*keba* tsukaremasu. (If I walk to school, I will be tired).
Potential	2. *masu* (can, able to). Aru*kemasu* (I can walk).
Imperative	3. This base can be used as abrupt imperative. Aru*ke* (Walk!).

E. | ARUKOO + |

The following endings are added to the fifth base:

"tried to"	1. *to suru* (about to, tried to). Aru*koo to shita* ga dame deshita. (I tried to walk, but it was impossible).
"let's"	2. This base can be used alone to mean, "Let's walk!"—Aru*koo*.

II. ICHIDAN VERB (n.c.v.) (TABERU)

Since there are no bases for *ichidan* verbs (n.c.v.), use the stem in attaching all endings, except for the third base, where the root form of the verb is used (*taberu koto ga dekiru, taberu hazu desu,* etc.)

For the fifth base, replace *ru* with *yoo,* viz., *tabeyoo, miyoo,* etc.

Passive

Where the subject is the recipient of the action, the following construction is used:

I. YODAN VERBS (c.v.) (UTSU)

UTA	(first base) + RERU = *utareru*

Doroboo wa junsa ni pisutoru de ashi o *utaremashita.*
(The robber was shot in the leg by the police with a pistol.)

II. ICHIDAN VERBS (n.c.v.) (MIRU)

MI	(stem) + RARERU = *mirareru*

Otoko no ko wa uchi e hairu no o koochoo ni *miraremashita.*
(The boy was seen entering the house by the principal.)

Causative

This is the form used when you "cause" or "have" another person do something, viz., "Please *have* the maid bring a glass of water," or "The teacher *made* the student go home."

The rule for forming this expression is:

FIRST BASE (of YODAN VERBS—c.v.) + SERU

or

STEM (of ICHIDAN VERBS—n.c.v.) + SASERU

I. YODAN VERBS (c.v.) (ARUKU)

ARUKA	(first base) + SERU = *arukaseru*

a. Isha wa anata o aru*kaseru.*
   (The doctor will *make* you walk.)
b. Sensei wa gakusei o kae*raseta.*
   (The teacher *made* the student go home.)

II. ICHIDAN VERBS (n.c.v.) (TABERU)

TABE	(stem) + SASERU = *tabesaseru*

Isha wa kudamono o *tabesaseru.*
(The doctor will *make* you eat fruit.)

Causative Passive

A construction where both causative and passive are used is not uncommon. For example, "I was made to wait," or "We were forced to see some slides," "I was made to walk," etc.

I. YODAN VERBS (c.v.) (MATSU)

A. First, form the causative: MATA + SERU.
Note that this is now an *ichidan* verb—n.c.v. ("eru" ending).

B. Now form a passive of this n.c.v. by adding *RARERU* to the stem: MATASE + RARERU.
Ma*taserareru* no wa kirai desu.
(I do not like to be made to wait.)

II. ICHIDAN VERBS (n.c.v.) (MIRU)

A. MI + *SASERU*—causative

B. MISASE + *RARERU*—causative + passive
Omoshirokunai suraido o *misaserareta.*
(We were forced to see [some] uninteresting slides.)

Note: You can add the desiderative *(tai)*, negative *(nai)*, or conditional *(ba)* suffixes to these *ichidan* verbs (n.c.v.) endings and get the following complicated, but commonly used, constructions.

A. mi + se + tai—(I) want (you) to see.

B. mi + se + rare + tai—(I) want to be forced to see.

C. mi + se + rare + taku + nai—(I) don't want to be forced to see.

D. mi + se + rare + taku + nakereba—If (you) don't want to be forced to see. . . .

E. Now, see if you can translate:
If you don't want to be made to wait . . .
If you want to be elected . . .
I don't want to be sent . . .
I like to be forced to study . . .
The children were made to go home . . .
My child was made to wear a kimono . . .
I was made to write . . .
I don't like to be made to do . . .
I was made to drink . . .

Examples:

If you don't want to be made to wait . . .,
(cond.) (neg.) (desid.) (passive) (causative)

This sentence contains the conditional, negative, desiderative, and causative.

1. causative of *matsu* = ma*ta* + *seru* (cause to wait)
2. passive of *mataseru* = mata*se* + *rareru* (to be made to wait)
3. desiderative of *mataserareru* = matasera*re* + *tai* (want to be made to wait)
4. negative of *mataseraretai* = mataserare*ta* + *ku* + *nai* (do not want to be made to wait)
5. conditional of mataseraretaku + *nai* = mataseraretaku + *na* + *kereba* (if you do not want to be forced to wait)
   The verb we want is *mataseraretakunakereba.*

Note: *Miseru* and *misaseru* are often confused in usage.

Miseru, a transitive verb, simply means "to show something" or "to let a person see."

i. Tanaka-san wa rippa na bonsai o *misete* kuremashita.	Mr. Tanaka showed me a splendid bonsai.
ii. Iminkan ni ryoken o *mise-nakereba narimasen.*	You must show your passport to the immigration officer.

On the other hand, *misaseru* has the implication of force or compulsion, compelling someone to see.

i. Kore wa gakusei ni *misasetai* eiga desu.	This is a movie which I would like to have my students see.
ii. Gakusei wa mitakunakatta ga *misaserareta.*	The students did not want to see it, but they were forced to.

FIVE BASES AND SUFFIXES

FIVE BASES		CONJUGATION	SUFFIXES
1st base	mizen NEGATIVE	ka-KA	1. nai 2. nakute mo ii 3. nakereba narimasen 4. zu ni, nai de 5. seru 6. reru 7. nakereba
2nd base	renyoo CONTINUATIVE	ka-KI	1. masu, masen, mashoo 2. tai 3. nasai 4. ni (iku, kuru, kaeru) 5. nagara 6. nikui 7. yasui
3rd base	1) shuushi CONCLUSIVE	ka-KU	1. no ni 2. koto ga dekiru 3. tokoro 4. hoo ga ii (desu) 5. hazu 6. hima ga aru 7. soo desu 8. tsumori 9. mae 10. tochuu
	2) rentai MODIFIER	ka-KU	1. koto ga dekiru 2. tokoro 3. hoo ga ii desu 4. hima ga aru 5. mae 6. tochuu
4th base	katei CONDITIONAL	ka-KE	1. ba 2. ru, masu 3. imperative
5th base	VOLITIONAL	ka-KOO	1. to suru 2. "let's" 3. to omou

APPENDIX II

POSTPOSITIONS

Following is the summary of the more common usage of postpositions emphasized in this book and also other not too common usages. Remember that postpositions are used mainly with substantives (noun or noun equivalent) and indicate the function and the relation of the substantives within the sentence.

The numbers below indicate the pages.

WA— (a) indicates the subject (p. 27)
Ano kata *wa* sensei desu.

NO— (a) shows possessive (p. 38)
Watakushi *no* hankechi . . .
(b) used in place of a noun in the sense of "one" (p. 155)
Ookii *no* wa watakushi no desu (large one).
(c) forms a noun modifier (p. 38)
Tomodachi kara *no* tegami . . .
(d) *NO* used for *ni aru* in relative clause (p. 279)
Tsukue no ue *no* (ni aru) hon wa . . .
(e) *NO* used for *ni iru* in relative clause (p. 279)
Tookyoo *no* (ni iru) ani wa . . .
(f) This can be used as *de aru* in relative clauses.
Hisho *no* (de aru) Tanaka-san wa . . .
(Miss Tanaka who is a secretary . . .)
(g) subject of a relative clause
Kodomo *no* kaita e . . . (picture which the child drew . . .)
(h) used as a nominalizer (to make a noun) (p. 334)
Noboru *no ga* muzukashii desu (difficult to climb).
Toru *no o* mimashita.

O— (a) shows the object of a verb (p. 52)
Jidoosha *o* uru.

(b) indicates the action occurring in space (p. 291)
Hashi *o* wataru (cross the bridge).

(c) points to where the action occurs—"from"
Gakkoo *o* deru (leave the school).

NI— (a) shows location "where" (p. 62)
Gakkoo *ni* atsumaru (gather at the school).
(b) after a specific time (p. 124)
Shichi-ji *ni* shuppatsu suru (depart at 7 o'clock).
(c) place of arrival
Kyooto *ni* tsuku.
(d) shows the result of an action—"naru" (p. 244)
Gakusha *ni* naru (to become a scholar).
(e) specifies the indirect object
Tomodachi *ni* hon o okuru (send a book to a friend).
(f) indicates the purpose of an act (p. 176)
Sensei o yobi *ni* iku (go to call the teacher).
(g) used to show the doer, or the originator of an act in the passive form (p. 271)
Inu *ni* kamareru. (to be bitten by a dog).

E— (a) shows direction (p. 116)
Nihon *e* iku.
(b) indicates point of arrival
Koko *e* kinasai.

DE— (a) shows the instrument—"by means of" (p. 117)
Tetsu *de* tsukuru (make with steel).
(b) place of action (p. 155)
Toshokan *de* benkyoo o suru (study at the library).
(c) indicates the reason, or the cause
Byooki *de* yasumu (stay away due to illness).
(d) used in comparison (p. 172)
Nihon *de* ichiban ookii (largest in Japan).

APPENDIX III

CONNECTIVES

Following are the commonly used connectives which come at the *end* of the subordinate clause, and combine it with the principal clause. * indicates usage not mentioned in this book.

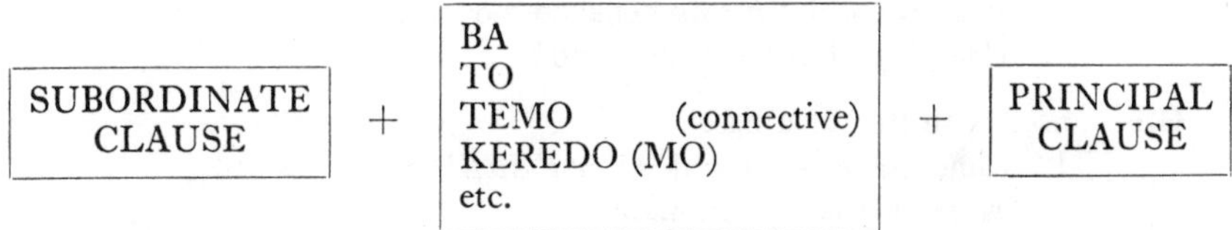

Note that this is the opposite of English. In English, "when," "if," "because," "while," etc., are used at the beginning of the clause.

BA— used with the fourth base

1. shows conditional, "if" (p. 329).
   Yome*ba* wakaru. (If you read, you will understand.)
2.* inevitable results arising from a certain situation.
   Haru ga kure*ba* atatakai. (When spring comes, it will be warm.)
3.* used to list several facts.
   Kisha mo are*ba* densha mo aru. (There are trains and streetcars, too.)

TO— used with the third base (abrupt form)

1. as a conditional "if" (p. 228, p. 329).
   Yomu *to* wakaru. (If you read, you will understand.)
2. inevitable result (same as #2 of *BA*).
   Kaze ga fuku *to* samui. (When the wind blows, it is cold.)
3. has the meaning of "when," "on the occasion" (p. 228, p. 329).
   Tookyoo e iku *to* Kabuki o miru.
   (When I go to Tokyo, I will see Kabuki.)

4. used to indicate the relation of one action to another, or one action preceding another.
Dekakeyoo to suru *to* denwa ga natta.
(When I was about to leave, there was a telephone call.)
Eki o deru *to* takushii ni notta.
(When I came out of the station, I took a taxi.)

TEMO (DEMO)—attach *MO* to "te" form of the verb

1.* used to express ideas contrary to expectation.
Mi*temo* wakaranai. (Even if you see it, you will not understand.)

KEREDO (KEREDOMO)—used with the third base

1.* contrary to expectation usage.
Atama ga itai *keredo(mo)* iku.
(I have a headache, but I'll go.)

2.* to show contrast of two ideas.
Kare wa asobu *keredo* benkyoo mo suru.
(He plays, but he studies, too.)

GA— used with the third base

1. same usage as #1 and #2 of *KEREDO.*
Kaze wa fuku *ga* samukunai.
(The wind blows, but it is not cold.)

NONI—used with the third base

1.* same usage as No. 1 of *KEREDO* and *GA,* used to put in contrast two opposing ideas to express unexpected, displeased feeling.
Ame ga futte iru *noni* yama e iku.
(Even though it is raining, I will go to the mountains.)

NODE—used with the third base

1. shows cause and the reason (p. 136).
Atama ga itai *node* gakkoo o yasumu.
(Since I have a headache, I will not go to school.)

KARA—used with the third base.

1. same usage as *NODE* (p. 135).
Atama ga itai *kara* gakkoo o yasumu.
(Since I have a headache, I will not go to school.)

SHI— used with the third base

1. has the meaning of "furthermore" when listing several features (p. 390).
Jidoosha mo unten suru *shi* ryoori mo suru.
(He drives a car; in addition, he cooks.)

NAGARA—used with the second base

1. two actions taking place simultaneously (p. 404).
   Shokuji o *shinagara* shimbun o yomu.
   (He reads a newspaper while eating.)

TARI (DARI)—"ri" added to abrupt past

1. shows alternate action (p. 275).
   Benkyoo shi*tari* ason*dari* suru.
   (Sometimes I study, other times I play, etc.)

VOCABULARY

The following vocabularies are found in the text. Words *followed* by an asterisk do not appear in the text, but have been selected because of their frequent use. Words *preceded* with an asterisk can be used as Chinese verbs by the addition of *suru*. (For example, *benkyoo* is a noun meaning "study." By adding *suru* to it, *benkyoo suru* now means "to study.")

A

AA—Oh!
ABUNAI—dangerous
ABURA*—oil
ACHIRA KOCHIRA*—here and there
AIDA—between
AINIKU*—unfortunately
AIRON*—iron
*AISATSU—greetings
AJI—taste
AKAI—red
AKABOO—red cap
AKACHAN—baby (affectionate term)
AKAMBOO—baby
AKI—autumn
AMAI—sweet
AMARI—very
AME—rain
AMERICA GASSHUUKOKU—U.S.A.
AMERICAJIN—American
ANATA—you (singular)
ANATAGATA—you (plural)
ANE—elder sister
ANI—elder brother
ANNA—that kind of
ANNAIJO—information place
ANO—that (over there)
ANO KATA—that person (polite)
*ANSHIN—peace of mind
ARASHI*—storm
ARE—that (over there)
ARIGATOO—thank you
ARU—certain
ARU HI—one day
ARU TOKI—once upon a time
ARU TOKORO NI—at a certain place
ASA—morning
ASAGOHAN*—breakfast
ASATTE—day after tomorrow
ASE*—perspiration
ASHI—leg, legs, foot, feet
ASHITA—tomorrow
ASOKO—over there
ASU—tomorrow
ATAMA—head
ATARASHII—new
ATATAKAI—warm
ATENA—(forwarding) address
ATO—after

ATSUI—hot
ATSUI—thick

B

BAKA—fool
BAKA NA—foolish
BAKARI—only
BAN—evening, night
BANANA—banana
BANGOO—number
BASU—bus
BATAA—butter
BEIKOKU—America
BENGOSHI—attorney
BENJO*—toilet
*BENKYOO—study
BENRI—convenience
BENTOO—box lunch
BIIRU—beer
*BIMBOO—poor
BIMBOONIN—poor person
BIN—occasion
BIN*—bottle
BOOEKI—trade
BOOI-SAN—waiter
BOKU—I (used by men only)
BOOSHI—hat
BOOTO NORI—boat ride
BUDOO—grapes
BUMPOO*—grammar
BUNSHOO—sentence
BUTANIKU—pork
BYOO—second
BYOOIN—hospital
*BYOOKI—illness
BYOONIN*—sick person

C

CHA—green tea
CHAIRO—brown
CHAWAN—rice bowl
CHICHI—father (intimate term)
CHIHOO—district
CHIISAI—small
CHIISA-SUGIRU—too small
CHIKAGORO—nowadays
CHIKAI—near
CHIKAKU—nearby
CHIKATETSU—subway
CHIPPU—tip
CHIRI—geography
CHIZU—map
CHOODO—exactly
CHOOJO—eldest daughter
CHOONAN—eldest son
CHOOSHOKU—breakfast
CHOTTO—a moment
CHOTTO NO AIDA—short space of time
CHUUGAKKOO—junior high school
CHUUGOKU—Communist China
CHUUKA RYOORI—Chinese food
*CHUUMON—order
CHUUSHINCHI—center
CHUUSHOKU—lunch

D

DAIGAKU—university
DAIGAKUIN—graduate school
DAIJI—importance, great thing
DAIJOOBU*—all right
DAIKIRAI—dislike greatly
DAISUKI—like very much
DAITOKAI—large metropolis
DAITOORYOO—President (of a country)
DAKE—only
DAME—no good
DAN-DAN—step by step
DARE—who?
DE—by, with, in, at
DE—is, and
DEMO—even
DEMPOO—telegram
DENSHA—street car
*DENWA—telephone
DEPAATO—department store
DEWA—then, in that case

DEWA—between (in comparison)
-DO—classifier for number of "times"
DOA—door
DOCHIRA—which
DOO ITASHIMASHITE—Don't mention it.
DOKO—where
DONNA—what kind of
DONO—which
DORE—which
DOREI—slave
DORU—dollar
DOOSHITE—why, how
DOOSHITEMO—by all means
DOTCHI—which
DOYOOBI—Saturday
DOOZO—please

E

E—picture
E—postposition showing direction
EE—yes
EHAGAKI*—picture-postcard
EIGA—movie
EIGAKAN—movie theater
EIGO—English
EIKOKU—England
EIWA*—English-Japanese
EKI—station
EMPITSU—pencil
*ENRYO—hesitation
EREBEETAA—elevator

F

FOOKU—fork
FUBEN—inconvenience
FUDE—writing brush
FUJISAN—Mt. Fuji
FUN—minute
FUNE—boat
FURO—bath
FUROBA—bathroom
FURUI—old
FUTARI DE—together (two persons)
FUTATSU—two (items)
FUUTOO—envelope
FUTOI*—thick
FUTSUU—ordinary
FUYU—winter

G

GA—but
GA—postposition used in the nominative case
GAIKOKU—foreign country
GAIKOKU BOOEKI—foreign trade
GAIKOKUJIN—foreigner
GAKKI—school term
GAKKOO—school
*GAKUMON—studies
GAKUSEI—student
GAKUSHA—scholar
GEKIJOO—theater
GENRYOOHIN—raw material
GETA—wooden clogs
GETSUYOOBI—Monday
*GIMBURA—a stroll along Ginza
GINKOO—bank
GINZA—name of a famous street in Tokyo
GO—five
-GO—suffix "language"
*GO-CHISOO—good things to eat
GOGATSU—May
GOGO—p.m.
GOHAN—cooked rice, meal (in general)
GOMEN—pardon (me)
GORO—about
GOZEN—a.m.
GUN—county
GUNJIN—soldier
GURAI—about
GYUUNIKU*—beef
GYUUNYUU—milk

H

HA*—teeth
HABA*—width
HACHI—eight
HACHIGATSU—August
HAGAKI—post card
HAHA—mother
HAI—yes
*HAIKINGU—hiking
HAJIME—beginning, first
HAJIMEMASHITE—I am happy to meet you (for the first time).
HAKARI—scale
HAKKIRI—plainly
HAKO—box
HAKURAIHIN—imported goods
HAMBUN—one-half
HANAMI—flower-viewing
*HANASHI—story
HANKECHI—handkerchief
*HANTAI—opposition
HARU—spring
HASAMI—scissors
HASHI—chopsticks
HASHI—bridge
HAYAI—fast, early
HAYAKU—quickly
HEIYA—plain
*HENJI—answer
HETA—unskillful
HEYA—room
HEYADAI—room rent
HI—day
HIDARI—left side
HIDOI—severe
HIGASHI—east
HIJOO NI—very
-HIKI—classifier for animals
HIKOOJOO—airport
HIKOOKI—airplane
HIKOOYUUBIN—airmail
HIKUI—low
HIMA—leisure time
HIRU—noon
HIRUGOHAN—lunch
HISASHIBURI—after a long time
HITO—person
HITOBITO—people (plural)
HITORI—one person
HITOTSU—one (thing)
HITSUYOO—necessity
HOO—direction, side
HOOCHOO—kitchen knife
HOMBAKO*—bookcase
HON—book
-HON—classifier for counting long slender objects
HONSHUU—main island of Japan
HONYA—bookstore
HOORITSU—law
HOSHI*—star
HOSHII—desirable
HOTERU—hotel
HOTONDO—almost all, hardly
HYAKKATEN—department store
HYAKU—hundred
*HYAKUSHOO—farmer

I

ICHI—one
ICHIBAN—No. 1, most
ICHIDO—once
ICHIGATSU—January
ICHIGO*—strawberry
IE—house
II—good
IIE—no
IKAGA—how
IKKA—family household
IKURA—how much
IKUTSU—how many
IMA—now
IMI—meaning
IMOOTO—younger sister
INAKA—(rural) country
INDO—India
INKI*—ink

INU—dog
IPPAI—full, one cupful
IPPON—one (long, slender object)
IRIGUCHI—entrance
IRO—color
IRO-IRO—various
ISHA—doctor
ISOGASHII—busy
ISSATSU—one volume
ISSHO NI—together
ISSHOOKEMMEI NI—with all one's might
ISSHUUKAN—one week
ISU—chair
ITAI*—sore, painful
ITOKO—cousin
ITSU—when
ITSU GORO—about when
ITSU-MO—always
ITSUTSU—five

J

JAMA—hindrance, obstacle
JI—letter
-JI—time of the day
JIBIKI—dictionary
JIBUN—oneself
JIDAI—period, era
JIDOOSHA—automobile
JIKAN—hours
JIKANHYOO—time table
JINKOO—population
JINSHU—race (human)
JITENSHA—bicycle
JOOBU*—healthy, strong
JOCHUU—waitress, maid
JUU—ten
JUU—throughout
JUUGATSU—October
JUUICHIGATSU—November
JUMBI—preparation
JUUNIGATSU—December
JUNSA—policeman
JUUSHO—address

K

KA—or
KA—used to make an interrogative sentence
KABAN—bag
KABE—wall
KABIN—vase
KABUKI—classical Japanese drama
KADO—corner
KAGAMI—mirror
KAIDAN—steps
*KAIHOO—emancipation
*KAIMONO—shopping
KAISATSU GUCHI—ticket-gate
KAISHA—firm, company
KAIWA*—conversation
KAKARI—charge, responsibility
KAKITOME—registered mail
KAMI—hair (on the head)
KAMI—paper
KANAI—(one's own) wife
KANARI—fairly
KANASHII—sad
(O)KANE—money
KANEMOCHI—rich man
KANGAE—idea
KANJI—Chinese written symbols
*KANJOO—check or bill (for a meal, etc.)
KANKOKU—South Korea
KAO—face
KARA—from
KARA—since, because
KARADA*—body
KARAI—hot, peppery
KAREE RAISU—curry rice
KASHIKOMARIMASHITA—certainly
KATA—person (polite)
KATAI*—hard
KATAMICHI—one way
KAWA—river
KAWAKAMI—up-stream

KAWASE—money order
KAYOOBI—Tuesday
KAZOKU*—family
KEIKAN—police
KEIZAI—economics
KEIZAITEKI—economical
*KEMBUTSU—sightseeing
KEMBUTSUNIN—sightseer
KERAI—servant, follower
KEREDOMO—but, however
KESHIKI—scenery
KESSHITE—never
KI*—tree, wood
KIBIDANGO—kind of dumpling
*KIBOO—hope, desire
KIBUN—mood, feeling
KIIROI—yellow
KIJI—pheasant
KIMI—you (used by men only)
KIMOCHI—feeling
KINOO—yesterday
KINYOOBI—Friday
KIPPU—ticket
KIREI—clean
KIRO—kilogram
KISEN—steamship
KISHA—train
KISOKU*—rule
KISSATEN—tea house
KITA—north
KITTE—postage stamps
KOOCHA—black tea
KOOCHOO—school principal
KODOMO—child
KOOEN—park
KOOFUKU—happiness
KOOGAI—suburb
KOOGYOO—manufacturing industry
KOOHII—coffee
KOOJOO—factory
KOKO—here, this place
KOKONOTSU—nine
KOKUBAN—blackboard
KOKUMIN—people of a country
KOMBAN—tonight
KOMBAN WA—good evening
KONDATEHYOO—menu
KONO—this
KONO AIDA*—the other day
KONO ATARI—around here
KONOGORO—nowadays
KORE—this
*KOOSAN—surrender
KOSHI—waist
KOOSHUU—general public
KOTOBA—word
KOOTOOGAKKOO—senior high school
KOTOSHI—this year
KOZUKAI—pocket money
KOZUTSUMI—package
KU (KYUU)—nine
KUCHI—mouth
KUDAMONO—fruit
KUGATSU—September
KUNI—country
KURAI*—dark
KURAI—about
KURASU—class
KUROI—black
KURUMA—vehicle, car
KUSURI—medicine
KUTSU*—shoes
KYOO—today
KYOODAI—brothers and sisters
KYOOJU—college professor
KYOOKAI*—church
KYOOKASHO—reader, primer, textbook
KYOKUIN—postal clerk
KYONEN—last year
KYOOSHI—teacher
KYOOSHITSU—classroom
KYUUKOO—express train
KYUURYOO*—salary

M

MACHI—town
MACHIAISHITSU—waiting room
MADA—still, yet

MADE—up to, until
MADO—window
MAE—front, before, past
-MAI—classifier in counting flat objects
MAI- —prefix meaning "every . . ."
MAINICHI—everyday
MAN—ten thousand
MANNAKA—center
MANNENHITSU—fountain pen
MANSHUU—Manchuria
MASSUGU—straight
MATA—again
ME—eye(s)
MEISHO—famous place
MEKATA—weight
MICHI—road
MIGI—right side
MIJIKAI—short
MIKAN—orange
MIMI—ear
MINAMI—south
MINASAN—everybody
MINATO—harbor
MINNA—all, everything
MIRUKU—milk
MISE—shop
MIYAGE—gift, souvenir
MIYAKO—(archaic) capital
MIZU—water
MIZUKUSAI—taste which lacks sufficient seasoning
MIZUPPOI—watery taste
MIZUUMI—lake
MO—also, too
MOO—already, more
MODAN—modern
MOO ICHIDO—once more
MOKUYOOBI—Thursday
MOMO—peach
MON—gate
MONO—person, fellow
MONO—thing
MOSHI MOSHI—hello, oh say, if you please!
MOO SUKOSHI—a little more
MOTTO—more
MUKASHI—long time ago
MURA—village
MUSHIATSUI—sultry
MUSUKO (SAN)—son
MUSUME (SAN)—daughter
MUTTSU—six
MUZUKASHII—difficult
MYOOBAN—tomorrow night
MYOOJI*—surname

N

NAGAI—long
NAI—is not (abrupt form)
NAIFU—knife
NAKA—in, inside
NAKA NAKA—quite, very
NAMAE—name
NAN (nani)—what
NANATSU—seven
NANI-KA—something
NAN-NIN—how many persons
NARA—if
NATSU—summer
NATSUYASUMI—summer vacation
NAZE—why
NE—isn't it?
NEDAN—price
NEKO—cat
NEN—year
NI—indicating location
NI—two
NICHI—days of the month
NICHIYOOBI—Sunday
NIGAI—bitter
NIGATSU—February
NIHON—Japan
NIHONFUU—Japanese style
NIHONGO—Japanese language
NIHON-ICHI—No. 1 in Japan
NIHONJIN—Japanese (people)
NIHONKAI—Japan Sea
NIHONSEI—Japanese-made
NIHONSHOKU—Japanese food

NIKU—meat
-NIN—classifier to count people
NIOI—smell
NI-SATSU—two volumes
NISHI—west
NI-TOO—second-class
NI TOTTE—for
NO—of (possessive)
NODE—since, because
NODO*—throat
NOOGYOO—agriculture
NOMBIRI—relaxed
NOOTO (BUKKU)—notebook
NURUI—lukewarm
*NYUUGAKU—school entrance
NYUUGAKU SHIKEN—entrance examination

O

O—tail
OBA—aunt
OBAASAN—grandmother, old woman
ODORI—dance
*OOFUKU—round trip
OFUKURO—mother (used by men only)
OHAYOO GOZAIMASU—good morning
OISHII—delicious
OJI—uncle
OJIISAN—grandfather, old man
OJOOSAN*—young lady
OKAASAN—mother
OKASHI*—candy
OOKII—large, big
OOKINA—large, big
OKUSAN—(someone else's) wife
OMEDETOO—congratulations
OMOI*—heavy
OMOSHIROI—funny, interesting
OMOTE—surface, face, front
ONAJI—same
ONAKA—stomach
ONEESAN—elder sister
ONGAKU—music
ONGAKUKAI—concert
ONI—ogre
ONIISAN—elder brother
ONNA—female, girl
ONNA NO KO—girl
ONSEN—hot spring
OOBAA—overcoat
ORE—I (used by men only)
OSOI—slow, late
O-TAKU—(your) residence
O-TEARAI—toilet
OOTOBAI—motorcycle
OTOKO—male, man
OTOKO NO KO—boy
OTONA—adult
OTOOSAN—father
OTOOTO—younger brother
OYASUMINASAI—good night
(O) YU*—hot water
OYAJI—father (used by men only)
OOZEI—many (people)

P

PAN—bread
PANYA—baker
PEEJI—page
PEN—pen
PIANO—piano
POKETTO—pocket
POSUTO—mail box
-PUN—minute

R

-RA—plural suffix (human beings)
RAISHUU—next week
REKISHI—history
REKISHITEKI—historical
RESSHA—train
RINGO—apple
RIPPA—magnificent
ROKU—six
ROKUGATSU—June
ROKUNIN—six persons

RONDON—London
RUSU—absence
RUSUCHUU—during the absence
RYOOHOO—both
RYOKAN—Japanese inn
*RYOKOO—trip
*RYOORI—cooking
RYOORININ—cook
RYOORIYA—restaurant
RYOOSHIN—both parents
RYOOTE—both hands
RYUUGAKUSEI—foreign student

S

SABISHII—lonesome
-SAI—classifier to count age
SAIFU—purse
SAKABA—bar
SAKANA—fish
SAKE—Japanese rice wine
SAKI—ahead, point
SAKUNEN—last year
SAKURA—cherry blossoms
SAMBANME—third
*SAMPO—stroll
SAMUI—cold
SAN—three
SAN—Mr., Mrs., Miss
SANGATSU—March
SARARII-MAN—salaried man
SARU—monkey
SASSOKU—immediately
SATOO—sugar
-SATSU—classifier for books
*SEIBATSU—extermination, conquest
SEIJI—politics
SEIJIGAKU—political science
SEIJIKA—politician
SEIJITEKI—political
SEINEN—young man
SEISANHIN—manufactured goods
SEITO—student
SEIYOO—west
SEIYOO-FUU—western-style
SEKAI—world
SEMMENJO—washroom
SEN—thousand
SENGEN—proclamation
SENGO—postwar
*SENKYO—election
SENSEI—teacher
*SENSOO—war
*SENTAKU (MONO)—washing (clothes)
SENTAKUYA—laundry
SHASHOO—conductor
SHI—four
SHI—city
SHIBAI—play (act)
SHICHI—seven
SHICHIGATSU—July
SHIGATSU—April
SHIGOTO—work
SHIKA—only
SHIKASHI—however, but
SHIKATA GA NAI—It can't be helped
*SHIKEN—examination
SHIMA—island
SHIMBUN—newspaper
SHIMIN—citizen
*SHIMPAI—worry
SHINAMONO—merchandise
SHINDAI—bed
SHINDAI-KEN—sleeper ticket
SHINDAI-SHA—pullman car
SHINRUI—relative
SHIO—salt
SHIOKARAI—salty
SHIROI—white
SHITA—down
*SHITAKU—preparation
*SHITSUMON—question
SHIZUKA—quiet
*SHOOBAI—business
SHOOGAKKOO—grade school
SHOOGATSU—New Year's Day
SHOOGO—noon
SHOOGYOO—commerce
*SHOOKAI—introduction
SHOKUDOO—dining room

SHOKUDOOSHA—dining car
*SHOKUJI—meal
SHOONIN—merchant
SHUU—state
(GO)SHUJIN—(your) husband, boss
SHUUKAN—week
*SHUKUDAI—homework
*SHUPPATSU—departure
SHUPPATSU JIKAN—time of departure
SOO—"so" as in, "that is so"
SOBA—near
SOBO—grandmother
SOFU—grandfather
SOKO—there
SOKO DE—therefore
SOKUTATSU—special delivery
SONNA—that kind of
SONO—that
SORE—that
SORE DEWA—in that case
SOREKARA—and then
SOSHITE—and
SUU- —prefix for a few, several
SUGI—after
SUGOI—horrible
SUGU—immediately
SUI—sour
SUIKA—watermelon
SUIYOOBI—Wednesday
SUKI—like
SUKII—ski
SUKIYAKI—name of Japanese dish
SUMIE—brush painting
SUMIMASEN—I'm sorry
SUTEKI—wonderful, marvelous
SUUPAA MAAKETTO—supermarket
SUPPAI—sour
(O)SUSHI—name of Japanese dish
SUUGAKU—mathematics
SUZUSHII—cool

T

TABAKO—tobacco
TABEMONO—things to eat
TABITABI—often
-TACHI—plural suffix (for people)
TADAIMA—I am back (greeting)
TAIHEIYOO—Pacific Ocean
TAIHEIYOO SENSOO—Pacific War, World War II
TAIHEN—very
*TAIKUTSU—weary, boredom
TAISEIYOO—Atlantic Ocean
TAISETSU—important
TAISHOO—leader, head, general
TAISOO—very
TAITEI—usually
TAIWAN—Formosa
TAKAI—high
TAKA-SUGIRU—too expensive
TAKIGI—firewood
TAKUSAN—considerably
TAKUSHII—taxi
TAMA NI—occasionally
TANJOOBI—birthday
TANOSHII—pleasant, delightful
TASSHA—well, in good health
TATEMONO—building
TE—hand
TEATE—treatment
TEBUKURO—gloves
TEGAMI—letter
TEISHAJOO—railroad station
TEKI—enemy
TEKKYOO—bridge
TENIMOTSU—hand baggage
TENIMOTSU TORIATSUKAISHO—hand baggage department
TENIN—store clerk
TENKI—weather
TEMPURA—popular Japanese food
TENUGUI—towel
TEREBI—T.V.
TESAGE KABAN—suitcase
TO—door
TO—and
TO—when
TOO—ten
TOOBUN—for a while

*TOOCHAKU—arrival
TOOCHAKU JIKAN—time of arrival
TOCHUU*—on the way
TOOFU—soybean cake
TOOI—far
TO IU—called
TOKAI—city, metropolis
TOKEI—watch, clock
TOKI—time
TOKIDOKI—sometimes
TOKKYUU—special express train
TOKORO—place
TOMODACHI—friend
TONARI—neighbor
TONNERU—tunnel
TORANKU—trunk
TORI—bird
TOORI*—street
TOSHI—year
TOSHIYORI—old, aged (person)
TOTEMO—very
TOOTOO—finally
TSUGI—next
TSUITE—concerning
TSUKAIKATA—how to use
TSUKI—moon
TSUKI—month
TSUKUE—desk
TSUMA—(one's own) wife
TSUMETAI—cold
TSUMORI—intention
TSUNA—rope
(O)TSURI—change
TSUYOI—strong

U

UCHI—home
UE—top, above
UMA—horse
UMI—ocean
URA—back
URAYAMASHII—envious
URESHII—happy
USHI—cow
USHIRO—rear, back
USUI—thin

W

WA—postposition used in nominative case
WAKAI*—young
WARUI—bad
WASHOKU—Japanese food
WATAKUSHI—I

Y

-YA—suffix for shops
YAA—oh!
YA—and
YACHIN—house rent
YADOCHOO—hotel register
YAKAMASHII—noisy
*YAKUSOKU—promise
YAMA—mountain
*YAMA NOBORI—mountain climbing
YASAI—vegetable
YASUI—inexpensive, cheap
YASUMI—holiday
YATTSU—eight
YOI—nice, good
YOOJI—business
YOKU ASA—following morning
YON—four
YOO NA—like (followed by a noun)
YOO NI—like (followed by a verb)
YORI—more than
YOOROPPA—Europe
YOOSHOKU—Western food
YOOSU—condition
YOTTSU—four
YUBI*—finger
YUUBE*—last night
YUUBIN—mail
YUUBINBAKO—mail box
YUUBINKYOKU—post-office
YUKI—snow
YUUMEI—famous

YUUSHOKU—supper

Z

ZA—denote a theater
ZASHIKI—Japanese style room
ZASSHI—magazine
ZEHI—by all means
ZU—diagram
ZUIBUN—extremely, very

VOCABULARY—VERBS

Words *followed* by an asterisk do not appear in the text. Words *preceded* by an asterisk can be used as nouns. For example, *kaeru* means "to return (home)." The 2nd base of *kaeru* is the noun form *kaeri,* which has the meaning of "return, return trip." Similarly, for *ichidan* verbs, the stem is the noun form: *hajimeru* (v.), "to begin"; *hajime,* (n.) *"beginning."*

A

AGARU—humble term of *iku*, go
AGARU—honorific term of *taberu*, eat
AGARU (v.i.)—go up
AGERU (v.t.)—give, raise
AI SURU—love
AKERU—(v.i.) open
AKU—(v.t.) open
ARAU—wash
ARU—there is
ARUITE KAERU—walk back (home)
ARUKU—walk
*ASOBU—play
ATSURAERU—make to order
AU—meet
AZUKERU—place (something) in someone's care

C

*CHIGAU—differ

D

DASU (v.t.)—put out, produce, send
DEKAKERU—leave for
DEKIRU—able to do
DERU (v.i.)—leave, depart
DESU—is

E

ERABU—select, elect, choose

F

FUKU*—wipe
FUKU*—blow
FURU—(rain) fall

G

GAKKARI SURU—be disappointed

H

HAJIMARU (v.i.)—begin
*HAJIMERU (v.t.)—begin
HAIRU—enter
HAKU*—wear (on feet)
*HANASU—talk, speak
HARAU—pay

HARERU—become clear (weather)
HASHIRU—run
*HATARAKU—work
HIKKAKU—scratch
HIKU—pull
HIKU—run over
HIROU—pick up, find
HOMERU—praise

I

IKU—go
IRASSHARU—go, come, be
IRERU—put in
IRU—need
IRU—there is
ISOGU*—hurry
ITADAKU—receive (humble)
IU—say, tell

K

KABURU—wear (on one's head)
*KAERU—return, go back, go home
KAESU*—return (something)
KAGU*—smell
KAKARU—take (time)
KAKARU—cost
KAKERU—hang
KAKERU—sit (on a chair)
KAKU—write
KAMI-TSUKU—bite
*KANGAERU—think
KARIRU—borrow
*KASU—lend
*KATSU—win
KAU—buy
KAZOERU—count
KIKU—listen, ask, hear
KIRAI DESU—dislike
KIRU—cut
KIRU—wear
KOMARU—to be troubled
KOMU—be crowded
KOROSU—kill
KOSHIKAKERU—sit
KOTAERU—answer
KOWARERU (v.i.)—break
KOWASU (v.t.)—break
KUDASAI—give (me)
KUDASARU—give (me)
KUMORU—become cloudy
*KURASU—live
KURU—come

M

MAGARU—turn
MAIRU—come (humble form)
*MAKERU—lose
MA NI AU—be on time
MATSU—wait
MAWARU (v.i.)—turn
MAWASU (v.t.)—turn
MESHIAGARU—eat
MIERU—can see
MIRU—see, look
MISERU—show
MOCHI-KOMU—take in
MORAU—receive
MOTSU—hold
MUKAERU—meet, call

N

*NAGARERU (v.i.)—flow
NAGASU (v.t.)—flow
NAI—there is not
NAKU—cry
NAKUNARU—pass away, lose, die
NA O TSUKERU—give a name
NARAU—learn
NARITATSU—be composed of
NARU—ring
NARU—become
NAORU (v.i.)—become better, fix
NAOSU (v.t.)—fix
NERU—sleep
NIRU—resemble
*NOBORU—climb

NOMU—drink
NORERU—able to ride
*NORI-KAERU—transfer (bus, train)
NORU—ride, get on, board
NUGU—undress
NUSUMU—steal

O

*ODOROKU—be surprised
OERU (v. t.)—finish
OGORU—treat
OKIRU (v.i.)—get up
*OKORU—start, break out
OKORU—get angry
OKOSU (v.t.)—awaken, cause to happen
OKU*—put, place
OKURERU—be late
OKURU—send
ORIRU—get off
*OSHIERU—teach
OSU—push
OWARU (v.i.)—end
OYOGU—swim

S

SASU—point
SASOU—invite
SEME-KOMU—attack and enter into
SEMERU—attack
SHIKARU—scold
SHIMARU (v.i.)—close
SHIMERU (v.t.)—close
SHINU—die
*SHIRABERU—investigate
SHIRU—know
SODATERU—raise, bring up
SUGIRU—exceed
SUKI DESU—like
SUMASERU—complete, finish
SUMU*—live
SURU—do
SUU—inhale, smoke

T

TABERU—eat
*TANOMU—request
*TATAKAU—wage a battle
TATAKU*—hit, strike
TATSU—stand up
TATSU—depart
TAZUNERU—visit, ask
TEKI SURU—be appropriate
*TETSUDAU—help
TOBU—fly
TOMARU (v.i.)—stop
TOMERU (v.t.)—stop
TOORU—go through
*TORIATSUKAU—handle
TORU—take
*TSUKARERU—be tired, get tired
TSUKAU—use
TSUKERU—attach, put
TSUKERU—turn on (a light)
TSUKU—reach, arrive
TSUKURU—make
TSUMU—load
TSURERU—take, bring
*TSUTOMERU—work
TSUTSUKU—peck
*TSUTSUMU—wrap
TSUZUKERU (v.t.)—continue
*TSUZUKU (v.i.)—last, extend

U

UGOKASU (v.t.)—move
UGOKU (v.i.)—move
*UMARERU (v.i.)—be born
UMU (v.t.)—give birth to
URIKIRERU—be sold out
URU—sell
UTSU—shoot, strike
UTSURU (v.i.)—move
UTSUSU (v.t.)—move

W

WAKARU—understand
WAKASU*—boil
*WARAU—laugh
WARERU (v.i.)—crack, break
WARU (v.t.)—crack, break
WASURERU—forget
WATARU—cross

Y

YAKUSU—translate
YAMERU* (v.t.)—stop (something)
YAMU* (v.i.)—stop
YARU—give
*YASUMU—rest
YATOU—hire
YOBU*—call
YOMU—read
*YOROKOBU—be pleased, happy
YORU—drop by
YUKU—go
*YURUSU—forgive

INDEX

F

G

H

I

K

M

N

O

P

Q

R

S